UNIDIR/2009/2

Unfinished Business

The Negotiation of the CTBT and the End of Nuclear Testing

Rebecca Johnson

UNIDIR
United Nations Institute for Disarmament Research
Geneva, Switzerland

UNITED NATIONS

New York and Geneva, 2009

About the cover

The cover shows the control room of the International Data Centre, part of the International Monitoring System of the Preparatory Commission for the Comprehensive Nuclear-Test-Ban Treaty Organization.
Photograph courtesy of the Preparatory Commission for the Comprehensive Nuclear-Test-Ban Treaty Organization.

NOTE

The designations employed and the presentation of the material in this publication do not imply the expression of any opinion whatsoever on the part of the Secretariat of the United Nations concerning the legal status of any country, territory, city or area, or of its authorities, or concerning the delimitation of its frontiers or boundaries.

*

* *

The views expressed in this publication are the sole responsibility of the individual authors. They do not necessarily reflect the views or opinions of the United Nations, UNIDIR, its staff members or sponsors.

UNIDIR/2009/2

UNITED NATIONS PUBLICATIONS

Sales No. GV.E.09.0.4

ISBN 978-92-9045-194-5

The United Nations Institute for Disarmament Research (UNIDIR)—an autonomous institute within the United Nations—conducts research on disarmament and security. UNIDIR is based in Geneva, Switzerland, the centre for bilateral and multilateral disarmament and non-proliferation negotiations, and home of the Conference on Disarmament. The Institute explores current issues pertaining to the variety of existing and future armaments, as well as global diplomacy and local tensions and conflicts. Working with researchers, diplomats, government officials, NGOs and other institutions since 1980, UNIDIR acts as a bridge between the research community and governments. UNIDIR's activities are funded by contributions from governments and donor foundations. The Institute's web site can be found at:

www.unidir.org

CONTENTS

ACKNOWLEDGEMENTS

There are many people I would like to thank for making this book possible. I am indebted to Patricia Lewis, who first had the idea of shipping me off to Geneva in 1994, and who has been a wonderful friend over the years. I am particularly grateful that Patricia lent me her windswept cottage in West Cork so that I could get away from work for a month, breathe fresh air and finally write my doctoral thesis on "The 1996 Comprehensive Test Ban Treaty: A Study in Post Cold War Multilateral Arms Control Negotiations". I wish to express my appreciation to my supervisor at the London School of Economics and Political Science, Nicholas Sims, especially for his wisdom and kindness during the ups and downs when the demands of my more-than-full-time job took precedence over my studies. Particular thanks are also due to Sean Howard (editor of *Disarmament Diplomacy* until 2003) and his wife Lee-Anne Broadhead for commenting so helpfully on my thesis draft.

Kerstin Vignard, John Borrie, Jason Powers and the rest of the team at UNIDIR did a fine job of helping me convert the thesis into a more readable book, and were patient and helpful even when I missed my deadlines. I am also grateful to the governments of Finland, Japan and Norway for their support in enabling UNIDIR to publish the book and hold meetings on promoting entry into force of the CTBT. Thanks are also due to colleagues at the Acronym Institute for Disarmament Diplomacy, especially Nicola Butler, Frances Connelly, Lorna Richardson and Stephen Pullinger; and to John Edmonds, not only for being a very supportive Chair of our Board for many years, but also for generously sharing with me his recollections and writings on early test-ban negotiations, notably the tripartite talks, in which he headed the UK delegation. Others deserve medals for putting up with me as I struggled to finish first the thesis and then the book, usually late at night when Acronym's other work was done. Along with my long-suffering sweetheart and friends, this includes the Johnson siblings and offspring, for believing in me whether or not they agreed with what I was doing (and of course for the chocolate ice cream and hikes).

I also want to thank the diplomats and government officials of many countries who gave so generously of their time and coffee during and after the CTBT negotiations, and to staff of the CTBTO for responding to my queries and updating me on developments since 1996, notably on the verification regime and the North Korean test. I will not embarrass them by naming names, but they know who they are, and I am eternally in their debt. In addition to uncounted informal discussions throughout the negotiations, I was grateful to be given one-to-one recorded interviews for the thesis, notably with Ambassadors Grigori Berdennikov, Wolfgang Hoffmann, Stephen Ledogar, Jaap Ramaker, Sha Zukang and Sir Michael Weston, as well as detailed (but not taped) interviews with Arend Meerburg, Onno Kervers and Victor Slipchenko. Though they may not agree with all of my analysis, I hope I have treated their recollections fairly in my efforts to understand what had gone on behind closed doors. While I thank all who shared their thoughts and insights with me, any errors of recollection or analysis are of course my own.

This book is dedicated to the non-violent activists for peace and human rights everywhere, who imagine a better world and then work passionately to build it, and to the next generation, represented in my life by my nieces and nephews and by Lindi, Edda-Lara and Joe, whose healthy, peaceful future we have an obligation to secure.

ABOUT THE AUTHOR

Dr Rebecca Johnson is Director of the Acronym Institute for Disarmament Diplomacy, which she co-founded in 1995, and has edited its journal, *Disarmament Diplomacy*, since 2003. Parts of this book are based on contemporaneous notes and research conducted for her PhD, which she received from the London School of Economics and Political Science in 2004. Johnson began reporting from Geneva on the CTBT negotiations in January 1994 on behalf of The Acronym Consortium of four UK-based NGOs, which disseminated her "Acronym Email" reports to a wide international audience. As a long-time campaigner and organizer on peace and women's issues and then as Greenpeace International's Coordinator on a Nuclear Test Ban from 1988 to 1992, Johnson participated directly in some of the events that are recorded in this book. With a background in physics as well as international relations, she also holds degrees from the University of London School of Oriental and African Studies (MA) and the University of Bristol (B.Sc Hons). She is a prolific author and policy analyst on security and non-proliferation issues and has served as an adviser or board member for several organizations, including the International Weapons of Mass Destruction Commission (2004–2006), the Bulletin of the Atomic Scientists (2001–2007), the Middle Powers Initiative (2007–present), and the Women's Network of the International Action Network on Small Arms (IANSA). She has twice been nominated for the Nobel Peace Prize, most recently in 2004, as one of a thousand peace-women from all over the world who were put forward collectively.

FOREWORD

The Comprehensive Nuclear-Test-Ban Treaty (CTBT) was a child born following a long gestation. From the test of a nuclear weapon in 1945 to the first call for a "standstill agreement" on nuclear testing in 1954 by Jawaharlal Nehru, Prime Minister of India, to the 1963 Partial Test Ban Treaty, there have been repeated and intense efforts to halt the qualitative and quantitative nuclear arms race by preventing nuclear weapons testing.

Following the end of the Cold War, having prepared the ground for several years through the establishment of a Group of Scientific Experts (GSE), the Geneva-based Conference on Disarmament formally began negotiations on the CTBT in 1993. The negotiations ran from January 1994 to September 1996, culminating in a treaty that was opened for signature in New York on 24 September 1996.

In 1993, a group of British non-governmental organizations, The British American Security Information Council (BASIC), Defence Fax (DFAX), International Security Information Service (ISIS) and the Verification Research, Training and Information Centre (VERTIC) formed a collaborative project called the Acronym Consortium (a witticism reflecting the acronyms used to name the organizations and the myriad of acronyms used in the linguistically obtuse world of arms control) and engaged Rebecca Johnson to report on the proceedings of the Conference on Disarmament from Geneva.

There were many grandfathers, grandmothers, mothers, fathers, aunts and uncles of the CTBT. There were surrogate parents, godparents and a number of would-be siblings. However, there was one outstanding doula—a professional birthing assistant—and that was Rebecca Johnson.

Dr Johnson saw the negotiations through from beginning to end, and like all professional birth assistants, is still there with the Treaty, helping ensure its viability as it eventually comes into force and onto the statute books.

Her reports were sent out, via the internet and paper copy, all over the world. Other organizations were able to follow the goings on in Geneva. Weekly (sometimes daily) blow-by-blow accounts of detail and nuance were transmitted to expert researchers, government officials and journalists. Everyone involved in the effort relied on Rebecca Johnson's reports, summaries and analysis. She did not report just what people wanted to hear; she reported fact and opinion, carefully delineating both. She thus alerted national experts and activists to the actions of their countries' representatives so that governments were held to account in a timely manner. The media relied equally heavily on her reports and their quality. That the Treaty was delivered to the UN General Assembly after a difficult labour and traumatic birth in Geneva was, in large part, as a result of Rebecca's efforts in supporting the whole process and helping keep the focus.

It has now been over 12 years since the CTBT was opened for signature. As of 31 December 2008, 180 states have signed the Treaty and 148 have ratified. But entry into force depends on more than just numbers. There are 44 named states in Annex 2 of the Treaty and each of those has to ratify before the CTBT can enter into force. Of those 44, all but three have so far signed and all but nine have ratified. And thus the Treaty is kept in limbo.

In the belief that the CTBT would only thus be successfully agreed, states burdened the Treaty with provisions that still hinder its entry into force. To move forward, to obtain and keep this Treaty so necessary to nuclear security and prosperity, it would be wise of us to study how it is that we have arrived in these circumstances—and perhaps learn the lessons of the CTBT negotiation. The history presented here provides an uncommon opportunity to do just that.

Political transition in some of the 44 named states has either just occurred or is possible in the future. This potential for change allows us to hope that the entry into force of the CTBT is on the horizon. The importance of such an event should not be underestimated. If the terms of the Nuclear Non-Proliferation Treaty are ever to be met, if further progress toward nuclear disarmament is to be made and if the prevention of nuclear war could ever become a reality, the CTBT will be there at the heart of such transformation.

It is my hope that this project, generously funded by the Governments of Finland, Japan and Norway and written by Dr Rebecca Johnson, with all the authority she bestows on the historical account, will provide the international community with insights and signposts as to how to bring this important Treaty into force and give it the teeth, through the International

Monitoring System embodied in the Treaty, that the world needs and demands.

Patricia Lewis
Director, UNIDIR (1997–2008)

SPECIAL COMMENT

The publication of this book is indeed very timely.

As the threat posed by the existence of nuclear weapons once again comes to the fore of the international agenda, a new political momentum gathers behind the comprehensive test.

For too long now this Treaty has been a hostage of fortune: left on the sidelines because circumstances in the international arms control regime were not conducive to agreement of any kind, let alone those measures already widely supported and enacted around the globe, such as the Comprehensive Nuclear-Test-Ban Treaty.

It is time to write a new chapter in the fight against nuclear weapons. A chapter that will see no more countries entering the nuclear weapons club and no new nuclear weapons entering the arsenals of existing members. A chapter that will erase once and for all the scar of nuclear weapons testing from the Earth. The time has come for this Treaty, and the global alarm system that supports it, to enter into force.

We are ready to begin.

One hundred and eighty nations have signed up to the Treaty's principles, 150 of whom have ratified their commitment. A de facto norm against testing waits to be inscribed in the international rule book proper.

The global alarm system supporting the Treaty—the verification regime being built around the world to ensure compliance with the ban—moves toward completion. It has already proven itself admirably. In 2006, with only 60% of the system complete, a low-yield nuclear test conducted by North Korea was detected by 20 stations (both seismic and radionuclide) around the globe. Since then more than 60 monitoring stations have been added to the system, and the capacity to detect noble gases—the smoking gun of a nuclear explosion—has been doubled from 10 systems to 20.

In short, the Treaty is standing at the door, waiting to enter. This opportunity is knocking and we must answer. It is a call for determined leadership, a call to action. The time of the Comprehensive Nuclear-Test-Ban Treaty is now.

Tibor Tóth
Executive Secretary
Preparatory Commission for the Comprehensive
Nuclear-Test-Ban Treaty Organization

CHAPTER 1

INTRODUCTION

They were not told what had happened, why it had happened, what was wrong with them. Their hair was falling out, finger nails were falling off—but they were never told why.

Darlene Keju-Johnson, Marshall Islands, speaking about the impact of first thermonuclear bomb test, codenamed Bravo, on Bikini Atoll, 1 March 1954.[1]

From the first atomic explosion above New Mexico in July 1945 to the underground nuclear test conducted by North Korea in October 2006, nuclear testing has defined the nuclear age.

The first nuclear explosion was codenamed *Trinity* and carried out in Alamogordo, New Mexico. It was followed by the detonation of a uranium bomb over Hiroshima on 6 August 1945. Three days later, a plutonium bomb exploded directly above Japan's largest Catholic cathedral, in the port city of Nagasaki. These explosions carried materials from the surface—soil, vegetation and the remains of people and buildings—miles into the sky in pillars of radioactive dust that folded and billowed, dripping streams to the ground in what onlookers likened to huge suppurating mushrooms. These explosions heralded the nuclear age, in which tens of thousands of weapons were made, deployed and nearly unleashed.

During the 1950s and 1960s, conducting nuclear test explosions became the public proof that a states' scientists had mastered the technology to make nuclear weapons. When even more powerful thermonuclear bombs were developed in the 1950s, some explosions yielded a force equivalent to several millions of tons of TNT. The radioactive mushroom clouds rising high above the Pacific, the United States, Kazakhstan and Siberia prompted calls for a Comprehensive Nuclear-Test-Ban Treaty (CTBT). Launched in the mid-1950s, as fallout from nuclear explosions spread around the world, the campaigns to end nuclear testing engaged nuclear and non-nuclear governments and a wide cross-section of civil society, starting with doctors and scientists, women's groups and grassroots activists. When dentists found radioactive strontium from these tests in children's teeth and doctors and scientists raised concerns about long-lasting damage to human health and the Earth's environment, public opposition to nuclear weapons accelerated.

In 1954, India and Japan separately called for a total ban on nuclear testing, a demand taken up by civil society as a first step toward nuclear disarmament. Despite widespread calls for a CTBT, efforts to negotiate were derailed time and again. In 1963, in the wake of the Cuban Missile Crisis, the Soviet Union, the United States and the United Kingdom finally managed to agree the Partial Test Ban Treaty (PTBT), which banned nuclear testing in the atmosphere, under water and in outer space, and so halted the most visible and environmentally dangerous explosions.[2]

The 1970 Treaty on the Non-Proliferation of Nuclear Weapons (NPT) prohibited the development of nuclear devices—and therefore any testing—by its non-nuclear-weapon states parties, who comprised the majority of members of the United Nations. But nuclear testing by the five nuclear-weapon states defined in the NPT (China, France, Russia, the United Kingdom and the United States, which are also the P-5 permanent members of the UN Security Council) continued, mostly underground. China and France, which were further behind in their nuclear weapon programmes, refused to join the PTBT and continued testing in the atmosphere over the next decade.

Twenty years and more than 2,000 nuclear tests later, a CTBT was finally put back on the negotiating table. The main purpose by this time was to cap nuclear weapon development by the P-5 and apply additional constraints on three states outside the NPT with de facto nuclear weapons programmes (the D-3: India, Israel and Pakistan). Yet little serious consideration was given to holding plurilateral negotiations solely among the P-5 and D-3. The negotiations were undertaken multilaterally as a process of intentional regime-building not only to impose legal restraints on these eight, but because of the higher normative value and collective "ownership" associated with multilateral regimes.

By the time negotiations on a CTBT opened in the Conference on Disarmament (CD) on 25 January 1994, the dynamics among the key negotiating states illustrated not only different views on the value of a test ban, but competing motivations for and against nuclear disarmament. Only six states had conducted a nuclear explosion prior to 1994 when the negotiations opened. Those in favour of a test ban argued that it would contribute to preventing the development of new and destabilizing weapons, protect against further environmental damage, curb proliferation and contribute to the process of disarmament. Those that sought to prevent a test ban, by contrast, regarded nuclear weapons as conferring deterrence or stability and opposed a CTBT on grounds that it would close off options to develop or modernize nuclear arsenals and might impair the ability of the laboratories to maintain the safety and reliability of existing weapons.

Three years later, after intense and sometimes dramatic negotiations, the CTBT was overwhelmingly adopted by the UN General Assembly. On 24 September 1996, it was opened for signature. The President of the United States signed first, using John F. Kennedy's pen. The foreign ministers from China, France, Russia and the United Kingdom followed, as others queued up. By 7 March 1997, when the treaty was handed over to Vienna, the host city for the Comprehensive Nuclear-Test-Ban Treaty Organization (CTBTO), 142 states, including Iran and Israel, had signed.

In accordance with the treaty, the CTBTO's Provisional Technical Secretariat established an international monitoring system with seismic, radionuclide, hydroacoustic and infrasound sensors located around the world, feeding information into the International Data Centre in Vienna. Scientists and technicians from many of the signatory states have been trained to work with these technologies, while diplomats and experts have negotiated sensitive issues such as what procedures, rights and responsibilities should go into the operations manual for the conduct of on-site inspections.

As of 31 December 2008, 180 states have signed the CTBT. Of these, 148 have ratified. The CTBTO looks ready to implement the treaty, but is stuck in legal limbo. Incompatible political objectives between some of the key states during the final months of the negotiations resulted in treaty text that made entry into force contingent on the signature and ratification of 44 states with nuclear programmes or capabilities, which were listed in an annex to the treaty. Though the CTBT is one of the best-supported treaties in history, nine of the necessary 44 have not ratified, so the treaty is prevented from entering into force.

Nuclear-weapon states France and the United Kingdom ratified together in 1998, and Russia ratified before the NPT Review Conference in 2000. In the United States, by contrast, ratification by the Senate failed in 1999 after being turned into a partisan referendum that had little to do with the real security interests of the United States and the world. China continues to express support for the treaty, but has not yet ratified it. India, North Korea and Pakistan have to date not signed, and each has conducted one or more nuclear tests—India and Pakistan in May 1998[3] and North Korea in October 2006.[4] Among the remaining nine who must ratify for the CTBT to come into full effect are Egypt, Indonesia, Iran and Israel, which signed early on but have yet to ratify. After their nuclear testing in 1998, India and Pakistan joined the P-5 in announcing moratoria on further tests. But moratoria can be unilaterally revoked and do not carry the force of treaty obligations.

The US role in international security is such that the Senate's failure to ratify and the subsequent repudiation of the CTBT in speeches and votes by members of the administration of George W. Bush from 2001 to 2008 did more than the actions of any other state to weaken the test ban and non-proliferation regime. Despite Bush's opposition to the treaty, opinion polls continued to show not only enduring global support for bringing the CTBT into force, but that more than 70% of Americans back US ratification of this treaty. While the CTBT's future remains in question, the credibility of the non-proliferation regime as a whole is weakened, as has been acknowledged by successive UN Secretaries-General, the Weapons of Mass Destruction Commission, and a number of former generals and senior officials from the United States and other countries. The importance of the CTBT is underscored time and again in statements from world leaders and from the 188 states parties to the NPT, the cornerstone of the non-proliferation regime. Recognizing the importance of increasing the CTBT's legal and political authority, especially in the wake of North Korea's nuclear test, an eminent and bipartisan group that included former US Secretaries of State and Defense, led by George Shultz, Henry Kissinger, William Perry and Sam Nunn, published an essay in the *Wall Street Journal* entitled "A World Free of Nuclear Weapons".[5] After receiving a positive response from around the world, they published a second essay a year later, in which they called for the adoption of a "process for bringing the Comprehensive Test Ban Treaty (CTBT) into effect, which would strengthen the NPT and aid international monitoring of nuclear activities".[6]

This book tells the story of how the CTBT was fought for, achieved, and also undermined. At the centre are the dynamics, objectives and tactics of the main nuclear and non-nuclear players as the treaty was multilaterally negotiated in the CD from January 1994 to September 1996. Particular emphasis is given to four key elements: the campaigning that impelled the nuclear-weapon states to the table; the zero-yield scope[7] that means that this treaty bans all nuclear explosions in all environments; the multilateral verification regime and the CTBTO; and the entry-into-force provision that many consider the treaty's greatest weakness. This history charts several earlier attempts to ban testing and looks at the prenegotiation phase that framed disarmament objectives for the 1990s and put the CTBT back onto the negotiating table. It does not gloss over the problems encountered and created in the process of negotiation, but seeks to understand how they came about in order to suggest ways to overcome the obstacles now faced by the treaty and non-proliferation regime. Bringing the story up to date, the last two chapters consider what lessons can be learned for future multilateral negotiations and what now needs to be done to bring the CTBT into force.

Although efforts to get a total test ban were an enduring feature of the Cold War, the 1994–1996 negotiations were influenced by broader multilateral dynamics and concerns, making the CTBT an unmistakable product of post-Cold War security considerations. Some things went right, and some went wrong. The negotiations simultaneously reflected Cold War attitudes and the transition to a "new world order", though not, perhaps, what President George H.W. Bush had envisaged in 1991.[8] As attitudes toward nuclear weapons began to change with the end of the Cold War, the test-ban negotiations posed new or different challenges for the P-5, the D-3 and the international community as the restraints and expectations of Cold War relations were transformed.

Reading the standard textbooks on arms control and international relations, it often appears as if politicians and governments wake up one morning and decide to change their policies—to have a moratorium, for example, or start negotiating a treaty. Accounts of treaty formation usually dwell on a handful of leaders and the formal processes among diplomats and governments. When dealing with nuclear arms control, they tend to focus most on the interests of the nuclear weapon states. Few go beyond the official sources to look at the movements, pressures and processes that bring leaders to the negotiating table and shape the way governments think about what kind of agreements are desirable and possible.

While paying due attention to powerful and dominant states with nuclear arsenals and significant military and political resources, this history tells a story that is often missed, showing how the interests and strategies of national and transnational civil society influenced the timing and created the conditions for negotiations to commence, and how civil society specialists and organizations worked with middle powers and less well-resourced states committed to building a stronger non-proliferation regime, with the aim of achieving a CTBT that would genuinely contribute to international security, disarmament and non-proliferation. That these alliances and strategies were not always successful is also part of the story.

The CTBT was formally negotiated from 1994 to 1996. The full negotiating history, as described here, was longer and more complex, with many more players than could fit into the CD. Among the false starts and disappointments, political posturing, exaggerated technical demands and diplomatic showdowns, there were also passionate advocates, scientists, analysts and diplomats offering proposals to overcome every obstacle. In telling the story of the CTBT negotiations, this history also brings to light ideas that can contribute not only to bringing the CTBT into effect but also to an improved understanding of the dynamics of multilateral arms control and how outcomes can be more effectively shaped and implemented.

The chapters that follow reveal that the CTBT negotiations were essentially a process of conflict resolution between the objectives, postures and politics of fewer than 25 of the negotiating parties, informed and influenced by a number of civil society actors in a range of expert and advocacy capacities. The outcomes on scope, verification and entry into force were wrought by three levels of simultaneous policy-shaping interactions: domestic, international and transnational. Agendas, options and interests were contested and determined not only by government representatives, but also among national and transnational civil society actors, between government and non-governmental actors within a particular state, and also across these levels, with information exchange and links occurring between governments and domestic actors on different sides.

The final chapters deal with two kinds of conclusions and recommendations: lessons to enable future multilateral negotiations to be conducted more effectively, and mechanisms to strengthen the test ban and promote the CTBT's entry into force. In addressing the challenges of multilateral disarmament and arms control in the post-Cold War for practitioners and theorists, this history demonstrates that though a state's attributive (military, economic and political) power and the linkage between nuclear interests and expectations were important, they did not determine outcomes to the extent that analysts trained in the realist or neoliberal traditions would have predicted. While nuclear interests were a major feature in determining a state's expectations and negotiating posture, other factors were important in determining many of the outcomes, especially those with high political salience, such as the scope of the treaty.

In addition to considering states' expectations and perceived interests, it becomes clear that the conduct and outcomes of multilateral negotiations are heavily influenced by civil society engagement, norms and regime values, knowledge and ideas, partnerships and alliances, internal policy cohesion or division, and the level of domestic and international political attention and support in key states. By choosing to incorporate transnational civil society as a principal unit of analysis, along with states, this history develops a fuller understanding of how government calculations of national interest and security can be influenced, expanded and shaped, opening up alternative solutions for agreement than those initially envisaged. This history starts with consideration of early efforts to persuade the major powers to agree on a test ban, from the first nuclear test and subsequent use nuclear weapons in 1945 to the end of the 1980s.

CHAPTER 2

COLD WAR ATTEMPTS TO BAN NUCLEAR EXPLOSIONS

The longest sought, hardest fought prize in arms control history.

US President Bill Clinton describing the CTBT,
24 September 1996[1]

Nuclear weapons developed a public visibility not generally accorded other weapons,[2] largely as a consequence of the dramatic devastation of Hiroshima and Nagasaki in 1945. The terrible events of the Second World War prompted a renewal of interest in multilateralism as a mechanism for building collective security, resulting in the establishment of the United Nations and its various associated institutions, as well as regional alliances and arrangements. Arms control developed, as the Baruch Plan succinctly stated, "to make a choice between the quick and the dead".[3] The earliest calls for a test ban came in 1954, when India's Prime Minister Jawaharlal Nehru and the Japanese Parliament made separate appeals for nuclear testing to be stopped. From then until the end of the Cold War, there were three phases[4] in nuclear arms control, during which test-ban efforts fluctuated between hope and frustration:

Settling for the Partial Test Ban Treaty (1954 to 1963)—during which the Soviet Union, the United Kingdom and United States abandoned the search for a comprehensive test-ban treaty, but agreed to ban testing in the atmosphere, underwater and in outer space, leaving underground testing unregulated. During this period the first anti-nuclear movements were born, involving professionals (notably scientists and physicians) and citizens, including women's groups.

Non-proliferation and arms control, while testing continues (1964 to 1980)—during which concepts of strategic deterrence and arms control dominated policy thinking in Washington and Moscow. Test-ban advocates were marginalized as proliferation and the arms race were addressed by governments through the Treaty on the Non-Proliferation of Nuclear

Weapons, détente, the Strategic Arms Limitation Talks and the Anti-Ballistic Missile Treaty. This period was one of Cold War superpower diplomacy, with diminished public interest in nuclear issues. Two interim agreements set testing thresholds at 150kt, but talks on banning underground testing failed.

Public mobilizing against nuclear weapons (1981 to 1989)—during which deteriorating strategic relations between the Soviet Union and the United States led to nuclear weapons becoming highly salient public and political issues. Civil society engagement was transformed during this period: traditional single-issue politics was challenged, stimulating the rise of democratic (anti-communist and anti-capitalist), environmental, feminist and anti-nuclear actors, linking Western movements with dissident civil society actors in the Soviet bloc demanding greater democracy and human rights. Nuclear testing was at best a marginal issue of broader anti-nuclear campaigns. However, the goal of a CTBT was kept on the international diplomatic agenda by civil society actions against the French, US and Soviet test sites, a 19-month Soviet moratorium, and political strategies in which non-governmental organizations (NGOs) worked with non-nuclear-weapon states to highlight the issue in international fora. To recognize the role played by civil society in keeping test-ban hopes alive and understand how and why some positions—on thresholds and on-site inspections for example—assumed so much importance during the 1994–1996 negotiations, it is useful to have an overview of the main events on the long road to the CTBT.

1954–1963: SETTLING FOR THE PARTIAL TEST BAN TREATY

After 1945, the United States turned down international proposals that would have prohibited nuclear arsenals, and intensified the development and testing of new types of these weapons. Rather sooner than Washington had anticipated, the Soviet Union conducted its first atomic explosion in 1949. The nuclear arms race was launched. The United States accelerated its programme with one underground test in 1950 and 15 above-ground explosions in 1951. In 1952, when the United States carried out 10 nuclear tests, the United Kingdom joined the club with an atmospheric explosion on the Australian island of Monte Bello on 3 October. In 1953, in the midst of the Korean War, US planners were shocked when the Soviet Union demonstrated its mastery of nuclear weapon technology by detonating a thermonuclear device just one year later than the United States had managed.

In March 1954 the rest of the world woke up to the dangers when a US thermonuclear test, codenamed Castle Bravo, produced a much greater yield than anticipated.[5] The huge blast vaporized part of the Bikini Atoll and contaminated nearby islanders. It also caused severe radiation sickness and at least one death among Japanese fishermen on a nearby trawler, the misnamed *Lucky Dragon*, provoking protests in the Japanese parliament, which demanded a suspension of nuclear testing. On 2 April 1954, Prime Minister Nehru of India called for an immediate "standstill agreement" on nuclear testing. Nehru's proposal for a test ban was submitted for consideration to the UN Disarmament Commission on 29 July 1954, and from then on a CTBT became a consistent demand from the growing number of developing states that formed the Movement of Non-Aligned States, of which Nehru became a leading light.[6]

Meanwhile, the Cold War rivals carried out more nuclear tests—by 1958, the United States had conducted 197, the Soviet Union 103 and the United Kingdom 21. Not all policymakers in these states supported the race to acquire nuclear weapons, however, and the mid-1950s witnessed a flurry of disarmament initiatives. The United Kingdom, together with France, put forward a three-stage plan for nuclear disarmament in June 1954. The Soviet Union submitted similar proposals in May 1955, which it followed by declaring a moratorium on nuclear testing in June 1957, later extended by General Secretary Nikita Khrushchev, on condition that no other state tested.[7] By 1957, as the United Kingdom conducted its first thermonuclear test, nuclear testing had become "a burning public issue",[8] with women's groups, scientists and doctors at the forefront of raising public awareness of the dangers of radioactive fallout.

Peace-oriented organizations, such as the Nobel-prize-winning Women's International League for Peace and Freedom, the Fellowship of Reconciliation, and the Religious Society of Friends (the Quakers), had begun protesting against nuclear weapons soon after the first bombs were detonated, but they received little attention initially. Scientists involved in the Manhattan Project raised ethical, political and technical questions about controlling and using nuclear weapons and materials, and in 1945 some of them founded *The Bulletin of the Atomic Scientists*.[9] These scientists were among the earliest non-governmental actors to integrate and publish information on the risks of nuclear proliferation and the health and environmental dangers of nuclear testing.[10]

During the 1950s, additional groups were formed specifically to address nuclear weapons and testing. Of these, the most important in the West were the US Women's Strike for Peace, the US National Committee for a Sane Nuclear Policy (commonly known as SANE), the international Pugwash Conferences of scientists,[11] and the British Campaign for Nuclear Disarmament (CND). Together with doctors and dentists, who became concerned when studies showed significant levels of strontium-90 and other radioactive isotopes in children's teeth in the United States and Europe, scientists were prominent in efforts to lobby against nuclear testing, using their professional expertise and standing to raise awareness.[12] At the same time, grass-roots initiatives such as the Women's Strike for Peace, SANE and CND organized rallies, petitions and public demonstrations in major cities. In 1958, CND held its first protest march from London to the United Kingdom's main nuclear research and production facility at Aldermaston, arriving with over 10,000 people. Subsequent rallies and marches between Aldermaston and London attracted even more supporters and were given significant media coverage. Through demonstrations and local organizing, these campaigns sought to influence government policy by raising public concern and fostering direct contact with legislative representatives. Sections of the Women's Strike for Peace and CND also formed direct action wings, prepared to block roads or trespass at nuclear test sites and facilities. Famous academics such as the Cambridge philosopher Bertrand Russell joined the growing number of activists that risked arrest and imprisonment to bring governments to their senses and halt nuclear weapons testing and development.[13]

The Soviet Union's launch of *Sputnik I* on 4 October 1957, together with its tests of intercontinental ballistic missiles, shook US confidence.[14] Soon after, President Eisenhower announced that he too favoured a nuclear test ban. Acknowledging growing public concern about testing, he cited radioactive fallout and the need to curb the nuclear arms race.[15] Eisenhower offered the Soviet Union a two-year moratorium on nuclear testing, combined with a halt in the production of fissile materials for weapons purposes. Then, in a diplomatic game of distrustful two-step that became all too familiar during the Cold War, Moscow pulled back from its earlier offers and accused Washington of seeking to freeze a status quo in which the United States retained superior nuclear weapon capabilities.[16]

Eisenhower persisted, and proposed a joint study on verification. Broadened to involve scientists from Canada, Czechoslovakia, France, Poland, Romania, the Soviet Union and the United States, the Conference of Experts to Study the Possibility of Detecting Violations of a Possible Agreement on Suspension of Nuclear Tests was subsequently convened from 1 July to 21 August 1958 in Geneva, Switzerland. The conference report proposed a verification system based on four technologies—seismic, radio, acoustic and sensors to detect "radioactive debris"—along with on-site inspection of unidentified and suspicious events. According to the report, this combination of verification approaches would be able to "detect and identify nuclear explosions, including low yield explosions (1–5kt)".[17] In order to get this far, Eisenhower had found it necessary to go beyond the advice he was receiving from the US nuclear weapon laboratories, where a majority of scientists opposed a test ban.[18] In addition to the conference report, he needed convincing support from US-based scientists to present to the Congress and the military. In 1957, therefore, he established the President's Science Advisory Committee (PSAC), comprising scientists who were considered to be more independent of the nuclear bureaucracy. The committee, chaired by James Killian,[19] advised Eisenhower that a test ban could be adequately verified and would be in the best interest of the United States.[20]

With the support of Khrushchev and British Prime Minister Harold Macmillan, Eisenhower then initiated tripartite talks—the Conference on the Discontinuance of Nuclear Weapon Tests—which opened on 31 October 1958, with the objective of a total ban on nuclear tests.[21] To build confidence in the talks, the three nuclear powers suspended their test programmes. Led by Edward Teller, a brilliant and determined advocate of US nuclear dominance, a vociferous group of US nuclear weapon scientists based at the Lawrence Livermore and Los Alamos laboratories published data intended to show how the detection of underground tests could be evaded. These studies on evasion scenarios were deliberately constructed to undermine Eisenhower's test-ban initiative and the experts' report by highlighting ingenious ways in which the signals from underground nuclear tests could be concealed or minimized.[22] Unable to counteract arguments that a comprehensive ban would be difficult to verify, the Eisenhower administration decided in 1960 to offer a partial ban based on what they considered to be verifiable by remote sensing or other national technical means (NTM).[23]

By the end of the year, however, the trilateral test-ban talks had been put on hold as US–Soviet relations deteriorated after a US reconnaissance flight was shot down over Soviet territory, leading to accusations and feeding into the agendas of military hawks on both sides.[24] Meanwhile, three atmospheric tests in 1960 had signalled France's entry into the nuclear club. In an increasingly toxic atmosphere of distrust and recrimination, the Ten-Nation Disarmament Committee convened in Geneva.[25] It considered a joint US–Soviet initiative that set general and complete disarmament as an ultimate goal, but did not get far.[26] In August 1961, the Berlin Wall went up.

President John F. Kennedy had decided to revive Eisenhower's test-ban initiative when he took office in January 1961, but was unable to take the issue forward in his first couple of years. Using the French tests as an excuse, first the United States and then the Soviet Union broke their moratoria and resumed testing, both with greatly accelerated programmes. After September 1961 and throughout 1962, the Soviet Union conducted an estimated 93 atmospheric tests, and the United States 39. During that time the United States also experimented with 67 underground tests, while the Soviet Union and the United Kingdom each conducted two.[27]

As nuclear tests continued across the world, the Soviet Union issued another test-ban proposal in November 1961, which fell on deaf ears. Protests against the resumed nuclear tests were now spreading almost as fast as the fallout. In March 1962, the issue was taken up multilaterally in Geneva, where the Eighteen-Nation Disarmament Committee (ENDC) had been established under United Nations auspices, replacing the Ten-Nation Disarmament Committee.[28] With President Kennedy taking a more active role in response to public concern, the United Kingdom and the United States initiated a joint draft test ban on 18 April.[29] Moscow then reiterated its earlier proposal, after which the United Kingdom and the United States tabled draft partial-test-ban treaties intended to ban explosions that would spread radioactive contamination beyond the territorial limits of the state.[30] The main issues of contention concerned verification, particularly inspections.

These talks might have continued with little progress for years, despite mounting public anger about the frenzy of testing sending tonnes of radioactive dust into the atmosphere. It was the "shared danger"[31] of the Cuban Missile Crisis, which nearly resulted in the use of nuclear weapons in October 1962, that shocked the governments back to the negotiating table and reinvigorated pressure for a test-ban treaty as a first step toward complete nuclear disarmament. During the UN General Assembly in late 1962, a high-profile debate was held on nuclear testing in which 37 non-nuclear states, including the eight non-aligned members of the ENDC, demanded an end to atmospheric testing by 1 January 1963, and called for a comprehensive treaty or limited agreement accompanied by an interim moratorium on underground testing. The United Kingdom and the United States sponsored a second resolution, calling for a CTBT with international verification or, alternatively, a limited, partial ban covering testing in the atmosphere, underwater and in outer space.[32]

When the ENDC met again in Geneva in early 1963, the test-ban talks got quickly bogged down, as both Soviet and US representatives lobbied the non-aligned delegates to support their opposing positions on inspections. Moreover, as the demand for a CTBT began to look more realistic and serious, opposition intensified in the United States, spearheaded by the Joint Chiefs of Staff and the Senate's Joint Committee on Atomic Energy. The United States appeared divided: as test-ban opponents in the military and the nuclear laboratories called for an even more vigorous programme of nuclear testing and declared a CTBT to be unverifiable, US Senators were being "showered with letters, phone-calls and petitions" calling for an end to testing.[33]

With talks in the ENDC going nowhere, tripartite negotiations were suggested in April 1963, following which Kennedy cancelled three nuclear tests and made positive overtures to the Soviet Union in what became known as his "peace speech" at American University in June.[34] The Soviet Union and the United Kingdom responded positively, and so tripartite negotiations commenced in Moscow on 15 July. Although Kennedy, Khrushchev and Macmillan had at different times all said that they wanted a comprehensive test ban, the verification problems emphasized by the US nuclear laboratories and their backers in the Pentagon resulted in Kennedy's team submitting three separate proposals for partial bans. With US concerns about verification presented as insurmountable, it was decided by the Soviet Union to put the verification issues aside and settle for prohibiting test explosions in only three environments. On 5 August 1963, after more than five years of intermittent negotiations, the three governments signed the Treaty Banning Nuclear Weapon Tests in the Atmosphere, in Outer Space and Under Water, widely known as the Partial Test Ban Treaty (PTBT).[35]

The political mood facilitated prompt ratification by all three negotiating partners, which enabled the PTBT to enter into force on 10 October 1963. International verification was not part of the agreement, which would rely on NTM and intelligence for monitoring compliance. No mention was made of a verifiable threshold for underground testing, which had been so much a part of discussions in the late 1950s. Nor was there any mention of a moratorium on underground testing pending agreement on verification. Although negotiated by only three states, others were invited to accede to the PTBT, and over a hundred did. France declined to join and carried on testing in the atmosphere over the Pacific until 1974, when Australia and New Zealand initiated a case in the International Court of Justice, citing the PTBT as applicable law in their bid to halt French testing. China, which conducted its first nuclear test in 1964, also chose not to join. Although Chinese and French atmospheric tests challenged the PTBT regime and caused abiding concern to the other nuclear and non-nuclear states and international civil society, they were not permitted to derail the treaty.

The PTBT was hailed as a victory, but it contained an important element of defeat and some bitter lessons for disarmament advocates. Weakly echoed in Article I, only the preamble referred directly to a comprehensive test ban: "Seeking to achieve the discontinuance of all test explosions of nuclear weapons for all time, determined to continue negotiations to this end, and desiring to put an end to the contamination of man's environment by radioactive substances …". Although they favoured a total test ban, NGOs had focused most of their public and political mobilizing on the harm to public health from radioactive fallout. By banning testing in the atmosphere, outer space and underwater, the PTBT reduced the risks to public health and the environment. This was undoubtedly worthwhile, but technological advances in the nuclear programmes of the major powers meant that it did not contribute much to disarmament. On the contrary, the PTBT made disarmament efforts harder to pursue because it removed an important visible reminder of the nuclear arms race. After 1963, nuclear testing continued out of sight. The PTBT left the nuclear scientists free to experiment with underground testing technologies, which were then refined to fuel the next three decades of the arms race with new and advanced weapons systems. The treaty might have enshrined in its preamble the objective of the "discontinuance of all test explosions of nuclear weapons for all time", but in practical terms, much of the driving force to achieve a comprehensive ban was dissipated once testing had gone underground.

1964–1980: NON-PROLIFERATION AND ARMS CONTROL, WHILE TESTING CONTINUES

The bitter rivalry and brinkmanship that characterized strategic relations between the US and Soviet blocs from 1945 until the 1962 Cuban Missile Crisis were succeeded by a period of relative accommodation, with mutual efforts to reduce nuclear dangers, including proliferation. The US–Soviet détente continued through most of the 1970s, during which time US security policy was dominated by theories of balance of power, deterrence and arms control. Although there were vigorous peace movements in the United States and elsewhere, they focused mainly on the Vietnam War, not nuclear weapons. The period witnessed some crucial developments in multilateral non-proliferation and bilateral arms control, of which the most important was the Treaty on the Non-Proliferation of Nuclear Weapons (NPT).

With its origins in slightly different resolutions from Ireland and Sweden to the UN General Assembly in 1961,[36] the NPT was concluded in 1968 and entered into force in 1970. The need to prevent proliferation began to be taken more seriously after the Cuban Missile Crisis, as President Kennedy famously raised the spectre of a vulnerable world with twenty or more nuclear-armed states locked in regional and international rivalries. While popular culture in the form of songs, films and books echoed ordinary people's fears of nuclear annihilation, policymakers in the Soviet Union and the United States were as much if not more concerned that a world with many nuclear-armed states would undermine nuclear deterrence and erode the marginal utility of their own nuclear forces. Once these two superpowers decided that a non-proliferation treaty would accord with their interests and began pushing in 1965, negotiations moved forward in earnest.[37]

Progress was initially slow, according to Swedish ambassador Alva Myrdal, who noted, "Confident of their power, [the Soviet Union and the United States] attempted to hold unrestricted rights to possess, deploy, and develop nuclear arms quantitatively and qualitatively, while showing overbearing disregard for the three minor nuclear weapon powers, and resolutely closing the options for all other nations to go nuclear".[38] India, which by that time had a significant nuclear programme of its own under way, in 1964 put forward a proposal for a UN agenda item on non-proliferation, and then joined forces with Sweden to demand an integrated approach, including "some other measures affecting directly the nuclear weapons capability of the nuclear powers".[39] This was supported by the eight non-aligned members on the ENDC. After China joined the nuclear club, and "to retain the initiative", according to Myrdal,[40] the Soviet Union and the United States coordinated submission of their own draft treaties to the General Assembly in 1965, based on the Irish approach, which drew distinctions between the obligations on states possessing nuclear weapons and those without.[41] In the following debates in the ENDC and the General Assembly, some states pushed hard for the treaty to contain disarmament-related commitments, such as a CTBT, a cut-off of fissile material production for weapons purposes, as well as support for regional nuclear-weapon-free zones.

In August 1967, the Soviet Union and the United States again submitted identical draft treaties to the ENDC, superseding the previous drafts of 1965.[42] The new drafts were hardly more welcome to the non-nuclear state negotiators, who made further proposals linking non-proliferation to nuclear disarmament. In January 1968, the superpowers introduced revised (and still identical) draft treaties at the ENDC, incorporating a number of the non-nuclear-weapon states' concerns. A special session of the General Assembly was held in April 1968, at which the Soviet Union and the United States jointly tabled their draft treaty.[43] The draft contained a preambular reference recalling the PTBT pledge to seek the discontinuance of nuclear tests. Reflecting some of the other states' concerns not to lose out on cutting-edge technological developments, the superpowers had also revised the Article IV provision on "peaceful uses of nuclear energy", included a new Article V on "peaceful nuclear explosions" (PNE) and a new Article VII on nuclear-weapon-free zones. A rather vague commitment to pursue nuclear disarmament appeared in a new Article VI. This bilateral draft was debated and slightly amended by the ENDC members and then finalized. Adopted by the General Assembly just three months later, on 12 June, the NPT was opened for signature on 1 July 1968. Although marginalized from the bilateral negotiations on the draft treaty, the United Kingdom was invited to become the third depositary state, joining the Soviet Union and the United States. China and France, the other two countries defined in the treaty as nuclear-weapon states—having "manufactured and exploded a nuclear weapon or other nuclear explosive device prior to 1 January, 1967"—did not join the NPT until 1992.

Though the NPT now has wide multilateral membership, with 188 states parties at the time of writing, history shows that the treaty did not really emerge from a multilateral negotiating process, but pre-eminently reflected the strategic interests of the Soviet Union and the United States. With the right to nuclear energy emphasized as the primary incentive for non-nuclear-weapon states, the NPT's reflection of a prevalent belief that this technology could provide cheap, safe and clean energy for all has become increasingly problematic in the twenty-first century security environment. The NPT's recognition of the status quo with regard to the five defined nuclear powers led to more stringent and heavily policed obligations being imposed on the rest, whose only option in joining the NPT would be as non-nuclear-weapon states. Although the ENDC played a significant role in ensuring that the NPT would link disarmament with non-proliferation, the Cold War powers maintained overall control by tabling identical treaty drafts and, finally, their joint draft treaty. One immediate consequence of the treaty's "inequalities" was that a number of states with nuclear programmes or aspirations (for example, Argentina, Brazil, France, India, as well as several African states) abstained on the UN resolution recommending adoption of the NPT in June 1968, and—in a move that was to be echoed 28 years later with the CTBT—India publicly declared its refusal to join the NPT, on the grounds that it was discriminatory.[44]

The NPT's connection with the CTBT went beyond the exhortation in the preamble to discontinue nuclear testing. A number of negotiators, unsure of the future effectiveness of the non-proliferation regime, insisted on review conferences every five years, with the NPT's duration limited to 25 years, requiring a decision to be made in 1995 on any future extension. The review conferences and the finite duration of the treaty provided mechanisms for the non-nuclear-weapon states and civil society to use in raising concerns about the nuclear arms race and the lack of progress on nuclear disarmament, with particular emphasis on nuclear testing. Confined largely to diplomatic declarations, concerns raised at review conferences had little effect on the policies of the major nuclear-weapon states for the first two decades. This changed in the 1990s, as the date for the decision on extending the NPT drew near, presenting an opportunity to exert unprecedented leverage on the nuclear-weapon states.

DÉTENTE, ARMS CONTROL AND TESTING LIMITS

Opening with entry into force of the NPT, the 1970s was a decade of détente, appearing to vindicate theories of bipolar stability, popular in the late 1950s and early 1960s. Nuclear arms control was dominated by bilateral negotiations between the Soviet Union and the United States, both of which had begun to recognize the need to show they were making some effort to curb their spiralling arms race—not just to give greater credibility to the NPT, which they were encouraging others to join, but also because of the consequences of an uncontrolled arms build-up for their economics and national security. Early in the 1970s they developed a linked offence–defence approach to arms control, exemplified by two closely related US–Soviet treaties, the Anti-Ballistic Missile Treaty, which enshrined the concept of deterrence based on mutual vulnerability, and the SALT I Interim Agreement, the first to limit strategic nuclear weapons. The two treaties were designed as a package and entered into force together in 1972. During this time, the superpowers also commenced negotiations on SALT II.

In 1974 and 1976, two bilateral treaties limiting to 150kt the yield of underground nuclear test explosions were also concluded, the 1974 Threshold Test Ban Treaty (TTBT), which covered military explosions, and the 1976 Peaceful Nuclear Explosions Treaty (PNET), which covered nuclear explosions for civil purposes, such as large scale excavations.[45] John Edmonds, who led the UK delegation at the later trilateral talks, characterized the contribution of these two treaties as "negative", saying, "their prohibition of tests yielding 150 kt imposed no serious limitation on further nuclear weapons development by the two superpowers".[46] Myrdal was even more damning, calling the TTBT a "disgraceful conspiracy between the two superpowers" and characterizing it as a sham, intended to present the public with an image of restraint and of commitment to arms control, when it actually "strangles all attempts to reach international agreements on a total ban".[47] The scepticism of these two senior diplomats was shared by many others, including Jimmy Carter, who chose not to push for ratification when he became president in 1976. Carter criticized the TTBT threshold as too high to provide a genuine restraint on weapons development, and preferred to use his political capital in trying to get a CTBT.[48] Less criticism was levelled at the PNET, signed two years later. Critics of arms control were prepared to view this as a useful confidence-building measure, providing exchange of data and inspections at proposed sites for PNE.[49]

The United States terminated its PNE programme in 1977, and the Soviet Union, which did not conduct PNE large enough to trigger an inspection under the treaty, finally halted its programme in 1989. The PNET may have been associated with a larger US policy objective of opening the Soviet Union up to inspection, if only for the relatively rare events of a nuclear explosion for large-scale engineering or mining. Whether or not this objective was explicit, it appears to have been an outcome. Roland Timerbaev, a senior Soviet arms control negotiator at the time, wrote that the PNET "put to test the willingness of both sides, above all of the Soviet Union, to accept highly intrusive verification procedures ... [and] may have laid at least some of the groundwork for subsequent verification schemes".[50] Similarly, Nancy Gallagher commented that they "served as a dry run in which the superpowers first made a political commitment to limit underground tests and then worked out the details of a cooperative verification system that balanced the risks of cheating and spying, and allocated the costs of verification in an equitable fashion".[51]

Tripartite talks, 1977–1980

Once the TTBT was concluded, the Soviet Union tried to reinvigorate efforts on a total ban by submitting a draft CTBT to the UN General Assembly in 1975. Reacting to criticism from the United Kingdom and the United States that its draft was inadequate, particularly on the issues of verification and PNE, Moscow took soundings from a number of states and tabled a revised treaty in February 1977. This elicited a more positive response from President Carter, who had made a CTBT a major plank of his election platform.[52] Following preliminary discussions, tripartite talks were established later that year between the Soviet Union (under General Secretary Leonid Brezhnev), the United States (under President Jimmy Carter) and the United Kingdom (under Prime Minister James Callaghan).[53]

The negotiations began in earnest with a meeting held at the UK Mission in Geneva on 3 October, on the twenty-fifth anniversary of the first British nuclear test. Edmonds describes three "differences of principle" in the opening positions of the Soviet Union, on the one hand, and the United Kingdom and the United States, on the other: the level of intrusion required for verifying a comprehensive test ban; PNE, which the Soviet Union did not want banned; and the Soviet demand that the treaty should not come into force until France and China acceded.[54] During the first year the talks made progress. The Soviet Union was willing to include a moratorium (but not an outright ban) on PNE, and moved closer to the US–UK position on verification, while the United States slightly modified its stance on on-site inspections. It is interesting to see how versions of these positions—with the same or different advocates—were to become crucial to the outcome of the CTBT 15 years later.

The prospect that a CTBT might become possible concentrated minds in the nuclear laboratories and relevant government departments. Rather than opposing outright, test-ban opponents in the US Department of Energy and the Joint Chiefs of Staff reprised the verification obstacles that had served so well in the past. Claiming that the verification under consideration would be inadequate to prevent or detect Soviet cheating at low yields, they pressed for a new, lower threshold instead of a comprehensive ban. With support from their British counterparts at Aldermaston, the US nuclear laboratories also asserted that they needed periodic nuclear tests to have confidence in the safety and reliability of stockpiled nuclear weapons.[55] President Carter tried to appease domestic opponents of a ban by proposing a comprehensive test ban of five years' duration, hoping that this would begin to embed the norm. Intensified pressure from the US military and nuclear establishments forced Carter to reduce this to three years and to add the requirement of Senate ratification before renewal. In addition, he was drawn into permitting underground testing of up to 100lbs yield for nuclear triggers and "to keep weapon scientists up-to-date".[56]

Carter's compromise, described by the US House Armed Services Committee as "the worst of both the political and military worlds", [57] was derided by all sides. The British were disappointed, the Russians cynical, civil society refused to endorse the continuation of low-yield nuclear explosions, and there was media speculation that the three-year duration was designed to free the hands of the next president. Carter therefore lost the initiative and time ran out on the talks. Margaret Thatcher replaced Callaghan as the UK Prime Minister following elections in May 1979, and brought a very different set of priorities and interests. The Conservative Party under Thatcher embarked on modernizing the nuclear forces, taking the decision to replace Polaris with the more powerful Trident system, capable of carrying multiple warheads that the United Kingdom would need to design—and also test—to be compatible with US missile specifications. The talks continued, but Carter subsequently became mired in crisis when Iranian revolutionaries seized 52 US diplomats in Tehran on 4 November 1979 and held them hostage for over a year. After Ronald Reagan was elected president in November 1980, the United States requested that the tripartite talks be suspended. They were never resumed and the Reagan administration formally withdrew in 1982.

1981–1989: PUBLIC MOBILIZING AGAINST NUCLEAR WEAPONS

By the end of the 1970s, détente was failing and though SALT II was signed in 1979, it never entered into force. Despite his best intentions, President Carter had proved unable to sustain any significant challenge to the dominance of the nuclear weapons lobby in US strategic decision-making. The deterioration in US–Soviet relations had a nuclear dimension, but was largely due to a mix of geostrategic and political factors, which included the Soviet invasion of Afghanistan, and the exercise of a Soviet veto to block UN Security Council action to support the United States during the hostage crisis with Iran. Such events and tensions contributed to the ousting of the Carter administration.[58]

The period from 1981 to 1989 spanned from the Cold War's depths to its sudden end. As the Soviet Union began to deploy a new generation of intermediate range missiles, known as SS-20s, the North Atlantic Treaty Organization (NATO) took the decision to deploy 464 ground-launched cruise missiles in five West European states, and 108 Pershing II ballistic missiles in West Germany. The "dual-track" approach, so called because deployment was coupled with calls for negotiations, reflected concerns among European members of NATO that their security was being compromised by the new Soviet deployments, changing US nuclear doctrine and Washington's dysfunctional bilateral arms control relationship with Moscow.

Reagan entered his presidency eager, he said, to consign the Soviet Union to the "ashcan of history" and determined to modernize US nuclear and other military capabilities.[59] He ended it in partnership with Mikhail Gorbachev, who transformed Soviet politics when he took over the Communist Party in 1985. In the early 1980s, however, US–Soviet relations hit a dangerous low, as US strategic doctrine shifted toward prevailing in a "limited" nuclear war, in which the deployment of nuclear weapons could be envisaged as part of a wider conflict without automatically escalating into all-out mutual annihilation.[60] Such notions, combined with NATO's deployment of the cruise and Pershing II missiles, viewed as having a first-use capability more suited to warfighting than deterrence, contributed to the dramatic rise of the peace movements in the 1980s. European governments found themselves squeezed between domestic public opinion and a US–Soviet game of diplomatic combat and counter-accusation, fuelled by Reagan's zealous anti-communism.

Doctrines of nuclear deterrence had helped reconcile many people to the presence of nuclear weapons since 1963 because they emphasized that the purpose and role of nuclear forces was to prevent nuclear war. Talk of limited nuclear war wrecked that uneasy complacency, and provoked vociferous opposition. NATO tried to win public opinion in 1981 by proposing a "zero option"—the elimination of all intermediate-range nuclear forces from Europe.[61] In March 1983, Reagan launched the Strategic Defence Initiative—a programme of missile defences meant to protect the United States from a Soviet attack and thereby escape the contradictions of nuclear deterrence and dilemmas of mutual vulnerability. But the initiative—soon ridiculed as "Star Wars"—was attacked from all sides as technologically unfeasible and politically destabilizing.[62] Half-way through his first term, as anti-nuclear movements grew across Europe and the United States, Reagan was reportedly shaken by a film titled *The Day After* that fictionalized a nuclear attack on Kansas, which was shown on US television in November 1983. This was around the time that the United States suffered a further close encounter with nuclear war when Soviet intelligence misconstrued NATO's Able Archer nuclear exercise of October–November 1983 as preparation for attack. The President of the United States began to dream of a world without nuclear weapons as the last option to escape mutually assured destruction.

The screening of films like *The Day After* was Hollywood's response to the volcanic eruption of anti-nuclear activism provoked by the deployment of the new generation of nuclear missiles. As the Reagan–Thatcher axis sought to recreate an Atlanticist consensus and dominate with their "special relationship", they provoked the most significant upsurge in anti-nuclear protests since nuclear testing went underground in 1963. There was a dramatic increase in the membership of established anti-nuclear organizations such as CND but, even more significantly, new kinds of peace movements and civil society engagement developed, reflecting feminist and environmentalist concerns.[63] In Germany, one of the peace movement's roots was in church organizations, reinvigorated politically by the post-

Second World War emphasis on the Lutheran imperative of conscience and dissent. Another was with the trade unions and socialist Left. A third constituency, which grew into the Green Party, formed in the late 1970s in an attempt to overcome the disillusionment many felt with the fragmented, male-dominated, "radical" Left and to integrate the adversarial single-issue politics of previous decades into a more coherent political movement for social and international change. The Greens rode to prominence on the wave of anti-nuclear feeling in the early 1980s, attracting some 5–10% of public support in Germany. In addition to mobilizing opposition to the policies and deployments of NATO, the Greens, independent women's groups and Western churches made strong efforts to build links with dissidents in the East. Academics and activists also developed links across Western and Eastern Europe, through national peace organizations and networks such as European Nuclear Disarmament (END).

A noted example from the United Kingdom was the Greenham Common Women's Peace Camp, which was established in September 1981 at the gates of the first US Air Force base scheduled to receive ground-launched cruise missiles, and became a dramatic focus for grassroots direct action. Peace camps arose at many nuclear bases across Europe, but Greenham's influence on subsequent anti-war movements was unique. The Women's Peace Camp provided the crucible for a feminist, anarchist challenge that directly undermined US military deployments while also provoking the established political and peace movements to change their ways of working. But this was not the only feminist challenge. European and Scandinavian women took the lead in networking across borders, with marches and train journeys traversing Europe, raising awareness of the risks of nuclear weapons and war in the towns and communities along the way, and promoting discussion on alternatives to Cold War militarism.

In the United States too, anti-nuclear opposition mobilized in response to growing fears about nuclear war. Where the European movements called for nuclear disarmament, US activists coalesced around the demand for a freeze on the production and testing of nuclear weapons, as represented by Randall Forsberg's "Call to Halt the Nuclear Arms Race", issued in April 1980. The Freeze Movement organized large demonstrations in Washington and other cities, but also worked with legislators, only narrowly failing to have Freeze legislation passed through Congress. When Greenham women took a legal case to the New York courts in November 1983, seeking an injunction to prevent the deployment of cruise missiles, they were joined by two Congressmen, Ron Dellums and Ted Weiss, arguing that the constitutional requirement of Congressional approval on any decision to go to war would be nullified by nuclear first use. Though the US movement played little role in combating the "Euromissiles", as cruise and Pershing missiles were known to Americans, it took on the Strategic Defense Initiative and the MX missile. Through public and political mobilization aimed at Congressional denial of funds to the programme, Freeze advocates were influential in the cancellation of the MX missiles, while the arms control organizations contributed to the discrediting of the Star Wars programme through effective use of technical, strategic and financial analyses. The MX programme, which Carter had surprised many by backing, may have been the price he paid to buy off opponents in time to get SALT II signed, so there was a certain irony that as SALT's main critics came to power in the Reagan administration, they saw the MX cancelled by a fiscally conscious Congress responding to the upsurge of anti-nuclear concerns across the public spectrum.

The turning point occurred when Mikhail Gorbachev took power in 1985. Badly bogged down in Afghanistan and beset by growing social and economic crises across the Soviet bloc, Gorbachev undertook a programme of *glasnost* (openness) and *perestroika* (reconstruction), which included significant concessions in arms control. In a speech on 15 January 1986, which Lawrence Freedman compares to Reagan's star war visions, Gorbachev offered a plan for total nuclear disarmament.[64] Nine months later, at the US–Soviet summit in Reykjavik, Gorbachev and Reagan "began to outbid each other" in visions of how to remove the nuclear threat through disarmament.[65] As senior officials on both sides scrambled to prevent the two leaders' nuclear disarmament ideas from becoming adopted, NATO was confronted with an unanticipated Soviet acceptance of its "zero option". The direct outcome of the Reykjavik Summit was the Intermediate-Range Nuclear Forces (INF) Treaty, signed on 8 December 1987. This ground-breaking treaty was made possible not only because of the two leaders' apparent desire to see progress in disarmament and arms control but because, under Gorbachev, the Soviet Union was more willing to accept intrusive verification.

Despite the upsurge of protests, however, little attention was directed toward nuclear testing, and hopes for CTBT negotiations continued to be thwarted.[66] One tragic incident briefly returned nuclear testing to the international headlines. The environmental organization Greenpeace, which had campaigned against nuclear testing since 1971, was preparing to lead a protest flotilla to the French nuclear test site in the South Pacific, when French secret service agents sank its flagship, the *Rainbow Warrior*, in Auckland Harbour on 10 July 1985. A Greenpeace photographer, Fernando Perreira, was killed.[67]

Greenpeace had planned to draw attention to nuclear testing by combining direct action and diplomatic pressure. Its diplomatic strategy was based on the NPT's preambular commitment to the discontinuance of nuclear testing and made use of the fact that this was one of the priority issues raised by the non-nuclear-weapon states at the review conferences of the NPT. Utilizing lobbying and media strategies, Greenpeace tried to prevent consensus on the final document of the Third NPT Review Conference in July 1985 unless the nuclear-weapon states agreed to negotiate a CTBT. They managed to make allies among NPT parties, especially the non-aligned states, but failed in their bid to get a binding commitment on a test ban.[68]

Despite this diplomatic defeat, test-ban advocates were rewarded when Gorbachev declared a moratorium on testing on 5 August 1985, the twenty-second anniversary of the signing of the PTBT. The moratorium was both a bid for international public opinion at the height of the stand-off over the intermediate-range nuclear forces in Europe, and a response to non-aligned and non-governmental pressure. Two noted examples of organized pressure were the Five-Continent Peace Initiative, coordinated by Parliamentarians for Global Action, an NGO whose membership consisted of democratically elected representatives from parliaments and legislatures around the world, and the recently formed International Physicians for the Prevention of Nuclear War (IPPNW). This latter group had been founded by American and Russian physicians in an attempt to highlight the need for nuclear disarmament. Its authority rested on the physicians' scientific and medical assessment of nuclear testing and the effects of using nuclear weapons, including the dangers of nuclear war and nuclear winter. They also conveyed moral authority, derived from the traditional respect that doctors command and from their bilateral efforts to transcend the Cold War political culture and appeal to the common cause of humankind's survival, a point emphasized when IPPNW and its founders were awarded the Nobel Peace Prize in 1985.

The Soviet moratorium lasted 19 months, despite receiving no positive response from the other nuclear-weapon states. During this time, the

US House of Representatives attempted to exert pressure on the Reagan administration with an initiative to cut off funding for nuclear tests above a yield of 1kt. Once again, however, scepticism about the verifiability of a CTBT was marshalled by the Pentagon and intelligence advisers to boost the positions taken by test-ban opponents. To discredit these familiar—but unsubstantiated—claims of non-verifiability, scientists from a Washington-based environmental organization, the Natural Resources Defense Council (NRDC), proposed a joint verification experiment with the Soviet Academy of Sciences. Despite official opposition from the Reagan administration, supporters in the State Department made it possible for scientists from the Soviet Union and the United States to meet, plan and carry out the placement of seismic stations around the main test sites in Nevada (USA) and Semipalatinsk (Kazakhstan). The Soviet participants enjoyed the support of Gorbachev, but had to contend with resistance from the Foreign and Defence Ministries.[69]

The joint experiments lasted for 14 months. Making use of chemical explosions of 10–20t and a small, local earthquake for the purposes of comparison and control, the experiments showed that regional monitoring could detect a de-coupled (masked) 1kt explosion and distinguish between similarly located earthquakes and explosions. While the project was credited with assisting Gorbachev to win the support needed to extend the Soviet moratorium in 1986, the impact in the United States was initially small, and mostly assisted Congressional attempts to build verification confidence for ratifying the much-maligned TTBT and PNET. More importantly, the project flushed out a number of contradictions in the positions of US test-ban opponents, causing the Reagan administration to waver between welcoming the pressure on the Soviets to engage in cooperative verification and portraying Gorbachev's support for the project as an attempt to "confuse the domestic debate about the need for American nuclear testing" and to "promote an inequitable and unverifiable ban on nuclear testing".[70]

Although the nuclear weapon laboratories again sought to use science to blindside the politicians into rejecting a CTBT, they were no longer able to rely on verification arguments to do the job. The belief of many Americans that verification was apolitical and that the scientists from the national labs were simply providing neutral facts and assessments had begun to give way to greater awareness of the manipulative potential of scientific presentations. Losing verification as their main source of leverage, the laboratories started pushing more with arguments related to the safety and reliability of the nuclear arsenal. Although they were successful in intimidating some non-scientist policymakers, the safety and reliability arguments were more obviously politicized from the beginning, and therefore less effective than verification arguments had been in the earlier attempts to block a CTBT.

Applauded for their attempts to bridge the confidence gap on verification, the joint experiments had diminished the potency of the politics of verification.[71] Even so, under pressure from his own military and nuclear establishments, and having failed to get significant political gains from the Soviet moratorium, Gorbachev resumed testing in February 1987, after the first US test of the year. The role of civil society in inducing him to start a new moratorium in October 1991 and why France and the United States undertook moratoria of their own the following year are considered in the next chapter, which deals with the prenegotiation phase of the CTBT, 1990 to 1993.

CHAPTER 3

PUTTING THE TEST BAN BACK ON THE TABLE

I salute all those officials in governments and citizens who have struggled for so long to achieve this Treaty. Thank you all for making the world a safer place for our children and grandchildren.

Boutros Boutros-Ghali, UN Secretary-General,
24 September 1996[1]

On 2 October 1992, President George H.W. Bush signed into law an appropriations bill that mandated a nine-month moratorium on US nuclear testing and required the government to seek to conclude a comprehensive test-ban treaty by September 1996. Described as "a fascinating story of Senate politics and procedures",[2] this ground-breaking US moratorium joined the French testing moratorium that President François Mitterrand had undertaken six months earlier, which itself followed the second Soviet moratorium in five years, which General Secretary Gorbachev declared in October 1991. These three national moratoria on testing played a crucial, arguably a causal, role in bringing the parties to the negotiating table in the CD 16 months later. Each was important in its own way, but the die was cast when President Bush signed the US moratorium legislation, which not only mandated a pause in testing, but also set a target date for conclusion of a negotiated CTBT.

Analysts in the realist tradition would seek to explain the US moratorium in the following terms: the hegemonic power was adapting to the post-Cold War strategic environment by down-grading its reliance on nuclear weapons. As part of its nuclear policy shift, the US government decided that its security interests would now be served by a multilaterally negotiated nuclear test ban, and so took appropriate measures to ensure that the issue was given priority and prominence on the international arms control agenda. Put like this, the US moratorium is made to appear the outcome of a rational decision-making process, but that is not how it happened. In fact,

President Bush opposed the CTBT at that time, and his Secretary of Defense, Dick Cheney, and National Security Advisor, Brent Scowcroft, had actively lobbied against the moratorium. Even as he signed the bill, President Bush declared the provision limiting US nuclear tests to be "highly objectionable" and complained that it "unwisely restrict[ed]" tests necessary "to maintain a safe and reliable nuclear deterrent".[3] Far from being a strategic decision undertaken by a rational government, the US moratorium was put in place despite the highest levels of opposition in the Bush administration.

The hostility to a CTBT in President Bush's administration followed in the steps of President Reagan's reversal of President Carter's pro-CTBT policy in 1982,[4] but their opposition was not shared by the majority of voters. Similarly, despite opinion polls that showed overwhelming British public support for a CTBT, the Conservative government in the United Kingdom opposed joining the French and Russian moratoria. The United Kingdom, which had for three decades conducted its nuclear explosions in cooperation with the US Department of Energy at the Nevada Test Site, had at least three more nuclear tests scheduled for its new Trident warhead, and strongly rejected any suggestion of a US moratorium, knowing that this would require a halt in UK testing as well.[5] The depth of opposition by these two governments to a test ban had been clearly demonstrated at the Fourth NPT Review Conference in 1990, when the United States, supported by the United Kingdom until the very last minute, allowed this important meeting to collapse without a Final Document rather than agree to a one-sentence commitment to negotiate a CTBT.

The US moratorium was a pivotal moment in moving the world toward CTBT negotiations, but far from reflecting a change in government policy or posture, the moratorium was actually forced on a reluctant president by legislative action in the US Senate and House. The nine-month moratorium and target date for the CTBT were attached and carried as amendments to the 1993 Energy and Water Development Appropriations Act.[6] This clever strategy was to a large extent designed and organized by pro-CTBT pressure groups, but it was carried out by legislators. What, then, impelled US Senators and Representatives to take up the issue of a nuclear test ban in the early 1990s? How and why did they force the moratorium through despite attempts to trade it away for other benefits? How did this political strategy take shape?

The French moratorium announced on 8 April 1992 gave powerful impetus to the advocates of a US moratorium. Before it was declared, many would have regarded a voluntary suspension of French testing to be more improbable than a US moratorium. It certainly took many by surprise, though it followed on the heels of the Russian moratorium and took place at around the time France acceded to the NPT. Moreover, it appeared to come as a surprise to the French military and Atomic Energy Commission (*Commissariat à l'énergie atomique*), which had already begun preparations for the 1992 programme of tests at Moruroa[7] and Fangataufa.[8] What induced President Mitterrand to initiate France's first ever moratorium since French testing began in 1960? Mitterrand, who had presided over dozens of nuclear tests in the South Pacific, had for years ignored the protests of Australia, Japan, New Zealand and the Pacific Island peoples. Moreover, as discussed later, the *Commissariat à l'énergie atomique* pushed to conduct further nuclear tests in 1995 and France was by no means an enthusiastic participant during the early stages of the CTBT negotiations, suggesting some level of policy conflict or confusion between the moratorium decision and its consequences. To understand how these political leaders came to declare a halt in their nuclear testing programmes, it is necessary to consider the strategies and tactics used by civil society to raise public awareness and exert pressure on the nuclear-weapon state governments.

RAISING AWARENESS OF THE NEED FOR A TEST BAN

As the Cold War ended, eyes were beginning to turn toward the NPT, which would be up for renewal in 1995. The priority for test-ban advocates was to increase public and political interest in the issue and exert pressure on the nuclear-testing states so that they would agree to start negotiations. The period of 1990 to 1993 was characterized by the interplay of three diplomatic and direct-action strategies involving non-aligned states and NGOs: utilizing the political commitment to a CTBT enshrined in the NPT to exert pressure through the 1990 NPT Review Conference, direct action at the major nuclear test sites and symbolic locations in the nuclear-weapon states, and convening an Amendment Conference for states parties to the PTBT to consider an amendment adding "underground" to the prohibited environments, thereby converting the partial ban into a comprehensive test ban.

The first opportunity for action arose when NPT states parties met in Geneva for the Fourth NPT Review Conference in 1990. A group of non-nuclear-weapon states updated the strategy tried by Greenpeace in 1985 and insisted that the final document from the review conference contain a clear commitment by the nuclear powers to negotiate a CTBT. Russia supported, but the United Kingdom and the United States held out against language that would commit to a CTBT.[9] As the conference was coming to an end in the early hours of 15 September 1990 with all other issues agreed, its President, Oswaldo de Rivero of Peru, stopped the clock, hoping that private negotiations among a group of 16 parties would reach agreement on CTBT language.[10] The Chair of the drafting committee, Carl-Magnus Hyltenius of Sweden, obtained widespread support and the President's endorsement for a compromise text that called for early bilateral and multilateral action. The United States insisted on adding a further paragraph that asserted the primacy of "step-by-step negotiations" between the two superpowers on intermediate limitations on testing "leading to the ultimate objective of the complete cessation of nuclear testing as part of an effective disarmament process".[11]

Mexico led non-aligned opposition to the US language. Arguing that it contradicted the intentions contained in Hyltenius' text, Mexico's ambassador, Miguel Marín Bosch, refused to go beyond the compromises already contained in this language. In the early hours of the morning, the UK delegation at last accepted the compromise text, but the United States continued to hold out for its own paragraph.[12] With the United States still refusing to join consensus, and Mexico determined not to budge any further, the Review Conference collapsed without a final document, amid mutual recrimination.

The strategy of holding out for a CTBT commitment in the NPT final document had been widely supported by non-nuclear states. Mexico's persistence at the end was also backed by a significant number of non-aligned states. NGOs were divided. Parliamentarians for Global Action and Greenpeace, which attended the Conference, strongly supported Mexico's stand, but a number of influential non-proliferation and arms control NGOs argued that Mexico should have given in to the United States to prevent the loss of the Conference's other hard-won agreements on safeguards, inspections and nuclear smuggling.[13] As it later transpired, however, Mexico's refusal to concede on its CTBT demand sent an essential signal about the importance of the CTBT just as Western diplomats were planning their campaigns to get the indefinite extension of the NPT in 1995.

Public mobilization halts testing in Kazakhstan

Of the three nuclear-weapon states in the NPT at the time of the 1990 Review Conference, only the Soviet Union supported the CTBT. While Gorbachev appeared genuinely committed to a test-ban treaty, he was also under pressure from Kazakh nationalists, who vowed to shut down the largest Soviet test site comprising four areas, known locally as "Polygons", near Semipalatinsk. After giving up on the August 1985 moratorium when none of the other nuclear-weapon states responded, the Soviet Union had renewed nuclear testing. Provoked to anger by two nuclear explosions that vented unexpected amounts of radioactive substances in February 1989, Olzhas Suleimenov, a popular Kazakh poet, launched a grass-roots movement that linked environmental and anti-nuclear concerns with nationalist appeal. The beginning of this movement appeared spontaneous. Suleimenov used his appearance on a television broadcast to condemn the tests and to call on the viewers to march to the centre of Almaty, at that time the capital city.[14] Surprising Suleimenov as much as the Soviet government, tens of thousands of people joined the demonstration, and so the Nevada–Semipalatinsk Movement was born.[15]

The name was deliberately chosen to make links with US opponents of nuclear testing who demonstrated each year at the Nevada Test Site. After initiating this movement, Suleimenov recruited local doctors and nationalists and made contact with international NGOs, notably Greenpeace, IPPNW and the Nevada-based American Peace Test network. He also gained support from the Western Shoshone Nation, whose tribal lands (known as Newe Segobia) lay at the centre of the test site in Nevada. During 1989–1990, the Nevada–Semipalatinsk Movement held meetings and demonstrations in several Kazakh and Russian cities. Working with physicians, they conducted epidemiological research, and released a series of filmed documentaries that mixed medical data with harrowing pictures of deformed and brain-damaged children. Suleimenov's tactics are widely credited with forcing the Soviet Union to cancel 11 out of 18 scheduled tests in 1989. In May 1990, the Nevada–Semipalatinsk Movement and IPPNW jointly organized an International Citizens Congress for a Nuclear Test Ban, attracting 600 international participants to Semipalatinsk, who joined with thousands of local people in demonstrations at villages adjacent to the test site. The

Kazakh movement against testing grew, attracting widespread support from the villages and towns all round the site, as well as politicians and businesses in the towns. As central control of the Soviet republics slipped as the Cold War drew to an end, Moscow cancelled more planned tests and announced that the Semipalatinsk site would be closed by 1993. This meant that from then on, all Soviet underground testing would have to be conducted at the less convenient test sites on Novaya Zemlya, in the Arctic Ocean, home to the indigenous Nenets people.[16]

Direct action to make the test sites publicly visible

After a few years of relative inactivity on nuclear issues following the events of 1985, Greenpeace returned in the late 1980s with a plan to highlight testing at Novaya Zemlya, Nevada and Moruroa as part of a strategy to raise public awareness and exert political pressure for a CTBT. On 10 July 1989, exactly four years after the sinking of their flagship in Auckland Harbour, Greenpeace launched a converted trawler, naming it likewise *Rainbow Warrior*. At the launch, Greenpeace pledged to build an even stronger campaign for a CTBT, together with a new drive toward the objective of "nuclear free seas". Capitalizing on growing public concern about protecting the environment, Greenpeace combined its disarmament message with raising awareness about the scale of the international environmental and human rights problems associated with nuclear testing. This "soft" strategy was particularly important for building support in France, which retained a strong, national consensus on nuclear defence policy despite growing environmental consciousness and concern.

From 1990 to 1992, successive direct actions were carried out at these test sites.[17] Greenpeace had made links with the Nevada–Semipalatinsk Movement and joined in the May 1990 International Citizens Congress for a Nuclear Test Ban in Kazakhstan. Receiving intelligence that Moscow was planning to conduct its next nuclear tests on Novaya Zemlya later in the year, Greenpeace sent a ship there in October 1990. A team of four campaigners with radiation detectors landed a small boat on the northern island and then hiked to some shafts left from earlier tests, where they measured high levels of radioactivity. The four were apprehended by the Soviet Union, which then arrested the *MV Greenpeace* and its entire crew. The international crew members were detained for nearly a week, while Greenpeace offices around the world generated massive publicity and a barrage of letters calling on President Gorbachev to release the prisoners and end all nuclear testing. Even Boris Yeltsin joined in, publicly demanding that Gorbachev call another moratorium. On 18 October 1990, shortly after the campaigners had been released and deported, the Soviet establishment went ahead with the planned nuclear explosion at Novaya Zemlya. Because of the publicity and shock generated by Greenpeace publishing the radiation levels they had measured at the site, this nuclear test provoked an unprecedented storm of criticism at the United Nations and in the international media. That turned out to be the last Soviet nuclear explosion. Instead of preparing the frozen ground at Novaya Zemlya to receive further tests the next year, Gorbachev instead announced another unilateral moratorium.

One month after its ship was released from custody, Greenpeace put the spotlight on Anglo-American nuclear collaboration, with simultaneous actions in London and Nevada to draw attention to a British underground test scheduled for November 1990. A dramatic photograph of climbers hanging above the Thames with a huge banner suspended from London's iconic Tower Bridge with the words "Stop UK Nuclear Tests" made the front pages of several UK newspapers. At the same time, Greenpeace sponsored four activists, including three Greenham women, to disrupt the planned UK test at the Nevada Test Site. Hiking, camping and avoiding detection by the military and police for three days, they found their way to the prepared location of the British test just before the device was due to be detonated. When a site camera showed the four converging on the ground zero site six minutes before detonation, the explosion had to be halted while the US Department of Energy sent police to remove the protesters from the test site. The explosion proceeded several hours later, but the action and subsequent trial of the protesters served an important purpose by generating significant media coverage and interest on both sides of the Atlantic, not to mention raising embarrassing questions about nuclear security.[10] The Tower Bridge and Nevada Test Site actions carried the political message about nuclear weapons testing to a much broader public. Opinion polls revealed that the majority of British people were not even aware that nuclear weapons were still being exploded in such tests. Building on the publicity and renewed interest, other disarmament activists and groups boosted their campaigns against nuclear weapons as well.

The next month, December 1990, Greenpeace took the new *Rainbow Warrior* to the French test site at Moruroa, where several nuclear tests were being prepared. Having chosen to focus more on the "soft" issues of environmental contamination and human rights, where there was better hope of eroding French support for nuclear testing than a confrontation over nuclear weapons per se, Greenpeace published a compilation of personal testimonies from Tahitian witnesses and workers involved in the French nuclear testing programme in the South Pacific, with information on accidents, health effects and environmental problems that appeared to be linked with the tests.[19] Film and data from a French cultural hero, the explorer Jacques Cousteau, were employed to present evidence that plutonium and caesium were leaking into the surrounding ocean and to raise questions about the atoll's fragility. With public fanfare, Greenpeace applied to the French government for permission to take samples "to quantify present and short to medium term releases of radioactivity from the underground nuclear explosions at Moruroa and Fangataufa".[20] When their request was ignored, Greenpeace went ahead with a planned sampling mission as a form of non-violent direct action, with media on board to record every move. In a tactic similar to the one used at Novaya Zemlya, a small team with scientists took a boat close to the test site to take samples of water and fauna. As anticipated, they were arrested for breaching the 12-mile exclusion zone, but they managed to retain some of their samples.[21] The arrests and subsequent deportations received worldwide media coverage, with significant—and unusually positive—reporting in France. Analysis of the samples revealed radioactive contamination. Although the levels were relatively low, there were traces of plutonium—enough for Greenpeace to publish a report in September 1991 and persuade Members of the European Parliament to call on the French government to permit an independent international study of the Moruroa and Fangataufa test sites. Vowing to keep taking scientists to Moruroa until France halted nuclear testing and allowed a full and open study of the environmental situation and rate of failure of containment from the nuclear tests, Greenpeace prepared to return the following year.[22]

The PTBT Amendment Conference

In January 1991, the PTBT Amendment Conference was held at the United Nations in New York against the strong opposition of the governments of the United Kingdom and the United States. This conference was initiated by Parliamentarians for Global Action, and took three years of partnership between civil society and non-nuclear governments to convene.[23] Drawing on the provisions in Article II.1 of the PTBT, Parliamentarians for Global Action managed by August 1988 to persuade six states (Indonesia, Mexico,

Peru, Sri Lanka, Venezuela and Yugoslavia) to table a proposal for amending the PTBT to cover all environments, which would have transformed it into a CTBT.[24] Over the next two years, Parliamentarians for Global Action worked on gathering signatures from one third of the states parties to the treaty, thereby obliging the three PTBT depositary governments, the Soviet Union, United Kingdom and United States, to convene a conference to consider the proposed amendment. This conference was held 4–18 January 1991, chaired by Ali Alatas, ambassador of Indonesia.

Spokespeople for the key NGOs, including Greenpeace, IPPNW, the Nevada–Semipalatinsk Movement and Parliamentarians for Global Action, addressed the delegates to the PTBT Amendment Conference, along with representatives of indigenous peoples affected by nuclear testing. The United Kingdom and the United States had made it clear that they would block consensus on any amendment banning underground testing, so a compromise amendment was proposed giving the president, Ali Alatas, the authority to keep the issue on the diplomatic agenda, with the possibility of reconvening the PTBT Amendment Conference at some time in the future. This proposal was carried by 74 votes to 2 (the United Kingdom and the United States), with 19 abstentions (mainly NATO states). Since the decision was procedural, the depositary states could not exercise their vetoes.

The Amendment Conference had been preceded by a conference in Las Vegas and a mass trespass on the Nevada Test Site, resulting in 750 arrests.[25] Despite the numbers, neither the arrests nor the Conference received much media coverage because of the imminence of the Gulf War. The Conference outcome, and especially the device of keeping the conference potentially alive acted as a useful lever that Alatas and his non-aligned colleagues used to exert pressure over the next few years.[26] Some NGOs also used the conference as an opportunity to present up-to-date arguments and research on the feasibility of a CTBT, including its verifiability. Attached to the amendment, for example, was a proposal for a verification protocol that had been drawn up by the Verification Technology Information Centre.[27] Such information was an important resource for diplomats and officials in countering the pessimism of the nuclear-weapon states during the next few years.

RUSSIA, FRANCE AND THE UNITED STATES SUSPEND NUCLEAR TESTING

In order to bring conflicting parties to the negotiating table, it is often useful to have a "bridge", or temporary suspension of conflict behaviour, such as a ceasefire.[28] The moratoria provided such a bridge toward the CTBT. As discussed above, the first was the Soviet declaration on 5 October 1991, made by General Secretary Gorbachev under pressure from a combination of political and environmental factors, including negative international publicity about radioactive contamination at the Semipalatinsk and Novaya Zemlya test sites and the growing popularity of the Kazakh movement against testing. But there had been Soviet moratoria before. The real breakthrough came when President Mitterrand declared the French moratorium on 8 April 1992.

Three levels of interacting civil society pressure appear to have contributed to Mitterrand's decision. Most immediately, the March 1992 regional elections had gone badly for the Socialist Party and marked the first significant success for the French Green Party, which garnered almost 15% of the vote. The Greens had listed a nuclear test ban high on their political platform of environmental priorities. They had also been instrumental in the January 1992 launch of a European Campaign for a Moratorium on French Nuclear Tests in the Pacific by a coalition of French ecologists and peace activists, members of the European Parliament, and the Protestant and Catholic churches of France and other European countries.[29] After publishing information on radioactive leakage from samples taken at Moruroa in 1990, Greenpeace took the *Rainbow Warrior* back to the Pacific test site in late 1991/early 1992. Since official permission for sampling was once more denied by the French authorities, Greenpeace was able to attract further international—and French—publicity as its boat was again blocked by the French military. Polls suggest that through such actions and publicity about radioactivity at the site, Greenpeace and the Green Party had begun to erode public confidence in government statements about the environmental safety of the French testing programme, thereby increasing pressure on Mitterrand.[30]

At the same time, the president was undoubtedly reassessing French policy after the Cold War, as evidenced by the withdrawal of tactical nuclear weapons from the Plateau d'Albion, the cancellation of the Hadès programme, and the announcement that France would join the NPT, made on 3 June 1992, soon after the nuclear testing moratorium was announced. Prime Minister Pierre Bérégovoy also alluded to the necessity to stop the massive build-up and stockpiling of nuclear weapons.[31] Was the moratorium a reflection of a desire to halt nuclear testing or a political manoeuvre designed to counteract political pressure from the Greens? The president's own statement just days after the moratorium was announced was revealing: "If the other nuclear powers are stubborn, France will have to continue to assure its defence. It will regret the lost opportunity. It will have done its duty".[32] This statement lends credence to the view that Mitterrand had calculated that temporarily suspending the tests would allow France to take the moral high ground, address some of its safety and technical problems at the Pacific test site, and appear to meet the environmentalists half way. In a political climate dominated by the Conservative Party in the United Kingdom and the Republicans in the United States, there was every reason to assume that the other governments would carry on testing. France could then resume when it was ready. By such a strategy, undertaking the moratorium would bring political gains with little or no military cost.

At the time, there were also grounds for believing that the Russian moratorium would not hold. At the end of 1991 Boris Yeltsin had taken over from Gorbachev as the head of the newly formed Russian Federation. A leaked memo dated 27 February 1992 revealed that despite calling for testing to be halted in 1990, Yeltsin was willing to breach Gorbachev's moratorium and resume nuclear explosions at Novaya Zemlya. After NGOs highlighted the memo and called on Yeltsin to honour Gorbachev's suspension of nuclear testing, he backed down and declared that Russia would extend the moratorium.[33] Whatever the original intentions of Mitterrand and Yeltsin, they became locked into their respective moratoria by the US moratorium and decision to support the completion of a CTBT by 30 September 1996.

As noted above, President Bush was no supporter of a test ban when he signed the Energy and Water Appropriations Bill into law, thereby requiring the United States to adhere to a nine-month moratorium and work toward a CTBT. The October 1992 timing was particularly significant for the United Kingdom, which had a nuclear device already placed in an underground shaft at the Nevada site, and at least two further nuclear tests planned. Joining Russia and France, the US legislation paved the way for the UN General Assembly's annual CTBT resolution to be adopted without a vote for the first time.[34] This consensus resolution served as a multilateral instruction to the CD to come up with a mandate to negotiate a test-ban treaty.

So how did the US administration come to initiate a nuclear testing moratorium and commit to a CTBT against the wishes of the President, the Secretary of Defense Dick Cheney and political allies in the UK government, Ministry of Defence and nuclear weapons laboratories? The impetus came from Senator Mark Hatfield, who had co-sponsored the "Freeze" resolutions with Senator Edward Kennedy in the 1980s, and Senator James Exon, who had reportedly been shocked by the devastation he saw during a visit to the Nevada Test Site in 1991. The French moratorium gave impetus to Hatfield's initiative, enabling him to recruit 53 co-sponsors, the most important of whom was Senate Majority Leader George Mitchell. Meanwhile, the Bush administration tried to carry on business as usual, and detonated a nuclear device on 30 April 1992, three weeks after the French moratorium was announced.

As civil society erupted with criticism and petitions for an end to US nuclear testing, House Majority Leader Richard Gephardt and Representative Mike Kopetski responded by introducing the Nuclear Testing Moratorium Bill, which quickly gained 216 co-sponsors in support of a one-year moratorium. Hatfield's initial draft legislation was attached to the Senate Defense Authorization Bill for 2003. Hatfield, Exon and Mitchell entered into negotiations to get bipartisan support. Talks with Sam Nunn, the Chair of the Senate Armed Services Committee, resulted in modifications to allow for a limited number of safety tests, and the Bush administration successfully lobbied for language to allow the United States to resume testing if any other state conducted a test.[35] In a shrewd tactical move, Hatfield duplicated the moratorium provision as an amendment to the Energy and Water Appropriations Bill. This proved vital, for the moratorium provision fell in the House–Senate conference committee on the Defense Authorization Bill after its Chair, Senator Sam Nunn, prioritized other provisions. By contrast, Hatfield, the ranking member on the Senate Appropriations Committee, was able to ensure that the moratorium survived the House–Senate conference committee on the Energy and Water Appropriations Bill. Cheney and Scowcroft lobbied the Senate, urging them to vote against the Hatfield-Mitchell-Exon Amendment, but in vain.[36]

During this time, there was intensive lobbying from arms control proponents and a massive grass-roots campaign of letter writing to Congressional representatives and editorials in local newspapers. After a tough round of negotiations and trade-offs, the moratorium amendment was passed by the Senate on 13 September 1992 by a vote of 55 to 40. On 24 September, the House of Representatives adopted the same amendment, 224 to 151. Elsewhere in the bill were provisions desired by political allies of President Bush.[37] Without a line item veto, Bush had the choice of either signing the bill with the moratorium or vetoing the whole package. The United Kingdom, dependent on the US test site, had no say. With his eyes on the forthcoming election and the bill's allocation of funds for several key states, including Texas, President Bush ignored British lobbying and signed the bill, while making clear that he did not support a test ban.

The text of the Hatfield-Mitchell-Exon Amendment mandated a nine-month moratorium, with the possibility of seeking approval for up to 15 tests before 30 September 1996 (of which the United Kingdom could conduct one per year, up to a maximum of three, if the president determined that it would be in the US national interest).[38] Significantly, despite the French and Russian moratoria and evidence that pressure was mounting for a test ban, Bush took no steps to prepare the nuclear establishment for the test ban. A triumph for legislative strategy, the moratorium was meant to be a bridge towards the CTBT, but few expected it to last.

That it did last, despite efforts by the nuclear laboratories and the UK government to overturn it, was due to a combination of political pressure and conditions embedded in the cleverly drafted legislation. When Bill Clinton became president in January 1993 he was expected to support a CTBT, a measure that he had advocated as a candidate, but in his first few months he came under pressure from members of his own administration, CTBT opponents and the UK government on three testing-related issues: to pursue a treaty with a 1kt threshold, not to renew the moratorium after its first nine months, and to consider proposals that would limit the duration of any testing treaty.[39]

In February 1993, Robert Bell, Director for Arms Control at the National Security Council, advocated that the CTBT should have a 1kt threshold and argued that "no-one was supporting continuation of the moratorium imposed by the Hatfield-Mitchell-Exon legislation after the expiry of the nine-month period in June 1993".[40] Clinton's National Security Advisor Anthony Lake initiated a mid-level interagency review lasting several months, with a principals' meeting involving senior officials scheduled for

14 May. During this time, the British nuclear establishment and Ministry of Defence, in close collaboration with their opposite numbers in the Pentagon and the US nuclear labs, mounted a well-orchestrated offensive against the moratorium. Arms control proponents in London and Washington responded by working with Representative Mike Kopetski to table a bill that would make the United Kingdom pay the full costs of its testing, including the environmental clean-up.[41]

Thomas Graham, at the time Deputy Head of the US Arms Control and Disarmament Agency, recollected that, at the first principals' meeting of the interagency process to consider whether to continue the moratorium, he was the only one to argue that "the tests were not necessary and should not jeopardise NPT extension".[42] The newly appointed Secretary for Energy, Hazel O'Leary, surprised the other principals by insisting on a postponement of the decision until she could receive full briefings from the nuclear labs and other interested parties connected with her department. O'Leary heard arguments for and against conducting further tests. The officials from the nuclear labs at Livermore, Los Alamos and Sandia were mostly in favour, and cited safety and reliability, test-ban readiness, Anglo-American relations, and future ratification considerations.[43] Others, such as Frank von Hippel, who later became Clinton's science adviser, maintained that no further safety tests were needed, although he supported allowing hydronuclear experiments up to 4lbs (1.8kg).[44] O'Leary concluded that, notwithstanding the desires of some in the nuclear establishment, further nuclear tests were not actually *needed* for stockpile safety and reliability.

The Hatfield-Mitchell-Exon Amendment had been drafted to require that if any safety or reliability tests were to be conducted before 30 September 1996, there must be a plan and intention to install potential warhead safety or reliability upgrades into the arsenal. This made any decision to resume testing after the initial nine-month moratorium less attractive, as it would have entailed a considerable additional financial commitment, as well as necessitating adjustments to the armed forces' operational procedures for handling certain warheads.[45] When the principals reconvened in late May, they were divided: Secretary of Defense Les Aspin and Secretary of State Warren Christopher argued that a "deal" had been made in Congress to allow 15 tests; Graham and O'Leary pushed to extend the moratorium; and Colin Powell, head of the Joint Chiefs of Staff, remained undecided.[46]

Fearing that a resumption of US testing would derail the possibility of treaty negotiations, civil society focused on preventing the transgovernmental collaboration between US and UK opponents of the CTBT from being successful in their aim to resume testing in Nevada. On both sides of the Atlantic, NGOs mobilized campaigns including thousands of letters to the President and Congress supporting the moratorium and opposing proposals for a 1kt or 500t threshold. In particular, Washington arms control proponents provided technical information and assisted the Senators at the forefront of the moratorium legislation to organize almost 200 letters to the Clinton administration from their congressional colleagues. They published poll data showing that 72% of the US public favoured continuing the moratorium.[47] Greenpeace, Physicians for Social Responsibility and a coalition of test-ban advocates put pro-CTBT advertisements into major US newspapers. One of these showed a photograph of the saxophone-playing President Clinton, and admonished: "Don't Blow it Bill".

In the United Kingdom, the Test Ban Action Group (T-BAG), a network of anti-nuclear organizations and Greenham feminists, handed out anti-testing leaflets around the country. They also worked with Labour and Liberal Democrat Members of Parliament to raise questions about the Ministry of Defence's lobbying activities in Washington against the moratorium. When newspapers published news of the US administration's internal debates, British and US civil society intensified their lobbying, with letters to the Prime Minister and President from church leaders and dignitaries, a slew of newspaper editorials and a barrage of information to congressional representatives who, in turn, lobbied the Clinton administration.[48] With the US interagency process unable to come to a clear decision, Lake consulted senior politicians, receiving their assurances that there would be congressional support for extending the moratorium. On 3 July 1993, Clinton announced that the US moratorium would continue indefinitely. This decision effectively ensured that France and Russia would continue with their moratoria as well. It also left the United Kingdom with no choice but to finalize its Trident warhead programme without the further tests it had planned.[49]

Although China continued to conduct underground nuclear explosions until the CTBT negotiations concluded in 1996, Beijing was put under pressure when VERTIC exposed the first Chinese test after the US and other moratoria were extended. Using publicly available satellite imagery and seismic monitoring hooked up to some laptop computers, VERTIC identified the likely timing and location of the Chinese test of 5 October 1993, and then published details within a few hours of its occurrence.[50] Beijing initially tried to counteract the negative publicity by passing the event off as a mistakenly identified earthquake. As further data from other sources backed up VERTIC's claim, the government was forced the next day into admitting the test, provoking widespread public and diplomatic condemnation from around the world. VERTIC's coup had two positive outcomes. Occurring just as the United Nations met in New York for the 1993 First Committee,[51] it gave reassurance and credibility to the concept of verifying a total test ban by showing how even a small NGO could successfully detect and locate an underground test. The exposure of this nuclear test also led to China becoming more open about its future nuclear explosions. Although China conducted about two tests per year until it signed the CTBT in September 1996, the government avoided a repetition of its October 1993 embarrassment by releasing its own announcements to the media. Equally importantly, the exposure and news coverage caused China for the first time to make a public commitment to a CTBT "no later than 1996".[52]

THE CD ADOPTS A NEGOTIATING MANDATE

President Clinton's decision to extend the US moratorium gave the final push that was needed for the CD to agree a mandate to negotiate the CTBT. Commonly considered the sole multilateral negotiating forum of the international community, the CD is the successor to the ENDC.[53] In setting out its terms of reference in 1978, the First UN Special Session on Disarmament had specified that the CD would conduct its work by consensus, adopt its own rules of procedure, adopt its own agenda taking into account the recommendations made to it by the General Assembly and members' proposals, submit reports to the General Assembly at least once a year, and permit open public access to its plenary meetings, unless otherwise decided.[54]

After a decade of frustration in the 1980s, when the dominant US–Soviet rivalry prevented any significant progress on multilateral arms control, the end of the Cold War gave the CD new opportunities. By 1993, the CD had just concluded the negotiations that resulted in consensus agreement on a Chemical Weapons Convention (CWC), which included the most intrusive verification provisions in the history of multilateral arms control. Buoyed up by its success in handing a strong treaty to the United Nations, where it opened for signature in January 1993, the CD was keen to start negotiations on a CTBT, which had been near the top of its formal agenda for many years.

Stimulated by the more positive political environment fostered by the testing moratoria, the consensus test-ban resolution that was adopted by the 1992 UN General Assembly made it finally possible for the CD to develop a negotiating mandate for its Ad Hoc Committee on a Nuclear Test Ban. After several months of negotiations under the leadership of Ambassador Yoshitomo Tanaka of Japan, the CD on 10 August 1993 agreed that the CTBT was to have both a disarmament purpose and a role in non-proliferation, and adopted a mandate as follows:

> The Conference directs the Ad Hoc Committee to negotiate intensively a universal and multilaterally and effectively verifiable comprehensive nuclear test ban treaty, which would contribute effectively to the prevention of the proliferation of nuclear weapons in all its aspects, to the process of nuclear disarmament and therefore to the enhancement of international peace and security.[55]

By finally adopting this mandate, the CD showed that it was ready to build on the constructive work of its last few years negotiating the Chemical Weapons Convention. Yet, as the next chapters detailing the CTBT negotiations illustrate, the CD remained hampered by its Cold War legacy—a membership of 38 states[56] that did not adequately represent the geopolitical players of the post-Cold War era, a rigid adherence to the rule of consensus and an outdated group system. Throughout 1993, negotiations had been underway on enlarging the membership by 23 states. These 23 were part of a list that the special coordinator, Australian ambassador Paul O'Sullivan, had carefully balanced to reflect post-Cold War regional and political realities. On advice from existing CD members, O'Sullivan had not only added new democracies and regional powers, but also included weak and highly militarized states, in the hope that their inclusion would enable the wider community to address the challenges they posed more effectively and directly. The enlargement decision was planned for September 1993, but failed to go through because of last minute opposition from the United States over admitting Iraq. Other states refused to drop Iraq from what became known as the "O'Sullivan List" on grounds that the list was the result of painstaking negotiations to balance geostrategic and regional concerns, with the significant criterion being relevance for disarmament negotiations rather than US or international approval.

During the negotiations, some 30–40 states participated in the CD as observers, of whom fewer than 10 engaged actively in the test-ban negotiations. The failure to enlarge the CD in 1993 meant that some key nuclear players, including Israel and South Africa, were able to participate only as observers for the first two-and-a-half years, though efforts were made to ensure that they could put in working papers and have their concerns and proposals properly heard. Talks on enlargement continued in parallel with the CTBT negotiations and, in June 1996, a formula was finally agreed that enabled the long-awaited induction of the 23 new members, bringing the membership formally to 61.[57]

Before detailing the CTBT negotiations in the next chapters, the structure and limitations of the negotiating forum are worth brief consideration. Although its close relationship with the United Nations leads many to assume that the CD is a UN body, it is legally and technically autonomous. Nevertheless, the CD meets on UN premises, is serviced by UN personnel and its budget is included in the UN budget. The Secretary-General of the CD is appointed directly by the UN Secretary-General and acts as his or her personal representative. As illustrated by the important role played by the CTBT resolutions in the UN General Assemblies of 1992 and 1993, the CD is expected to take into account UN resolutions, especially where consensus has been obtained. As the final phase of the CTBT negotiations illustrated, it is also assumed that the CD should transmit the texts of any treaties or agreements to the General Assembly to be formally adopted and opened for signature. By 1984, the US and Soviet co-chairs of the ENDC had been replaced with a presidency that rotated among the CD member states in alphabetical order every four weeks.[58]

The rotating presidency and Bureau (comprising the past, current and next presidents, coordinators of the principal groupings within the CD and China) are supposed to manage the taking of decisions, flow of information and exchange of views. As can be seen from their names, the groups represented—and to this day continue to represent—Cold War political affiliations, outdated even at the time of the CTBT negotiations: the Group of Western States and Others, the Group of Eastern European States and Others, and the G-21 Group of Non-Aligned States and Others. China has chosen to remain as a "group of one".[59] These are subsets of groupings found in wider multilateral fora and the United Nations.[60] Since the Cold War there has been some shifting of group alliances in the CD, but the group system itself has remained deeply embedded in multilateral diplomacy, resisting all efforts to bring it up to date.[61] However, taken together with a rigidly applied rule of consensus, they have also made it easy for objectors to block decision-making and hide behind others. The consensus rule is arguably the most crucial determinant of how the CD operates. A multilateral body of rival regional and international powers, the CD must, according to Rule 18 of its rules of procedure, "conduct its work and adopt its decisions by consensus". From its inception, the CD members have interpreted Rule 18 as conferring the power of veto on every member.[62] Objectors to a decision are not obliged to give their reasons for opposing and may choose to conceal their identities since decisions can be blocked if the group coordinators simply report that there is no consensus in their groups, without providing any details or explanations.

In order to understand some of the problems and constraints that beset the negotiations it is important to understand how the CD's Cold War origins and continuing adherence to a rigid consensus rule contributed to its persistent problems of participation, management and decision-making and were important factors in the CTBT's endgame, where India's single opposition to consensus in effect vetoed the CD's adoption of the finalized treaty.

In multilateral conferences with a specific objective and time frame, the need for consensus is more likely to produce frenetic endgame negotiations, sometimes requiring that the clock be "stopped".[63] Alternatively, application of a consensus rule may foster managed convergence on the basis of lowest-common-denominator compromise agreements.[64] Alternatively, consensus could be interpreted and applied in ways that promoted shared responsibility for decision-making without requiring unanimity for each and every decision. As civil society groups working with consensus have long known, there must be effective procedures to manage group decision-making and for the individuals in a group to register their support, opposition or acquiescence in an accountable manner. The CD interpretation of consensus is more rigid than it needs to be. Rule 18 is currently interpreted as requiring that even the agenda, programme of work, presidential statements and the establishment of ad hoc committees or personnel as chairs or coordinators are decisions that require unanimity. The procedures for registering views other than agreement are woefully inadequate. One consequence of this is that the consensus rule is manipulated by different players to accomplish a variety of objectives. Instead of being a helpful tool to bring about inclusive agreement, it is as likely to be employed by regional or political adversaries to block progress that might benefit others. Used in this way, the consensus rule enables individual governments to deadlock the CD's work by exerting linkages between issues or agreements that may have little intrinsic connection at all.

The rule of consensus, originally insisted on by the superpowers to ensure that they could not be outvoted by other states, can give any delegation the formal power to prevent work from getting started. In practice, consensus still serves the interests of the major powers and a deadlock is allowed to persist only when the dominant CD members are content with it (regardless of their public relations statements to the contrary). If opposition is exerted by other delegations when the major powers have decided they want to negotiate, behind-the-scenes pressure or cheque-book diplomacy will be used to break the deadlock. In effect then, under its non-discriminatory exterior, the rule of consensus hides informal rules concerning not just the degree of positive agreement required (as opposed to abstaining acquiescence), but which of the parties are most important and must be included.[65]

Negotiating tactics

Before moving on to consider the CTBT negotiations and states' strategies in detail, it is useful to summarize the kinds of tactics that diplomats—and other actors—have at their disposal.[66] Some tactics are used to promote constructive outcomes, while others are intended to obstruct or delay negotiations or increase a state's relative gains in negotiating contexts that are traditionally viewed as zero sum. The boundaries between constructive and obstructive tactics are not always clear, and can depend on the interests and preferences of both the user and the perceiver. Depending on a negotiator's intention and the circumstances of the interaction, a particular demand or action—calling for an inquiry, for example—can either be used as a delaying tactic or as a constructive cognitive tactic aimed at unpacking difficult issues in order to facilitate convergence through shared understanding.

To obstruct negotiations, strategies of delay, defection and concealment are employed. These are frequently seen in the prenegotiation phase and also as negotiations approach their endgame. Johann Kaufmann identified three kinds of delaying tactics, which he called "waiting for Godot", "quicksand" and "ping-pong". In waiting for Godot, a negotiator continually insists that the time for something is not yet ripe, while impeding all attempts by others to create more positive conditions. Quicksand is the tactic of bogging down a proposal or initiative in questions, objections or demands for definitions, or by insisting on an inquiry or further consultations. Ping-pong is the apt name Kaufmann gave to the oft-used tactic of getting an initiative or issue referred to another committee, forum or authority and then to keep on shunting it between different bodies for as long as possible.

To conceal their real objectives, intentions or interests, states may employ a variety of techniques. Concealment tactics are often used by weak states that are acting contrary to stated ideology, national policy or public opinion. They may also be deployed by alliance or group members that do not wish to be exposed as pursuing national self-interest at the expense of collective policy, or even by diplomats that disagree with their instructions or government policy, which is more common than might be admitted. Frequently observed examples of concealment tactics are characterized here as "hide and seek", "slipstreaming", "fronting" and "faking". The hide-and-seek tactic is a perennial favourite, in which states mask their real objectives with high-sounding rhetoric or a mass of technical data and extraneous detail. When slipstreaming, a delegation will maintain a low profile or keep quiet about its preferences and allow another delegation that holds the same position to engage more openly (and, if necessary, take the brunt of any criticism). Delegations in whose wake a slipstreamer is concealing its positions may or may not be aware that they are assisting in this way. By contrast, fronting is a collaborative form of slipstreaming, in which one delegation deliberately leads on an argument or position knowing that others will benefit by following in its wake. In some but not all cases, the fronting delegation may adopt a position that is stronger than its own interests would require in order to assist those slipstreaming in its wake. In general, the fronting delegation is the stronger, but there are notable exceptions. A less powerful ally will sometimes front for a stronger delegation in situations where that state does not wish to be exposed. Similar to a diplomatic practice identified by Kaufmann as "two-faced", faking is the tactic of pretending to support a proposal that you actually oppose, or vice versa. It may also involve manipulating another state to take the lead in advocating or opposing a position, leaving them to bear any criticisms or penalties if the position fails. As is sometimes the case in slipstreaming, faking is deployed by states that want to keep favour with allies or dominant states, or by states with positions that they know would attract domestic or international criticism if made public.

The third category of tactics covers obstruction of agreement through linkage and defection. With the general aim of providing grounds for pulling out of any agreements that might be reached, two common defection tactics are "moving the goalposts", in which agreement is rendered more inaccessible by altering objectives if it begins to seem as though the previously established objectives will be achieved, and "best versus good", in which a remote or unobtainable ideal is persistently evoked to prevent agreement on a more practical, achievable measure. It is sometimes difficult to determine whether a state genuinely desires a more radical solution or is deploying best-versus-good tactics for the purposes of obstruction or defection. One basis for judgement would be the degree to which a government actively works toward achieving the "best" outcome or merely evokes it in criticism every time it appears as if the "good" alternative might be achieved.

Another way to obstruct a decision or prepare the ground for defecting is by invoking the "all or nothing" demand. This is closely related to the linkage tactics that tie progress on agreement on one issue with agreement or gains on another issue. The hallmark of the all-or-nothing tactic is the frequently heard mantra "nothing to be agreed until everything is agreed". This phrase is deployed in multilateral diplomacy to ensure that a state's core objectives cannot be dropped or sidelined once the dominant states have got what they want. As such, it may reflect not an intention to obstruct the negotiations as such, but an assertion of a political objective that outweighs the perceived gains of agreement in a particular context.

Linkage is a double-bladed tactic that may be used for positive reasons but which frequently contributes to deadlock. The CD has long been bedevilled by the assertion of linkages that prevent negotiations being started on one issue until there is agreement to work on or omit some other, which may or may not be related. Several times during the CTBT negotiations, a dominant state was accused of "hostage-taking" after its delegation insisted that not winning on its positions would be a "treaty-breaker". "Tit for tat" is the name given to a further linkage tactic, in which an actor will thwart the plans of another in retaliation for a real or imagined offence. Because tit-for-tat reprisals tend not to be issue-based in origin, the tactic is associated more with rivalries and negative dynamics among negotiating parties than with substantive disagreements. Such tactics may backfire on the user.

Linkage can also contribute to agreement, for example through bridging strategies and concession trading.[67] Concession trading is a very familiar bargaining process in which allowances are made on one issue to win compromises on another, even if the issues are not related substantively. Other bridging tactics include "mediation", in which underlying causes of disagreement are addressed; "bridge-building", in which demands and positions are modified or conceded for the sake of agreement; and "third-party bridging", in which a broker—for example, a third party or group of middle powers—facilitates agreement by exploring solutions somewhere between the extremes, perhaps by identifying and fostering concessions that bring antagonistic parties closer together.

Cognitive strategies, associated with regime-building and integrative convergence, are often employed by civil society. Knowledge and norms may be shaped to reframe an issue or recast and expand the zone of possible agreement. Among tactics used to facilitate cognitive strategies are "step-ladder", where new insights are introduced to enable parties to surmount obstacles or at least to perceive them differently, and "unpacking", in which complex issues are disaggregated and then resolved incrementally.[68] Cognitive strategies may be pursued with new technical information, projections or data highlighting the probable consequences of particular choices, psychological and cultural insights, or a mixture of some or all of these components.

In extreme circumstances, when obstacles appear intractable, negotiators can choose to bypass the problem, for example by changing the rules or conventions that sustain the opposition or status quo. The Ottawa Process provided a recent, renowned example of effective use of a bypass operation to create an alternative forum where the landmine ban could be negotiated.[69]

As illustrated in the next chapters, in which the 1994–1996 negotiations of the CTBT are analysed in detail, many of these tactics were utilized at different times by different states, and with varying degrees of success.

NEGOTIATING TACTICS AT A GLANCE

Delaying tactics

- Waiting for Godot—interminably delaying for the arrival of some mythical moment when the time is perfectly ripe.
- Quicksand—bogging an initiative down in questions, objections or demands for definitions or an inquiry.
- Ping-Pong—shunting an issue back and forth between different committees, fora or institutions.

Concealment

- Hide and seek—concealing real objectives, for example in high-minded rhetoric or a mass of technical data and extraneous detail.
- Slipstreaming—concealing preferences behind the positions of another delegation.
- Fronting—a form of collaborative slipstreaming, in which one delegation adopts a position that is stronger than its own interests would require, enabling others to benefit by coasting in its wake.
- Faking—a two-faced tactic of pretending to support a proposal that you actually oppose or vice versa.

Defection and linkage tactics

- Moving the goalposts—whatever is achievable becomes by definition inadequate so that the reachable is perpetually ditched for a more inaccessible position.
- Best versus good—rejecting adequate or useful agreements on the grounds that they do not match up with some grander but less practical or accessible ideal.
- Linkage—tying progress or agreement on one issue with achievement of agreement or gains on another issue.
- All or nothing—a linkage tactic asserting that nothing is agreed until everything is agreed.
- Hostage-taking—coercively presenting a contested point or outcome in your favour as a "make or break" issue for the whole negotiations.
- Tit for tat—you have done something to thwart or annoy me, so I will do something to thwart or annoy you.

Bridging and trading

- Concession-trading—a bargaining process of trading concessions to facilitate convergence.
- Mediation—when a third party or parties help to promote agreement by enabling antagonists to address underlying causes of disagreement.
- Bridge-building—in which one or more of the antagonistic parties are prepared to concede or modify demands to promote convergence.
- Third-party bridging—by an "honest broker" (which can be officials, states or civil society), exploring ways to bring antagonistic parties closer together.

Regime-building "cognitive" tactics

- Norm-shaping—stigmatizing the weapon or problem and presenting alternatives and solutions.
- Reframing—recasting hurdles, problems or solution options in less adversarial terms, offering integrative solutions with mutual gains.
- Step-ladder—deploying new information to enable parties to view problems from a different perspective and so surmount the obstacles impeding agreement.
- Unpacking—in which a problem is disaggregated or separated into its constituent parts to facilitate incremental agreement or progress.

Bypassing the obstacles

- Bypass operation—can be used to radically redefine the context or, alternatively, to create or adapt an alternative forum for negotiations or adoption of a measure or agreement if the established forum is inadequate or obstructed.
- Leap-frogging—a more dramatic means of avoiding deadlock, such as when a group of like-minded states carry an issue by jumping over a structural or political obstacle.

CHAPTER 4

THE STRUGGLE FOR A ZERO-YIELD TEST BAN

The CD is the only multilateral forum to address global arms control and disarmament issues on a continuing basis. Its membership covers every region of the globe and reflects a wide range of concerns and interests. We have all come to accept the CD as both a market place of ideas and a place where nations get down to practical business and conclude the agreements that enhance international security.

John D. Holum, Director of the US Arms Control and Disarmament Agency, 25 January 1994[1]

On 16 December 1993, the General Assembly gave consensus to a resolution that endorsed the negotiating mandate agreed by the Conference on Disarmament in August of that year.[2] The stage was now set for CTBT negotiations to begin in earnest when the CD reconvened on 25 January 1994. The CD got off to a good start by adopting Ambassador Tanaka's negotiating mandate at its first plenary, but there was a simultaneous disruption over confirming the nominee of the non-aligned states as Chair of the Nuclear Test Ban (NTB) Committee. The Group of Non-Aligned States and Others (usually called the G-21) had chosen Mexico's ambassador Miguel Marín Bosch because of his enduring and high-profile commitment to a CTBT. This included his refusal to back down on the CTBT commitment at the 1990 NPT review conference and his leadership during the 1991 PTBT Amendment Conference. For these same reasons Marín Bosch was opposed by the United Kingdom, which also considered him too radical on nuclear disarmament. Although France's ambassador Gérard Érrera shared the United Kingdom's reservations, he was constrained from openly opposing the G-21 nominee by his position as President of the CD when the 1994 session opened. The rest of the Western Group, particularly the United States, made clear their desire that the G-21's choice should be respected so that the negotiations could have a positive start. After a week of concerted pressure, the UK delegation acquiesced. In accordance with its mandate, the NTB Committee immediately established two working groups. The first, known as "Working Group 1", was devoted to verification issues, and chaired by Ambassador Wolfgang Hoffmann of Germany. The second, "Working Group 2", chaired by Ambassador Ludwik Dembinski of Poland, focused on legal and institutional issues, which included scope and basic obligations, as well as the implementing organization and entry into force. During the course of the year, the working group Chairs appointed various Friends of the Chair to coordinate specific aspects of the work. Responsibilities were allocated among the delegations according to expertise and regional representation.[3]

1994: STARTING POSITIONS AND STALLING TACTICS

Differences over the treaty's objectives, role and timing were immediately revealed as states put forward their opening positions. At the beginning, the two working groups respectively prioritized the central issues of the international monitoring system (IMS), which was to be built around an international network of seismic and radionuclide monitoring stations, and scope—the basic obligations and what would be prohibited and permitted. While the majority of negotiators viewed a CTBT as a major step toward nuclear disarmament, the nuclear-weapon states in their different ways wanted to make sure that a test ban would not significantly constrain the further development of their nuclear arsenals. The P-5 employed the term "comprehensive", but in truth wanted to sew up the issue of scope in secretive P-5 meetings on what they called "activities not prohibited". Put in terms of safety tests, low-yield and hydronuclear tests, laboratory experiments, simulations and peaceful nuclear explosions (PNE), "activities not prohibited" were desired by the P-5 as a means of protecting and maintaining nuclear weapon capabilities. Nevertheless, because of asymmetrical technological capabilities and political rivalries, the nuclear-weapon states competed with each other over which activities to exempt from the treaty, and so failed to achieve a treaty scope that would have optimally met their shared interests.

At first there appeared to be collaboration between France, Russia, the United Kingdom and the United States, all seeking to avoid a definition of nuclear explosions in the treaty so as to maintain a degree of ambiguity that would allow them to carry out low-yield testing for "safety and reliability".

Beijing took a different approach, arguing that a CTBT should cover only nuclear weapon test explosions and should not hamper the use of nuclear explosions for other purposes. Russia, which prioritized keeping low-yield explosions outside the treaty's prohibition, took an ambiguous stance on PNE. Even as scientists from Russia's Ministry of Atomic Affairs provided technical information and arguments to Beijing to reinforce China's advocacy of PNE, the official diplomatic position was that Moscow "would not oppose consensus" on this issue.

But the appearance of collaboration was superficial. Moreover, though alliances shifted on some issues, the P-5 dynamic in the first 15 months of negotiations differed markedly from what might have been expected. In the test-ban talks of 1958–1963 and 1977–1980, the United Kingdom and the United States had presented a more or less common front against the Soviet Union. In 1994, the dynamic was very different. Until May 1995, France and the United Kingdom acted in close cooperation with each other on a number of issues that were not supported by the United States, while US and Russian positions coincided more often than not. A characterization of the P-5 dynamic in the first phase of negotiations would therefore be 2:2:1 (Russia with the United States; France with the United Kingdom; China).

From the beginning, the United States had an explicitly stated position that a CTBT should be comprehensive, declaring, "the treaty should constitute a comprehensive ban. It should not be a threshold treaty; rather, it should focus on nuclear-weapons explosions" and (in language derived from the PTBT) prohibit "any nuclear weapon test explosion or any other nuclear explosion".[4] Contrary to the impression this was intended to give, it was widely known in US policy circles that, after an internal debate in 1993 over a 1kt-threshold treaty, the Clinton administration had come down in favour of a comprehensive ban, but designated "zero" yield as 1.8kg. This threshold was chosen because the United States characterized warheads as "one-point safe" if the probability of the nuclear yield exceeding 1.8kg following a sharp collision (resulting from being hit by a bullet or heavy implement or dropped, for example) was judged to be less than one in a million. In setting the permitted yield at the 1.8kg level, the United States considered this was a reasonable margin for possible error, and not a threshold.[5]

Russia saw no reason why the basic obligations did not simply reprise the "time-tested language" of the PTBT and add "underground" to the list of test environments prohibited in that treaty.[6] An early reference to nuclear tests "which are not dual-purpose in nature"[7] opened suspicions that Russia wanted to keep its options on PNE, which were being forcefully advocated by China. Together with France and the United Kingdom, Russia also wanted to continue conducting hydronuclear experiments, so these three set their sights on higher yields than the 1.8kg limit advocated by the United States. After some initial bargaining in the first few months of 1994, reports from the negotiations indicated that Russia wanted an activities-not-prohibited exemption that would allow testing up to a yield of 10t. The United Kingdom favoured a level of around 45kg, but France required a much higher threshold of 100–300t. China refused to enter this numbers game, having proposed a PNE provision that, combined with a no-yield scope, would cover all military explosions "which release nuclear energy". Although the activities-not-prohibited threshold levels were never discussed openly in the CD, it was understood that if thresholds were to be agreed at all, China would favour something higher, perhaps around 500t.[8]

China's first major statement to the CD called for "strict, precise and clear-cut texts", with "no loopholes or ambiguities which will give rise to different interpretations, misunderstandings or disputes in the future".[9] Concerned that the more technologically advanced nuclear-weapon states would benefit from loopholes for "further development and improvement of nuclear weapons", China pushed for more in-depth negotiations and clarity on definitions and scope than any of the other nuclear-weapon states wanted.[10] Beijing, which had not signed the PTBT, rejected using it as a basis for a CTBT. Deliberately echoing non-aligned states' concerns that the CTBT should not become another partial test ban, China argued that it should "prohibit at any place and in any environment any nuclear-weapon test explosion of any form which releases nuclear energy". Instead of "copying the text of some agreements of the 1960s and 1970s", China wanted "definitions and provisions truly in conformity with the purposes of the CTBT in the light of today's reality and possible future situations".[11]

The United Kingdom took the view that the test-ban objective should be non-proliferation:

> The United Kingdom Government continues to attach importance to the role of nuclear weapons for the preservation of our security now and in the foreseeable future. But we recognize also that the need to ensure effective measures to prevent the proliferation of weapons of

> mass destruction has increased. ... For us, a successful outcome will mean the conclusion of a treaty which makes a real contribution to non-proliferation by interposing a substantial obstacle in the process of developing nuclear weapons.[12]

The United Kingdom was prepared to base the treaty's scope on the PTBT language, but was more interested in securing provisions for conducting occasional tests in order to maintain the "safety and reliability" of weapons in its arsenal. When the UK delegation tabled a proposal to allow nuclear explosions to be carried out in "exceptional circumstances" to test the safety of nuclear weapons, France agreed and suggested that the nuclear-weapon states ought to retain the option to conduct a safety test every 5 or 10 years.[13]

France explicitly framed the CTBT as "a treaty to prohibit nuclear tests, not a treaty to prohibit nuclear arms", and insisted that it should not harm France's nuclear deterrence posture or the reliability of its arsenal. France said it favoured a comprehensive treaty provided it was universal and verifiable, and with the understanding that deterrent capabilities should be able to be maintained through technological advances, including "the acquisition of simulation capabilities".[14] France had not at that time refined its simulation capabilities, so this was an early indication that Paris was likely to break its moratorium and test before the CTBT came into force unless the data to ensure these capabilities could be secured through a provision for safety tests, or activities not prohibited were set at a sufficiently high threshold.[15]

Though the other states were not participants in the P-5 discussions on threshold and yield, the G-21's paper on purposes and objectives of the treaty made clear its opposition to safety tests.[16] Since Algeria and Iran had expressed some interest in PNE early in the negotiations, and in view of sensitivity over PNE being enshrined in Article V of the NPT 25 years before, the early G-21 positions avoided taking a position on this issue, although many individual states opposed PNE. Some of the Western non-nuclear states also put forward their positions on scope and circulated papers and information that built on the long years of prenegotiations.[17] While the P-5 in their private negotiations tried to agree a treaty scope that would leave them with some testing options, Iran led some of the non-aligned states in pushing for the verified closure of the nuclear test sites, while Germany and Sweden made a proposal for the treaty to outlaw *preparing* to conduct nuclear explosions, as well as prohibiting the actual nuclear tests.

Where much of the verification system is aimed at detecting and identifying nuclear tests after they have been conducted, such proposals would have strengthened the CTBT to deter would-be violators. Although they attracted wide-spread support from NGOs and non-nuclear-weapon states as ways to diminish the nuclear powers' options, amplify the verification regime beyond the task of monitoring after the event, and enable the regime to take preventive action if test preparations were detected, these proposals ended up being dropped. The German–Swedish proposal lasted the longest, but France, Russia, the United Kingdom, the United States, and, to the surprise of many, Australia lobbied hard against, claiming that "preparations" would be difficult to define and distinguish from legitimate activities, and would add considerable expense and complication to verification requirements. Sweden's ambassador Lars Norberg accepted that it would be difficult to define and verify preparations for a nuclear test, but argued that it is "logical in this context to include at least direct preparations leading up to a nuclear test".[18] Although Germany and Sweden were unsuccessful in their bid to incorporate preparations, it was useful to have raised preparations as a matter of serious concern, as this would be reflected in the negotiating record and may be invoked if the need arose in the future.[19]

Iran put forward the first proposal for closing the existing nuclear weapon test sites and destroying the testing infrastructure, arguing that this would be a more effective way of preventing as well as prohibiting nuclear testing than the German–Swedish proposal.[20] Unspoken, of course, was the concern that including preparations in the scope would entail a provision for intrusive inspections at nuclear facilities other than recognized test sites. Iran's proposal for closing the test sites was endorsed by Algeria, Indonesia, Nigeria, Pakistan and Ukraine, and received the backing of several more, including Brazil, Cuba and Mexico; India also expressed interest for a time. The United States fronted for the P-5 when it refused to countenance the proposal on the grounds that the test sites were also research laboratories. Although the idea of permanently closing down the test sites and dismantling the infrastructure for testing was supported by many non-nuclear-weapon states and NGOs, the initiative's supporters did not propose any actual text on closing the test sites.

In an alternative approach on scope, Indonesia went against all the nuclear powers by arguing that a CTBT should "cover peaceful nuclear explosions as well as testing through super-computer simulation".[21] Arguing that "comprehensive coverage is needed to prevent vertical proliferation of nuclear weapons in the future",[22] Indonesia carried forward these arguments with a formal proposal in 1995 to prohibit any nuclear weapon testing activity, whether explosive or not.[23] Despite these statements of intent, the NTB Committee and its Working Group 2 held few multilateral discussions on scope during 1994–1995 because it was assumed that until the P-5 came to their decision on activities not prohibited, there was little for the rest to talk about.

Outside the P-5 meetings, most energy was devoted to the least politically contentious issue, the development of the IMS. While scientists, most of whom were attached to the P-5 and the more engaged or well-resourced delegations including the D-3, argued about the technologies most suitable and cost-effective for verifying a test ban, the diplomats sketched out the range of options for the basic treaty articles. By half-way through the first year of negotiations, there appeared growing agreement on the verification technologies but little consensus about the more sensitive issues, such as scope, composition and powers of the implementing organization and Executive Council, whether the treaty's duration should be indefinite, and so on. Entry into force was barely addressed, as most delegations assumed it would fall into place near the end. Through the efforts of the Working Group Chairs and the various Friends appointed to coordinate the negotiations on specific issues, sections of language were already being collated into a draft text, with various states' proposals appearing in square brackets as alternatives and options. Known as a "rolling text" because the proposals and language it contains are continuously added to during negotiations, this draft fulfils the important function of highlighting areas of agreement and contention.

The politics of timing

In passing the moratorium legislation in 1992, the US Congress had mandated 30 September 1996 as the target date for conclusion of the treaty, so this was the timetable many had in mind.[24] The G-21 argued that the CTBT was achievable before the NPT, and expressed the hope of holding the signing ceremony at the United Nations in New York at the same time as the four-week NPT Review and Extension Conference, scheduled to open on 19 April 1995. Russia and the United States may have regarded this signing date to be unrealistic, but they seemed willing to support trying to get the CTBT concluded or substantially agreed by then to create a positive climate for the NPT Conference.

China, France and the United Kingdom wanted a much slower timetable. France's strategy for the first 18 months was driven by the desire to delay all major political decisions relating to nuclear testing until after the French General Election in May 1995.[25] A new administration was expected to replace the long-running presidency of François Mitterrand, and the nuclear establishment wanted to hold open its options. China was continuing to conduct two nuclear tests per year, indicating that its nuclear and military establishments were not yet ready to stop. However, Beijing held publicly to its statement of 5 October 1993 that it was committed to a CTBT "no later than 1996".[26] During the negotiations, China's delegation often complained of being rushed, and frequently reiterated the 1996 target date to make clear that this meant no earlier than 1996.[27]

The United Kingdom had no comparable reason for delay, other than the Conservative government's apparent antipathy to the idea of a CTBT and the deep unhappiness in the nuclear establishment and Ministry of Defence about the 1992 US moratorium having forced a premature halt to the UK nuclear testing programme. France and the United Kingdom tried to undermine the link the non-aligned states were making between conclusion of a CTBT and extension of the NPT by reversing it. In the argument put forward by Gérard Errera in a French statement to the NTB Committee, "A satisfactory result [on the extension of the NPT] would confirm our participation in negotiations on a test ban. On the other hand, failure to extend the NPT [indefinitely] could put in doubt our commitment to a CTBT".[28]

Half-way through the first year, Chairman Marín Bosch assessed that to achieve a treaty by the 1995 NPT Review and Extension Conference, as the G-21 wanted, there needed to be a draft text by August 1994. Accordingly, he began to put one together, intending to table it as a Chair's text before the second part of the CD's 1994 session ended on 1 July. The timing was chosen so that the delegations could get their governments' instructions and be ready to negotiate on the basis of the Chair's text when the session resumed at the end of July. Marín Bosch had intended to table a "clean" draft text, without any square brackets containing alternative language, in order to direct attention to the main questions, thereby accelerating the negotiations by encouraging the delegations to abandon any possessiveness over particular bracketed proposals. Before the draft could see the light of day, however, France, the United Kingdom and, with greater restraint, China had declared strong opposition to the very concept of a Chair's text at this time.[29]

Worried that Paris' strategy of delaying the conclusion of the treaty until after the French elections would be upset if Marín Bosch's text turned out to be a good basis for accelerating the negotiations, Érrera's opposition was regarded as particularly vociferous. According to reports, he whipped up anxiety over what he dubbed a "vision text" and accused the Chair of attempting to pre-empt the negotiations. Sir Michael Weston, head of the UK delegation to the CD, reportedly declared that a Marín Bosch text would be consigned to the waste-paper basket and be taken no more seriously than the Australian or Swedish texts then being drafted.[30] Though US ambassador Stephen Ledogar said he preferred to see the content of the Chair's draft before taking a position, Érrera's threats to pull out of the negotiations if presented with Marín Bosch's draft text made a number of delegations very nervous. This led the Chairs of the two Working Groups and around ten other delegations to express concern that a Chair's clean text would be premature and counterproductive. To the surprise of many, this group included not only European Union allies of France and the United Kingdom, but a handful of G-21 states, notably Algeria, Indonesia and Pakistan.

Up to this point, there had been a relatively good atmosphere in the negotiations, with positive talk and generous efforts to bring everyone's concerns on board. The United States had made it a priority to keep the P-5 together and talking, and European Union states made a point of not criticizing French positions that they disliked.[31] However, there was also concern that in view of the French and Chinese interest in delaying conclusion, these attempts to keep everyone together would sacrifice a timely treaty. In common with most of the G-21, the Chair feared that the CTBT could be allowed to fall off the disarmament agenda if the nuclear powers managed to extend the NPT before the test ban had been substantially finalized. On the basis that all the relevant questions had been discussed, Marín Bosch's strategy in developing a clean draft text was to accelerate toward the endgame and provoke the delegations to confront the genuine options and clarify their real objectives and issues that might be construed as treaty-breakers (also referred to as "red lines"). In the hope of concluding the treaty by April 1995, he wanted to stimulate states to negotiate in earnest on a practical draft text before the end of 1994.

The strategy failed because of the intensity of the French opposition and the rumours and speculation that Érrera and others fomented about the kind of "vision text" that Marín Bosch might produce. In this, they were aided by the fact that the Chair had kept his text very close to his chest, with no hints about its content or approach, and no one admitting to having seen it. As a compromise, several delegations suggested that instead of tabling a completely clean draft text, the Chair should issue a substantially cleaned, streamlined text that would nonetheless retain some of the most contested options in brackets. Had Marín Bosch chosen to take this course, he might have met his objective of focusing and clarifying the negotiations and distinguishing the crucial areas of debate. With a better chance of gaining the full support from the Working Group Chairs than any clean text, such an approach might have enabled the Chair to carry the majority of the CD with him and marginalize those whose primary objective was to delay the negotiating process until a time more suited to their national political needs. Such "might have" speculations tantalize the analyst, but in the end the diplomats must make their judgments based on the environment and information that they have at the time. Given the strategies of delay underlying the vigorous opposition by France and China, under pressure from national militaries to ensure that September 1996 would be the earliest possible date for conclusion of a treaty, it is not certain that any attempt by the Chair to speed up negotiations would have worked at that stage. In any case, Marín Bosch abandoned the idea of presenting a Chair's draft and in July 1994 asked the CD Secretariat to prepare a compendium of the options and proposals so far discussed.

Compiled by the Working Groups, this compendium turned out to be an unwieldy 93 pages full of square brackets indicating myriad alternative proposals, some but not all of which were formulated in treaty-appropriate language. In response to suggestions from the US delegation, the proposals were sorted into three categories, to reflect the varying levels of discussion and support they had received. On legal and institutional issues, Working Group 2 had produced a substantially clean text that they referred to as "category 1" (meaning that there were very few brackets) on the following standard treaty articles: measures to redress a situation and to ensure compliance, including sanctions, settlement of disputes, privileges and immunities, signature, ratification, accession, depositary, status of the protocol(s) and annex(es), and authentic texts. On the more contested issues, the "category 2" text collected the main options for scope, the implementing organization, entry into force, duration and withdrawal, and review of the treaty.

Working Group 1 had made much progress, but its text on verification was limited to a compilation of technical and political proposals and options, much of it not yet developed into treaty language. Agreement was hampered by continuing arguments over how fully defined the verification requirements should be. By this point, candidate technologies for supplementing the envisaged seismic network included radionuclide, hydroacoustic, infrasound, optical, and electromagnetic pulse monitoring, with China still keen for satellites to be added.[32] There were differences over which should be incorporated into the international data-processing centre that would need to be established under the auspices of the implementing organization, paid for by states parties, and which should be provided through national or multinational technical means.[33] Russia, which was concerned to limit costs and favoured what it called an "evolutionary approach", proposed that NTM be used to supplement the basic seismic and radionuclide networks already broadly agreed. While many non-aligned states initially appeared to support this pragmatic approach, a handful of others, particularly India and Pakistan, joined China in opposing the incorporation and legitimation of NTM.

Although the outgoing ambassador for the Netherlands, Hendrik Wagenmakers, rather disparagingly described 1994 in the CD as the "year of the questionnaire",[34] others portrayed the first year as one of diligent preparations, aimed at laying a careful, thorough foundation for the treaty. The defeat of Marín Bosch's attempts to table a Chair's text was a pivotal moment, making clear that a CTBT would not be concluded before the 1995 NPT Review and Extension Conference. From then on the target date was accepted as September 1996, as contained in the US moratorium legislation of 1992 and endorsed by China and others. The Chair's initiative did however have a positive impact. Expert papers and Working Group discussions became more tightly focused in an attempt to bring a coherent rolling text out of the plethora of written and verbal proposals. Furthermore, the pressure flushed out into the open proposals and positions that were being kept back for tactical or political reasons. Thus, states known to have particular interests but which had hitherto provided a low-key presence, notably China and Israel, suddenly issued working papers with specific proposals to ensure their inclusion in the rolling text. China, in particular, began to engage more directly in the multilateral negotiations, a factor also credited in part to a change in the head of delegation. Fluent in English, Ambassador Sha Zukang arrived in Geneva with considerable confidence and political authority, and brought a stronger team to counsel him on the test ban's technical and legal issues. As a consequence, China became better equipped to pursue its interests, whether among the P-5 or with middle powers and civil society.

Losing the pre-NPT target date had further important consequences, unrecognized until many months later. As hope for an early treaty faded, the option of a simplified CTBT also vanished. Although some had initially favoured a primarily political and norm-building instrument, with a streamlined verification system backed up by NTM, it was clear after August 1994 that a treaty would not be concluded unless it met stringent technical and compliance criteria. Paradoxically, given the role of certain nuclear-weapon states, the longer time frame also meant the P-5 lost whatever opportunity might have existed to get the other negotiators to go along with a low-threshold treaty that would permit sub-kiloton hydronuclear experiments.

1995: BREAKTHROUGH ON ZERO YIELD

As the CD closed its 1994 session in September, the 93-page compilation was already being treated as a de facto rolling text.[35] When the 1995 session opened in January, it was the turn of the nominal Eastern European group to choose a new Chair for the Nuclear Test Ban Committee. They nominated the Polish ambassador Ludwik Dembinski, who was confirmed as Chair by the rest of the CD. As before, the Committee established two Working Groups. The Netherlands' new ambassador, Jaap Ramaker, was made Chair of Working Group 2 on legal and institutional issues, following a dispute within the Western Group. The majority had favoured the candidacy of Australia's ambassador Richard Starr, but France objected to Starr, reportedly because of Australia's hostility to French testing in the Pacific and because Starr was seen by the French as too "active" and anti-nuclear.

With some of its key ambassadors due to leave the CD during the year, the G-21 had difficulty finding a candidate to chair Working Group 1 on verification. As one of the G-21 delegations with the most technical expertise and a track record of participating fully during the previous year, India was strongly encouraged to put forward a candidate. To the regret of its G-21 colleagues and many others, India declined, citing overstretch of its diplomatic resources. India's reluctance prompted private speculation in the CD corridors that New Delhi had strategic reasons for avoiding responsibility for the process of negotiations. Once it became obvious that India would not be persuaded to chair Working Group 1, the G-21 agreed to nominate Sweden, which had been a G-21 member until 1993 and was not yet admitted formally into the Western Group. Considering that the major posts were traditionally supposed to be rotated for geopolitical reasons among the three CD groups, it was considered by some to be politically undesirable that all three Chairs in 1995 were held by states in the European Union's sphere of influence: the Netherlands and Sweden as EU members, and Poland as an applicant.[36] However, in the circumstances, no one chose to make any open objections.

As the NTB Committee worked to clean the 93 pages of text it had inherited from the previous year, progress in 1995 was heavily influenced by political events outside the negotiating chamber. Chief among these was the 1995 NPT Review and Extension Conference and changes of government or other political processes affecting decision-making in some of the key states, especially France and India. China, meanwhile, continued its testing programme, but appeared more engaged in the detail and progress of the negotiations.

Thwarted in its bid to chair Working Group 2, Australia made an impact early in 1995 by tabling draft language on scope that over the course of the year would prove to be the winning text. It prohibited "any nuclear weapon test explosion or any other nuclear explosion" and from the moment it was presented became the front-runner for attracting consensus, even by some who were not yet ready to abandon their own preferences.[37] In addition, Australia called for the pace to be accelerated and proposed that negotiations should focus on six outstanding clusters of issues: scope; verification, the implementing organization, entry into force, review and amendments, duration and withdrawal.

WINNING THE ARGUMENT FOR A PERMANENTLY ESTABLISHED CTBT

Most states went into the negotiations assuming that once the CTBT entered into force, it would have indefinite duration and be, in effect, permanent. At the same time, they expected that there would be some version of the standard treaty article permitting a state to give notice of its intention to withdraw if "extraordinary events" related to the issues covered by the treaty were deemed to threaten its "supreme interests". To their surprise, in August 1994, the United States and France each put in new proposals relating to mechanisms and justifications for withdrawal from the treaty. France's proposal would give the right of withdrawal if a state decides that "extraordinary events ... in particular, developments which have altered the conditions which have allowed the entry into force of this treaty".[38] This was perceived as meaning that a state could withdraw from the treaty if it were concerned about the reliability of its nuclear forces or decided that it needed to conduct tests to modernize its arsenal. Widely viewed as a step too far beyond the standard "supreme national interests" justification in most treaties, France's proposal was not considered likely to be successful. The US proposal, which was taken more seriously, caused greater consternation.

The United States proposed that the article relating to review of the treaty (not, significantly, the article relating to duration and withdrawal) should provide for a state to exercise a fast-track mechanism for withdrawing from the treaty at the first review conference, 10 years after entry into force. This 10-year "easy opt-out" proposal was immediately condemned from all sides, most vociferously by US allies, who viewed it as a mechanism to enable the Pentagon to keep its testing infrastructure operative in perpetuity. Clearly intended to provide impetus to the second year's negotiations, the genesis and subsequent abandonment of this provision by the Clinton administration reveals some of the internal disputes and ambivalence that continued in US policy circles. The 10-year opt-out provision was meant to reassure test-ban sceptics in the United States by making it comparatively easy to pull out of the treaty at a review conference, rather than having to make the argument that its supreme national interests were jeopardized. The language was not tied to national security or the safety and reliability of nuclear weapons, although the US delegation justified the provision in those terms. The concept echoed President Carter's attempts to appease test-ban opponents during the 1977–1980 tripartite test-ban talks when he offered a CTBT of only five-, then three-years duration. Opponents also raised concerns that having a mechanism that facilitated easy withdrawal from the treaty at an early stage by the nuclear-weapon states would trivialize commitment to the treaty and be regarded as discriminatory, with negative consequences for the arms control and non-proliferation regimes. Even the US delegation appeared ambivalent, feeding speculation that this unpopular proposal was the outcome of an internal power struggle between pro- and anti-CTBT forces among competing US agencies.

After the CD session had closed in September 1994, when diplomats conducted intersessional talks and politicking on the CTBT during the UN General Assembly and First Committee meetings in New York, many US allies and non-aligned states put Washington under pressure about the proposal, while a number of NGOs and think tanks ran campaigns to have it withdrawn.[39] Most notable among these was the Campaign for the Non-Proliferation Treaty, whose support for indefinite extension of the NPT gave it access to and influence with the Clinton administration.[40] Underlining the importance of the CTBT to the US government's goal of indefinite extension of the NPT, the Campaign strongly backed a zero-yield scope and viewed the easy opt-out provision as counterproductive to US interests in strengthening the credibility of the NPT.[41]

There was considerable relief all round when the Deputy Director of the US Arms Control and Disarmament Agency, Ralph Earle, announced at the first plenary of 1995 that the United States had decided to drop the opt-out proposal.[42] Hopes that the US decision would boost the negotiations were short-lived, however. Negotiations progressed rather slowly between January and April 1995, with a determined but plodding concentration on verification. Though the withdrawal of the easy opt-out proposal had been widely welcomed in Geneva, some continued to express scepticism. Marín Bosch, for example, characterized the provision as a distraction from the CTBT's deeper challenges: "you take a white elephant into the living room, everyone objects; you take the white elephant out again and everyone cheers you as if you have accomplished something wonderful".[43]

France, for its part, modified its proposal a couple of times before finally dropping it in August 1995. At that time, having changed its stance on the scope of the treaty, France accepted the standard text on treaty withdrawal that the rest of the negotiators had assumed would be adopted, while stating on the record its interpretation that since the nuclear-weapon states were responsible for the safety and reliability of their nuclear weapons, this constituted a matter of "supreme interest".

France and the United Kingdom withdraw the safety test proposal

Arguing that Russia and the United States had larger and more diverse arsenals and could retire weapons if their reliability came into question, France and the United Kingdom saw themselves as lacking such flexibility, and so clung to the proposal for safety tests "which may be authorized in exceptional circumstances".[44] Between the two states, however, there were emerging differences over the reasons why they might want to exercise an exceptional right to test. British representatives spoke of the necessity for tests to enable safety improvements of a design.[45] France appeared more interested in testing to ensure the reliability of a design. China, Russia and the United States opposed a routine provision for safety tests in the treaty, preferring their alternative approaches to "activities not prohibited". These larger nuclear powers appeared to share the concerns of non-nuclear-weapon states that the provision might be abused, since it would be impossible to verify that such tests were not being used to modernize or enhance nuclear weapon designs.

The delegations from non-nuclear states unanimously opposed having explicit exceptions enshrined in the treaty. The G-21 specifically ruled out safety tests, and both India and Pakistan made individual statements saying, in effect, that weapons whose safety was in doubt should be eliminated.[46] With the United Kingdom appearing to lead the push for safety tests, British civil society was at the forefront of the opposition, concerned that persisting with the demand would delay, undermine or even derail the CTBT. British NGOs worked with the Labour Party to raise questions in parliament about the UK position, the responses to which revealed confusion in the Conservative government. In June 1994, for example, Defence Procurement Minister Jonathan Aitken said that the British government would "look for a verifiable and effective prohibition of all nuclear tests, with the aim of making a contribution to our international non-proliferation objectives". Acknowledging that a "minimal programme of nuclear testing" had "previously" been important, Aitken added "we now aim to use and develop alternative technologies".[47] When this was reported as a shift in the United Kingdom's attitude, Weston denied that there had been any policy change and reiterated that his country still wanted the CD to consider the possibility of the treaty having a provision for testing in exceptional circumstances.[48] A week later Lynda Chalker, Minister of State at the Foreign and Commonwealth Office, added to the confusion by insisting that "we never made a demand that safety tests should be excluded from the treaty".[49]

One explanation for the mixed messages was that British policymakers had decided to do without safety tests but were continuing to protect the position as a delaying tactic—either to maintain bargaining leverage or to assist the French who hoped to be free to test after the May 1995 elections.[50] With no friends on this issue, France and the United Kingdom were put under considerable pressure, especially from Western colleagues, including other European Union states. Yet they insisted that the option should go forward into the 1994 rolling text and only withdrew the proposal on 6 April 1995, at the very last CD plenary before the opening of the NPT Review and Extension Conference in New York. Making a point of sounding as if he was responding to the views of other delegations, Weston announced that the United Kingdom had decided to withdraw its language on "exceptional tests" from the rolling text, and would support the general scope formulation tabled by Australia in March.[51] In what was interpreted as a reference to the P-5 discussions on hydronuclear experiments, Weston stressed that the "'scope' article in the treaty should not be interpreted as prohibiting the United Kingdom, in common with the other nuclear-weapon States, from fulfilling its responsibilities to maintain the safety and reliability of its nuclear weapons".[52] For its part, France indicated that it would not oppose the deletion of the bracketed language (which it had effectively co-sponsored), but carefully refrained from making any direct comment on the Australian text.[53]

CTBT issues in the 1995 NPT Conference

A CTBT, which had been a major source of contention in past NPT review conferences and the principal factor in the failure of the Fourth Review Conference in 1990, was a focus of considerable discussion but did not cause significant problems at the 1995 Review and Extension Conference. As discussed earlier, the NPT, regarded as the corner-stone of the non-proliferation regime, entered into force in 1970 but was not designed to be permanent. Instead, the treaty provided for an initial period of 25 years, and would not continue to have legal effect beyond 1995 without a further decision being taken by its states parties. Since a CTBT and nuclear disarmament were enshrined in the NPT as aspirations, the poor record of the nuclear-weapon states on disarmament—not least of which was their failure to conclude a CTBT within the treaty's first 25 years—was a major point of contention as the extension decision approached. Although there were few if any advocates for allowing the NPT to lapse, debate raged over whether the treaty should be extended indefinitely, as favoured by France, Russia, the United Kingdom, the United States and many of their allies, or whether there should be a specified extension or new extension mechanism. Some NGOs, and several states including Indonesia and Iran, argued that the treaty should be extended for successive periods of 25 years, with automatic "rolling" extensions unless states parties took a decision to halt a future extension. Venezuela and Kenya preferred a "roll-over" of the treaty in its entirety, with retention of the Article X.2 requirement for a conference to determine any further extension after the next 25 years. Others wanted a single fixed period, with proposals ranging from "long term" or "25 years" down to just 10 years.[54] For some, it was axiomatic that indefinite extension of the NPT was necessary for the credibility and sustainability of the non-proliferation regime, while others thought that a shorter, conditional extension would provide better leverage to bring about nuclear disarmament.[55]

As it turned out, enough had been done to build confidence in the prospects for conclusion of the CTBT by 1996, so that it did not become a major stumbling block to consensus at the 1995 NPT Review and Extension Conference, unlike in previous review meetings. Although a large number of states took the opportunity to emphasize their opposition to thresholds or PNE, almost all expressed positive support for the CTBT. Indeed, the NPT conference was an opportunity especially for states that were marginalized in the negotiations, both members and non-members of the CD, to make representations on behalf of the CTBT. While the Western states party to the NPT tended to applaud CTBT progress, concerns were expressed by others about what Zimbabwe characterized as the "current snail's pace" of negotiations. In common with others, Switzerland, an observer to the CD waiting to be accepted for membership as part of the O'Sullivan List, expressed disappointment at the "little progress reached so far" and warned that to allow "exceptions to the principle of a complete test ban is … incompatible with the spirit of Article VI of the NPT … [and would] raise certain doubts as to the commitment to renounce all nuclear test explosions forever". Viet Nam called the CTBT "a hope rather than a reality", while the Philippines complained that "nothing substantial had been accomplished" in the CD.[56]

The only serious CTBT-related division manifested during the NPT Conference concerned PNE. The issue was addressed in statements to the general debate and in Main Committee III.[57] This Committee focused mainly on the provisions for the peaceful uses of nuclear energy under Article IV of the NPT, but it also included consideration of Article V on "the potential benefits from any peaceful applications of nuclear explosions".[58] China continued to press for PNE and raised the issue during its opening statement to the NPT Conference, with reference to both Article V and the Article IV text regarding the "inalienable right ... to develop research, production and use of nuclear energy for peaceful purposes without discrimination ...". To undermine China's rationale for PNE, Australia put in a working paper that proposed language to be included in the final document of the NPT Conference to the effect that the potential benefits from PNE had not been demonstrated and that there were serious concerns about the environmental consequences and the implications for nuclear non-proliferation.[59] Australia's paper immediately gained co-sponsorship from 41 states, cutting across group lines and engaging non-aligned states as well as Western and Eastern European states. To reassure states that wanted to make certain that any diminution of Article V would not affect the general principles enshrined in Article IV, the paper stated that "a ban on all kinds of nuclear explosions [does] not constitute a detriment to the peaceful utilization of nuclear energy".[60]

The working paper's co-sponsors pushed for their language to be included in the report from Main Committee III. Isolated on this issue, China found it difficult to argue against the paragraphs, as the paper had been cleverly drafted as a series of factual statements. It noted, for example, that the International Atomic Energy Agency (IAEA) had received no request for consideration of PNE services and that no state party had an active programme on PNE. China successfully argued for the removal of some sentences and the insertion of wording that the CD should "take this situation and future developments" into account.[61] Russia, which had exhibited ambivalence on the question during the negotiations in Geneva, joined consensus and did not impose any brackets around the PNE language, but Ambassador Berdennikov said Russia reserved the right to raise the issue at a later stage. Despite China's obvious discomfort and Russia's verbal reservation, the three paragraphs on Article V were accepted by consensus for inclusion in the report of Main Committee III and were passed to the Drafting Committee.[62]

On 11 May 1995, the penultimate day, the President of the Conference, Ambassador Jayantha Dhanapala of Sri Lanka, brought the gavel down on a package of three decisions—Strengthening the NPT Review Process, Principles and Objectives for Nuclear Non-proliferation and Disarmament, and the indefinite extension of the NPT. In addition, the states parties adopted a resolution on the Middle East, sponsored by the three depositary states, Russia, the United Kingdom and the United States. Unable to get consensus for a stand-alone decision to make the NPT permanent, the package constituted a politically binding set of commitments, with the decision to continue the NPT in force indefinitely predicated on the decision to accept the fact that a majority of states parties supported indefinite extension.[63] With reference to the CTBT, Paragraph 4(a) of the agreed Principles and Objectives provided a target date of "no later than 1996" and stressed that the nuclear-weapon states "should exercise utmost restraint" pending a CTBT's entry into force.[64] No mention was made of PNE or Article V.

After consensus had been given to adopting the decisions on extending the NPT and strengthening its review process, attempts to get agreement on the Final Declaration encompassing the review of the treaty foundered, chiefly over issues relating to nuclear disarmament. In the end, to the immense frustration of many NPT parties, the Conference closed without adopting a Final Declaration. Despite the fact that three quarters of the Drafting Committee's text—essentially everything in the reports from Main Committees II and III—had received consensus agreement, they were formally lost. In an interview after the Conference ended, Dhanapala ascribed the failure to two principal causes: poor management of Main Committee I by its Chair and the consequent failure to agree large parts of its review of Article VI; and intransigence on the part of the P-5, once they had achieved their objective of extending the treaty indefinitely.[65]

NPT aftermath: more nuclear tests from China and France

The details of the NPT statements and discussions related to nuclear testing had far less impact on CTBT negotiations than the divisive politics of the NPT Conference, the perceived loss of the NPT's restraining leverage on the nuclear-weapon states once the decision on indefinite extension was secured, and the impact that the NPT's indefinite extension had on policymakers in India.

The ink was barely dry on the NPT agreements when on 15 May China detonated a nuclear bomb with a yield of 85–110kt at its test site at Lop Nor in Xinjiang Province.[66] China's military decision makers—thinking chiefly of conditions on the ground, including weather—had actually planned the test for early May, which could have put it in the middle of the NPT Conference. That China waited until after the NPT Conference had concluded was claimed to have been solely due to the efforts of other P-5 diplomats when they were apprised of China's test preparations.[67] As it was, China's nuclear explosion occurred during the 1995 meeting of the UN Disarmament Commission, which followed immediately after the NPT Review and Extension Conference. The Commission heard ritualistic expressions of regret, but it was left to a few states and international civil society to condemn the explosion as inconsistent with the NPT obligations and the just-agreed commitment in the adopted Principles and Objectives to show "utmost restraint" on nuclear testing pending completion of a CTBT.

Meanwhile, the newly installed French President, Jacques Chirac, waited only a month before announcing on 13 June that France would resume nuclear testing to conduct up to eight explosions between 1 September 1995 and 31 May 1996. Just before that public statement, Érrera communicated the decision to resume testing to the P-5 and European allies in the CD, who made little or no public comment.[68] When Chirac's decision was made more widely public, however, states in and around the Pacific were outspoken in their opposition, and many alluded pointedly to the commitments recently undertaken at the NPT Conference. Japan called the French announcement a "betrayal of the trust that the non-nuclear-weapon States had in the nuclear-weapon States".[69] New Zealand expressed "outrage" and rejected the argument that further tests were needed to ensure the safety of the French nuclear arsenal before the CTBT entered into force.[70] Richard Starr read statements on behalf of Australia and also from the South Pacific Forum governments, rejecting France's assertion that the nuclear tests were consistent with the agreement on "utmost restraint" adopted unanimously by NPT parties six weeks earlier. Australia temporarily froze cooperation with France on defence-related matters.[71] Outside the Pacific, Switzerland referred to the "moral incompatibility" between the resumption of nuclear tests and the NPT commitments undertaken at the recent conference, noting that "experts are not unanimous on the technical need to conduct tests in order to maintain the safety of [nuclear] weapons".[72] Mexico's new ambassador, Antonio de Icaza, noted that the proposal for adoption of an immediate moratorium on nuclear testing, tabled by his country during the NPT Conference, had not been accepted because of the opposition of "certain nuclear powers". Linking the French resumption of testing with China's test of 15 May and "the statement by a senior United States representative to the effect that his country might also resume nuclear testing", Mexico's ambassador Antonio de Icaza warned that such developments "do not create a propitious climate" for implementing the NPT obligations.[73]

Iran's ambassador, Sirous Nasseri, remarked that the P-5's concerns to achieve their preferred NPT extension outcome had served as a greater deterrent to nuclear testing than the moratoria. He reminded the CD that there had been two views at the NPT Conference: that indefinite extension would promote a climate of confidence, which would lead to nuclear disarmament; or that indefinite extension would allow the nuclear-weapon states to pursue their own agendas and objectives with even greater freedom. It was clear from his remarks—and similar comments from other representatives of non-aligned states—that the French and Chinese tests were seen to exemplify the latter view.[74] Earlier, at the penultimate preparatory committee meeting before the 1995 Review and Extension Conference, Iran had warned that the non-nuclear states could lose whatever leverage they had if the P-5 obtained their desired objective of indefinite extension of the NPT. Raising doubts that the nuclear-weapon states would honour the commitment to complete the CTBT negotiations once the NPT had been extended, Iran suggested that the PTBT should be amended quickly to ban underground testing "pending finalization of the CTBT".[75]

The temporal proximity of the decision to extend the NPT, the Chinese test, Chirac's decision to resume French testing and reports of a reopening of the US interagency debate over higher thresholds (referred to in Ambassador de Icaza's statement to the CD) greatly increased anxiety among the non-nuclear-weapon states and hardened the positions of some non-aligned states. On 18 June, US Secretary of Defense William J. Perry publicly acknowledged that yields from zero to "a few pounds" to "even several hundred tons" were being considered by the Clinton administration.[76] UK government support for efforts by the Pentagon and US Joint Chiefs of Staff to obtain a half kiloton threshold were also exposed.[77] Despite Perry stressing that the United States did not plan to break its moratorium and that no decisions had yet been taken on whether to support a threshold, press reports began to speak of a possible resumption of testing by the

United States.[78] In Washington, Ambassador Thomas Graham, who had led the US delegation at the NPT Review and Extension Conference, argued that adoption of such a threshold would be "a serious breach of trust".[79]

Although the US Arms Control and Disarmament Agency and the Department of Energy were formally opposed to a 500t threshold, the Director for Arms Control at the National Security Council, Robert Bell, and several important State Department officials backed this demand, reasserted as a compromise by the Pentagon and others who had earlier advocated that tests up to 1kt should be allowed.[80] Bell, who had previously advocated the 1kt threshold, was reportedly frustrated with the inability of the rest of the P-5 to agree on the scope of the CTBT ("activities not prohibited" in particular), and saw a 500t threshold as a way to end the dispute.[81] In believing that a CTBT would be possible with such a threshold, Bell had misread the mood of the non-nuclear states. Even in July 1994, when many negotiators were willing to accommodate hydronuclear experiments in order to make certain of the CTBT before the NPT extension decision, a 500t threshold would have been difficult for them to accept. By June 1995, that chance had gone completely.

In view of the dismay expressed about French testing and the renewed US debates over a 500t threshold, the Chair of Working Group 2, Jaap Ramaker, decided to hold a meeting to discuss scope. Ramaker's initiative recognized the growing disquiet over what some delegates called the "privatization" of the scope discussions among the P-5. With the aim of reasserting the multilateral responsibility and role in determining the treaty's basic obligations, he made a point of encouraging G-21 delegations to participate.

Convened on 27 June 1995, the session on scope may not have constituted a turning point as such, but it sent some strong signals that if the CTBT were to have credibility in the wider world, the P-5 would need to change their approach. India and Indonesia both tabled proposals to tighten the scope so as to exclude hydronuclear experiments and laboratory testing. Indonesia sought to ban all nuclear testing, including laboratory tests and simulations.[82] India seized on an approach put forward in March by the US environmental organization, Natural Resources Defense Council (NRDC), and proposed draft text to define a nuclear explosion. Prior to taking this initiative, India's new ambassador, Arundhati Ghose, had consulted with fellow members of the G-21, gaining some but not unanimous support for the following proposal:

> 1. Each State Party undertakes to prohibit and to prevent, and not to carry out, any nuclear weapon explosion, or any other nuclear test explosion, or any release of nuclear energy caused by the assembly or compression of fissile or fusion material by chemical explosive or other means, at any place under or beyond its jurisdiction or control.
> 2. Each State Party undertakes, furthermore, to refrain from causing, encouraging, assisting or in any way participating in the carrying out of any nuclear weapon test explosion or any other nuclear explosion.[83]

Australian, British and German diplomats publicly derided India's proposal, which differed from the NRDC's language in three significant respects: it would permit PNE, which India said it opposed, and prohibit inertial confinement fusion experiments, which India was interested in developing. Furthermore, it would extend the obligation to areas beyond a state's jurisdiction or control, which would be impossible to implement. The Indian delegation offered to discuss revisions and invited sceptics to explain their difficulties and help to develop a more satisfactory text. India's invitation to participate in reworking its scope text received no reply from Western delegations or NGOs, as they preferred to work for a zero-yield understanding based on the majority-supported Australian formulation on scope.[84]

Though it did not result in a direct breakthrough on scope, the 27 June debate crystallized opposition to any threshold. At the time, the attitude of many CD delegations was summed up thus:

> if the [nuclear-weapon states] want a threshold ban they will have to conclude it among themselves outside the CD, but if they do that, it will fail to have a positive effect on the non-proliferation regime and could even be counterproductive; the only CTBT that will emerge from the CD now will be zero threshold … . The [nuclear-weapon states] need to evaluate the whole proliferation picture and decide which they want more: a CTBT or continued testing. They will not now get both.[85]

This perception was reinforced by a hard-hitting G-21 statement to the CD at the end of June that expressed the deep concern of non-aligned parties to the NPT that the resumption of testing will "run counter to the decisions adopted at the 1995 NPT review and extension Conference ... and [jeopardize] the credibility of the NPT regime".[86] Addressing the CTBT negotiations directly, the G-21 statement continued:

> Conducting or intending to conduct nuclear-weapon tests over and above the substantial number of tests already conducted raises serious questions about the nuclear-weapon States' real intentions with regard to continued development of nuclear weapons. Recent reports about discussions among the nuclear-weapon States on a threshold for a test ban have also given rise to deep concern. ... [T]he CTBT should be an instrument against both horizontal and vertical nuclear proliferation and should effectively contribute to nuclear disarmament. To admit low-yield nuclear testing or to permit testing below a certain threshold by using any technique would defeat such purposes. ... No tests should be allowed for any reason or justification including the so-called safety and reliability of the nuclear weapons and perfecting the techniques to further develop nuclear weapons. The ban should be comprehensive.[87]

The G-21 statement was able to challenge the private P-5 negotiations on scope and threshold so explicitly in part because of the activities of civil society in exposing and discussing the internal debates on activities not prohibited.[88] Arguing that all aspects of the CTBT should be multilaterally and openly negotiated, the G-21 called on the Chair of the NTB Committee to take "appropriate measures to ensure that negotiations are held for a clear understanding on the scope of the future CTBT".[89] Viewing the G-21 statement as posturing, the nuclear-weapon states dismissed their concerns, and relations between the non-aligned CD members and the P-5 continued to deteriorate.

The sense of betrayal and frustration that pervaded the CD session of 29 May to 7 July 1995 was largely due to the post-NPT immediacy of China's first test of 1995 and President Chirac's termination of the French moratorium. Meetings were characterized by rancorous exchanges between some of the nuclear-weapon states and key delegations from the Western Group and G-21.[90] One senior US diplomat called the polarization and hostility a "post-NPT hangover" and predicted that it would improve over the summer.[91] He was right; the first clear political breakthrough of the CTBT negotiations occurred during August: not, as some anticipated, through the process of negotiations, but as the result of a dramatic resurgence of civil society protests against nuclear testing. These caused a reappraisal at the highest levels and led directly to President Clinton's decision to take the moral and political high ground and commit to a zero-yield scope.

The United States and France commit to a zero-yield scope

French diplomats have claimed credit for bringing about the essential breakthrough on scope, and undoubtedly the international shock of President Chirac's decision to resume testing caused a crisis that affected the negotiations.[92] However, the road to zero yield had been paved earlier by the failure to conclude the CTBT in early 1995, and by the combined efforts of a small number of civil society experts, who decided to go public on the disputes among the P-5 over hydronuclear experiments on nuclear warheads.[93]

During 1994, the difficulties of verifying the nature of explosions at very low yields had been evoked as part of a strategy to accommodate hydronuclear experiments. From January 1995, the argument had been reversed and verification doubts became an effective weapon *against* accepting such experiments. As it became clear that agreement among the P-5 on the issue was far from a done deal, arguments involving non-governmental scientists, US government scientists and officials came to a head in journals, conferences and Washington policy circles. As Acronym brought the debates to the attention of Geneva diplomats, pressure intensified on Washington policymakers. A growing number of delegations began to emphasize that the CTBT must be "non-discriminatory", diplomatic code for opposing differential privileges for the nuclear powers, such as those that had been codified in the NPT three decades earlier. A growing number of diplomats in the CD put forward the argument derived from civil society sources that permitting hydronuclear testing would complicate verification and risk compliance ambiguities and challenges that could weaken or discredit the operation of the treaty.

Although reinforced buildings could theoretically be used (which had provoked some suspicions about the Russian preference for listing prohibited environments based on the PTBT), US hydronuclear experiments were all conducted underground for safety reasons, including the risks associated with larger-than-expected explosions or nuclear yields, and the need to satisfy more stringent environmental regulations if explosions were carried out in above-ground facilities. The US facilities were located at the Low-

Yield Nuclear Explosion Research (LYNER) complex at the Nevada Test Site. Conducted at test sites, the preparations and procedures for conducting hydronuclear experiments could appear similar to those for underground nuclear testing. Without intrusive verification and transparency procedures, such experiments would be difficult to distinguish from tests that might be conducted to develop new types of low-yield or "micro" nuclear weapons.[94]

Early in 1995, Marín Bosch, freed from the constraints of his position as NTB Committee Chair, warned about technological advances and hydronuclear experiments subverting the disarmament objective of the CTBT:

> What is happening now with regard to nuclear testing is no different from what has been happening in the disarmament field for years: the technologically more advanced nations reach a point where they can discard a certain weapon or weapon-related activity and then they move to ban that weapon or activity for the rest of the world through a multilateral treaty … .[95]

Such concerns were shared by many and, as the year wore on, the G-21 became more vocal against allowing the nuclear powers to conduct tests that would enable them to continue to develop and modernize their nuclear weapons. Delegations from the Middle East, most vocally from Egypt and Iran, were particularly concerned by the widely distributed assessment by some NGO scientists that Israel already possessed laboratory-based hydronuclear testing capabilities and could thus benefit from a provision in the CTBT permitting hydronuclear experiments below a certain threshold.[96]

A report from NRDC physicists Thomas Cochran and Christopher Paine was particularly influential. Publicly disagreeing with the US characterization of hydronuclear experiments as solely to assure the safety and reliability of nuclear weapons, Cochran and Paine showed that the tests "indisputably constitute nuclear weapon test explosions".[97] According to their assessment, "At nuclear yields of 100–200 tons, fusion phenomena can be investigated, allowing partial yield verification of the performance of new boosted-fission weapons, including new designs for the 'primary' or triggering component of much more powerful two-stage thermonuclear weapons".[98] They concluded, "Since the marginal value of hydronuclear and other low yield tests for insuring the safety and reliability of existing stockpiled weapons is small in comparison to their associated verification complexities and proliferation risks, such tests should be explicitly banned under the CTBT".[99] Cochran and Paine's proposed treaty language for an Article I scope provision that would explicitly encompass a ban on these experiments was intended to be helpful, but India's advocacy of a modified version, discussed above, backfired.[100] The report was, however, influential in the US debates.

During June and August 1995, the CD became a hive of rumour, leaks and suspicions. Although the United Kingdom, like China and Russia, refrained from making any formal comment on US and French activities and developments, Lord Henley, UK Parliamentary Under-Secretary of State for Defence, provoked anger among civil society and Labour parliamentarians when he refused to rule out further British tests if the United States lifted its moratorium. He also shrugged at the idea that France could jeopardize the negotiations with its tests, saying: "it is entirely a matter for the French themselves to decide whether or not they wish to test".[101] Such statements helped to fuel conspiracy theories that the P-5 would ratchet up the threat of a high threshold or another failure to achieve a CTBT in order to panic the non-nuclear negotiators into accepting a non-explicit provision on hydronuclear experiments at a level that would appear more reasonable than the threatened threshold. In fact, as borne out by subsequent interviews, there was no conspiracy and little strategy among the US agencies or the P-5.[102] Even at the time there was no evidence beyond circumstance and coincidence to justify any conspiracy theories, which chiefly testified to the atmosphere of hostility and negativity in the CD in the aftermath of the NPT Conference.

As the mood in the CD grew more and more negative, a heated debate over the purpose and scope of the CTBT took place within the Clinton administration.[103] Fearing that the prospect for a genuinely comprehensive test ban was slipping away, US NGOs increased their activities. Arguing that a 500t threshold would sustain the nuclear arms race and encourage would-be proliferators, they circulated information showing that if testing were permitted up to half a kiloton, then not only hydronuclear experiments, but also the field testing of new low-yield or miniaturized warhead designs could be conducted.[104] The Physicians for Social Responsibility, NRDC and other Washington-based NGOs mobilized 137 Congressional representatives, including 24 Senators, to sign letters urging President Clinton to support a total, zero-yield test ban. In less than two months, grass-roots networks had collected over 35,000 letters and messages from all over the United

States, which they dispatched to the White House and the Department of Energy.[105]

Energy Secretary O'Leary had already shown she was willing to challenge the US military establishment when she hired experts from the NRDC, the Carnegie Endowment and other think tanks to advise on issues relating to the nuclear laboratories and cooperative threat reduction programmes with Russia. Not only was O'Leary viewed as a supporter of the test ban, but she had also demonstrated her commitment to more open government by releasing substantial documentation, hitherto classified, covering nuclear-related accidents, health and safety issues, and information from health and environmental studies concerning US nuclear facilities.[106] In early 1995, O'Leary commissioned the JASON Group—highly qualified experts from the US nuclear laboratories and scientific establishment who had previously written an influential report on stockpile stewardship[107]—to do a further report on nuclear testing. This report, made public on 4 August during a Senate debate on testing and hydronuclear experiments, concluded that low-yield, sub-kiloton nuclear explosions would be of only marginal utility in ensuring stockpile safety.[108] Test-ban advocates in the United States, the United Kingdom and Geneva made sure that the JASON Group's findings were widely distributed and reported outside of Washington policy circles, particularly to governments and media. The group's technical arguments reinforced O'Leary and senior officials in the Department of Energy and the Arms Control and Disarmament Agency in their opposition to the 500t threshold pushed by Bob Bell and the Pentagon. Moreover, it became clear that even the nuclear laboratories were divided: some scientists wanted to be able to continue conducting nuclear explosive testing, but others had vested interests in the highly funded projects contained in the stockpile stewardship programme that had been established in 1994 to persuade the US labs to move away from nuclear testing.[109]

Throughout July and early August 1995, test-ban advocates had ensured that the White House was flooded with letters from all over the United States, backed up by copious pro-CTBT editorials in regional and national newspapers (an important way to influence congressional representatives). The White House also received higher than usual levels of correspondence from members of the US Congress and from abroad, especially from parliamentarians and retired, senior military officials, and churches and schools in countries allied with the United States.[110] Faced with the greatest pressure exerted on a US President on nuclear issues in over a decade, Clinton took the decision to back a zero-yield CTBT.

France was also coming under pressure, but not from the CD. It was clear that the French had prepared for opposition. To mitigate the political damage France recognized might result from its resumption of testing, Chirac sought to build confidence in the CTBT by pledging that the "campaign" of eight tests would be the last that France would conduct and promising that he would sign the CTBT, if concluded, in 1996. What took France by surprise was the international reaction outside governmental circles, as demonstrations disrupted French diplomatic residences and companies all over the world.[111] Despite Chirac's assurances, the prospect of more French nuclear explosions in the South Pacific ignited public anger and protests across much of the world, and created a particularly strong backlash in the Pacific. European Union solidarity meant that few European governments criticized France openly or in the CD, but spontaneous demonstrations hit the streets in Australia, Germany, Japan, New Zealand and Sweden. A French mission in Australia was set on fire (though most Australian NGOs were quick to condemn this and dissociate themselves from such an attack). Boycotts against French goods, especially wine, were started in several regions, not insignificantly affecting trade in Australasia, parts of North America, and affecting a number of major importers in Japan and Scandinavia. In news stories that were covered in France as well as around the world, bottles of French wine were shown being poured down drains. Although Germany's government said little, German shoppers boycotted French goods in surprising numbers. The boycotts were largely a spontaneous response by citizens, though they were encouraged and in some cases facilitated by various national and international NGOs, some of whom produced boycott stickers and publicity materials.[112]

Once again, French nuclear testing put Greenpeace in the limelight. Ten years after the *Rainbow Warrior* had been sunk by French agents in Auckland harbour, a dramatic and violent boarding of the second *Rainbow Warrior* by French commandos near the Moruroa test site in July 1995 was recorded by media and broadcast around the world.[113] Such sounds and images helped to galvanize public outrage against France and muster support for the consumer boycotts. In France too there were more demonstrations against nuclear weapons than ever before, though these were small by comparison with the protests in other countries. In July and August 1995, French radio and television news and discussion programmes carried interviews with farmers and wine producers on the nuclear tests and their consequences for French commerce. While most of the French public appeared relatively unconcerned about the nuclear testing as such, the government was accused of not doing enough to mitigate the bad publicity and economic damage to French producers.[114] While it is difficult to be certain which forms of protest were most effective, Thomas Graham recorded in his memoirs that their combined effect caused Chirac to complain to an aide, "Why didn't someone tell me that this was the 50th anniversary of Hiroshima?"[115]

The first indication of a shift in the French position came on 9 August, in a US radio interview with French Foreign Ministry spokesperson Yves Doutrieux and Australian ambassador to the United States Don Russell. Pre-empting the announcement scheduled to be formally made by the French delegation to the CD the following day, Doutrieux declared that France would accept the Australian scope text, as tabled in March 1995. When asked if the French decision meant zero and if it ruled out hydronuclear testing, Doutrieux confirmed "zero".[116] The next day, Ambassador Érrera informed the CD that France envisaged a "truly comprehensive prohibition" and would endorse the Australian scope language prohibiting "any nuclear weapon test explosion or any other nuclear explosion". He went on to say that this proved the falsity of criticisms that the resumption of French nuclear testing would harm the negotiations. Érrera also emphasized France's commitment to the CTBT by telling the CD that a new approach to the negotiations was needed in order to achieve conclusion of the treaty by September 1996.[117]

The French announcement was followed just one day later, on 11 August, by a speech in Washington from President Clinton, who committed the United States to "a true zero yield ban" on all nuclear explosions. By linking this announcement on zero yield with a renewal of US approval of the Australian scope text, and by exactly quoting the relevant part of that text as "any nuclear weapons test explosion, or any other nuclear explosion", the Clinton administration placed on the record its new interpretation that the Australian text excluded low-yield and hydronuclear testing.[118] At the same time, to appease critics in the nuclear laboratories and bolster support for the CTBT in Congress and the Pentagon, Clinton specified six conditions for the United States to join a CTBT, including a well-financed long-term commitment to further development of the "Science-Based Stockpile Stewardship" programme. These conditions were referred to as "safeguards", and included stockpile stewardship; the maintenance of modern, well-financed nuclear laboratories; the retention of a "basic capability" to resume nuclear testing; continuation of research and development programmes to improve treaty monitoring and operations; and continuing resources for and development of intelligence gathering to ensure accurate information relating to nuclear arsenals and related nuclear programmes worldwide. The sixth safeguard, repeated in his speech, was that Clinton would "be prepared, in consultation with Congress" to exercise the right under the treaty article allowing for withdrawal on grounds of "supreme national interests" and conduct whatever testing was required in the event that he were:

> informed by the Secretary of Defense and Secretary of Energy … advised by the Nuclear Weapons Council, the Directors of [the] nuclear weapons laboratories and the Commander of the United States Strategic Command—that a high level of confidence in the safety or reliability of a nuclear-weapon type [considered] to be critical to our nuclear deterrent could no longer be certified.[119]

The last qualification, allowing "supreme national interests" to be interpreted in terms of the assessed function and condition of the US nuclear arsenal, resembled France's argument that the CTBT must be compatible with the continuing reliability of its nuclear arsenal, a justification that underpinned both the dropping of France's earlier text on treaty withdrawal and, more notably, its explanation for conducting a further series of tests.[120] The other conditions echoed the safeguards which the nuclear weapon laboratories and the Pentagon had extracted from President Kennedy more than 30 years earlier. Clinton's decision was a trade-off, but though some have criticized the compromise since, it was necessary for him to act when he did to save the CTBT negotiations. Responding to advice from some of the most respected nuclear scientists in the United States, Clinton's decision to support a zero-yield obligation and the Australian text on scope boosted the CTBT in the CD and circumvented the disagreements over threshold and yield among the P-5, as well as within the US administration.

Following the French and US commitments to zero yield and the Australian scope, CD members pushed China, Russia and the United Kingdom to agree as well. Bypassed and disgruntled, British Ministry of Defence officials were furious at having been sidelined by the United States, which informed the UK government just before Clinton's announcement, and by France, whose delaying tactics the UK delegation had faithfully supported during the previous 18 months. Without a test site of its own, and dependent on the US Nevada Test Site since 1962, the United Kingdom had no choice but to accede more or less gracefully. In September 1995, therefore, Weston told the CD that, having carefully studied the statements by Clinton and Érrera, he wanted now "to put on record my Government's position that the CTBT should not permit any nuclear-weapon test explosion involving any release of nuclear energy, no matter how small". Echoing the US position linking the safety and reliability of nuclear arsenals and supreme national interests, Weston said that the United Kingdom attached the same conditions as the United States, related to the retention and maintenance of its nuclear stockpiles and design resources. Twice emphasizing that, as a nuclear-weapon state, the United Kingdom continued to bear responsibility for maintaining "the safety and reliability of our nuclear deterrent", Weston asserted that the CTBT "must not prevent us from fulfilling this responsibility". With this new-found virtue, Weston could not resist challenging China and Russia to do likewise: "it would contribute greatly to the progress of the negotiations if those nuclear-weapon States who have not already done so would confirm that they share this view too".[121]

Russia was furious about the zero-yield decision, and took its anger out in the negotiations. Although President Yeltsin stood beside Clinton and nodded and smiled when the American President closed a summit meeting on 23 October 1995 with the announcement that both supported a fully comprehensive, true zero-yield test ban, it took another six months before Russia formally accepted that position.[122] Clinton again tried to include Russia when, at a summit in April 1996, he said that "we have all agreed to go with the so-called Australian language which is a strict zero yield comprehensive test ban treaty. That is the only kind of treaty that can give the people of the world the certainty that they really are seeing the end of the nuclear age of the big weapons".[123] Yeltsin voiced agreement this time, saying that "all, to the very last one, agreed that this year we've got to sign the treaty on banning ... any size of test forever".[124] The position was subsequently formalized by Russia's ambassador to the CD on 14 May 1996. Remarking, somewhat to the surprise of his diplomatic colleagues, that "the Russian delegation has always argued that this treaty should contain no threshold restrictions whatsoever", Berdennikov confirmed Moscow's support for the Australian scope on the understanding that it did not contradict the provisions of the PTBT. Accordingly, Russia accepted that "any nuclear weapon test explosion or any other nuclear explosion in any environment will be banned forever and without any 'thresholds'".[125]

In relation to this, Berdennikov added, Russia would need to conduct "nuclear stockpile stewardship activities". He listed five measures that closely resembled Clinton's August 1995 safeguards: implementation of a programme to ensure the safety and reliability of the nuclear arsenal without conducting nuclear explosions; continued support and resources for research infrastructure and expertise; retention of a "basic potential" for renewing nuclear test explosions if need be; the continuation of activities aimed at improving capabilities in monitoring the nuclear test ban; and further improvement in information gathering and intelligence related to "possible covert nuclear armament projects or other activities conducted by other countries that are of significance for nuclear weapons purposes". The statement also contained a sixth condition, similar to that of the US, British and French assertions on supreme interests, that "if [Russia's] supreme interests are threatened, [it] will make use of its right to withdraw from the treaty in order to conduct all necessary tests which may be called for if there is no other possible means of confirming a high level of confidence in the safety or reliability of any of the key types of Russian nuclear weapons".[126]

By the end of March 1996, Beijing, which had appeared to sit on the fence over the scope issue, made virtue of necessity by reminding everyone that China had consistently advocated that the CTBT scope should exclude any threshold and "welcoming" that other states had come to this position.[127] In view of the continuing resistance to defining a nuclear weapon test or explosion, and since there appeared now to be a common understanding that the Australian scope formulation would be interpreted to mean zero-yield, China agreed to withdraw the phrase "release of nuclear energy" from its scope proposal in the rolling text. At the same time, Ambassador Sha Zukang signalled a review of China's position on the use of satellites and electromagnetic pulse monitoring for remote sensing verification. In making these concessions, he called for similar flexibility from others and reiterated China's requirement that the treaty should not ban nuclear explosions conducted for peaceful purposes.[128]

Despite the zero-yield breakthrough, by the end of 1995 the CD continued to struggle with a 97-page rolling text that contained more than 1,200 pairs of brackets containing disputed text.[129] Much of the technical work was accomplished, but political troubles were looming. As 1995 drew to a close, two events occurred with ominous implications for the CTBT: accusations that India was preparing to conduct a nuclear test in Rajasthan (and counter-accusations about US spying and lying), and a US Department of Energy announcement about starting subcritical tests in Nevada.[130] The next chapter will examine how these events played out as the CTBT negotiations approached their endgame.

CHAPTER 5

MAKING THE TREATY BAN CIVILIAN AS WELL AS MILITARY NUCLEAR EXPLOSIONS

> *… as an important principle, any disarmament or arms control treaty should not hinder the development and application of science and technology for peaceful purposes.*
>
> Sha Zukang, China's Ambassador to the CD,
> 28 March 1996[1]

The fiftieth UN General Assembly in December 1995 adopted the annual CTBT resolution without a vote, giving a political boost to the objective of concluding the treaty in 1996. The resolution called for the negotiations to be concluded as "a task of the highest priority", and urged the CD to complete the final text of the treaty "as soon as possible in 1996".[2] As CD delegations reconvened in Geneva in January 1996, three issues dominated the third year of the CTBT negotiations:

- finalizing the verification regime, with particular reference to how difficult to make the conditions for triggering an on-site inspection and whether NTM would be permissible as evidence to back an inspection request;
- whether the treaty should include language explicitly prohibiting the qualitative development of nuclear weapons (related to the broader question of how the CTBT should be linked with the wider goal of nuclear disarmament); and
- what conditions would have to be met before the CTBT could enter into force—particularly whether to specify in some way the signature and ratification of certain states.

Underlying these central questions were deep divisions between the perceived interests of the P-5, the D-3 and the rest of the world—civil society as well as the non-nuclear-weapon states. In the aftermath of the

US decision to base scope on zero yield and the French decision to conduct a final series of tests to ready its laboratories for maintaining the arsenal without nuclear testing, the positions and relations among the key states with nuclear weapons programmes or aspirations had shifted. As noted in the previous chapter, the P-5 dynamic from January 1994 to April 1995 could be characterized as Russia with the United States, France with the United Kingdom, and China. After August 1995, France moved into a more constructive posture on many issues, including verification and entry into force, bringing it closer to the United States, which still tried to be "out front pulling", as John Holum had promised back in January 1994.[3] Russia shifted into a less constructive posture, digging in its heels on a number of minor questions, refusing to endorse the zero-yield decision for months and siding with China on several verification-related issues. The United Kingdom's posture remained ambivalent. Its scientists continued to provide constructive leadership on verification issues, but in the broader CD and P-5 negotiations, the United Kingdom was perceived as hostile to a zero-yield CTBT and rigid in its determination to make the treaty serve a non-proliferation rather than disarmament purpose. For China and India, which had entered the negotiations in 1994 without having taken definite political decisions to join the CTBT, this question could no longer be avoided in 1996. As the final year of negotiations progressed, it became clear that China was choosing to commit to the multilateral treaty it had participated in negotiating, while India was leaning toward rejecting it.

Entering the year with a heavily bracketed rolling text, it was clear that, to conclude the treaty in 1996, the CD would have to change the form and conduct of its negotiating processes. It being the turn of the Western Group to chair the Nuclear Test Ban Committee, Australia again put forward its CD ambassador, Richard Starr. His nomination was supported by many other delegations, non-aligned as well as Western, which felt that the final year of negotiations would require strong leadership. However, despite its change of posture in the second half of the negotiations, France again blocked the Australian candidacy and encouraged the European Union to throw its weight behind the previous year's Chair of Working Group 2, Jaap Ramaker.[4]

On being confirmed as the Chair, Ramaker convened the two Working Groups and appointed several Friends of the Chair for the key issues. He maintained this structure between January and May 1996, but suspended the Working Groups after that in order to coordinate the endgame directly, though he retained some of the Friends of the Chair as "moderators". Once again, Western representatives dominated the decision-making processes, particularly on technical issues.[5]

1996: END OF AN ERA

As the CD resumed negotiations in January 1996, France conducted its sixth nuclear test, which President Chirac declared would be the last.[6] Having completed its programme with six rather than the originally-announced eight explosions, France pledged to dismantle its test facilities at Moruroa and Fangataufa, presenting this decision as proof of the French commitment to a CTBT that would be in force indefinitely.

The United States opened the final year's negotiations with a statement from President Clinton reiterating the CTBT's promise of "a true-zero-yield comprehensive test-ban treaty that will endure for all time" and pledging the "full and energetic support of the United States to conclude promptly a treaty so long sought and so long denied".[7] US efforts to ensure the final year would progress smoothly, however, were undermined by an announcement from their own Department of Energy in November 1995 that it would conduct a programme of subcritical tests on nuclear warhead components, starting June 1996. The announcement, which specified that the tests would contain small quantities of weapon-grade plutonium, was so clumsily managed that it caused speculation among Washington insiders that it was a sabotage attempt, engineered by opponents of the treaty in the nuclear weapon laboratories. Ledogar did his best to reassure CD members in private, but the effect of the announcement was to dissipate much of the positive impact of the zero-yield victory of the previous August and to erode confidence in the CTBT's significance for curbing nuclear weapon modernization.[8]

John Holum, director of the soon-to-be-dismantled Arms Control and Disarmament Agency, tried to counteract the concerns raised by CD delegations by emphasizing the constraints that a CTBT would impose. He argued, for example, that the treaty would prevent the nuclear-weapon states from pursuing new or advanced nuclear-weapon technologies and that it would "sustain today's trend toward smaller nuclear arsenals with shrinking roles in national defences".[9] However, despite these assurances, the announcement of subcritical tests in 1996 provoked some

CD delegations—notably Egypt, Pakistan and Sri Lanka—to make critical statements during the first weeks of 1996.[10]

Despite such concerns about the subcritical tests, the declared end to French testing and positive indications from China resulted in greater confidence about the commitment of P-5 states to the CTBT. By contrast, concerns about India's intentions came to the fore in the third year of negotiations. Following US intelligence analyses at the end of 1995, the *New York Times* carried reports that India was making what appeared to be nuclear test preparations at the Pokharan test site in Rajasthan.[11] Soon after, it appeared that Prime Minister Narasimha Rao had cancelled the preparations at the test site. The reports unleashed a turbulent debate in India about nuclear policy, national interests and the CTBT, much of which took place in the pages of India's print media. It became clear that a large majority linked the retention of India's nuclear option with independence, status and future security.[12] In her first CD statement of 1996, India's ambassador Arundhati Ghose publicly reacted against the US accusations and remarked dryly that 1996 would be "a testing time for all of us". She derided the 1995 NPT extension as legitimizing "the possession of nuclear weapons by a few states and their possible use as a currency of power" and tabled three working papers.[13] These contained proposals that linked the CTBT's preamble and entry into force with commitment to a 10-year timetable for nuclear disarmament and also contained explicit language on preventing qualitative developments or new weapons systems.[14]

That India would push for the CTBT to contain language committing to a timetable for nuclear disarmament was not unexpected. Atal Behari Vajpayee, Indian Member of Parliament and soon-to-be Prime Minister, had told the UN First Committee in October 1995 that "Developing new warheads or refining existing ones after a CTBT is in place, using innovative technology, would be as contrary to the spirit of [the] CTBT as the NPT is to the spirit of non-proliferation". Arguing that the CTBT should be "an integral step in the process of nuclear disarmament", Vajpayee stated that the test ban's scope should cover "complete cessation of nuclear tests by all states in all environments and for all time" and that the treaty must "contain a binding commitment to take further measures, within an agreed time-frame, towards the total elimination of nuclear weapons".[15]

CD negotiators had expected India to propose strong disarmament language for the preamble, where it would probably have received support from the rest of the G-21. Instead, and to the surprise of its non-aligned colleagues, India sought to attach the nuclear disarmament time frame as a condition of CTBT entry into force.[16] Such an explicit link between the CTBT and a 10-year target date for nuclear disarmament would no doubt be popular with the public and dismissed by the nuclear-weapon states. Hence, use of these linkage tactics, combined with ignoring G-21 strategies and taking a high-minded but impractical stance on disarmament, gave the first clear sign that India wanted to establish its grounds for refusing to join the CTBT despite having participated fully in the negotiations. Although Indian diplomats insisted that their proposals and target dates were negotiable, it appeared to many negotiators that, in mounting its challenge in this way, India was deliberately creating conditions to justify rejecting the treaty later on. India's tactics and the perception they created that it wanted to hold open the option to conduct nuclear tests became a topic of concern and corridor discussion in Geneva, though no one alluded to it publicly until much later.[17]

Finding a PNE compromise

While India appeared to lay the groundwork to reject the CTBT, China seemed to be moving closer to the treaty. This was illustrated by its determined negotiations on institutional and verification issues, but there was still the issue of PNE to resolve. During the first two years, most CD members and observers had assumed that PNE were in reality an expendable bargaining chip, guarded by China until they could be traded for a provision more vital to its interests. However, doubts began to creep in as Beijing continued to devote considerable resources and prestige to fighting for this provision against the almost unanimous opposition of the rest of the CD.

Despite acknowledging that the Soviet Union and the United States had abandoned their PNE programmes amidst concerns about environmental impact and few if any economic benefits,[18] a senior Chinese general told the NTB Committee that "these differences are not sufficient to negate the potential technological benefits of PNE or to provide a good ground to ban PNE as a technology".[19] China's case was put forward by Sha Zukang in public meetings as well as the CD: "As a populous developing country with insufficient per capita energy and mineral resources, China cannot abandon forever any promising and potentially useful technology that may be suited to its economic needs".[20]

India complicated things for China by a clever tactical manoeuvre. To counter the fear expressed by many negotiators that allowing any nuclear explosions would provide a back door to nuclear proliferation, China had proposed that PNE be conducted only by the nuclear-weapon states and under the strictest conditions of international monitoring and control. India, which had conducted a nuclear explosion in 1974 that it claimed was for peaceful purposes,[21] put forward an amendment that included "States Parties which had conducted a peaceful nuclear explosion" among those who could carry out PNE.[22] India's intention appears to have been twofold. Firstly, the amendment was another tool in the quest for recognition and status among the nuclear powers, consistent with its strategic objective of undercutting the exclusive definition of nuclear-weapon state contained in the NPT. Since India did not expect to win this recognition, its second purpose was to cause additional problems for China, which it perceived as a strategic and regional rival. Pakistan, whose primary concern was to prevent India from being able to benefit militarily in any way, had already taken a position against the inclusion of any PNE provision. Despite having close relations with China, Pakistan's position was that "the so-called peaceful nuclear explosions contribute towards nuclear proliferation".[23]

In February 1996, China's solitary campaign for PNE was unexpectedly given a boost. First, Russia began circulating some ideas for a PNE provision based on a suggestion that had arisen during the 1977–1980 tripartite talks. Then, in a draft treaty presented by Iran in February 1996, a provision was included for considering and permitting PNE in exceptional circumstances. Russia's ideas, which were never formally proposed, were for a treaty-endorsed moratorium on PNE until they could be conducted so as to preclude any military benefit. Iran's draft text gave the Conference of States Parties responsibility for considering, "in exceptional circumstances and in the case that the real benefit of nuclear [explosions] for the sole purpose of purely peaceful scientific research and civilian applications are demonstrated … a specific request for conducting a peaceful nuclear explosion". A PNE would only go ahead if four fifths of the Conference of States Parties agreed, and with verification "to ensure that it will be conducted for purely peaceful purposes".[24] Assessing that this condition would never be met, several states that had hitherto opposed PNE expressed interest in the proposal.

The Iranian and Russian approaches for regulating but not prohibiting PNE generated interest from states that feared that China's refusal to give up PNE could destroy the chance to secure the CTBT.[25] What then happened reveals a significant difference between those among the non-nuclear states that prioritized obtaining agreement at any price and those for whom agreement had to be on the basis of the right substance and content. The former were prepared to accept any workable compromise, and so looked favourably on the Iranian or Russian suggestions. The latter, though some initially welcomed the initiatives, were persuaded to oppose them once it was brought to their attention that the proposed solutions contained underlying threats to the broader disarmament objectives of the CTBT and non-proliferation regime.

The generally positive diplomatic response given to the Iranian proposal for including PNE for consideration by the Conference of States Parties shocked opponents into action. The right to unlimited laboratory research was implied in the requirement to provide information to support a PNE request. Moreover, under the treaty's founding principle of non-discrimination, Iran's formulation appeared not to be limited to the P-5, but could in principle allow all states parties the right to research and develop nuclear devices for PNE. If so, it would contradict the NPT restrictions; if not, it would enshrine and perpetuate nuclear research and development by the five nuclear-weapon states and any non-NPT member that became a state party to the CTBT. Either way, it was dangerous. Questioned about what they intended, Iranian diplomats gave ambiguous responses, reiterating that the CTBT should be non-discriminatory, but also in conformity with the NPT.[26] However, since the nuclear device used in a PNE is essentially indistinguishable from one which could be used as a bomb, it would be a very difficult task to prove that there would be no military benefit; hence both the Iranian and Russian suggestions could be construed as an invitation to nuclear physicists, laboratories and interested governments to set up design teams to develop ways to satisfy the requirement that no military benefit should be obtained. Concerned that the CD delegations were getting ready to accept a compromise along such lines, civil society acted fast to bring to the diplomats' attention that:

> what started out as a seemingly benign way of making concessions to China while ensuring that PNEs would never be conducted, may well turn out to be a life-saver for the nuclear weapon laboratories, reinforcing more strongly than ever the privileges of the nuclear-weapon States, and setting in place a barrier which would make further restrictions on nuclear weapon development and production more difficult in any future negotiations.[27]

After having shown initial enthusiasm for Iran's proposal, the delegations from a growing number of non-nuclear-weapon states, led by Australia, Canada, Germany, Japan and Mexico, were persuaded to oppose the Iranian and Russian approaches for dealing with PNE. Mexico's Deputy Foreign Minister, Sergio González Gálvez, for example, moved Mexico completely away from its initial interest in the Iranian position and reiterated the position that the CTBT should put an end to the qualitative improvement of nuclear weapons and that it should prevent the development of new nuclear weapons. Acknowledging China's argument that there may be some future reason why states would wish to reopen the question of PNE, González instead suggested that an amendment process could offer a solution to the impasse. Mexico made the suggestion to ensure that the treaty's scope should unequivocally prohibit PNE, but sought to reassure China that "the absence of any mention of peaceful nuclear explosions does not in our view mean that this option is ruled out".[28] As it turned out, an amendment provision was indeed incorporated as part of the solution, but not for some months, as China was not yet ready to give in.

Agreeing to the main provisions and understandings contained in the Australian scope proposal, now accepted by almost all the negotiating parties, Sha Zukang emphatically underlined China's continuing opposition to banning PNE. Echoing an earlier public speech, he evoked a series of arguments based on development principles and former treaties:

> Any disarmament or arms control treaty should not hinder the development and application of science and technology for peaceful purposes. This is an important matter of principle. Therefore, it would be incorrect if the CTBT should ban PNEs. … As a populous developing country with insufficient per capita energy and mineral resources, China cannot abandon forever any promising and potentially useful technology that may be suited to its economic needs.[29]

Stressing that China shared and understood the concern over the possible misuse of PNE, Sha Zukang argued that the issue could be "resolved by establishing a strict application and approval procedure and an effective international on-site monitoring mechanism for the whole process of PNEs".[30] This was precisely what the Iranian draft sought to do, but by the end of March, the majority of CD delegations had been convinced that this provision could—intentionally or not—legitimize nuclear weapon research under the guise of PNE. With India's 1974 example in mind, few now wanted to take that risk in the CTBT.

After failing to convince the majority to accept either the Iranian or Russian proposals, China next tried to obtain a PNE provision through concession-trading among the P-5. According to sources in the P-5, Sha proposed an additional Article II of the treaty in return for Chinese acceptance of the Australian language for Article I. China's proposed Article II would, "notwithstanding the provisions of Article I", offer the possibility of permitting PNE, providing that the Conference of States Parties agreed to this by consensus.[31] When news of this latest proposal was made public, it was again necessary for civil society observers and non-nuclear delegations to mobilize opposition. As a consequence, when Ramaker tabled his first Chair's draft treaty at the end of May 1996, it contained no provision for PNE.

Nevertheless, information leaking from the P-5 negotiations suggested that the other nuclear powers were still discussing a possible deal with China to include an additional article or paragraph in the review section of the treaty providing for periodic review of the prohibition on PNE. Sha Zukang himself brought this into the open on 6 June 1996, stating that "in order to facilitate the conclusion of the treaty within the time-frame as planned, the Chinese delegation is now ready to go along with a *temporary* ban on PNEs".[32] In an informal proposal put forward on 18 June, China advocated a new Article II for the treaty, in which PNE would be considered by the review conferences. If the parties agreed by consensus, then the conference of states parties would "immediately commence its work with a view to agreeing on arrangements for the possible approval and conduct of such explosions", intended to ensure that military benefits were precluded.[33]

Though this went further than most delegations wanted, there appeared to be a growing apprehension that the Chinese delegation had little room to manoeuvre. Whatever the original purpose underlying Beijing's insistence on PNE, a great deal of investment and prestige had now been staked on retaining some form of PNE option. Despite China now strongly signalling its intention to sign the completed treaty, PNE seemed to have been elevated from a bargaining chip to a potential treaty-breaker.[34] A face-saving formula needed to be found that would not compromise the test-ban regime.

Despite being one of the states that had consistently declared an "allergy" to PNE,[35] Canada offered to work with China on the text and managed to produce a modified version of China's proposal that the rest of the states opposed to PNE could accept.[36] Significantly, while maintaining a reference to PNE, which had become necessary to China, Canada won Chinese agreement to relocate the provision to Article VIII, which provided for reviews of the treaty. PNE would not be automatically considered at review conferences, as China had proposed, but could be considered if a state party put in a special request. If the review conference agreed to the request by consensus, the next step would be recommending an amendment to the treaty to enable a PNE to be carried out. The recommendation would then have to be dealt with under the amendment procedures laid out in Article VII, requiring consensus among all states parties at a specially convened Amendment Conference. After a brief discussion in the NTB Committee, Ramaker incorporated the Canadian–Chinese compromise text directly into Article VIII of his second draft text, which was tabled on 28 June 1996, as follows:

> On the basis of a request by any State Party, the Review Conference shall consider the possibility of permitting the conduct of underground nuclear explosions for peaceful purposes. If the Review Conference decides by consensus that such nuclear explosions may be permitted, it shall commence work without delay, with a view to recommending to States Parties an appropriate amendment to this Treaty that shall preclude any military benefits of such nuclear explosions … .[37]

This is the only provision for PNE in the CTBT. The majority of states were able to accept it because, in accordance with the Article I basic obligations, PNE are unequivocally prohibited. They can only be conducted if the treaty is amended at some time in the future. In fact, the Article VIII provision is more stringent than the normal amendment process, as it requires two stages of consensus: at a Review Conference and again in an Amendment Conference. The likelihood of amending the treaty to permit PNE is now so remote that the possibility should not be regarded as a justification for any research programmes by nuclear weapon laboratories. The Canadian–Chinese compromise met that desirable criterion in bargaining—sufficient ambiguity to allow China to interpret that a door had been left open on PNE, while the other states parties are reassured that the ban on PNE would not be lightly set aside or the amendment provision evoked to justify research into nuclear explosions.

Competing draft treaties from Iran and Australia

As negotiations near the endgame, it can sometimes be useful for a delegation other than that of the Chair to table a draft text that tries out certain options to see if they will fly. The CD had been expecting such a draft from Australia, which had made a positive contribution with a draft text during the final year of the negotiations on the Chemical Weapons Convention.[38] Iran, however, stole Australia's thunder by delivering its own draft text on 22 February 1996, a week before Australia's presentation. Iran had kept secret its intention until its draft was presented by Foreign Minister Ali Akbar Velayati, who emphasized that the purpose was to help the CD "to perceive a middle ground—a package ... which may constitute a compromise amongst the various and, at times, contradictory positions".[39] A week later, Michael Costello, Secretary of Australia's Department of Foreign Affairs and Trade, offered his delegation's model treaty to "demonstrate, tangibly, that a CTBT ... is indeed within reach".[40]

Both drafts built on the rolling text and synthesized the areas already substantially agreed. There were also noted similarities in their conceptual approach to resolving some of the most difficult issues such as entry into force, on-site inspections and the composition of the Executive Council. This "near coincidence" was noted by Sirous Nasseri, who used the tabling of Australia's draft as an occasion to remind the CD that Iran's initiative had come first and had been just as comprehensive.[41] The fundamental difference between the two drafts was on scope. Australia reproduced the scope text from its own March 1995 working paper, with the understanding of zero yield adopted by France, the United States and the United Kingdom in August–September 1995.[42] Iran's draft reintroduced language that would prohibit all nuclear weapon tests (not only explosions), despite Indonesia's withdrawal earlier that month of its June 1995 proposal to that effect.[43] As noted above, Iran offered China a substantial concession on PNE, whereas the Australian model unequivocally banned all nuclear explosions, making no distinction between military and non-military purposes.

Iran's draft preamble retained a commitment to nuclear disarmament in a time-bound framework, while Australia's preamble favoured NPT-related language referring to a "systematic process" leading to nuclear disarmament. For entry into force, both attempted to balance early implementation of the treaty with its political credibility. Each proposed that entry into force should be based on accession by a list of specified countries that included, among others, the P-5, India, Israel and Pakistan, but with a mechanism to prevent any particular state on the list being able to block the treaty or hold it hostage. Australia proposed ratification by all CD members plus observers, with a waiver conference after two years. Iran proposed ratification by at least 65 of the 68 states on the IAEA list of states with nuclear technologies.

With regard to verification and on-site inspections, both proposed a two-phase process with quick access for the first, less intrusive phase, and a more rigorous decision-making procedure for any subsequent, more complete inspection. Australia's draft would permit any kind of information to be used to back an inspection request, but also considered ways of making data generated by NTM more accessible to the international community to meet non-aligned states' concerns about bias. Iran would base an inspection request solely on data from the IMS, but left a small opening for NTM to be used to provide supplementary information.

Many diplomats were agreeably surprised that both texts were conceptually so similar. While some worried that the texts could complicate the solutions that the Chairs and their Friends were trying to hammer out and might narrow the Chair's room to manoeuvre, rather than assist him, China, India and Pakistan made the strongest objections, insisting that the drafts must not be allowed to pre-empt the rolling text.[44] Australia was clearly disappointed with the lukewarm reception its draft text received and the fact that it was not sufficiently distinguished from Iran's initiative.[45] Both drafts were generally commended, however, and their tabling was regarded as a useful, perhaps even necessary, mechanism to pave the way for a Chair's text. Having let these drafts test the waters, Ramaker decided not to introduce a clean Chair's draft text before the end of the first part of the 1996 session.

Chair's first draft text

Choosing what he characterized as a two-stage process, on 28 March Ramaker prepared the ground for his draft treaty text by tabling a working paper with an "Outline of a draft Comprehensive Nuclear Test Ban Treaty".[46] This working paper was structured as a treaty and outlined the key elements, with a preamble and 17 articles, but still contained a large number of brackets. Where states' individual proposals were hard fought, such as on scope, Ramaker presented the heavily bracketed rolling text, together with an indication of a clean formulation that had attracted wide support, in this case, the Australian text on scope. In other cases, for example the composition of the Executive Council, the outline offered text developed by a Friend of the Chair after consultations with the delegations. Four bracketed articles were put at the end, covering China's proposals on the peaceful use of nuclear energy, PNE, security assurances and the relation of the treaty to other international agreements. By this time, there were no supporters for China's proposal on PNE. Some of its other proposed articles, such as on security assurances, may have been supported in principle by many non-aligned states, but they were not going to push for them in the context of the CTBT. By attaching them at the end of his outline in this way, Ramaker provided a strong indicator of the general view that these proposals should not remain in the treaty, while at the same time meeting China's insistence that its decision on these issues should not be pre-empted by others.

In his statement to the 28 March meeting of the NTB Committee before it recessed for April, Ramaker highlighted six outstanding issues: the preamble, scope, the composition of the Executive Council, some of the functions of the international data centre (particularly the level of information and analysis it should provide to states parties), on-site inspections and entry into force. He gave the Committee the six weeks of the intersessional break to consider the structure and various options.[47] Two weeks after the CD resumed in mid-May, and after discussions with most of the delegations, Ramaker tabled a clean draft treaty on 28 May 1996.[48]

A Chair's draft treaty text invariably heralds the endgame when negotiators are faced with tough choices, including whether to compromise or defect. It came as no surprise, therefore, to hear vociferous complaints from delegations that were reluctant, unready or out-manoeuvred. On 23 May, the day after Ramaker announced when he would be tabling his draft, Pakistan's ambassador Munir Akram warned that "A treaty which descends from heaven or elsewhere may arrest rather than accelerate our negotiations and the fulfilment of our deadline".[49] As China, India and Russia joined Pakistan's protests, Ramaker sought to reassure these delegations by stressing that his draft was for the purpose of facilitating "the last and final stage of negotiations".[50] Despite the reluctance of some, there was a shared recognition that if the CD was to make its unofficial target date of finalizing the treaty text by the end of June, then Ramaker could not delay any longer in putting down a clean draft text. As delegations soon saw, the Chair's text held few surprises, and so was neither rejected nor called premature when it was presented.

Two particular issues took centre stage as a result of the Chair's text: entry into force and on-site inspections. During the next month, meetings of the NTB Committee went late into the night, but without achieving much. Ambassador Mounir Zahran of Egypt, coordinating negotiations on the preamble, managed to obtain agreement for India's proposal that the Review Conference should also ensure that the objectives and purposes of the preamble were being realized. That was the only language proposed by India in January that was accepted into the treaty. India's proposals regarding a timetable for nuclear disarmament, widely viewed as a tactic to prepare the ground for refusing to sign, were not addressed. In the last week of June, 13 G-21 delegations tried to strengthen the treaty's disarmament language with a four-paragraph proposal on preambular objectives and aspirations but they needed India to come on board to have any hope of getting the P-5 to take it seriously.[51] India, for its part, appeared unwilling to work with its G-21 colleagues on this, which reinforced perceptions that New Delhi was less interested in getting a more disarmament-oriented treaty than in catering to a sector of domestic opinion that wanted India to keep all its nuclear options open.

The 28 May draft treaty caused a significant shift in the negotiations. Although no formal decision was ever taken to replace the rolling text, the Chair's text became the focus of work from then on. Despite Ramaker's assurance to the NTB Committee that the draft had not been tabled with a "take it or leave it attitude",[52] multilateral negotiations among all CD members ceased to play a relevant role after the end of May. Instead, Ramaker continued consultations with states that still expressed outstanding concerns. He also convened the representatives of 16 key states to discuss the most difficult issues. In addition to the P-5, India, Israel and Pakistan, the group included Australia, Canada, Egypt, Germany, Indonesia, Japan, Mexico and Morocco, most of whom had acted as Moderators or Friends of the Chair on the major issues.

As addressed more fully in chapter 7, on-site inspections and the related question of whether to accept NTM had been categorized as "treaty-breakers" by China and the United States. These two issues therefore became the main focus of the P-5's meetings. For others, the entry-into-force problems had begun to cause anxiety, especially in light of the strident, largely pro-nuclear media debate in India. China, Russia and the United Kingdom were pressing as "non-negotiable" their demand that entry into force needed to bind all of the P-5 and D-3 declared and undeclared nuclear-weapon states from the beginning. The United States was preoccupied with ensuring that inspections would not be subjected to overly rigorous pre-conditions, and despite the size of its delegation, appeared unable to deal with other pressing issues. Although Washington would have preferred a more flexible provision on entry into force, and France had come round to this position, both failed to pay sufficient attention to the hostage-taking dangers of an overly stringent entry-into-force article until it was too late. Though Ramaker had intended his draft text to replace the rolling text as the basis for the final phase of negotiations, delegations had not expected to be locked into the draft's language so completely or so quickly. This miscalculation was most acutely problematic with respect to entry into force, as the next chapter will discuss.

CHAPTER 6

ENTRY INTO FORCE AND THE ENDGAME

> [India] *would not accept any language in the treaty text which would affect our sovereign right to decide, in the light of our supreme national interest, whether we should or should not accede to such a treaty.*
>
> Ambassador Arundhati Ghose, 20 June 1996[1]

In the next two chapters we come to the endgame, which was dominated by India's dilemma over whether to join the CTBT or stay outside, as it had done with the NPT. As India's domestic debate over its nuclear policies and options reached fever pitch in 1996, it penetrated into the test-ban negotiations, with serious consequences that persist to this day. Though the Indian delegation had participated fully in all aspects of the negotiations from the beginning, the challenges came to a head over the entry-into-force issue, as India became cornered by delegations with regional or strategic concerns seeking to ensure that all states with nuclear weapon capabilities would have to accede to the CTBT.

A treaty's provision on entry into force (EIF) needs to strike a credible balance between political reassurance and operational viability. Assessing the CTBT 12 years after it was opened for signature, it is hard to escape the judgment that the negotiators handicapped the treaty with a provision that denied it operational viability (for a long time) and gave political reassurance only to its opponents. The endgame dynamic of fierce but solution-oriented concession trading on all the other outstanding issues among key states such as China, France, Russia and the United States suggests that the major states were genuine in their endeavours at this stage to conclude an effective, practical and implementable treaty. So how did the CD slide so inexorably into a trap over entry into force? Many diplomats and observers have blamed India's domestic politics and some of the key personalities. But that is too simple: India had given several months' warning that it would not join the treaty unless it included a time-bound framework for nuclear disarmament, knowing that the P-5 would never accept such language in the treaty. Ambassador Ghose underlined the implications when she commented in July 1996 that if any countries insisted on including India in a list of states required to ratify the treaty in the article on entry into force, "then those countries did not want the Treaty to enter into force".[2] So why did some governments persist in making the CTBT's entry into force dependent on a state that had already declared its intention to defect?

Virtually ignored for most of the negotiations, entry into force turned into a battleground for the competing objectives of some of the P-5, India and Pakistan. For most if not all of the P-5, the chief purpose of the CTBT was to curb the development and spread of nuclear weapons outside the NPT-recognized nuclear-weapon states. India, for its part, was caught between nuclear ambitions and the remnants of its non-aligned, pro-disarmament ideology from the immediate post-colonial time of Gandhi and Nehru.[3] While India's national debate on its nuclear options was undoubtedly an important factor, this chapter is concerned with identifying what went wrong in the CTBT's negotiating dynamics. How was it that the most reluctant participant in the negotiations was at the end handed a de facto power of veto over the treaty's legal status and implementation? And what prompted one senior European diplomat to label Article XIV "Britain's Revenge"?[4]

The entry-into-force requirements for a treaty determine the conditions that must be met in order for the agreement to take full legal effect. Negotiators aim to set appropriate conditions to give national and international confidence that the agreement will enhance rather than detract from the participants' security. Entry into force is therefore a mechanism related to reciprocity and implementation. Because it confers authority on the full operation of the verification regime and implementing organization, compliance and enforcement are closely bound up with it as well. Where signing and ratifying an agreement formally express the national political will to comply, EIF gives confidence that a critical mass of others will do likewise. Viewing security as a public good, the greater the number of participants in the regime the greater the benefits for all.

The CD negotiators and civil society made the mistake of paying scant attention to EIF until very late in the negotiations, probably because they were seduced by the past. In many treaty negotiations, most recently on the Chemical Weapons Convention (CWC), the EIF provision had fallen into place during the final stage.[5] By mid-1996, when it was clear that this would not happen for the CTBT, it proved impossible to influence key states' positions quickly enough to prevent an endgame stand-off.

EIF provisions usually specify that before the treaty takes legal effect it must be ratified by a certain number of states. In addition, the relevant article will often set a specific time frame between the treaty being opened for signature and the earliest date it can enter into force, or it may specify a period between the final "triggering" ratification and EIF. As a state's decisions about whether and when to accede to a treaty may have implications for security, EIF conditions are frequently subject to close political scrutiny during national ratification debates. It is therefore important that the requirements give a treaty credibility, without being prohibitively stringent.

The simpler the arrangements for EIF, the easier it is for the treaty to take effect quickly. An example of this was the PTBT, which took just three months between signature and entry into force. The EIF provision in the PTBT only required the ratification of the three negotiating parties: the Soviet Union, the United Kingdom and the United States. At the time, these three had reason to worry about China, France and several other states pursuing nuclear technology. They opened the PTBT for all states to join, but chose not to make its entry into force contingent on the accession of any other specific additional states.[6] Indeed, China and France have never acceded to the PTBT, and yet France ceased atmospheric testing after Australia and New Zealand evoked the PTBT when they sought redress for nuclear contamination of the Pacific in the International Court of Justice in 1973. The argument was made that the PTBT had been so widely accepted and adhered to that it had established a norm, effectively becoming part of customary law applicable to all, regardless of whether a particular country had itself signed.

The NPT and the CWC are examples of successful multilateral arms control treaties from two different eras that set the bar low enough to be able to enter into force without undue delay, and which fulfilled their negotiators' hope that after EIF the number of acceding states would continue to build and strengthen the regimes that developed out of these treaties. Low-bar EIF approaches rely on political pressure to bring hold-outs into the regime as the principles and norms of the treaty become embedded in international law and expectations. The NPT required ratification by the three depositary nuclear-weapon states plus 40 others, unspecified.[7] Concluded in 1968, the NPT entered into force on 5 March 1970, and at the end of 2008 189 states had signed and ratified. The CWC, which opened for signature in January 1993, specified only that it would enter into force 180 days after the deposit of the sixty-fifth instrument of ratification.[8] Though no specific states were listed, it was recognized that EIF without certain parties would make enforcement difficult, so the treaty provided substantial incentives for states to be part of the group of 65 "original" signatories. Arguing that the United States would be excluded from important posts and decision-making if the Convention entered into force without it, the Clinton administration was able to overcome opposition in the Senate and secure ratification on 29 April 1997. This illustrates that flexible EIF provisions may actually provide more incentives and political pressure to accelerate ratifications than overly rigid specifications.

Although it has failed to bring in India, Israel and Pakistan, the NPT has over the years built a non-proliferation regime strong enough to convince many others that their security would be better served remaining as non-nuclear-weapon states parties than by pursuing their own nuclear weapon ambitions. Hence, the regime has strengthened as it has grown.[9] If instead of the rather flexible EIF provision in Article IX, the NPT had specified a list of all states with nuclear capabilities as of 1968, it is unlikely the NPT would ever have taken effect. China and France, for example, though defined as nuclear-weapon states in the NPT, refused to join until 1992. Trying to build a non-proliferation regime on an NPT that had uncertain authority and legal standing and had not yet come into force would never have worked as well as legally enforcing the treaty early and then building up membership through a mix of pressure and incentive. If the flexible EIF provisions in the NPT and the CWC were deemed sufficient, why and how did the CD come to impose on the CTBT a provision so tight and rigid that it has consigned the treaty to legal limbo for more than a decade?

NUMBERS, LISTS AND WAIVERS

The basic positions on EIF were drawn early on in the CTBT negotiations. The 1993 Swedish draft treaty took a qualified numerical approach similar to the NPT, proposing ratification by 40 states, including the five declared nuclear-weapon states.[10] This pragmatic baseline found many supporters. Australia led those who advocated a simple number, as in the CWC, taking the view that this would be in keeping with the multilateral and non-discriminatory intentions of the negotiations, and would prevent the treaty from being held hostage to the politics of any individual state. Australia and Indonesia suggested 60, while Japan favoured early EIF on the basis of 30 ratifications, reasoning that international and regional pressure could be exerted to encourage the rest to join.

Consistent with the Swedish draft, the United States held that a minimum condition must be ratification by the P-5. By contrast, the opening positions put forward by France, Russia, the United Kingdom and, later, China, were designed to ensure that ratification by the D-3 would be as fundamental a condition as ratification by the P-5. Acknowledging that most other states favoured the CWC model, Weston epitomized the reasoning of this group of nuclear powers when he argued that "adopting this formula would provide no guarantee of adherence by all—or indeed any—of the countries whose commitment to the treaty we would regard as necessary if it is to play the non-proliferation role we want from it". [11] This view flew in the face of past experience, especially with the NPT.

With the intention of not offending anyone, while deferring to widespread political sensitivities about not according states outside the NPT any special status that might be interpreted as recognition of nuclear-weapon status, Russia proposed a definition based on IAEA assessments, namely ratification by 65 states, including all that possessed nuclear reactors or nuclear research programmes on the date of the treaty being opened for signature.[12] With the same intention but a different solution, the United Kingdom proposed that "at a minimum, all members of the CD should ratify the treaty before it enters into force". By way of explanation, Weston argued, "Given that we proceed in this forum by consensus, it is surely not unreasonable to expect that a treaty whose terms we have all been prepared to agree should be ratified by all without undue delay".[13] Sharing the United Kingdom's expectations of the imminent expansion of the CD to 60 members, giving membership for the first time to states of nuclear concern such as Iraq, Israel and North Korea (India and Pakistan were already members), France adopted the same position. Austria, too, favoured basing EIF on CD membership, noting that the 1969 Vienna Convention on the Law of Treaties relates "consent to be bound by the treaty" to participation in negotiations.[14] Later that year, as the CD became deadlocked over its enlargement, the French and UK delegations shifted toward the Russian position.[15]

The first 30 months of negotiations on EIF did little more than identify the basic options. In Working Group 2, an early working paper from the Friend of the Chair, Alessandro Vattani of Italy, summarized the options:

> Should the treaty enter into force ... after the deposit of instruments of ratification by: (a) five nuclear weapon states; (b) five nuclear weapon states and all nuclear capable states; (c) all members of the Conference on Disarmament; (d) all members of the Conference on Disarmament after expansion; (e) all states (or 95% of those) possessing nuclear reactors or nuclear research programmes; (f) a fixed number of states (e.g. 40 or 65, including five nuclear weapon states or including members of the CD); (g) along the lines of the provisions of the Treaty of Tlatelolco; (h) a significant number of key states; (i) other?[16]

In March 1995, Stephan Keller, who had taken over as EIF Friend of the Chair, circulated a "non-paper" that identified three core options: a number (either simple or qualified); a defined list based on the IAEA or expanded CD membership; and some kind of waiver formula. Annexed to this paper were several lists, including one of 68 states assessed by the IAEA to have (or have had) nuclear capabilities and two that identified members, applicants and/or observers of the CD. Although the nature and limitations of the options had been exhaustively explored, the negotiators remained far from any convergence of views. Those who wanted to ensure early entry into force still preferred to replicate the CWC approach, based on a simple number. The United States favoured this too, but held to its condition of ratification by all the nuclear-weapon states, noting that the P-5 all endorsed this requirement as a minimum.

While concerned that making EIF conditional upon ratification by a specific list could render a treaty more difficult to achieve, the United States also recognized that its P-5 colleagues were very determined to achieve stringent conditions. Therefore the US delegation suggested two different approaches for consideration. In the first, EIF would occur if a high percentage (95%) of listed states had ratified. In the second, providing that the P-5 were among the ratifiers, the United States suggested that a "waiver conference" could be held if the treaty had not entered into force within two years after the treaty was opened for signature. According to this scenario, the conference participants, or at least all participants that had ratified the treaty, could then decide whether to waive the specific requirements and, in effect, behave as if the treaty had entered into force. Such an approach would enable them to establish the verification regime and implementing organization. US delegation members also argued that the conference could be a useful mechanism to apply pressure on non-ratifying states, threatening them with loss of influence and appointments in the establishment of the implementing organization.[17]

For most of 1995, France, Russia and the United Kingdom expressed scepticism about the waiver options and adhered to their advocacy of a list based on the IAEA's assessment of all states with relevant nuclear capabilities. Sharing their strict approach, China proposed that the treaty could enter into force one year after "ratification by all States that were members of the Conference on Disarmament at the time when the Treaty was opened for signature and by all States known by the IAEA to possess nuclear capabilities (i.e. to possess nuclear power stations or nuclear reactors)".[18]

Many delegations found the idea of a waiver conference interesting in principle but few supported the US stipulation that all the P-5 must ratify before such a mechanism could be invoked. Mexico called it "multi-hostage taking"[19] and argued that by making P-5 ratification a condition before even the waiver conference could be invoked, the United States was discriminating in favour of the existing nuclear powers, giving them a de facto power of veto. Others, including Japan and Brazil, agreed. Reversing this logic, China considered the US proposal "a kind of political discrimination against the five nuclear weapon states".[20] Some negotiators saw China's opposition as indication that it intended to continue its nuclear test programme until the CTBT had fully entered into force, however long that would take. Such concerns had been accentuated by Sha Zukang's assertion that "once a CTBT has entered into force, [China] will cease nuclear testing".[21] India stated that naming the P-5 as a special category was "discriminatory" and argued that a "reasonable and representative group of countries should be required to ratify".[22]

Australia, which said that it preferred the concept of a simple list combined with political pressure to ensure that key states would accede, also suggested a possible alternative based on the waiver provision in the 1967 Treaty of Tlatelolco, which established a nuclear-weapon-free zone in Latin America and the Caribbean. Mexico had also previously advocated that the CTBT should consider this innovative waiver provision, which was credited with preventing the Tlatelolco Treaty from being held hostage by the domestic or national considerations of any state or group of states, while enabling governments to take account of regional rivalries and political shifts and choose a time to accede deemed appropriate to their own security assessments.[23] Australia's proposal was to list the specific states deemed essential, but with each ratifying state having the right to waive the requirements and allow the treaty's provisions to become legally binding for them. While recognizing that the waiver provision had been successful in the Tlatelolco context, a number of delegations objected that such an arrangement would be impractical for the CTBT. They noted that the Tlatelolco formula had not been tried in other agreements and pointed out that although the implementing organization was established by acceding states, verification was by bilateral arrangements with the IAEA. Accordingly, most seemed to think that the Tlatelolco Treaty's mechanism would not work for the CTBT, where the core of the verification regime was to be a multilateral monitoring system, supported by on-site inspections. Australia envisaged that unless some mechanism were developed for a sufficient number of states to inaugurate the multilateral verification system, implementation pending full EIF would be based on national monitoring. The objections to such an approach, which was deemed by some non-aligned states to undermine the rationale for a multilateral CTBT, proved to be too strong for the proposal to survive very long in 1996.[24]

Australia tried again, reviving the US idea of a waiver conference in the "model treaty" it tabled in February 1996.[25] Curiously, Iran, which had tabled a draft treaty text a week earlier, modified another US suggestion for its EIF provision.[26] Although the particular solutions they proposed were different, the Australian and Iranian drafts surprised many with their similarity of approach on EIF, with both combining a list with a veto-avoiding mechanism. Nevertheless, there was criticism of the Australians for basing EIF on the concept of an expanded CD, since that proposal had been dropped from the rolling text, while others complained that Iran's proposal could result in implementation of the treaty without three of the eight most crucial nuclear-weapon possessing states. Although both initiatives were welcomed, they did not advance the EIF debate significantly.

By the time the Australian and Iranian drafts were attempting to identify workable compromises, the political struggle between the P-5 and D-3 that underpinned the EIF negotiations had fully surfaced. As noted in the previous chapter, India introduced a qualitatively different variable in January 1996, relating EIF to nuclear disarmament: "this Treaty shall enter into force only after all states parties have committed themselves to the attainment of the goal of total elimination of all nuclear weapons within a well defined time framework (of ten years)".[27] India's reasoning was that if nuclear testing were halted under the CTBT, nuclear weapons development would be frozen at different levels; this would perpetuate a discriminatory situation that advantaged the P-5 unless the treaty also contained an agreed timetable for complete nuclear disarmament. India maintained that it supported non-discriminatory nuclear disarmament but could not accept further discriminatory non-proliferation measures.

On 4 March 1996, during consultations held under the auspices of Ambassador Mounir Zahran of Egypt, Chair of Working Group 2, the UK delegation decided to sharpen the debate. Cutting through the euphemisms and exposing the real purpose of the various lists by floating a "non-proposal" aimed solely at the P-5 and D-3, the United Kingdom proposed specifying states on the IAEA list "not under a legally binding treaty obligation not to manufacture or acquire nuclear weapons".[28] Such a formula covered all states with unsafeguarded nuclear facilities and excluded the non-nuclear-weapon parties to the NPT or parties to regional nuclear-weapon-free zone treaties (Brazil, for example, had not at the time acceded to the NPT, but was party to the Tlatelolco Treaty). Although the British delegation never formally tabled the proposal, which was disliked by many, it was inserted into the rolling text by Pakistan. Pakistan's eager adoption of the formula had not been anticipated, but it caused little surprise, and was generally viewed as just another tactic in that country's geostrategic and diplomatic rivalry with India.

Of course it had long been clear to everyone that the purpose of the CTBT was to prevent nuclear testing by the P-5 and the D-3, since other states, including Iraq and North Korea, were already bound through their NPT obligations. But the United Kingdom's suggestion, which forced into the open the subtext underlying the lists, did not merely evoke criticism—it caused considerable dismay on all sides. Some non-nuclear states argued that it placed an undesirable power of veto in the hands of the targeted states. Others feared that linking the D-3 so directly with the P-5 would confer special status on India, Israel and Pakistan. For Japan and South Africa, the issue was legitimation of the D-3: they feared that putting what amounted to a new definition into the CTBT would set a precedent and undermine the NPT's demarcation between nuclear- and non-nuclear-weapon states. More particularly, Egypt and some of the other Arab states were determined to allow nothing that could be construed as legitimation of Israel's nuclear status as they continued to push for it to join the NPT as a non-nuclear-weapon state. Israel, for its part, argued that it needed to be convinced that a CTBT was in its security interests and would not be "captured" by targeted definitions or mechanisms.[29] Despite insisting on a provision that would bind the D-3, some of the P-5 also disliked the UK suggestion because it associated the D-3 too directly with the nuclear-weapon states defined in the NPT. Their objections were not solely based on the fear of weakening the NPT, but because the linkage could erode the special status they themselves enjoyed in the nuclear club.

For those less worried about the risk of setting a precedent that might undermine the NPT, the British suggestion was thought capable of avoiding India's objections to the wider list, as it provided the attractive payoff for India of appearing to recognize the nuclear-weapon status of the D-3, something that India has long sought. A few even harboured the hope that it offered a way for Pakistan to sign and ratify the CTBT, secure in the knowledge that it would not take legal effect without India's accession as well. But India, it soon transpired, was not interested in this kind of offer. On the contrary, India and Israel objected that the formula singled them out. China joined India in claiming that it violated the principle of non-discrimination. Israel, which was prepared to accept its inclusion in a list of over 40 nuclear-capable states, feared that a narrower P-5 plus D-3 provision would have the effect of taking away its politically convenient doctrine of nuclear opacity, and might expose it to even more pressure from NPT states parties in the Middle East.

By early 1996, the CD had begun to realize that the political requirements of the P-5 and the D-3, as well as the interests of Israel's neighbours in the Middle East, could make compromise on EIF very difficult to achieve. In this context, Austria drew attention to a proposal on provisional application that it had originally tabled in June 1995, but which had received scant attention at the time. After updating it in February 1996, Austria found more states willing to listen to its argument for a conference to be convened by all states that had ratified, if the treaty had not entered into force two years after the date of deposit of the first instrument of ratification. These states could then decide (by a process to be determined) to let the treaty, or parts of it, be applied provisionally.[30] Under provisional application, the states agreeing to be covered by the treaty would decide amongst themselves about verification and financing. In the event that fewer than the specified states have acceded in a reasonable length of time, provisional application would thus enable the international verification system and implementing organization to be inaugurated, with special financial arrangements able to be determined by the states concerned.

Austria's proposal for a mechanism to allow provisional application represented a different approach from previous waiver options because it was based on collective decision-making among states that had ratified, rather than individual waivers. It might potentially bypass the verification question, since the participating states could institute some if not all components of the multilateral verification system and would not necessarily have to rely solely on NTM. The strongest objection came from the United States, which regarded it as an inadequate and even dangerous solution, on the grounds that provisional application lacked full legal force and so would not be able legally or satisfactorily to address a suspected violation or initiate an on-site inspection without the cooperation of the suspect, which was unlikely to be given. Sharing some of the US concerns, others raised questions about the legal standing of decisions and the status and obligations for those states that, having ratified, were in the minority that voted against provisional application: would they be permitted to hold aloof from the provisional organization or would they be bound by the majority decision?[31]

After an inconclusive meeting on EIF on 23 May, which demonstrated the lack of a front-running option, and under severe pressure from Russia and the United Kingdom, Ramaker added to his first draft treaty text (issued on 28 May) a suggestion linking EIF with the monitoring system. Accounts differ about whether Canada or the United Kingdom had the original thought of making EIF contingent on the list of 37 states that hosted either a primary seismic station or a radionuclide laboratory as part of the IMS. No one had put this into a formal proposal, so there was no language to this effect in the rolling text. The United Kingdom, which was the most vocal of the P-5 proponents of a stringent EIF provision, related this approach to its earlier argument for preferring the expanded CD list to the IAEA list: as the agreement to host a component of the verification system could be construed as a form of commitment, listing the same states for EIF requirements appeared to be a logical extension. When first floated, the list received little enthusiasm. Mexico, for example, said it would give the power of veto to small states that had not even participated in the negotiations. Moreover, scientists involved in the negotiations who had devoted considerable time and energy to ensuring that the IMS was representative and would provide effective global coverage warned against making it hostage to the EIF politics.

In assessing what went wrong in the EIF negotiations, one has to ask why Ramaker inserted this controversial list into his first Chair's draft without wider consultation. Clearly he was up against the clock and under heavy pressure, especially from Russia and the United Kingdom, knowing also that several other states, notably China, Egypt and Pakistan, wanted to bind the D-3 into the EIF provision as tightly as possible. On the other hand, waiver options put forward by the United States and canvassed in both the Australian and Iranian drafts had received wide support, and the majority of CD members were expecting the final outcome to be along the lines of a list plus waiver combination. According to senior Dutch officials, the Chair was heavily influenced by the insistence from China and Russia that they would not accept any Chair's text as the basis for further negotiations unless it contained a stringent EIF provision based on ratification by the three nuclear-capable states outside the NPT as well as all the P-5. Ramaker appeared especially worried that if his first Chair's draft treaty text was rejected out of hand by any of the P-5, the negotiations would go "back to square one". It later transpired that he had deliberately chosen the British formula for his first draft because it had never been part of the rolling text or any formal proposal, and so he thought it would not suffer from "ownership" or "turf" difficulties. He meant it to be a placeholder and hoped that it would galvanize the negotiators into renewed determination to find a workable compromise.[32]

Instead, the formula became a flashpoint. Once in the draft treaty, it was condemned by many CD members, who worried about the effect of such linkage on the verification system, which was close to being agreed. Advocates of a more flexible EIF provision were also concerned that it placed inappropriate leverage and potential delaying power in the hands of certain states, a problem common to all the lists under consideration. Others reiterated the scientists' concerns that the formula would make the practical, technical decisions about where to locate IMS stations vulnerable to legal–political disputes about EIF. Soon after, two more countries added stations to the IMS, further exposing the contradictions inherent in making the monitoring system the basis for an EIF list. India denounced as "coercive" the tactics of some nuclear-weapon states over entry into force and threatened to withdraw all its seismic stations from the IMS. On 26 June, India did just that, sending a letter to the CD President to insist that all mention of monitoring facilities in India should be deleted from the treaty draft.[33] Thus, a formula based on the argument that participating in the verification system was tantamount to commitment to the treaty had the malign consequence of pushing India out of the kind of cooperative association with the treaty that could, over time, have been a lever for building confidence and bringing that country on board. The strategy had backfired badly. And foremost among those who deeply regretted the adoption into the Chair's first draft of this formula for entry into force were British scientists who had worked at the forefront of efforts to design an effective IMS architecture. Given the hard work put in by one part of the UK delegation to persuade states to accept and participate in the IMS, it was sadly ironic that this UK-promoted EIF provision resulted in India withdrawing its stations altogether.

Though behind the scenes Ramaker stressed that he was not committed to this provision, and that the purpose of his draft was to "test the waters",[34] his statement to the CD emphasized that "a number of delegations expressed an interest in this formula, and indeed it seems to indicate the way forward".[35] However, he also acknowledged that there was no "magic formula" and that the provision linking entry into force with states responsible for IMS facilities had met with criticism as well.[36] Whether at the time he really considered this could provide the solution or, as he later claimed, he put the British formula in as a placeholder in the hope of forcing delegations to negotiate something more practical, the Chair became trapped when Berdennikov declared that Russia was satisfied with the stringent EIF provision in Article XIV and regarded it as final. China and Pakistan speedily and directly endorsed this draft Article XIV, further reducing the Chair's room to manoeuvre.

In withdrawing its stations from the IMS, India severed its cooperative links with the CTBT, nullifying any lingering hope that its participation in the negotiations would bind it to the outcome. India's general election in May 1996 had brought the Bharatiya Janata Party (BJP) into power as the largest party in a new coalition that ousted the Congress Party. On 16 May 1996, Atal Bihari Vajpayee became Prime Minister and, according to later reports, immediately authorized the nuclear tests halted earlier by Prime Minister Rao.[37] Before any nuclear devices could be detonated, however, Vajpayee lost a vote of confidence and had to concede power to a different "United Front" coalition after only 12 days. The Indian nuclear establishment's demand for tests continued, but were neither acted on nor rejected.

Instead, the cautious new Prime Minister, H.D. Deve Gowda, "sought to delay a decision while the government attended to more pressing domestic matters".[38]

At the CD, India increased its demand that the CTBT must not enter into force without a timetable for nuclear disarmament accepted by all states parties. Whether intended as a defection tactic or not, this linked demand made it easier for the P-5 to ignore the rest of India's arguments. India was becoming increasingly isolated, and its proposals linking EIF with nuclear disarmament were not being addressed in large part because they were not considered genuine. Even the G-21 became sceptical of India's motives when the Indian delegation refused to engage with G-21 initiatives to insert disarmament language into the treaty's preamble.

Belated recognition was dawning in Geneva that the EIF negotiations carried serious risks for the treaty. But was it a real treaty-breaker, meaning that, without a binding "P-5 plus D-3" condition, China, Russia and the United Kingdom would defect from the agreement and refuse to sign? Or were the three delegations just playing a tough tactical game, expecting their price to be negotiated down to something more reasonable? China's concerns were international and regional: it wanted to play as an equal among the P-5, but did not want India to be accorded the same status or allowed to become a serious military or nuclear competitor in the future. The United States took China's position on EIF seriously.[39] Sha Zukang has confirmed that binding the D-3 was a very important objective for China, but he never referred to this as a "make or break" or "treaty-breaking" issue, as he did with regard to on-site inspections and PNE, on both of which China made significant concessions in order for the treaty to be concluded.[40]

Russia's motives for insisting on the adherence of the D-3 as a condition were less obvious, since it was hardly plausible that policymakers feared that India would constitute a significant national security threat if it stayed outside the CTBT. Clearly, an important reason was that Russia wanted to be sure that China would adhere to the treaty and may have associated this objective with an analysis that China might not accede to the treaty without India. By contrast, in the PTBT, NPT and CWC negotiations, Moscow had recognized the benefits of facilitating early EIF rather than requiring prior adherence from all states of concern, and had subsequently witnessed how states that did not immediately accede became drawn into compliance with a regime's norms and principles once the treaty had taken effect. The institutional process of incremental build-up had proved successful for the NPT and PTBT, and by 1996, progress on the CWC was looking positive, though it had not yet entered into force. Russia's insistence also appears to have been based on its view that the CTBT's chief function was as a mechanism to pull the D-3 into legal obligations with regard to nuclear weapons, especially given that they were unlikely to accede to the NPT in the near future. Establishing a non-discriminatory regime against testing was therefore treated as subordinate to universalization of the discriminatory non-proliferation regime.

Although China and Russia were clearly in favour of a stringent EIF provision, both had engaged actively in concession trading on other issues, notably the verification regime and the implementing organization. By June 1996, both China and Russia appeared to be on board the treaty, as signified by China's acquiescence on PNE and Russia's acceptance of the zero-yield scope. In light of such political developments, Berdennikov's continued assertion that Russia could not have compromised on EIF[41] may be open to question. Doubt that the P-5 plus D-3 condition was an actual treaty-breaker for Russia has been cast by a former US official in the State Department, who recalled a Russian memo sent to Washington direct from Moscow at the height of the impasse over EIF. Reportedly, Moscow proposed in this memo that if the CD could not finalize the CTBT by September 1996, the P-5 should conclude the treaty among themselves, sign it and then open it to other states, as had been done with the PTBT. Washington, determined that the CTBT should be multilateral, did nothing with the Russian suggestion, which was not followed up. Since few if any of the Geneva negotiators were aware of such a memo, it did not influence the CD options at the time, but the significance of Moscow's communication—if true—is that it indicates that Russia was prepared to join a treaty that included only the P-5 as a condition of entry into force.[42] Had Ramaker known that Moscow's bottom line was P-5 adherence, rather than the P-5 plus D-3 condition, he may have risked putting a more flexible provision in the 28 May draft text.

Russia was not Ramaker's only problem, however, for he also had to satisfy China's concerns and contend with an unusually vocal and intransigent British posture. Weston has subsequently expressed pride in keeping the UK delegation consistent with the initial principles it laid down for the CTBT, and it is true that he refused to yield on the British demand for a rigid, list-based provision put forward in his opening policy statement in January 1994.[43] While it was clear that John Major's Conservative government wished to portray the CTBT as pre-eminently an instrument of non-proliferation, the stridency of the British position baffled delegations and NGOs in Geneva, London and Washington. Apart from this ideological motivation it was difficult to see a significant security threat to the United Kingdom if India, Israel or Pakistan did not accede to the treaty immediately. Wondering about more personalized, political motivations, some speculated that the United Kingdom could be using this issue to get back at the United States, a possibility consistent with evidence that the UK Ministry of Defence was more determined to hold on to the rigid position than the Foreign and Commonwealth Office.[44] At one point, Weston explained that the United Kingdom's position was predicated on a strategy to obtain Pakistan's accession. Contrary to the main evidence from the NPT and PTBT experiences with states that were still considering their nuclear options, the British establishment had apparently concluded that a strict mechanism would reassure Pakistan, which would sign on that basis and so completely isolate India. The theory was that India would hate to be completely on its own outside the treaty, so this strategy would be more successful in bringing India on board than a flexible approach that was not legally binding.[45] This is not how it worked out, however. When the CTBT was adopted by the UN General Assembly on 10 September 1996, Ambassador Munir Akram stated that Pakistan supported the resolution to adopt the CTBT but would not sign the treaty until its regional situation warranted, understood to mean when India signed.[46]

France and the United Kingdom had started with the same opening position on EIF in 1994, but during 1996 France moved toward the more flexible US position. This development was consistent with its overall shift in posture following Chirac's election and the decision to resume testing. Having achieved its desired delay France relaxed its position, but the more constructive French posture was offset by its weaker position in the P-5 dynamic after the departure of Gérard Errera in late August 1995. Most of the middle powers among the negotiators, notably Australia, Canada, Germany, Japan, Mexico and much of the European Union, including the Netherlands (notwithstanding Ramaker's position as Chair), preferred a more flexible approach on EIF, but they were slow to organize on the issue, failing to recognize how close it would come to breaking the treaty. The G-21 was divided, with the Arab states generally advocating a strict P-5 plus D-3 provision to bind Israel, and the rest preferring something more flexible. Several delegations began to suggest ideas whereby states particularly concerned by certain others could coordinate their accession with that of another state.[47] One suggestion was for certain states to attach to their own ratification a condition that the treaty would not be deemed legally binding on them unless "State X" had also ratified. Such conditions are sometimes attached to ratification legislation at the behest of national legislatures but are not usually incorporated into a treaty itself.[48] In the event, none of these suggestions were turned into formal proposals.

Though EIF questions had been largely ignored by civil society in the first two years of negotiations, by the middle of 1996 some had begun to sound the alert about the dangers inherent in an overly rigid provision. George Perkovich, a well-known US analyst of South Asia's nuclear politics, circulated a memo to "Parties concerned about the CTBT" in early June. Perkovich's analysis directly contradicted Weston's, as he noted that:

> putting India in a make-or-break EIF position would create a hot-button political issue in India … . [N]o matter how this or any other scenario played out, it's hard to see any positive aspect to having Indian accession required for EIF, once you accept that Indian signature on the treaty is unlikely.[49]

Given the turbulence and fluidity of Indian politics at the time, Perkovich urged that:

> the best politically feasible outcome would be for the treaty to move enough in India's direction that Indian leaders would not foreclose future signature, and that diplomacy and international developments over the next months and years evolve to the point where India can be persuaded to sign, perhaps with additional inducements … . If Indian accession is unlikely, then making EIF contingent upon this accession is self defeating.[50]

Paying heed to such advice, several NGOs coordinated a letter-writing campaign to key governments and Geneva delegations, as well as to influential Members of Parliament and Congressional representatives in the United Kingdom and the United States respectively. Their objective was to focus political attention on finding a regime-enhancing resolution that would combine political reassurance and operational viability with treaty credibility. For this they needed to exert high-level pressure on the Clinton administration, which still did not seem very seized of this issue, and get some kind of intervention to make the British government take a more flexible and constructive stance. Although these civil society endeavours bore some fruit, as discussed below, they were too late to influence the outcome.

THE DIE IS CAST

On 17 June 1996, the pool of formal negotiators was increased from 38 to 61, as the CD finally managed to achieve consensus for its long-awaited enlargement.[51] This meant that Israel was at last able to participate formally in the negotiations, just in time for some difficult decisions on areas with particular sensitivity for Middle Eastern states, such as on-site inspections and the Executive Council, including regional allocations and decision-making processes.[52] CD enlargement came just as matters over EIF came to a head in June 1996, amid deteriorating personal and political relations among some of the key delegations. There was a full CD plenary on 20 June, including for the first time the 23 new members. Then followed a meeting of the NTB Committee, at which Ramaker introduced a Chair's working paper with a new and complicated formula for EIF.

In the CD plenary, Ghose underlined India's conditions for joining the CTBT in terms of time-bound disarmament commitments. In her long and combative statement, the Indian ambassador rejected attempts to coerce her country through the EIF provisions of the treaty and conveyed an unmistakable warning that India was preparing to exercise its power to block CD consensus unless the EIF provision was made less specific. In what was interpreted by many as an ultimatum, Ghose declared: "India cannot accept any restraints on its capability if other countries remain unwilling to accept the obligation to eliminate their nuclear weapons".[53] Ghose's statement was an extraordinary example of diplomatic judo, in which she manipulated fact, perception and threat to destabilize the opposition and create an impression of the inevitability of the outcome. She positioned India for defection, distracting attention from her state's nuclear ambitions by focusing on the failure of the nuclear-weapon states to disarm or reduce their core reliance on nuclear weapons; she then couched India's familiar linkage arguments in terms of national security, so that New Delhi's justifications for rejecting the CTBT could be cast as a response to threat and the fault of others, principally the P-5. As this statement set the scene for India's subsequent actions, it is illuminating to consider in more detail the words and phrases actually employed.

After quoting from the CTBT's negotiating mandate, Ghose asserted:

> India has participated actively and constructively in the negotiations. We have put forward a number of proposals, consistent with the mandate adopted by the CD. These proposals are aimed at ensuring that the CTBT must be a truly comprehensive treaty, that is, a treaty which bans all nuclear testing without leaving any loopholes that would permit nuclear-weapon States to continue refining and developing their nuclear arsenals at their test sites and in their laboratories. Through these proposals we have underscored the importance of placing the CTBT in a disarmament framework, as part of a step-by-step process aimed at achieving the complete elimination of all nuclear weapons within a time-bound framework.

Expressing India's disappointment with how negotiations had developed, Ghose called the scope "narrow" and said it did "not fulfil the mandated requirement of a comprehensive ban"; it was, rather, only a "nuclear-weapon-test-explosion-ban treaty". The preambular references to disarmament were too weak and "cannot meet our concerns". She listed ways in which the CTBT failed to reduce the nuclear-weapon states' reliance on nuclear arms, illustrating that the nuclear testing carried out by China and France during the negotiations were "justified as essential for national security and for permitting completion of work on new designs and gathering of data to enable computer simulation and modelling to preserve and refine capabilities into the distant future". Ghose concluded her statement on the treaty's shortcomings with the following denunciation of the draft text, signalling India's intention to defect: "The CTBT that we see emerging appears to be shaped more by the technological preferences of the nuclear-weapon States rather than the imperatives of nuclear disarmament. This was not the CTBT that India envisaged in 1954. This cannot be the CTBT that India can be expected to accept".[54]

A further paragraph drew comparisons with the NPT as a discriminatory and unacceptable treaty regime. Ghose then reiterated her criticism of the CTBT, declaring that "India ... cannot subscribe to it in its present form". Finally, addressing Article XIV, she derided the use of the EIF provision to exert improper pressure on India to accede to the CTBT, and in the quotation reproduced at the beginning of this chapter, warned that India "would not accept any language in the treaty text which would affect our sovereign right to decide in the light of our supreme national interest, whether we should or should not accede to such a treaty".[55]

Antonio de Icaza of Mexico had been appointed the 1996 Friend of the Chair on EIF, and continued to consult on the issue as "Moderator", but Ramaker was increasingly taking negotiations into his own hands. In a tense atmosphere, assailed by a number of competing demands and different priorities, Ramaker and the Dutch delegation frantically tried to work out possible compromises on the outstanding issues. Among the P-5, China, Russia and the United Kingdom continued to insist that the treaty must unequivocally bind the nuclear-capable states as well as the P-5. They appeared willing to take the treaty hostage on this issue, so the pressure on Ramaker to meet their demands was heavy.

In the NTB Committee that followed the plenary, Ramaker presented for consideration a new working paper on EIF that added a different element to the provision in his Chair's draft treaty. Containing a series of staggered provisions, the working paper differed from past waiver proposals in one primary respect: instead of ratifying states having to take action to allow the treaty to enter into force for them, Ramaker's proposal would have the treaty automatically enter into force unless this was specifically opposed by one or more states that had ratified.[56] The first and main condition was accession by all states with a primary seismic station or radionuclide laboratory, as in the 28 May draft. If this strict requirement was not met within five years, then states that had ratified would have a second chance to bring the treaty into effect by a combination of a simple number threshold, a waiver conference and a "deferment" option. If at least 75 states had signed and ratified, then the treaty would enter into force automatically five years plus 180 days from the date of its opening for signature, unless one or more of them requested a special conference to be convened. If a conference were requested, then this would be open to all states that had ratified. They would have the power to agree by a two-thirds majority to implement the treaty. Responding to concerns put forward by Egypt and Pakistan, Ramaker's working paper proposed that any state that had ratified but did not support the decision to implement the treaty could, at the time of the conference, defer its own accession to the treaty until all the original conditions had been met, or until it felt able to revoke its decision to defer (a kind of reverse Tlatelolco mechanism).

The formula was ingenious and might have worked, but it suffered from three major problems: it was too late, too complicated and reproduced the discredited IMS-based list from which India had already threatened to withdraw. Despite its complexity, a modified version of such a phased EIF proposal could possibly have succeeded, especially if something along these lines had been inserted into Ramaker's 28 May draft instead of the British formula. It might also have been taken more seriously if it had used as its baseline the IAEA list or the newly expanded CD. Some had liked the phased concept, and if this has been the placeholder in the Chair's draft, it would have given it greater authority, while allowing for further discussion of the details. As it was, the tactics and timing were wrong. China, Russia, Pakistan and the United Kingdom rejected it out of hand, though others, including India, the United States, Israel and Japan, expressed interest. It was too late in the process, however, and despite the valiant attempts of some civil society representatives and the Dutch delegation, even the supporters of flexible EIF did not regard the proposal as worth pursuing. On 24 June, Ramaker introduced a slightly revised draft text and announced his determination to conclude the negotiations by 28 June. He challenged delegations to give feedback on his EIF proposal or come up with something more acceptable.

During the final week of June, there were several political attempts to address the EIF decision, but they turned out to be insufficient or too late. On 24 June, responding to lobbying by British NGOs, Robin Cook, the Labour Party's Shadow Foreign Secretary, put down a series of five questions for the UK government on CTBT entry into force, calling for a response to Ramaker's 20 June EIF working paper and asking about the "implications for international security of a lengthy delay in the entry into force" of the CTBT.[57] The government's reply, given by David Davis, Minister of State, was:

> Her Majesty's Government's position is that, for it to be a fully effective non-proliferation measure, the comprehensive test ban treaty must have as parties the declared nuclear-weapon states and all other states with a nuclear capability and which are not otherwise prevented from testing by other international agreements to which they are parties. The formula proposed by Ambassador Ramaker on 20 June, but not incorporated into his revised text, does not meet this requirement.[58]

Ignoring the central challenge implied in Cook's questions, Davis also stated: "We believe that the earliest practicable entry into force of the treaty on the basis of universal adherence would best serve the interests of international security".[59]

As bilateral and plurilateral meetings and consultations with the Chair and various moderators over a host of endgame issues were being carried out throughout the days and well into the evenings, EIF had become the most contentious issue, followed by the composition of the Executive Council and the decision-making process for on-site inspections. As noted above, on 26 June, India cemented its objections to the EIF provision in the Chair's text by formally withdrawing its stations from the IMS, causing delegations from Australia, Germany, Russia and the United States to express their regret. That same day, in his last act as Moderator, de Icaza convened an evening session specifically devoted to EIF. In his opening speech he referred to the many letters from NGOs, expressing their concerns that what he called "the eight condition" (the P-5 plus D-3) could be discriminatory and result in "excessive delay". In his national capacity, de Icaza said that he fully shared the NGOs' concerns and favoured an EIF solution that "endows the treaty with credibility ... such as a list combined with a waiver".[60]

The meeting, which took place late in a packed room on a very hot evening, was convened to consider the Chair's working paper on EIF, but it turned sour following a rancorous exchange between Weston and Ghose, in which the UK ambassador reportedly asserted that India was "wriggling on the end of a hook".[61] Weston's comment provoked an acerbic response from Ghose to the effect that India was no longer a colony and could not be bullied. As tempers frayed, Weston also offended diplomats from Germany and Japan, who opposed the stringent list-based EIF requirement, by telling them that since the CTBT was essentially a non-proliferation measure aimed at the P-5 and states outside the NPT, their role was only to pay for it. According to diplomats in the room at the time, these exchanges poisoned the atmosphere of the meeting and killed the chance of constructive debate on the EIF conundrum.[62] Canada tried to focus attention on the substance by circulating a proposal it had made earlier for a "political conference", while de Icaza tried to get some feedback on a summary of the options that he had circulated on 18 June. He also sought to stimulate discussion of Ramaker's working paper, but the diplomats seemed too exhausted or pessimistic to respond. As the meeting stewed in summer heat and acrimony, de Icaza appears to have interpreted the lack of response as a lack of support for the phased EIF approach of the working paper. He then reverted to the Article XIV formulation in the Chair's 28 May draft and tried to revive discussion by asking each delegation to say whether it could accept this or not. It appears, however, that his question was understood by delegations in the narrowest of terms: not "does your country accept this as the best formula for the treaty?" but rather "do you have national instructions to oppose it?" On that basis, only India rejected it, although a number of others commented that they would have preferred something more flexible.

Rather than opening opportunities for renegotiating the EIF provision, the 26 June meeting appeared to close them. Ramaker was faced with pressure to keep the stringent provision, primarily from Russia and the United Kingdom, supported by China, Egypt, Pakistan and a handful of Middle Eastern states. Other non-nuclear-weapon states appeared to give up and hope for the best. Although it was widely speculated that India had already taken its decision to walk away from the treaty and that changing Article XIV would not make much difference at this point, a number of diplomats present at the time blamed Weston's remarks for the final breakdown in communication with India.[63] Be that as it may, it is important to note that Weston was accompanied on 20 June by Roland Smith, a senior Foreign and Commonwealth Office official, and that most of his remarks that day were not off-the-cuff comments (as many assumed at the time), but read from a written statement.[64]

The United States, though among those that had preferred a condition based on ratification by the P-5 plus a simple number of other states, tried to use EIF as a bargaining chip in P-5 negotiations with China and Russia over on-site inspections. Failing to achieve agreement on this, the US delegation shifted again, and publicly opposed the list of 37 just as India withdrew its IMS stations.[65] Michael Krepon of the Henry L. Stimson Center had been trying for months to bring a high-level group of scientists and former diplomats together (as he had done on the issue of scope a year earlier) to convince the White House to exert its political authority to get a more credible EIF provision. Finally, on 28 June, a delegation including Sidney Drell, Cyrus Vance, Andrew Goodpaster and McGeorge Bundy visited the White House and obtained a promise that Clinton would try to obtain agreement on a more flexible EIF provision.[66] In addition, the Foreign Ministers of several European Union and Commonwealth states, including the Netherlands (as the country holding the chair of the negotiations) sent letters to Malcolm Rifkind, the UK Foreign Secretary.[67] Joëlle Bourgois, who had replaced Érrera as French ambassador to the CD, also sought ways to persuade the United Kingdom to modify its posture. Whether because of French efforts or following the high-level meeting at the White House, Weston received a telephone call from British government representatives attending the meeting of the Group of Seven (G-7) heads of state in Lyon, 27–29 June 1996, instructing him to show more flexibility on EIF.[68] Although it is understood that the change in instructions occurred as a direct result of discussions between President Clinton and Prime Minister John Major, it arrived too late to have any effect.[69] Too little, too late; and the fact that the US delegation had first underestimated the EIF issue and then been prepared to bargain with it undermined what hope might have remained that the United States would rally support for an alternative proposal.

Despite the setbacks in late June, Ramaker continued to try to find a workable EIF compromise and draw India back into negotiations. With time running out, several delegations returned to the view that listing the members of the newly expanded CD, combined with a waiver provision, could facilitate wide adherence and early implementation and also exert pressure on the nuclear-test-capable states. But the United States reportedly considered 60 too large, and China, Russia and the United Kingdom continued to oppose any kind of waiver. At that point, Ramaker resurrected an idea floated some months previously by Canada (and re-circulated at the ill-fated EIF consultations on 26 June), which proposed a "political conference" that would be held by signatories if the treaty had not entered into force three years after it was opened for signature. It was envisaged that this conference would be less formal, with fewer decision-making powers than a waiver conference, and would be convened to discuss ways to persuade non-states parties to accede.

Meanwhile, Ramaker had also realized that he had to abandon the IMS-based list, and came up with a formula that set the primary condition as ratification by an annexed list of 44 states which were participating members of the CD on 18 June (after expansion) and appeared in the 1995 and 1996 IAEA lists of states with nuclear research or nuclear power reactors respectively. He issued his revised Chair's text with this new Article XIV and the list spelled out in Annex 2. The reference to "participating members" excluded Yugoslavia (a CD member by name but barred from participation during its wars of disintegration) and Iraq (to meet US concerns that Saddam Hussein should be denied any opportunity to exercise leverage by threatening not to ratify). In addition, the revised Article XIV stipulated that if the conditions were not met within three years, then states that had already ratified could convene a conference to decide on measures to "accelerate the ratification process" and facilitate early EIF.

Following concerns raised principally by India, that the term "measures" might imply sanctions and that the provision as a whole was a threat to states' sovereignty, Ramaker gave the Committee his understanding that "the current article on entry into force did not impinge on the sovereign right of any state to take its own decision about whether or not to sign and ratify the treaty". He also stated that Article XIV, paragraph 2, which related to the conference, "did not refer to United Nations Security Council measures in accordance with Chapter VII of the United Nations Charter".[70] The NTB Committee report also placed on record that Article XIV did not impose any legally binding obligations on a state not party to the treaty, regardless of whether or not ratification by that state was a condition of EIF.

CHAIR'S REVISED TREATY ACCEPTED WITH RESERVATIONS

Saying that "convergence has reached its peak", Ramaker tabled a revised version of his previous Chair's text on 28 June, the last day of the second part of the CD's 1996 session. Though a large majority of CD members had wanted a simpler, more flexible provision to encourage early entry into force, the chance was lost due to the unfortunate combination of overwork and pressure at the centre, political rivalries, lack of effective leadership in the P-5 and the looming deadline. Indeed, though intending to be helpful, some 20 delegations had added to the pressure by affirming in a written declaration their commitment to conclude the treaty by 28 June.[71] Although Ramaker was far from satisfied with EIF provision himself, when he presented his draft treaty to the Committee on 28 June, he said that the negotiations were over.[72]

The text that became Article XIV of the CTBT was formed out of bridging proposals from at least three delegations that were themselves actually opposed to basing EIF on the "eight condition" of the P-5 plus D-3. Running out of time and fearing to lose the treaty altogether, they tried to make the best of a difficult job in what appeared to be a lose–lose situation. Conditioning the treaty's entry into force on ratification by every state on a list of 44, Article XIV had rendered the treaty vulnerable to blocking tactics and hostage-taking, softened only by the offer of a conference which could be convened three years after the date of the treaty being opened for signature. By this time, India and others were reading not just the small print, but the subtext as well. Ramaker had inserted Canada's idea of a political conference but, for this to be accepted, any useful ambiguity that might have attached to the concept had to be removed. Hence, assurances were given on the record that the conference proposed in Article XIV was not a waiver conference and could not impose sanctions.

Despite misgivings about the implications of the Article XIV provision on entry into force, the Clinton administration decided in early July that it would be better to support Ramaker's text as it was than to risk reopening negotiations to find a more workable EIF solution. Hoping to deter others from believing that anything would be gained from further negotiations, which they feared could cause the whole treaty to unravel, the United States then secured public declarations of support from France, Indonesia, Russia, the United Kingdom and others for the 28 June text to be regarded as final. When the CD resumed its session on 29 July, just as China conducted its forty-fifth (and final) nuclear test explosion, the atmosphere was tense. As China's CD diplomats raised reservations about the draft treaty, Beijing announced that from 30 July it would observe a moratorium.[73] While some states regretted this test, they welcomed this signal that China would join the CTBT from the beginning and did not plan to keep testing until the treaty entered into force, as previously feared.[74]

As the CD reconvened, India voiced its strong criticisms of the draft treaty, followed by Egypt, Iran, Nigeria and Pakistan. Berdennikov reinforced the US position against reopening negotiations when he announced to the NTB Committee that a meeting of Russian Minister of Foreign Affairs Yevgeny Primakov and US Secretary of State Warren Christopher had decided to support the 28 June text, although it did not "fully satisfy" both sides.[75] However, he warned that if the text were opened up for further negotiations, Russia reserved the right to try to improve the draft. A spectrum of non-nuclear-weapon CD members declared that, though they retained some concerns about aspects of the text, they thought the 28 June draft should be forwarded to the UN General Assembly. They included Argentina, Australia, Bulgaria, Canada, Chile, Finland, Germany, Hungary, Israel, Italy, Japan, New Zealand, Norway, Poland, the Republic of Korea, Romania, Spain, Sweden and Turkey.

As it turned out, the United States then went back on its public stand against reopening the treaty in order to address China's concerns about the decision-making procedure for on-site inspections, discussed in the next chapter. Having finally conceded on PNE,[76] the issue of on-site inspections was a make-or-break issue for China. Under pressure from its allies, and believing that China's signature of the treaty could be hanging in the balance, the United States modified its position and accepted a decision-making majority of "at least 30 affirmative votes" by members of the Executive Council as necessary before an inspection could proceed. Ramaker agreed that this change was "essential to achieve consensus", and so the US–Chinese decision on inspections was presented together with some procedural modifications in the Chair's final text, issued as working paper CD/NTB/WP.330.Rev.2 on August 14.

This late US–Chinese modification may have secured China's signature, but India was furious that the 28 June text was amended at China's behest while no one was prepared to address India's own proposals on disarmament and EIF. By this time, there was a high level of public and political interest in the CTBT negotiations in India, where the endgame struggles were followed daily in the national press. Such concessions to China increased India's sense of grievance—sections of the media argued that the draft treaty had been reopened because China was a nuclear power, suggesting that India's needs and proposals were ignored because India was not a recognized nuclear-weapon state.[77]

Other non-aligned countries had also tried to reopen negotiations on the preamble and EIF, but were told that negotiations were closed. As the repository of the treaty-makers' political aspirations, the preamble provides a display case for concepts that underpin the treaty, a storage site for ideas that were dropped from the body of the text, and at times an assertion of lowest-common-denominator general principles that no one would disagree with. From the very beginning, many non-aligned states had wanted the CTBT preamble to enshrine a commitment to the concept of a timetable for nuclear disarmament, while the majority of non-nuclear delegations had argued for the preamble to reflect the treaty's role in curbing vertical as well as horizontal proliferation, a position supported by some of the Chinese statements. The other four nuclear powers insisted that consideration of the preamble should be delayed to the end of the negotiations. When attention turned to the preamble in June 1996, Canada and the G-21 played the largest roles in proposing text, while the nuclear-weapon states (other than China) rejected anything but bland assertions of aspiration tied to the treaty's basic obligations.

The preamble in the 28 June text opened by welcoming recent arms reduction measures and quoting from the negotiating mandate. Coordinated by Mexico and based on an earlier working paper from Pakistan, 13 non-aligned states submitted a late proposal to amend the preamble to say that the CTBT "should end the development and qualitative improvement of nuclear weapons" and be "an indispensable step towards the larger goal of a nuclear weapon free world".[78] The P-5 had rejected any text that talked of curbing nuclear weapon development as a purpose, objective or aspiration of the treaty, but in the end they were prepared to allow the preamble to refer to "constraining the development and qualitative improvement of nuclear weapons and ending the development of advanced new types of nuclear weapons" but only in the context of this being a *consequence* of the treaty. This linguistic sleight of hand was intended to avoid being held responsible if they made technological developments that circumvented these constraints. The P-5 also agreed to a preambular paragraph that reflected language from the NPT decisions adopted in 1995, recognizing the CTBT as a "meaningful step in the realization of a systematic process to achieve nuclear disarmament".[79]

Earlier, France had adamantly opposed Cuba's proposals linking nuclear testing to environmental harm, perhaps fearing that formalizing such linkage could make it possible for the nuclear-weapon states to be sued by communities affected by nuclear testing over the years. Cuba and its non-aligned partners had to be satisfied with a reversed linkage noting that the treaty "could contribute to the protection of the environment".[80] Having accepted some compromise language brokered by Ramaker and the Australian delegation, the Western nuclear powers made it clear that they would not negotiate on further strengthening the preamble unless India gave a commitment to sign the treaty.[81] Frustrated at their inability to place stronger commitments in the CTBT preamble, 28 of the 30 non-aligned states in the CD proposed a "programme of action for the elimination of nuclear weapons", arguing that this should be the basis for further discussions in the CD, for which it should reconvene an ad hoc committee on nuclear disarmament.[82]

Neither the assurances from Ramaker regarding Article XIV nor the references to nuclear disarmament in the preamble ameliorated India's objections sufficiently to alter a decision to reject the CTBT that now appeared irrevocable. With the treaty characterized as "discriminatory" in the debates raging in media and political circles in India, Ghose again told the CD that India would not sign a CTBT text that did not address nuclear disarmament in a time-bound framework. On 8 August, she put forward another EIF proposal based on the simple numerical formula of ratification by 65 states, apparently dropping India's earlier linkage between entry into force and a timetable for disarmament. She also warned that in the event that the text was not altered, and the treaty was put forward with an EIF provision that included India, then her country would block CD consensus on the treaty,[83] a threat that was subsequently carried out. Denounced by more than just India, Article XIV was derided by many.[84] Even so, despite many warnings, few CD diplomats appeared to recognize that they could fatally undermine the CTBT if they let it be finalized with an EIF provision requiring the ratification of at least one state that had already declared its intention not to sign.

BYPASSING INDIA TO BRING THE TREATY TO THE UN GENERAL ASSEMBLY

When the Chair sought consensus in the NTB Committee for his final treaty text, India carried out its threat to veto the draft treaty. Omitting the treaty text, Ramaker managed to persuade India to allow the basic procedural report of the NTB Committee to be transmitted to the full CD on 19 August. In addition to the standard description of activities, personnel and documentation related to the Committee, the report contained explanations, interpretations and assurances from the Chair on several issues in the draft treaty, including the preamble, the Executive Council, verification and the use of NTM, the "sole purpose" of on-site inspections, and the clarifications discussed above regarding sovereign rights and sanctions. In particular, he responded to objections from Iran and others that about Israel's inclusion in the Middle East region, by clarifying the CTBT-specific relevance of the six-region basis for determining the composition of the Executive Council, with the implication that this would not set a precedent for any other forum. To reassure those concerned about possible abuses of NTM and on-site inspections, he made statements on the record regarding the limitation of inspections to the treaty's subject matter and various safeguards in the treaty against the violation of a state's sovereignty and potential abuse of NTM.[85]

Unusually, the report also contained a summary of some 18 statements of national position on the CTBT. These statements ranged from the generally supportive to the critical. In support, Australia made a statement on behalf of 39 mostly Western-leaning and Eastern European states, including the P-5, Israel and four G-21 states, and separate statements were also made by Belgium, Canada, China and Kenya. Other statements that might be characterized as critical of various aspects but not opposed to the CTBT included G-21 members Algeria, Brazil, Colombia, Cuba, Egypt, Mexico, Pakistan, Peru and Viet Nam.[86]

Two countries—India and Iran—expressed serious opposition. Iran shared various G-21 states' criticisms of the treaty's inadequacies with regard to disarmament, NTM and the regional composition of the Executive Committee, but went considerably further. Joining India in arguing against attaching the draft treaty text to the NTB Committee report on the claim that the negotiations had not been properly concluded, Iran stated that "the appalling fact here is that failure could be avoided" and that the remaining issues could be resolved. Iran then tried unsuccessfully to propose further amendments.[87] India's statement reiterated its opposition to the treaty and refusal to let the treaty text be attached to the NTB Committee report or any CD document that might be transmitted to the United Nations, even if there was clear acknowledgement that there had been no consensus. Stating that "it is unprecedented in the history of international treaties that a sovereign nation is required to sign a treaty against its will under implied threats", Ghose ignored assurances by the Chair and others to the contrary and resisted CD members' appeals to allow the treaty text to be attached to the report.[88]

On 20 August, with a graceful speech thanking his colleagues, Ramaker presented the NTB Committee report to the CD and thereby handed over responsibility for the treaty.[89] The only other speakers at that plenary were the ambassadors of India and Pakistan, which served to underline how the fate of the CTBT had become hostage to South Asian politics. Ghose again detailed India's arguments against the treaty. To these were added justifications for blocking consensus not only on the treaty text, but in preventing adoption of the NTB Committee report as well, with the claim that the CD "has no text of a CTBT to recommend to the General Assembly at this time".[90]

Akram attacked India for "hypocrisy" and said:

> Today the mask of the smiling Buddha has been torn off, revealing the face of the goddess of war. The leaders of our neighbour have proclaimed that they will keep their nuclear options open; that they reserve the right to conduct nuclear tests; that they will go ahead with their short- and medium-range missile programmes.[91]

In a last ditch attempt to prevent the treaty from having multilateral legitimacy, India carried out its threat to block transmission of the NTB Committee report to the UN General Assembly, even though the treaty text was not attached. In this, it was supported by Iran, ostensibly on procedural grounds.[92] There was a sudden, panicked flurry of activity among Western states, which had not anticipated this final obstacle.[93] Some sought to assure India that it would not be coerced into signing the treaty as long as it did not block its transmission to the General Assembly. Akram argued that "these letters and gestures of appeasement have ensured, rather than lifted, the veto against the treaty" and criticized India for making "obviously unrealistic and unreasonable" demands as "a transparent device to avoid a commitment to a nuclear-test-ban treaty, to veto a vital disarmament measure which has virtually universal support".[94]

The CD had never before been unable to adopt a treaty text that it had negotiated. After several unsuccessful attempts to persuade India and Iran to allow the report to be adopted by the CD and transmitted to the United Nations, the CD met in plenary on 22 August. To an unusally packed chamber, Pakistan formally proposed that the NTB Committee report should be transmitted to the General Assembly "for information" and was supported by a number of delegations, including non-aligned states Mexico, Brazil, Egypt, Peru, Chile and Morocco, as well as the United Kingdom on behalf of the Western Group of states and others, Slovakia on behalf of the Eastern European Group, and China.[95] Iran and India queried the CD's ability to take such a decision, invoking the rules of procedure. After further lengthy discussions back and forth among over 15 delegations, Richard Starr made an impassioned speech noting that the report they were all arguing about was "a report shorn of [the treaty text] … a report that registered non-consensus despite our belief that the overwhelming majority … were prepared to accept that text despite perceptions of imperfections".[96] Recognizing that many delegations, including his own, had not been very happy about the entry-into-force provision "which is the cause of this veto",

Starr argued: "Whatever its limitations, it is simply not accurate to suggest that it is illegal or coercive". Declaring "We have a workable treaty", Starr concluded by announcing Australia's intention "to work with friends of the CTBT to fulfil the goal of the fiftieth General Assembly of a completed text, endorsed and ready for signature by the fifty-first Assembly this year".[97] So many delegations wanted to speak that the plenary was suspended for lunch and for the President to undertake informal consultations to try to get consensus on Pakistan's proposal to transmit the NTB Committee report to the General Assembly. When the meeting resumed late in the afternoon, the President stated that there was no consensus. Egypt then attempted to have the report transmitted to the General Assembly under the auspices of the CD President, by means of a letter.[98] India objected and following further discussion Egypt's proposal seemed to fall. Moments before the plenary was formally closed, the Belgian ambassador, Baron Alain Guillaume, took non-Western delegations by surprise when in the midst of a speech thanking the CD President, Ambassador Ramaker and others, he suddenly requested on his government's behalf that the draft CTBT text be issued as an official CD document.[99] While it is quite common for governments to have relevant notices of bilateral or regional agreements and treaties negotiated elsewhere issued as official CD documents to give them a wider audience and authority, it has never before been necessary for a delegation to make such a request for a treaty negotiated by the CD. Before anyone objected, the CD President quickly recorded the decision. As a consequence of Belgium's initiative, the CTBT text was accorded a CD reference number and official status, though not the standing that consensus adoption by the CD would have conferred.[100]

A few hours later in New York, the Australian Ambassador to the United Nations, Richard Butler, requested the UN Secretary-General to arrange for the General Assembly to convene in plenary to take action on the CTBT, pursuant to UN resolution 50/65.[101] India's strategy of objecting to the NTB Committee Report was further thwarted when Australia requested that the CD document containing the full treaty text, given the number CD/1427 following Belgium's request, be accorded status as a UN document and attached to the resolution proposing its adoption by the General Assembly.[102] It was duly accorded the document number A/50/1027, whereupon Australia followed with a resolution proposing the adoption of the CTBT as contained therein.[103] Though there was overwhelming support for the CD to transmit the draft treaty to the General Assembly, Australia was still criticized in some circles for using this bypass operation to get the treaty to the United Nations after the CD was prevented from doing so. Even as they participated in the General Assembly debate on the CTBT that could not have taken place without Australia's initiative, some non-aligned countries raised concerns that it undermined the CD's rule of consensus, rules of procedure, independence and autonomy, and argued that this manoeuvre should not set a precedent.

THE UNITED NATIONS OVERWHELMINGLY ADOPTS THE TREATY TEXT

On 9 September 1996, with 127 co-sponsors, Australia's resolution to adopt the CD as finalized in Geneva was put to the UN General Assembly. Almost all the statements made during the next two days were in strong support of the treaty, but many also referred to its flaws. Among those that criticized the treaty, four major areas of concern were revealed, though not necessarily shared by all or criticized for the same reasons: concern about the entry-into-force provision, including prophetic fears that its rigidity "virtually guaranteed indefinite hibernation";[104] disappointment that the treaty did not adequately prohibit non-explosive testing or prevent the further qualitative design and development of nuclear warheads; the need for more progress on nuclear disarmament, with references to a programme of action on disarmament put forward by 28 of the 30 members of the G-21 Group of Non-Aligned States in the CD on the G-28 programme of action, a time-bound framework and the July 1996 advisory opinion of the International Court of Justice on the use or threat of use of nuclear weapons;[105] and the distribution of Executive Council seats, complaints about which were mainly a vehicle for some of the Arab countries to object to Israel being part of the Middle East and South Asia region.

Prior to the UN debate, there had been rumours and anxiety that India or Iran might try to amend the treaty, and in fact India initially submitted a resolution containing amendments to the treaty's preamble, scope and Article XIV on EIF.[106] The co-sponsorship of the CTBT resolution by more than two thirds of the UN membership ensured that any amendment strategies were abandoned. When the vote was taken at 16h00 on 10 September, the CTBT was endorsed by 158 votes. Bhutan, India and Libya voted against. There were five abstentions: Cuba, Lebanon, Mauritius, Syria and Tanzania. The abstainers and Libya explained their position in terms of dissatisfaction with the negotiating process and objections to Israel's inclusion in the

Middle East regional group established for the purposes of electing the Executive Council. Additionally, 19 countries were counted as absent.[107]

Pakistan supported the resolution, but explained that it would not sign the treaty until its regional situation warranted.[108] Ghose gave a final, angry statement, arguing that the negotiations had been "skewed" and the treaty would "only succeed in perpetuating a discriminatory status quo".[109] She then concluded by declaring "that India will never sign this unequal Treaty, not now, nor later. As long as this text contains this article [XIV] ... this Treaty will never enter into force".[110]

THE CTBT IS OPENED FOR SIGNATURE

Opening the CTBT for signature at the United Nations on 24 September, UN Secretary-General Boutros Boutros-Ghali saluted civil society and the citizens who had "struggled for so long to achieve this treaty". He spoke of the "constant and passionate flow of petitions, appeals, and support from the peoples of the world," and appealed to all signatory states to ensure that they conformed with the purpose of the treaty.[111]

Calling the treaty "the longest sought, hardest fought prize in arms control history", President Bill Clinton was the first to sign, using the pen with which John F. Kennedy had signed the PTBT in 1963. Clinton described the CTBT as "a giant step forward" that would "help prevent the nuclear powers from developing more advanced and dangerous weapons".[112] Russia's Minister of Foreign Affairs, Yevgeni Primakov, said the treaty "would stimulate a gradual transition to nuclear disarmament". He also warned that "Testing of a nuclear explosive device by any country before the treaty enters into force will cardinally change the international situation, greatly prejudice the treaty itself, and may compel many countries to revise their attitude to it".[113] Foreign Minister Qian Qichen reiterated China's view that a CTBT was "only a first step in the entire process of comprehensive nuclear disarmament" and called for all the major nuclear powers to renounce their policies of nuclear deterrence, commit to no-first-use of nuclear weapons and give legally binding assurances not to use nuclear weapons against non-nuclear-weapon countries. China also advocated the withdrawal of nuclear weapons to the home territory of the nuclear-weapon states themselves and pressed for the commencement of negotiations leading to a convention on the complete prohibition and thorough destruction of nuclear weapons.[114]

French Minister of Foreign Affairs Hervé de Charette called the CTBT a "major turning point in the world's strategic balances" and said it opened the way to "a more stable, safer world which will cease to be haunted by the twin dangers of the nuclear arms race and the proliferation of these weapons".[115] The United Kingdom's Foreign Secretary, Malcolm Rifkind, who had opposed the CTBT when he was previously head of the Ministry of Defence, was notably less enthusiastic in his comments, remarking that the CTBT showed that "we can, by acting with determination and by making sacrifices, reap the benefits of the end of the Cold War".[116] Following the P-5, senior government representatives lined up to sign the treaty, and by the end of the first week over 70 countries had signed, including Iran and Israel. By 7 March 1997, when formally transferred to Vienna, the host city for the CTBT Organization, the CTBT had 142 signatories.

CHAPTER 7

DESIGNING A ROBUST VERIFICATION REGIME

> *The treaty is effectively verifiable. … a global network of [monitoring] stations is being set up … We know it will work. … The United States and its allies have worked side by side for a Comprehensive Test Ban Treaty since the days of President Eisenhower. This goal is now within our grasp. Our security is involved, as well as America's. For the security of the world we will leave to our children, we urge the United States Senate to ratify the treaty.*
>
> Jacques Chirac, Tony Blair and Gerhard Schröder,
> 8 October 1999[1]

During the Cold War, verification was regarded as one of the most difficult and divisive challenges in arms control negotiations, more than once contributing to the derailing of efforts to achieve a CTBT. As this chapter explains, the political restructuring of US–Soviet relations and expectations in the early 1990s meant that though verification issues were hard fought, they were less divisive during these test-ban negotiations. The negotiations to design and agree the International Monitoring System (IMS) were more fully multilateral and, indeed, reciprocal than negotiations on some of the other aspects of verification. It was particularly noticeable that the US delegation negotiated for a strong verification regime, but did not put the kind of unattainable demands on the system that had characterized US positions in the past. Nevertheless, the US delegation had a large team of technical and legal experts who negotiated hard to get a strong verification regime, at times making explicit reference to the need to reassure the US Department of Defense and intelligence community and win bipartisan support in the Senate in order for the United States to ratify the treaty. When other delegations balked at some of the more stringent US positions, Ambassador Ledogar held firm, arguing that failure to provide a strong verification system would be a treaty-breaker. It came as some surprise, therefore, when criticisms of the verification regime appeared to become a major plank of opposition to CTBT ratification in the US Senate in October 1999. To the contrary, the negotiating history, summarized in this chapter, shows that the United States succeeded in meeting all its essential requirements on verification, and contributed to the establishment of the most robust and effective international monitoring and verification system ever seen in a nuclear treaty.

Nuclear explosions produce four kinds of primary effects: explosive blast, intense heat and light, radiation and residual radionuclide contamination. These phenomena result in various short-, medium- and long-range effects able to be detected by a range of different technologies and techniques. Although the PTBT already prohibited nuclear testing in the atmosphere, outer space and underwater, the CD's NTB Committee decided early in its negotiations that the verification regime for the CTBT should be capable of detecting and identifying nuclear explosions in these environments as well as underground.

Agreement soon emerged that the verification regime would need to have at its heart an international system incorporating a set of mutually complementary monitoring technologies able to detect nuclear tests or suspicious events promptly and provide states parties with capabilities to detect and identify the source and location of such an event, as well as—if feasible—information enabling states to make judgments about the nature and attribution of a detected explosion. In addition, the verification regime would need to consider the dissemination, interpretation and analysis of data; how to distinguish false alarms;[2] the role, scope and provisions for on-site inspections; the political requirement for a multilateral and non-discriminatory regime and whether to incorporate information derived from national intelligence sources and NTM. The negotiators would also need to factor in such relevant issues as cost and cost-effectiveness, universality and regional concerns, and the time required for the various verification components to become operational.[3]

In a study prepared as a resource for the delegates to the PTBT Amendment Conference, VERTIC in 1990 had identified three main functions of a CTBT verification regime: to establish methods and procedures to detect significant cheating, to deter cheating by rendering a potential violator sufficiently unsure of escaping detection, and to build confidence in the treaty so that the security of all parties is enhanced, thereby providing a strong incentive for the widest possible number of states to join.[4] In essence, these functions reflected the verification principles developed by the Reagan administration for the Intermediate-range Nuclear Forces Treaty of 1987. They were still valid when the CTBT negotiations in Geneva commenced in January 1994, but the devil is always in the detail.

As the history of past efforts to achieve a CTBT testifies, verification has long been an area of political as well as technical contention. As noted by UK negotiator Sir Michael Wright in 1964, "What the West considered adequate, the Communist countries rejected as unbearable; what the Communist countries considered bearable, the West rejected as inadequate".[5] In the post-Cold War era too, verification must take into account advances in technology for observing and detecting clandestine activities, as well as potential technologies and opportunities allowing for the circumvention of an accord. At a critical intersection involving technical capabilities and political concerns, what nations want from verification is complex and multifaceted, relating to issues of compliance, deterrence and confidence, and requiring not only the capabilities to detect violations, but to identify and locate suspicious events and confirm their nature and implications. Though the ideological divisions were no longer as wide as during the Cold War, the CTBT negotiations still had to contend with deep-rooted sensitivities around military intelligence, espionage and national security secrecy that frequently pitted domestic and opposing military and political interest groups against each other. In her thorough study of attitudes about verification among US arms control proponents, Nancy Gallagher identified a key difference of approach between "deterrent verificationists", who see verification as primarily a confidence-building measure and deterrent against cheating, and "detection verificationists", who prioritize getting the highest levels of detection and proof to cover imaginable if not necessarily practical violation scenarios. The two purposes are related, as the detection, location and identification capabilities must be sufficiently credible for the verification system to function as an effective deterrent, but the different approaches have implications for negotiating postures.[6]

Recognizing that states came to the CTBT negotiations with various interests and expectations, the first Chair of Working Group 1 on verification, Germany's ambassador Wolfgang Hoffmann (who later became the first Executive Secretary of the Preparatory Commission for the Comprehensive Nuclear-Test-Ban Treaty Organization), sought to bring the competing approaches into the open from the start in order to enable the political and technical assumptions to be unpacked and disaggregated. In his first working paper, Hoffmann posed four fundamental questions and requested delegations to send him their written responses:

- What are the main objectives of the verification of the treaty's basic obligations?
- What would be the components of such a verification system? Aside from seismic monitoring and on-site inspection, should the treaty envisage other measures such as radionuclide and hydroacoustic monitoring?
- What do we mean by a "cost effective" verification? What could one reasonably expect to verify and how much would it cost?
- If one opts for an "evolutionary approach", should the treaty itself provide for a mechanism (and resources) to develop and evaluate other monitoring techniques?[7]

Though not all delegations responded, Hoffmann received enough replies to be able to assess the differing priorities more clearly. There was widespread agreement on having an IMS comprising four basic detection technologies—seismic, radionuclide, hydroacoustic and infrasound—and some sort of provision for on-site inspections. What Hoffmann called the "evolutionary approach" was advocated by Russia, and came to be widely supported among the non-aligned states. In contrast to China, which proposed the inclusion of satellites in the IMS, and some of the proposals from the United States, Russia wanted the verification system to begin with a pragmatic baseline, allowing for the gradual inclusion of "new methods and technical means that would increase the reliability and quality of the CTBT compliance verification".[8] The evolutionary concept was immediately opposed by France, the United Kingdom and the United States, which portrayed it as tantamount to agreeing to open-ended verification. To understand how these differences were resolved, the following section considers the development of the IMS in more detail.

THE INTERNATIONAL MONITORING SYSTEM

The development of the IMS was the most genuinely multilateral process in the entire negotiations. There were three related reasons for this: effective management and continuity of coordination, conscious attempts to disaggregate issues and depoliticize disagreements, and the direct, accountable engagement of scientists and technical experts from a number of non-nuclear-weapon as well as nuclear-weapon state delegations. With regard to the latter, the treaty also benefited from the years of scientific preparation by the Ad Hoc Group of Scientific Experts to Consider International Cooperative Measures to Detect and to Identify Seismic Events, known as the GSE, which was established in 1976 at the insistence of a group of non-nuclear and non-aligned states, in part to counteract CTBT opponents' portrayal of a ban on underground testing as unverifiable.[9] As negotiations commenced, four test sites remained operational: the Nevada Test Site was used by both the United States and the United Kingdom, under the auspices of the US Department of Energy; China's tests were carried out at Lop Nor in Xingjiang Province; the main French test site in the South Pacific encompassed the adjacent coral atolls of Moruroa and Fangataufa; and Russia retained operational facilities on both the north and south islands of Novaya Zemlya. The principal Soviet test site at Semipalatinsk in Kazakhstan had been closed in 1989 and was in the process of being dismantled.

Although there were many differences of view regarding the number, distribution and location of the various sensors, there were only three major disputes, each of which pitted one of the nuclear powers against the majority of participants in the negotiations.[10] The most difficult of these to resolve was China's insistence (with support from Pakistan) that the IMS must include satellites and electromagnetic pulse monitoring and should omit the infrasound network. The second problem concerned the analysis of data by the International Data Centre (IDC). The United States, the only country to have direct experience running a prototype IDC, argued that the massive amount of data from an IMS should only be processed to the extent of producing a bulletin of detected events, and then it should be disseminated and archived, leaving all interpretation to individual states parties. Fearing that the majority, lacking adequate resources to analyse such data, would be disenfranchised, the G-21 pushed for the IDC to provide more "user friendly" reports, with some analysis and at least preliminary identification of any events that could be clearly identified as of natural origin. As the IMS was being concluded in 1996, Russia also sparked a short-lived but politically problematic dispute over additional test site monitoring.

The principal coordinator throughout the IMS negotiations was Peter Marshall, a British scientist based at Blacknest, the verification wing of the Aldermaston Atomic Weapons Establishment. A seismologist by training,

Marshall had considerable expertise in monitoring technologies and had participated in the tripartite testing talks as part of the British delegation in 1977–1980. He also had significant multilateral experience, having been a member of the GSE since its inception in 1976. This gave him the advantage of being well known and already respected among many of the scientists from other delegations. In 1994, he was appointed Friend of the Chair on Non-Seismic Verification, with Ajit Kumar of India providing diplomatic oversight of the seismic component of the IMS, working closely with the GSE. In 1995, Patrick Cole of Australia was appointed Friend of the Chair for the IMS, tasked with negotiating treaty language on the technical options being worked out among the scientists. Marshall, made responsible for technical verification, carried on with his work to develop the IMS, while Ralph Alewine of the United States was appointed to coordinate negotiations on the IDC. These scientists and diplomats worked exceptionally well together and were reappointed to the same positions in 1996 in order to finalize agreement on the architecture of the IMS and its appropriate representation in treaty text. One of Marshall's most notable contributions was his ability to demystify verification approaches and technologies, unpack complex issues, and represent technical and financial options in ways that were more easily understood, thereby helping the less technically resourced delegations to be more confident about the decisions being taken. By deliberately highlighting the policy implications of different technical options that the Working Group put forward, his strategy (paradoxically, some might think) helped to depoliticize the disagreements.

In the first year, the competing claims of seven technologies were discussed in the verification working group: seismic, radionuclide, hydroacoustic, infrasound, ground-based optical, ground-based electromagnetic pulse detection, and satellite-based detection.[11] Under Marshall's direction, the experts developed six options for consideration, examining detection capabilities for explosions of three standard yields. Four options were offered for the anticipated baseline of 1kt yield. Options were also provided in case a higher baseline of 5kt were chosen or the negotiators decided to have a more extensive monitoring capability, using the much lower baseline of 100t.[12]

To be effective, the verification system would need to be closely linked with the scope of the treaty, and there was anxiety early on that the options might allow the P-5 to continue testing to the identified thresholds. When 1kt was formally accepted as the baseline criterion, Marshall addressed this concern, emphasizing that the baseline was a practical measure for designing a cost-effective system and must not be confused with a threshold.[13] The baseline determination reflected two kinds of assessment: the need to keep costs at feasible levels; and the scientists' confidence that the synergistic use of the IMS technologies would ensure that nuclear explosive testing at much lower levels would, in practice, be detected. The uncertainty factor was expected to provide a high deterrent value even for much smaller yields.[14]

The seismic signature

The core of the IMS is the seismic network. An underground explosion generates seismic waves which can be analysed to locate and identify the origin of the waves. As nuclear explosions have a characteristic signature, seismic stations can also distinguish between earthquakes and explosions. Much work had already been done on seismic verification, principally through the work of the GSE, including its three technical tests of potential seismic networks. As negotiations got underway in the verification Working Group, there was much discussion of the number and location of primary and auxiliary seismic stations that would be needed to provide cost-effective verification confidence.

Primary stations, as the name implies, were to form the essential network in strategically significant locations for detection and identification of any explosions carried out in violation of the treaty. Some were already in place under national auspices, but others would need to be upgraded or built. The auxiliary seismic stations were considered to be less vital, but could provide useful information. In most cases, these were already part of national or academic facilities, and most would be completely or partly funded from national resources. In both cases, arrangements would need to be agreed for how the data from these seismic stations would be transmitted to the IDC.

Some states were concerned about the expense and inconvenience of having stations on national territory, and some were wary of stations being located close to sensitive facilities. Others were keen to host a station, perceiving it as an opportunity for closer participation in international projects and research. With Marshall's careful management, the majority of such concerns were resolved. In January 1996, however, after the IMS was thought to be substantially finalized, Russia made a late proposal for four additional seismic and radionuclide stations close to the major P-5 test sites.

Claiming that Novaya Zemlya was more closely monitored than Nevada, Berdennikov publicly argued for "identical transparency".[15] The assumption of many diplomats at the time was that this demand was in reaction to the zero-yield scope decision, which Russia had not participated in making. This was later confirmed, with the explanation that the zero-yield decision altered Russia's view of IMS requirements since it would be necessary to have confidence that none of the nuclear-weapon states would be able to carry out clandestine nuclear testing at sub-kiloton yields using existing nuclear test facilities.[16]

Though the demand was mainly directed at the United States, it was China that objected most vociferously. In an oblique reference to mutual support between the Chinese and Russian delegations over issues such as PNE and on-site inspections, China objected that Lop Nor was more closely monitored than the global average in any case and rejected any further enhancement of the detection level as excessive and unacceptable.[17] Ignoring the fact that the P-5 were more capable of conducting (and concealing) nuclear tests than the global average, China based its objection on the principle that the verification system must be equal and non-discriminatory. Concerned to avoid a late rupture in agreement, the United States took the lead in bridge-building to resolve the conflict. After initiating hurried talks among the P-5, the United States then negotiated directly with Russia, to whom it offered bilateral confidence-building measures, and then addressed Beijing's concerns with the Chinese delegation. In the end it was agreed that the location of one seismic station would be changed from California to Nevada, closer to the US test site, and that the station located in Kazakhstan would be upgraded and moved nearer to the border with China, thereby bringing it closer to Lop Nor without requiring explicit Chinese agreement.[18] The incident took the CD by surprise because Russia had generally been very constructive in the verification negotiations, and the way in which the demand was made seemed to echo the Cold War times when arguments about verification masked other political, ideological or power struggles.

Detecting airborne radioactivity

The second network to be incorporated into the IMS was designed to detect and measure the radioactive products emitted from a nuclear explosion, which could take the form of particulates or gases. These emissions can be distinguished from similar fission products released by nuclear power plant operations or accidents. Although there was general agreement that radionuclide sampling would be necessary to detect and identify atmospheric tests or venting from underground or underwater explosions, there were two areas of contention: whether it was necessary to monitor for the emission of noble gases, such as argon-37, xenon-133 and krypton-85; and whether specially equipped aircraft could play a useful role. Experts from two delegations were charged with the task of analysing how radionuclides would disperse according to geographical and meteorological conditions. Aiming for 90% detection probability of a 1kt explosion within 14 days, the experts recommended a radionuclide detection network comprising some 70–80 stations and 5–10 radionuclide laboratories around the world.[19]

On the grounds that radioactive noble gases produced by nuclear explosions are known to leak from underground explosions,[20] eventually all but one delegation in the Radionuclide Expert Group (a subgroup of the verification committee) agreed that noble gas monitoring should be included in the IMS. They reasoned that noble gases could play a unique and valuable role in early detection and identification (within 10 days) of an explosion in several potential environments, contributing especially to early resolution of ambiguous events, which would be politically desirable. Noble gas monitoring would also assist in detecting a decoupled explosion (conducted in a deep cave or salt cavern, for example, with the intention of masking the signals) and increase the costs and risks to a potential violator, thereby maximizing the deterrent function of the verification regime. China's experts disagreed. They argued that the effectiveness of noble gas monitoring was difficult to judge but would significantly increase the overall costs of the IMS. In Beijing's view, noble gas monitoring would only contribute to the detection of underground or underwater testing if sensors were located very close to the event. China was willing to include testing for noble gas emissions as part of an on-site inspection, but pointed out that certain time-critical phenomena, such as the presence of xenon-133, would disappear after two weeks.[21] Appearing to endorse Russia's concept of evolutionary verification, on which it had remained hitherto silent, China argued that the question of adding a noble gas monitoring capability should be deferred; if more technical study showed that inclusion was warranted, such monitoring could be added at a later stage.[22] During the final concession trading of the endgame, China accepted Ramaker's draft incorporating noble gas sensors co-located with 40 of the 80 radionuclide stations.

A second disagreement arose because Russia wanted fewer ground-based radionuclide sensors than was being considered in any of Marshall's options. Russia proposed that it would be more cost-effective to equip three special aircraft instead, and that these could be quickly dispatched after a suspicious event was detected by other technologies. Russia's reasoning was that a CTBT violation was likely to be rare, and that maintaining a full radionuclide monitoring network in perpetuity would be very expensive, whereas appropriately equipped airplanes could be quickly made ready to fly over the suspected location of an event, with sensors to detect particulates and noble gases, enabling samples to be taken in various atmospheric layers.[23] Others, however, worried about the timing and terms (ownership, responsibility for equipping, personnel training, piloting and so forth) that would govern the deployment of the aircraft. In the end, this issue was resolved through US-brokered concession trading in conjunction with the P-5 negotiations on Russia's proposal for identical transparency at the test sites. In return for two seismic stations being moved closer to the US and Chinese test sites, Russia abandoned the proposal for aircraft and agreed to the network of monitors outlined in Ramaker's draft treaty text.

Hearing underwater explosions

From the beginning there was agreement that there should be a hydroacoustic network for detecting explosions conducted underwater or underground in marine environments, such as the French test sites at Moruroa and Fangataufa. Such explosions generate soundwaves that can be detected by sensors thousands of kilometres away.[24] Negotiations focused on the number and location of hydroacoustic stations deemed necessary and most cost effective. Initially there was enthusiasm for 16 stations: four each to cover the Atlantic, Indian, and Pacific Oceans, plus a station south of Africa to cover both the Atlantic and Indian Oceans, and three auxiliary stations to aid location identification and to cover in the event of failure of one of the primary stations. Because of the high expense, this system was modified by agreement to a total of 11 stations, comprising six fixed cable hydrophone stations and five T-phase stations near coasts or on islands.[25]

Picking up shockwaves

A further technology, infrasound, was advocated by the majority of delegations to provide enhanced detection and location capabilities for nuclear explosions conducted in the atmosphere. Infrasound technology detects the shockwaves produced by nuclear explosions once they have decayed into low-frequency sound waves. For maximum effectiveness, the network was designed with microphones and microbarographs, organized in arrays of three or more sensors. Apart from China and Pakistan, which argued that satellite and electromagnetic pulse detection would be more effective and would obviate the necessity for infrasound coverage, there was an early majority for including an infrasound network of around 60 sensors in the IMS. When Beijing finally accepted that satellite monitoring would not be included in the IMS, both China and Pakistan also withdrew their objections to incorporating an infrasound network into the treaty.

Satellites and electromagnetic pulse monitoring

China's proposal for the IMS to include a CTBT-specific network of internationally funded satellites and electromagnetic pulse monitors proved very controversial. Arguing that both these technologies were essential for detecting and identifying nuclear explosions at high altitude or in space, as well as being useful to monitor potential sites on the ground, China had proposed that a network of around 60 electromagnetic pulse sensors could be established at relatively low cost and would provide "high sensitivity, precise location and prompt response" for detecting nuclear explosions conducted in the upper atmosphere.[26] Viewing a CTBT-specific satellite system as prohibitively expensive, most delegations considered that the Comprehensive Nuclear-Test-Ban Treaty Organization (CTBTO) would be able to get such information as necessary from national and commercial satellites in any case.[27] By contrast with its position on satellites, which was shared only by Pakistan, there was wider interest in China's proposal for a ground-based system to enhance the location and identification capability for atmospheric and high-altitude tests. Concerns were raised about a high false-alarm rate due to lightning, however. China proposed that analytical software could be designed to discriminate between the EMP produced by lightning and by nuclear explosions, but other experts were sceptical that this would be possible. In the end, it was decided to leave satellites and electromagnetic pulse monitoring out of the IMS, though use could be made of such data provided from national or civilian capabilities.[28]

Interpreting IMS data

The IDC, modelled on the US experimental centre in Virginia, was intended to process huge amounts of data from the IMS stations. Among the many details that needed to be resolved, the question of IDC "products"—in effect, how often and in what form the IDC should transmit IMS data to states parties—became a focus for sharp disagreement in late 1995 and early 1996. Although discussed in the language of technical parameters for filtering and analysing data, the underlying issues were actually about participation, finance and cost effectiveness. Although some G-21 states would have preferred the IDC to be explicit if there were a violation, there was no serious or lasting dispute over the majority view that it was the responsibility of states parties to assess compliance, as this required the exercise of political judgement. In contention was what form of information, reports or bulletins the IDC should send out to enable states parties to exercise this role according to the treaty's purpose and requirements.

Though it was indisputable that the raw data would be unmanageable for most states parties, the United States took the view that the IDC should only process, compact and disseminate the data, arguing that anything more would usurp the responsibility of states parties to assess compliance. The US position ignored the fact that only a very few states had the technology to analyse the data in a timely, regular and effective manner. The US position was opposed by most of the delegations, who raised concerns that if the standard were based at the high level of US technological capability this would effectively exclude the majority from decision-making.[29]

The Friend of the Chair on the IDC for most of 1995 and 1996 was a member of the US delegation, Ralph Alewine. An expert on the technology, Alewine's attempts to resolve the issue failed to pay sufficient attention to the concerns of less technologically resourced countries. In February 1996, for example, Alewine put out a working paper with three options, presenting the one closest to the US position as the cheapest for the CTBTO to provide. Other negotiators, however, pointed out that for states wishing to participate fully in decision-making, this option would actually be the most expensive on a national basis.[30] Weighing in on the side of the less-developed states, whose concerns were being ignored, Germany was the first Western ally to take a public stand against the US position. Commenting that all the options put forward by Alewine were simply different degrees of technical evaluation and screening of data, Germany advocated making use of IDC expertise to provide substantial filtering for the data. This would be more cost effective in the long run and would ensure greater participation by states with limited technical capabilities of their own.[31] Germany's intervention and technical expertise enabled Ramaker to propose an alternative based on Alewine's second option, in accordance with which the IDC would screen data in accordance with internationally standardized criteria established by the CTBTO, filter it according to nationally requested criteria, and provide some additional technical assistance to states parties. Characterized as "enhanced option 2", this was finally accepted by the United States and others in May 1996.

With conclusion of the provisions for the IDC, the IMS was able to be agreed. It was to comprise 50 primary seismic stations and 120 auxiliary seismic stations; 80 radionuclide stations, of which 40 would be equipped to monitor noble gases; 11 hydroacoustic stations; and 60 infrasound monitors.[32]

ON-SITE INSPECTIONS

Negotiations about on-site inspections—the direct, physical examination of a suspected site or facility—and the related questions of whether and how data from NTM would be incorporated, were very different from the cooperative multilateralism of the IMS negotiations. Laying bare governments' concerns about national security and spying, as well as rights, sovereignty and equality under international law, these talks pitted the verification requirement of timely access to evidence against states' anxieties about interference in their internal affairs. In particular contention were "challenge inspections", which the implementing organization might initiate at short notice. Although it was generally assumed that challenge inspections would primarily be called for in the event of a suspicion being raised, there was an additional rationale: as with random drug testing of athletes, it was believed that if a state knew it could be required to allow an inspection at short notice at any time, it would be deterred from cheating.

Another issue that came up was that of "managed access" at sensitive sites, in recognition of the fact that sites of potential interest to test-ban inspectors might have commercially or militarily sensitive facilities and technologies outside of the CTBT's scope, which a state should have the right to conceal from inspectors. At issue was how a state party could participate in managing the inspection so as to give sufficient access to inspectors for them to have confidence in that state's compliance with the CTBT, while also protecting against espionage that could potentially undermine its commercial or security interests.

Such questions were not new for the CTBT. For much of the 1960s through the 1980s, disagreements over the requirements and modalities of inspections and access had pitted Soviet and US negotiators against each other. The Reagan administration raised the standard verification requirement from "adequate" to "effective", and for many American policymakers, effective verification meant on-site inspections (OSI); the terms were employed politically as if they were synonymous.[33] In this context, OSI were a potent tool of confrontation. The US government would call for intrusive inspections as a means of undercutting Soviet disarmament proposals, putting Moscow on the defensive and enabling Washington to take the political high ground, while garnering domestic and international support. Bureaucratic manoeuvring over OSI also became a tactic in Washington's domestic arguments over arms control.[34] After the inability to agree on intrusive inspections ruined the chances of the Eisenhower and Kennedy administrations to achieve a ban on underground tests, little progress was made until the mid-1980s when, in a radical departure from previous Soviet policy, Gorbachev accepted intrusive inspections in order to secure the Intermediate-range Nuclear Forces Treaty.[35] Gorbachev's reversal of the traditional Soviet position also had impact on the Chemical Weapons Convention (CWC), concluded just before the CD embarked on the CTBT. It is worth briefly recalling what happened when those talks wrestled with on-site inspections, as these recent experiences left their mark on the CTBT negotiations.

The requirements of inspections and access had been hard fought in the CWC, with the main protagonists switching positions, partners and priorities over the adequacy and "bearability" of levels of access and intrusion.[36] In 1984, US Vice President George Bush had tabled a draft treaty text containing provisions for a select group of states parties on a "fact-finding panel" to call for short-notice, "anytime, anywhere" inspections of suspected facilities and sites. After accepting the principle of intrusive inspections in the Intermediate-range Nuclear Forces Treaty, President Gorbachev in 1988 indicated his willingness to agree to "anytime, anywhere" inspections in the CWC. The Soviet acceptance of the US position threw Washington into confusion. Amid interagency vacillation and conflict between arms controllers and the intelligence agencies, the United States retreated from its own demands and then undertook a further interagency review. After reportedly fraught domestic negotiations, the United States in July 1991 proposed a much weaker, long drawn out process that contradicted the concept and purpose of short-notice challenge inspections. During the difficult negotiations that ensued, the United States was opposed by most of its allies, but found that China, India, Iran and Pakistan gave guarded approval to this weaker proposal. Overruling strong objections from their own experts, Australia, Japan and the United Kingdom took a formal position of supporting the United States for alliance reasons, while others, notably Canada, France, Germany and the Netherlands, opposed any weakening of the procedures for enabling intrusive inspections, if deemed necessary. This latter position was reinforced by post-Gulf War revelations in 1991–1992 that showed how Saddam Hussein had evaded the IAEA safeguards inspections. This led the majority of states to support wide powers of inspection for the Organisation for the Prohibition of Chemical Weapons (OPCW), including the right to conduct short-notice inspections at undeclared as well as declared sites. Australia subsequently put forward a modified provision for challenge inspections, including UK proposals for managed access and mechanisms to deter governments from making frivolous or hostile inspection requests. The United States accepted this Anglo-Australian compromise, which was then incorporated into the treaty.[37]

Opinions differ about why the US position changed so dramatically during the negotiations. Some suggest that the "anytime, anywhere" position of 1984 was political posturing to embarrass the Soviet Union, which was never expected to accept such a position.[38] An alternative, not incompatible, analysis emphasizes the role and intensified engagement of the US defence and intelligence communities and chemical industries once the convention appeared to be achievable. Some of the major US opponents of setting an "anytime, anywhere" precedent on inspections in the convention may well have had responsibilities for dealing with nuclear weapons, and on both sides there were concerns that such a precedent could provide spying opportunities for military or commercial adversaries.[39]

The CWC's provisions for mandatory, short-notice "challenge" inspections with procedures for "managed access" to protect sensitive information or sites not related to the convention have been described by one enthusiastic observer as its "crowning glory".[40] However, the impact on the CTBT was not all positive. Many CTBT negotiators were involved in this recent history, with some of the same people in positions of authority in their respective ministries or CD delegations. It was therefore inevitable that there should be some spillover from the chemical weapons negotiations into the CTBT, as some participants attempted to reinforce and others to renegotiate the precedents set by the CWC on inspections and other approaches.

The United States, for example, reverted to a more familiar posture and pushed for the CTBT to have a stringent inspections provision based on simplified decision-making and early access. France and the United Kingdom shared the US emphasis on quick access and the prompt gathering of time-critical evidence, such as aftershocks and the venting of short-lived radioactive gases. However, France and the United Kingdom were more prepared than the United States to compromise on questions of decision-making and access. Russia accepted some of these positions, but favoured early provision for consultations and clarification, though with greater flexibility about its terms and timing. Though a little further from US policy than the two European nuclear-weapon states, Russia sided with the United States on most technical issues while taking a more cautious approach on the procedures:

> On-site inspection is the most important part of the international regime for verifying observance of the CTBT. It is in the nature of an exception, being resorted to only in the most serious situations, when there are genuine doubts about the observance of the Treaty, based on the identification of an ambiguous event having the characteristics of a nuclear explosion.[41]

China took the opposite extreme, fearing interference in its sovereign affairs and raising objections about espionage.[42] China, India, Israel and Pakistan argued that OSI should be a tool of last resort, used rarely, and only undertaken if a mandatory period of consultations failed to resolve an ambiguous data record or suspicious event. Israel, which for most of the negotiations had kept a low profile and slipstreamed with US positions, on OSI took a line that was much closer to that of China than the United States. In this, Israel's principal concern was to prevent hostile neighbours using the provision to gain access to its sensitive facilities.[43]

Intrusion versus protection

Though deliberations on OSI began at the same time as other issues, actual negotiations did not get going until the final year. The first two years of negotiations focused on technical questions, bringing out—but failing to address—the conflicting sensitivities that were to polarize the endgame.

Marking the nuclear superpowers' new-found collaboration on this issue, Victor Slipchenko, Friend of the Chair, appointed US delegation member John Zucca to head an expert group to consider the detectable characteristics, termed "manifestations or residual effects", of nuclear detonations and evasion scenarios in various environments. After much discussion, in which experts from the P-5 were most prominent, Zucca's list of what evidence might reveal a clandestine nuclear explosion was similar to that developed by the Geneva Conference of Experts forty years earlier.[44] Ruling out OSI in space and the upper atmosphere, the experts' report focused on testing in the lower atmosphere, underground and underwater environments, with particular emphasis on underground scenarios. They identified time-critical manifestations such as aftershocks, radioactive xenon gas,[45] and human-generated artefacts such as roads, debris or tailings, which could be quickly concealed or altered. Less time-critical manifestations included surface cratering; underground cavities and rubble zones; residual underground radioactivity; alterations in topography, notably surface changes due to the effects of spallation; radioactive argon gas;[46] changes in ground water level; and anomalies of heat, pressure and gas flow within the fractured geology.[47]

Zucca's report was not intended to address political questions as such, but he did acknowledge the political sensitivity of questions relating to information and procedures for "triggering" and deciding on an inspection, timing, the size of the inspection area, restriction of access in the event of national security sensitivities, and the terms and requirements, if any, of a consultation and clarification process. Since there was general agreement on what on-site inspections would look for, discussion in 1995 tended to concentrate on those and avoid addressing the politically-sensitive issues. Until the scope was agreed, there was little pressure to resolve other issues. Many delegations put forward working papers, but they did little more than exchange information on national positions. By the end of 1995, the problems and disagreements relating to inspections could be summed up as a series of questions. First, and most importantly, by whom should an inspection request be made—states parties only, the CTBTO, or both? Secondly, there was the question of what kind of evidence would be permissible to use when making an inspection request: data from the IMS only, or would information acquired through national intelligence, other NTM or commercial satellites be acceptable as well? If so, should such information be evaluated on the same terms as IMS data or accorded different weight?

Observers were especially bemused to hear negotiators argue about the merits of "red light" or "green light" decision-making processes. Assuming an Executive Council with the right and responsibility to authorize inspections, should the procedure be made easy (given the green light), for the sake of speed, or more stringent, to avoid unnecessary intrusion on a state's sovereign territory? Confusingly for some, the "red light" was less stringent because it provided for a requested inspection to be conducted automatically unless the Executive Council voted to stop it (thus giving it the red light), for which it would require a specified majority (the options were for a simple, two-thirds or three-quarters majority). Under the "green light" procedure, the Executive Council would be required to consider any inspection request, which would only proceed if it were "given the green light" on the basis of Council agreement by a specified majority, with most interest in a majority of two thirds or three quarters of the members of the Council.

When negotiations reconvened in January 1996, the competing approaches to inspections had been narrowed down to three broad issues: the role of transparency, consultations and clarification; the informational basis on which an inspection could be triggered (that is, a determination of the role of NTM); and the questions relating to the decision-making process, access, timelines and whether inspections should be undertaken in phases. Each of these issues hinged to some degree on the others, and all required political decisions that carried sensitivities among powerful domestic interest groups dealing with intelligence and national security.

Transparency

During the negotiations on the CWC an important distinction had been drawn between routine inspections, aimed at verifying declarations (while also monitoring for signs of undeclared activity), and challenge inspections, triggered if there were suspicions that the treaty had been violated.[48] Given the nature of nuclear tests, routine inspections were dismissed as unnecessary, but suggestions were made to open certain areas or activities to transparency measures. The major concerns focused on the former nuclear test sites, mining areas, locations of large chemical explosions, and caverns with potential for decoupling or masking nuclear explosions. The proposed transparency measures included declaration and notification prior to activities that might be misinterpreted by the IMS, and information and clarification following any anomalous seismic event or release of radioactivity.

In addition to the nuclear-weapon states, some non-nuclear-weapon states were also divided about transparency and what would constitute effective—and cost-effective—verification. The possibility of having observers in the event of particularly large chemical explosions was raised, but this was rejected as overly expensive and time-consuming. Sweden advocated notifying the CTBTO of chemical explosions above 500t, but Australia and Canada (both of which had to pay attention to the concerns of their commercial mining companies) argued against, on grounds that this "would serve no useful purpose without an observer being present at the time of the blast".[49] Instead, they proposed that there should be transparency measures with respect to the former nuclear test sites, as well as declarations on the locations of frequent or significant explosions. They also proposed technology sharing to enable more states to make use of special mining techniques, such as ripple firing, that were regarded as less likely to be confused with the seismic signature of a nuclear explosion. Neither these ideas, nor potential requirements if Germany and Sweden were successful in their early proposal for the treaty scope to cover preparations for testing, survived the opposition of the nuclear-weapon states.[50] Associated with transparency and confidence-building measures, most states argued that there should be an opportunity for consultation and clarification following detection of an ambiguous event, but they disagreed on whether consultations should be mandatory, prior to an inspection request, and if so for how long and between whom—just the challenging state party and the challenged state party, or should the Technical Secretariat or the Executive Council be involved at this stage?

Phased inspections, decision-making and access

As some states questioned the actual importance of evidence deemed time critical, such as local aftershocks and the venting of xenon gas, the United States promoted the idea of challenge inspections in phases, augmenting the level of intrusion if successive phases were warranted by a failure to resolve the ambiguity or suspicion in an earlier phase. The concept of a three-phase process was first put forward in June 1994.[51] After refining its approach, more as a result of discussions among its domestic experts than negotiations with other delegations, the United States put forward further proposals in June and July 1995, this time advocating that there should be two discrete phases.[52] In the US view, a two-phase approach would "balance ... the competing requirements for ... quick and early access to an inspection site, cost effectiveness, limited intrusiveness, and prevention of frivolous and abusive [inspection] requests".[53]

If on-site inspections were to be conducted in phases, this would have implications for the decision-making process: for example, would an Executive Council decision be required for each phase or could the next phase proceed automatically if the inspection team considered it needed further data? In the US proposal, each phase would need to be requested by a state party, but there was also the option of choosing means other than inspections, including direct consultations, to clarify ambiguous events. A challenging state party would have to balance the political circumstances and risks of being judged to have made a frivolous or abusive request, but "if states parties act responsibly, the US approach will keep the number of [inspections and their] costs manageable".[54] In addition, the United States suggested that investigations into ambiguous events outside the jurisdiction of any particular state party, such as in international waters, could be undertaken by one or more states parties individually, with or without the involvement of the Technical Secretariat.[55] The G-21 immediately objected to extending an individual state's investigating rights in this way, countering that the CTBTO should have "exclusive responsibility" for inspections "in areas both within and beyond the jurisdiction or control of States parties".[56]

As the US delegation argued strenuously for phased inspections, the rest of the P-5 were divided along unusual lines. China and France appeared initially open but wanted to discuss ideas that would significantly modify the US concept. Russia and the United Kingdom opposed the two-phase approach altogether, preferring there to be one request and one decision, although they had different views about what the actual decision mechanism should be. China advocated a mandatory consultation and clarification process of up to three days and a consideration and preparation stage taking up to three weeks. The Chinese delegation consequently suggested that a less intrusive inspection, not exceeding 15 days, could be followed by a second phase of up to 30 days. Both phases would require a vote in favour by a two-thirds majority of the Executive Council.[57] Russia preferred either a voluntary or compulsory consultation and clarification process, arguing that inspections, though an essential part of the verification regime, should be presumed an exception. Reasoning that "as a rule, all other possibilities of clearing up the situation will be exhausted before a request is made for inspection",[58] Russia wanted there to be a single decision to undertake an inspection, taken within seven days of the initial request by a state party. The decision would need a vote in favour by a two-thirds majority of the Executive Council. Suggesting a maximum of 40 days per inspection unless drilling were necessary, Russia emphasized that there needed to be some flexibility. The time frame should be determined by the type of ambiguous event and evidence available: up to the designated maximum, an inspection should be able to be extended or terminated early depending on the evidence. If drilling were required, a separate decision should be taken by the Director-General and confirmed by the Executive Council permitting an additional 50 days for this purpose.[59]

Outside the P-5, the D-3 were the most active participants in the negotiations over OSI. Both India and Pakistan joined China in advocating a mandatory period of consultation and clarification; they argued that only if this had failed to resolve the ambiguity should the challenging state party's request for an inspection be submitted to the Executive Council, which would then have to provide authorization by a "green-light" vote of either a two-thirds or three-quarters majority for the inspection to proceed. Maintaining that on-site inspections should not be conducted in a "hasty manner", Pakistan also questioned the premise on which the two-phase argument rested, claiming that in a well-camouflaged test, noble gas releases and aftershocks could be made negligible.[60]

During the negotiations, Israel put in a number of working papers relating to inspection procedures and technologies, even proposing draft treaty text to ensure the protection of confidentiality and national security under the verification regime, particularly with respect to inspections. Up to that point, Israel—the only D-3 state not then a member of the CD—had participated in the CTBT negotiations, but was rather quiet and unobtrusive on most issues.[61] It was assumed that Israel was in close consultation with the United States and in agreement with its major positions. With respect to OSI, however, Israel's military and intelligence lobbies were active in pushing for a slower, more restrictive and much less intrusive provision than demanded by the United States. Concerned that some of its neighbours might use the provision to demand frequent inspections at the Dimona nuclear facility or elsewhere, Israel's positions were almost diametrically opposed to the US proposals on three major issues: elevating the role of the Technical Secretariat and diminishing the rights of states parties in making inspection requests, a long mandatory consultation period, and stringent decision-making procedures. For example, Israel opposed phased inspections and wanted authorization to be on the basis of one "green-light" decision, requiring the positive vote of a two-thirds majority. In the Israeli view, although a treaty party may submit a request, with evidence, it should be the Technical Secretariat rather than an individual state that would have the primary right to request an inspection. Moreover, Israel wanted a time frame of 10 days for mandatory consultation, clarification and consideration of relevant information before any request would go before the Executive Council. Israel also pushed for inspected states parties to have the right to "exclude locations and facilities at the initial stage" of an inspection and "to exempt sensitive facilities from access on the basis of national security, proprietary rights and health and safety reasons".[62] If denying access, a state party would be required to "make every reasonable effort to demonstrate through alternative means that a nuclear explosion has not been conducted there" and should not invoke denial provisions to conceal a clandestine test.[63]

Despite acknowledging Israel's concerns and accepting that there might be a need for "managed access" to "protect certain sensitive facilities within the requested area from … intrusion", the US delegation maintained its position that the presumption should be full access, with restrictions only as the exception.[64] Managed access was a problem for more than just Israel. Russia also referred to the right to protect national security during an inspection by means of managed or regulated access, and proposed that the inspected state party could provide convincing evidence "that the excluded part of the region had no connection with the ambiguous event".[65]

National technical means

An issue that was discussed from the beginning and only resolved at the very end of the negotiations was whether to permit information derived from NTM to supplement IMS data or to support a request for an inspection. The US position was at one extreme, pushing for any kind of data to be permissible in support of a state party's request for inspection.[66] Arguing that NTM must be admitted as a legitimate component of CTBT verification, the United States frequently cited the discovery of Iraq's well-developed nuclear programme in 1991 as vindication of its position that a multilateral verification system could not be solely or fully relied on.[67] China and Pakistan were at the opposite extreme to the United States, and opposed any inclusion of information derived from NTM. Both claimed to have been the victims of false US intelligence, a point underlined by Sha Zukang when he spoke of "a self-assumed mandate as a 'world police'".[68] As far as China was concerned, sovereign states were entitled to develop NTM for the purposes of conducting activities "within the scope of their sovereignty", but because NTM were "inherently selective, arbitrary and subjective" it would be "unacceptable" for states to take advantage of NTM outside their own jurisdiction.[69]

One difficulty for this debate was that NTM meant different things to different participants. France, Russia and the United Kingdom, and indeed most of the Western and Eastern European delegations, favoured incorporation of some kinds of NTM data to complement the IMS, but the major states disagreed about where and how to draw the line. Russia, for example, supported inclusion of IMS-type data but wanted definite exclusion of communications intercepts (COMINT) and human intelligence (HUMINT), which it characterized as espionage. G-21 members largely supported the concerns raised by China and Pakistan during the first two years of negotiations, basing their arguments more generally on the principle of non-discrimination and the mandate's injunction that the treaty should be "multilaterally verifiable". They did not want to legitimize a means of verification that would be available only to a few privileged states, and which could be exercised in exclusive, discriminatory or abusive ways.[70] Countering the G-21, the United States insisted that the mandate also required the treaty to be "effectively verifiable", which it would not be if it prevented nationally sourced information from being utilized to supplement potential inadequacies in the multilateral system.[71]

Ambassador Ledogar portrayed on-site inspections and the permissibility of NTM in its widest sense as treaty-breakers for the US government.[72] Anxious to avoid a deadlock, other negotiators put forward suggestions for the limited incorporation of NTM, both to meet some of the concerns from China and the G-21 about discriminatory use and also in the hope of developing a precedent for a more accountable incorporation of data and evidence acquired from national sources. Some of these bridging proposals avoided referring directly to NTM by using the euphemistic term "any other information" and while addressing US concerns, sought to soften the rigidity of its posture. France, for example, made the unusual proposal that inspections could be requested on the basis of information from the IMS or from national means, but that different weight should be accorded to each.[73] South Africa built on France's proposal, advocating an "objective" role for the CTBTO in evaluating nationally sourced data provided to it.[74] Israel proposed that states parties could put data from their national facilities at the disposal of the IDC, or even allow the IDC and Technical Secretariat direct access to some NTM data, thereby allowing for NTM but providing some level of screening and control of access and source.[75] Other states reinforced the concept of a limited legitimacy for NTM by offering to supply the IDC with data from their national laboratories.

As a consequence of a widening of the debate to include more middle-power non-nuclear-weapon states, a number of G 21 delegations began to show interest in considering how nationally or commercially acquired data could be used by the IDC. They became interested in ideas for how the verification regime might benefit from NTM without surrendering its independence to the power of certain states with extensive and sophisticated surveillance and intelligence resources. With the apparent aim of preventing such slippage among those whose backing it had cultivated, China underlined in further working papers its strongly held case for opposing NTM. In a textbook example of hostage-taking tactics, China reiterated in September 1995 that "no NTM should be allowed" in the IMS, and then stated that it would "not accept the triggering of OSI by NTM data or 'any other information'".[76]

The bridging efforts began to bear fruit in early 1996. When Iran tabled its draft treaty text, it revealed that one of the staunchest opponents of NTM was prepared to compromise. While maintaining that inspections be based solely on IMS data, Iran's draft allowed for supplementary information to be considered by the Technical Secretariat.[77] The US delegation continued to reject all such compromises, arguing that they would not be convincing to the US intelligence agencies and Senate when the time came to ratify the CTBT. Running out of time, and faced with intransigence from both China and the United States, Ramaker took the view that NTM should be "acceptable in principle, but not in any unqualified manner", and in his 28 June draft treaty text he included provisions that would allow any relevant information, including national technical means, "consistent with generally recognised principles of international law", a phrase understood to exclude espionage. This satisfied the United States and Russia, but a number of other delegations continued to raise concerns about legitimizing NTM.

Ramaker undertook further consultations, with particular emphasis on the objections from China and Pakistan, as well as similar concerns raised by India and Iran. Aware of the kinds of questions likely to be raised in the United States by Senators, the Department of Defense and intelligence officials during debates over ratifying the CTBT, Ledogar continued to insist that the issue was a treaty-breaker. As a consequence, Ramaker decided not to risk altering the treaty text. Instead, he made a statement on the record (incorporated also in his report) to allay some delegations' expressed fears about the possibility of abuse of NTM or on-site inspections. In this statement, he emphasized that verification activities would be based on "objective information ... limited to the subject matter of the Treaty" and carried out on the basis of "full respect for the sovereignty of states parties".[78] This gave the United States what it needed and, though it did not fully satisfy the others, they accepted that it was the best deal they were likely to get.

Make-or-break dilemmas

The Australian and Iranian model texts of February 1996 were also helpful in facilitating convergence on other aspects relating to on-site inspections because they encompassed broadly similar approaches, though there were also some important differences. Both favoured a presumption of access with two phases for inspections. For the initial phase, Australia echoed the French proposal for different decision-making procedures depending on whether the request was based on IMS data or solely on NTM. Iran proposed that an inspection request could rely only on IMS data and advocated a simple "red-light" process by which a positive vote of three-quarters of the Executive Council would be necessary to prevent the initial phase of an OSI from going ahead. Both drafts proposed a two-thirds majority to enable any subsequent phase to proceed.[79]

As most delegations shifted their positions toward the middle ground, Ramaker attempted to negotiate a compromise between the US and Chinese poles. The Chair's 28 May draft specified that a simple "green light" majority decision of the Executive Council would be necessary to initiate an inspection. As is often the case with bridging proposals that split the difference, neither the United States nor China was very happy with this. But the US delegation, which had been consulted by Ramaker prior to his tabling the draft, said it could "live with it", while Sha Zukang declared that China would not.[80] Pointing to the distinction made elsewhere in the text between procedural matters (requiring a simple majority) and substantive matters, Sha Zukang stated that "the launching of an OSI can only be considered as a substantive issue", which would therefore require at least a two-thirds majority of the Executive Council.[81] Declaring that resolving this issue in accordance with the principles of "equality and justice" would determine "whether we can successfully conclude a CTBT and whether the treaty can attract universal adherence",[82] Sha also echoed Ledogar in telling negotiators that this was a "make or break" issue. During the intensive P-5 negotiations that ensued, France, Russia and the United Kingdom attempted to persuade the United States to show more flexibility by indicating that they would accept a "green light" decision-making process requiring approval by three fifths of the Executive Council, as China wanted. The United States at first refused to go beyond the simple majority in the Chair's draft. When Ramaker repeated this formula in the 28 June text, Sha Zukang stated again that unless the decision-making process reflected China's concerns, his country would be unable to sign the treaty.[83]

Insisting on bilateral negotiations with the United States, Sha Zukang moved from Beijing's preferred two thirds (34 members of the council) to propose three fifths as a bearable compromise, having previously ascertained that Britain, France and Russia would go along with this.[84] Ledogar acknowledged (without giving credence to) China's fears of being numerically overwhelmed on the Council by the United States and its allies. Since China had already come so far toward accepting the CTBT, the United States did not want it to join India in walking away. Despite having previously insisted that the Chair's text should not be reopened, the United States therefore agreed to an amendment whereby an on-site inspection would be authorized by "at least 30 affirmative votes" of the 51-member Council. This was the only substantive amendment to the 28 June text.[85]

The United States was not the only delegation to be concerned that requiring a "green light" decision of the Council to permit an inspection could cause delays, enabling time-critical evidence to be dispersed or erased. The treaty text dealt with this by providing a practical but strict timeline for the various stages between an inspection request and arrival at the site to be inspected, so that the time taken must not exceed one week. Hence, once an inspection was initiated, it could only be halted by a majority decision of the Council, or by recommendation of the inspection team (unless countermanded by the Council). If drilling needed to be conducted, a further "green light" decision of the Council would have to be sought.[86]

With regard to the strongly expressed concerns of Israel and Russia about intrusion and effectiveness, the Chair's text contained provisions for overflight and managed access. Although neither felt these provisions dealt with all their concerns, both were persuaded not to reopen negotiations. The envisaged time frame for an inspection was finalized at 60 days, with the possibility of an extension of up to 70 days, subject to a majority decision of the Council. Provisions covering the conduct of inspections were intended to diminish the opportunity for abuse while ensuring that the inspection team was not prevented from carrying out its mandate by undue delays or impediments. Responding to concerns about espionage expressed by India, Pakistan and others, Ramaker underlined that the sole purpose of an inspection was to gather any facts which might clarify whether a nuclear weapon test explosion had occurred and to assist in identifying a possible violator, and that requesting states were under an obligation to keep any inspection request within the scope of the treaty.[87]

Ramaker's compromise meant that states would be allowed to protect sensitive facilities and information unrelated to compliance with the treaty. Inspections would move from less intrusive to more intrusive procedures. In all cases, the decision to conduct an inspection would have to include approval of a concrete inspection plan and mandate drawn up by the Technical Secretariat. It was also decided that within 30 days of the treaty's entry into force (or a state's accession), that state should provide the CTBTO with a list of potential inspectors and sites, which would then be updated as appropriate. Provisions were also worked out for unusual circumstances, such as if the site under one state's jurisdiction or control was on the territory of another state (as with US bases in Europe or Japan). It was agreed that three observers from the requesting party or parties would be permitted to accompany the inspection team, subject to the inspected party's agreement on the actual personnel. Arising from the experiences of the UN inspections in Iraq, the treaty also enshrined privileges and immunities for personnel carrying out an inspection, consistent with diplomatic status.

In response to some delegations' concerns that the inspection process could be misused for other purposes, the treaty contained references to penalties in the event that the Executive Council deemed a request to have been "frivolous or abusive". Penalties could be financial (requiring the requesting state party to bear the costs incurred) or any of the measures in Article V, which covers the redressing of a situation, compliance and sanctions. Accordingly, failure to comply with treaty obligations or abuse of the treaty's provisions could incur a range of penalties, including suspension of membership rights and collective measures in conformity with international law. Cases of "particular gravity" could be taken to the United Nations. An earlier reference in the rolling text giving a role to the UN General Assembly and Security Council in the enforcement of the CTBT (not specific to, but inclusive of OSI) was left out of the final treaty text. Deriving from the problematic fact that the nuclear-weapon states were also the permanent members of the Security Council, opposition to giving the Security Council a formal role was based on many states' concerns that giving the Security Council an enforcement role could result in bias or prompt a misuse of the P-5's veto power to protect themselves or allies.[88]

ESTABLISHING THE CTBTO

Having decided that the CTBT would have a multilateral verification regime, negotiators also had to decide on the structure, composition and powers of an organization to oversee the verification system and implementation of the treaty. Although there had been an early bid by the IAEA, supported chiefly by Sweden, to be given the additional responsibilities of implementing and verifying the CTBT, consensus emerged for an independent organization—which soon acquired the abbreviation CTBTO.[89] Though other cities, notably Geneva, put in bids to host the CTBTO, there were strong incentives for it to be established in Vienna, where it could be co-located with the IAEA, and empowered to cooperate with the IAEA and other international organizations to "utilize existing expertise and resources, as appropriate, to maximize cost efficiencies".[90]

It did not take long for the CD to agree that the CTBTO should comprise a Conference of States Parties, expected to meet annually, an Executive Council, and a Technical Secretariat headed by a Director-General. The number and composition of seats on the Executive Council was more contentious. In the end, it was decided to have 51 seats on the Council (increased from the 45 originally proposed, following pressure from African and European delegations). These were allocated to six regions: 10 seats for Africa, 7 for Eastern Europe, 9 for Latin America, 7 for the Middle East and South Asia, 10 for North America and Western Europe, and 8 for South-East Asia, the Pacific and the Far East.[91] The regions differ from the UN's traditionally recognized five regions, and provoked some objections, notably from Middle Eastern states, which did not want Israel counted within their region. Israel, for its part, feared that if it were in the Middle East regional group it could be excluded from ever taking a seat on the Council. Meanwhile, the P-5 (echoed by the D-3) all wanted permanent seats on a Council that might sit in judgment on them.

After much wrangling, a complicated formula for seat allocation was agreed whereby one seat per region would be allocated by alphabetical rotation; one third of the seats per region would take into account certain criteria, including political and security interests, relevant nuclear capabilities, IMS facilities and expertise, and budgetary contribution to the CTBTO; the rest would be decided regionally by either election or rotation. The formula was intended to provide equitable regional participation and ensure that no state could be permanently excluded. It gave states that regarded themselves as potential targets of a challenge about non-compliance the assurance that they would have continuous seats on the Council, while avoiding the discriminatory overtones of conferring "permanent" seats on the P-5 or nuclear-capable states outside the NPT.

As this chapter closes, the narrative moves from analysing the 1994–1996 negotiations to consider the implications of these processes and outcomes for the future. The next chapter draws out the lessons of the CTBT history for future multilateral negotiations, with the intention of contributing to a better understanding of the dynamics of multilateral arms control and how outcomes can be more effectively shaped and implemented. The final, concluding chapter takes a look at the CTBT today, including the impasse over entry into force, and considers how the CTBTO has developed the verification regime from agreements in text to monitoring stations on the ground and an advanced data centre in Vienna to process the streams of information that come in daily.

CHAPTER 8

LESSONS FOR FUTURE MULTILATERAL SECURITY NEGOTIATIONS

First and foremost is intensive work with leaders of the countries in possession of nuclear weapons to turn the goal of a world without nuclear weapons into a joint enterprise.

George P. Shultz, William J. Perry,
Henry A. Kissinger and Sam Nunn,
4 January 2007[1]

The CTBT was negotiated as international relations underwent profound transformation at the end of the Cold War. But by the time the treaty was concluded in 1996, the enthusiasm for multilateral agreements that characterized the early 1990s was already coming under question. For the next decade, the politics of US neoconservatism made it even more difficult to address arms control through multilateral agreements, as sought-after measures such as a fissile materials treaty and a verification protocol for the Biological and Toxin Weapons Convention became blocked. This may continue or change as political relations among major states adjust and realign in the next decade. We could, for example, see renewed opportunities and pressure for multilateral negotiations on a fissile materials treaty, a treaty banning weapons in space or even a nuclear weapons convention. Or we could see existing treaties discredited and weakened by neglect, non-compliance or withdrawals. If multilateral disarmament and security treaties are put back on the agenda, it will be important to make the negotiations function more effectively. For this, we need a better understanding of the dynamics of multilateral negotiations and the conditions that must be put in place for multilateral arms control and disarmament regime-building to make progress.[2]

This chapter takes a closer look at the political strategies and perceived interests of the nuclear-armed states that the CTBT aimed to constrain.

After considering the differences between distributive and integrative approaches for reaching agreement in negotiations, the next section draws out the main lessons from the narratives in Chapters 3 to 7, with emphasis on the outcomes and negotiating experiences on scope, entry into force and verification, as well as how agreement was forged to enable the negotiations to get started. The chapter closes with consideration of how these lessons might be applied to enhance the conduct and outcomes of future multilateral negotiations.

Political and institutional factors are critical elements shaping multilateral negotiations in disarmament and arms control. As the first nuclear-weapons-related multilateral treaty to be negotiated in the post-Cold War era, the CTBT negotiations were at the interface of old and new thinking. The character, cast and changes (including elections) that affected the governments in some key states were undoubtedly significant, as were the configuration and processes of the CD, which was hobbled by Cold War rules of procedure while undergoing transition to expand the number of member states. In addition to dealing with the Cold War legacy, the CTBT outcome was shaped by factors of particular relevance to future multilateralism. These include the value accorded to norms and regimes; civil society engagement; knowledge and ideas; partnerships and alliances among negotiators and between certain states and NGOs; the level of domestic and international political attention and support in key states; and whether there was internal policy cohesion or division among the policymakers in the relevant governments.

Where the term "states" is used in this book, it is with the recognition that this is not "states as rational actors with fixed interests" as assumed in realist theories, but as "conditional entities"[3] and representative institutions "constantly subject to capture and recapture, construction and reconstruction"[4] by social and political actors. If an administration is changed, through election, coup or other kind of governmental transition, the state's objectives and strategies may correspondingly change. This was clearly demonstrated when Jacques Chirac became President after the French elections of May 1995. A general election campaign—especially if it is close fought—can have a significant effect on a government's policy, as illustrated by India in the year leading up to the Bharatiya Janata Party's election victory in mid-1996. The degree to which a state's objectives and posture change depends on the magnitude of the political differences between the outgoing and incoming administrations. If the distinctions are relatively weak, a change of party or government may have minimal effect on foreign policy. A coup or the election of a party with political and ideological precepts that are fundamentally different from those of the preceding government can result in a very significant shift in foreign policy or negotiating posture.

Power struggles among multiple domestic actors, agencies and pressure groups (be they bureaucratic, diplomatic, civil, military or political) may also cause shifts, fluctuations and sometimes contradictions in foreign policies, and can alter a state's negotiating positions.[5] While this analysis of the CTBT has been concerned with negotiating dynamics in the international arena rather than foreign policy formation, it has been important to consider the domestic, international and transboundary processes that influenced the policies of key actors at critical moments. The CTBT experience has borne out analyses of foreign policy formation as simultaneous action, reaction and interaction on the domestic and international levels to bring about a mutual shaping of agendas, options and interests.[6] The negotiations also confirmed that in diplomacy there is seldom a one-way linear process from determination of a state's policies to instructions from capitals and implementation by diplomats in the field. Although diplomats are charged with the task of carrying out instructions, there is a discernible feedback loop between the perceptions and objectives of experienced practitioners in the forum and the decision-making processes back home.

NUCLEAR WEAPONS, PROGRAMMES AND PERCEPTIONS OF NATIONAL INTEREST

The test-ban negotiations got going a year before the NPT was due to be considered for renewal. The rhetoric from all sides about the linked importance of these treaties suggested a general assumption that non-proliferation was a common "good". Yet this ostensibly shared objective masked differences of negotiating goals that correlated significantly with where a state was located on the spectrum of nuclear capabilities and interests.

Certain states dominated the negotiations because they saw themselves as having direct national interests at stake in terms of nuclear capability or ambition. For those officially acknowledged as having nuclear weapons programmes or aspirations, the CTBT would close off options that were currently considered open. All the others had voluntarily agreed to renounce these options by acceding to the NPT as non-nuclear-weapon states. It was thus no surprise that the P-5, defined as nuclear-weapon states under the NPT, and the D-3, who had de facto nuclear weapons, programmes or ambitions outside the NPT, played major roles in how the test-ban negotiations played out. Interests and capabilities among these eight were asymmetric, depending on the sophistication of the nuclear programmes, the number or type of weapons in particular arsenals, and whether these weapons (or dependence on nuclear testing) were regarded as of strategic or marginal importance to national security or political identity and status.

The non-nuclear-weapon states, by contrast, were generally viewed as having only indirect interests in the outcome, a characterization that missed a very important point. The security interests of non-nuclear-weapon states in building an effective non-proliferation and disarmament regime are, if anything, more salient than those of the nuclear-weapon states. Without nuclear arms or capabilities of their own to use for offensive or deterrence purposes, it is of direct and crucial importance for these countries to devalue, curb and eliminate weapons that could keep them at a political or military disadvantage and remove incentives that might prompt their neighbours or rivals to seek nuclear weapons.

CD members viewed as non-nuclear-weapon states actually encompassed a spectrum, including "aspirants" believed to have nuclear weapon ambitions or clandestine programmes, "nuclear insurance states" with sophisticated levels of nuclear technology developed under the NPT's rubric of peaceful purposes, and allies of one or more nuclear power. At the end of the Cold War, this last category included NATO members and those with nuclear cooperation agreements with the United States, such as Japan. Finally, there were the majority of genuinely non-nuclear-weapon states, which mostly included the non-aligned, developing countries that had no investment in nuclear deterrence and no technically relevant capabilities to develop nuclear weapons now or in the future. Although the CD comprised 38 members at the start of the CTBT negotiations and 61 at the end, only about 25 delegations were active participants in the relevant debates and decision-making.

The nuclear-weapon states largely viewed the CTBT as a component of the wider non-proliferation regime, which had defined and (as far as they were concerned) legitimized their nuclear status, conferring prestige, leadership and special privileges. They agreed to negotiate a CTBT for four main reasons: to cap the nuclear capabilities of India and Pakistan before they became weaponized to any significant degree, to induce the D-3 to take this first step toward formal engagement in the established arms control and non-proliferation regimes, to place a further barrier in the way of any nuclear aspirants and to reinforce the credibility of the NPT so that it would be indefinitely extended in 1995.

The probability that the CTBT would also freeze the differences in capability among the P-5 was undoubtedly useful for the dominant United States. The others appeared willing to go along with this, perhaps in the recognition that economics largely determined the post-Cold War military asymmetries. Their important security concerns were to stabilize the status quo in relation to each other, secure and sustain their nuclear arsenals, and prevent the rise of additional nuclear-armed states or groups. The CTBT was perceived as having a vital role to play in NPT extension because it was a stated objective in the NPT's preamble and had long been demanded by the non-nuclear-weapon states and NGOs as the minimum step to show that Article VI of the NPT was being taken seriously.

Israel's nuclear arsenal, while ritually included in calls for the D-3 to accede to the NPT, was of less political salience for the P-5 than the nuclear ambitions of India and Pakistan, which were viewed as regionally destabilizing, less controlled and more likely to feed the ambitions of other potential proliferators. Though the P-5 might have had fewer worries about Israel themselves, its participation in the CTBT was required by them to bolster the viability of the non-proliferation regime and increase its credibility for the Arab states, whose consent to the extension of the NPT was considered politically crucial. The P-5 were particularly determined to prevent any future testing or developments by other nuclear aspirants, of which three had been of concern since 1990: Iraq, North Korea and Iran.

Negotiating a CTBT did not mean that any of the P-5 had been converted to the cause of nuclear disarmament.[7] Defining the CTBT's role and function mainly in non-proliferation terms, they negotiated with a view to normalizing the possession of nuclear weapons by their own privileged group, while strengthening the barriers for others. Although the P-5 differed in how bluntly they expressed the sentiment that the CTBT was to "ban the bangs not the bomb",[8] they all sought to protect as much of their research and development options and infrastructures as possible. Even when they adopted the zero-yield scope, they all made sure to offset its disarmament impact by developing more effective capabilities through, for example, stockpile stewardship programmes, enhanced subcritical and hydrodynamic testing, and inertial confinement fusion. Although recognized as the domestically negotiated price for supporting a zero-yield CTBT, such programmes provoked considerable criticism from NGOs and many non-nuclear states because they were seen as circumventing the CTBT's historical role and purpose, which was to halt vertical proliferation and put the nuclear-armed states on the road to nuclear disarmament.

The D-3 pursued different strategies in accordance with their perceived interests and political resources. Israel, for example, aided by its close alliance with the United States, chose to slipstream through most of the negotiations. Influenced also by the fact that it was not admitted as a full member of the CD until June 1996, Israel prudently adopted a low profile, except when it had to fight for national interests that diverged markedly from those of the United States. With on-site inspections, for example, the United States pushed for rapid decision-making and easy access, while Israel, like its D-3 cohorts and China, wanted to establish tough procedural hurdles to protect its facilities from most kinds of scrutiny. In contrast to India and Pakistan, Israel's confidence in its continuing collaboration with the United States and the ability of its nuclear arsenal to perform the political and military functions it required vis-à-vis its non-nuclear-armed regional adversaries enabled it to become an early signatory of the CTBT.

The political calculations of Pakistan and India were rather different. India, which conducted its first nuclear explosion in 1974 (outside of the 1967 date by which the NPT defined a nuclear-weapon state), was institutionally excluded from gaining the perceived status and privilege of a nuclear power under the NPT-based non-proliferation regime. India's computations were complicated because it had become trapped between desire for international recognition and power through increased nuclear capabilities and its long-touted advocacy of nuclear disarmament, which was linked to that part of its post-colonial identity and sphere of influence that derived from the Gandhi–Nehru heritage and leadership in the non-aligned movement. India's options were also influenced by its regional situation vis-à-vis China, an established nuclear-weapon state, and Pakistan, with nuclear potential and inferior conventional forces. Denied access to special status through the NPT, India has long sought to undermine the non-proliferation regime as it is currently structured. Seeming to reinforce India's perpetual exclusion from the nuclear club, the NPT's indefinite extension without a vote in 1995 was a political blow that its leaders portrayed as a retrogressive decision forced on the non-aligned states by the nuclear powers and their allies. As the CTBT would have closed off the option to test its nuclear warhead designs, India balked. Helped by the clumsy handling of the entry-into-force issue, India then used its rejection of the CTBT to underscore its repudiation of discriminatory non-proliferation and avoid having its nuclear options capped.[9]

India's dilemmas displayed some of the characteristics of Jean-Jacques Rousseau's famous representation of mixed-motive cooperation as a stag hunt.[10] In Rousseau's analogy, a band of hunters can all feed themselves and their families if they cooperate to capture a stag. If, at a crucial moment, one of the hunters leaves his place to chase a hare, he may succeed in satisfying his own short-term hunger, but risks losing the stag, which would have provided for the longer-term food needs of the group. Rousseau illustrated how in certain interactions where there is a shared, common interest in cooperating, one or more actors may nonetheless act on the basis of narrow perceptions of self-interest in ways that result in a detrimental outcome for everyone, including themselves. Perception and psychology can be important factors in negotiations that should not be underestimated. In the CTBT case, it appeared to India and many other developing countries that the nuclear powers wanted the cooperation of everyone else to capture a treaty that would allow them to retain their nuclear deterrent requirements while blocking the nuclear ambitions of others. Viewed in this way, non-proliferation as currently constructed around the NPT excludes states other than the P-5 (and allies that they choose to include in extended deterrence arrangements) from their fair share of security. India seems to have regarded the benefits of sharing in a CTBT as uncertain or, at best, paltry, whereas pursuing its own nuclear arsenal appeared to carry more obvious and immediate gains. India defected from the hunt for a non-proliferation CTBT in order to secure a "nuclear deterrent" capability of its own.

On the other hand, if the CTBT "stag" is recast as a non-discriminatory disarmament objective, as most of the non-aligned states and middle powers sought, India's defection appears much less reasonable, since it ensured a suboptimal outcome that undermined disarmament efforts worldwide. Viewed in the disarmament light, India satisfied its own immediate desire for regional power and nuclear-weapon status at the expense of a future security objective sought by most of the world, which would have offered greater satisfaction and security for all, including India itself. At the same time, this analysis shows that India's nuclear disarmament positions in the CTBT, derided by many as either idealist hypocrisy or cynical rhetoric, are better understood as a way of hedging bets. They represented a rational strategic objective, since nuclear disarmament could diminish the relative power of competitors, especially China, but at the same time they provided a tactical justification if India chose to defect from the CTBT. India hoped that by taking the moral high ground with its disarmament demands (a time-honoured way of employing the "best versus good" tactic) it would be able to avoid complete condemnation by its non-aligned allies and international public opinion when the time came to reject the treaty.

Pakistan was also outside the NPT and employed disarmament rhetoric, especially in appealing to non-aligned solidarity, but its role and objectives were different from those of India. Pakistan's interests were conditioned by its regional relations and conventional military inferiority with regard to its larger neighbour. Its primary objective was to ensure that India gained no relative advantage and, where possible, to use the negotiations to increase pressure on its neighbour. It was in Pakistan's interests to be a supporting adjunct to China on many issues, but it did not merely slipstream in China's wake. Occasionally Pakistan fronted an issue for China or the G-21, playing its D-3 ambitions against both the nuclear powers and the non-nuclear regime-builders. This, and its manipulation of the United Kingdom and others in the entry-into-force negotiations, show the shrewdness with which it maximized its position, despite being comparatively disadvantaged in terms of military and economic power.

While the interests and strategies of the P-5 and D-3 undoubtedly dominated the negotiations, a third category, comprising middle powers such as Australia, Canada, Egypt, Germany, Japan, Mexico and the Netherlands, had greater influence on the outcomes than realist theory would predict from their national levels of attributive power. These states did not seek to use their power to dominate the negotiations or secure outcomes of narrow national interest. They were, rather, regime-builders that accorded value to the principles of non-discrimination and diffuse reciprocity,[11] and were more likely to recognize and uphold the role of participatory processes and multilateral institutions in constructing, maintaining and adapting regime norms, principles and rules.

As illustrated in the negotiations on scope and verification, the regime-builders shared the P-5's objectives of capping the D-3 nuclear programmes, engaging them in the rules, procedures and institutions of arms control, and strengthening the NPT's credibility and longevity (though not all had advocated indefinite extension). But they were also interested in capping and constraining the nuclear programmes of the established nuclear powers and viewed reciprocity as an important component in multilateralism, enhancing incentives and contributing to the legitimacy of the outcome. For the regime-builders, disarmament was not just a tactically deployed incentive to keep the non-nuclear-weapon states committed to the non-proliferation regime—it was an important principle inherent in non-proliferation. At the same time, however, many middle powers were influenced by their alliances with nuclear states and sought to justify some of their positions in terms of pragmatism and the constraints of *realpolitik*, falling back on the argument that, however useful the process of undertaking steps toward nuclear disarmament, the abolition of nuclear weapons was an unattainable ideal, at least for the foreseeable future. Regime-builders were far more likely than the P-5 to welcome civil society as a player in multilateral arms control; they valued NGOs' knowledge and contributions and were at times willing to engage with civil society in partnerships aimed toward agenda setting, constructing political will and shaping policy preferences.

The CTBT negotiating history shows that, while the participating states without nuclear weapons generally behaved as regime-builders, even if they were classified by others as nuclear aspirants (as in the case of Iran), far too many of the non-aligned states were marginalized. Although the G-21 underscored as often as possible that their objective in negotiating a test ban was disarmament, which was portrayed, with due reference to Article VI of the NPT, as an obligation and objective of non-proliferation, they had difficulty putting forward a coherent, united position on many aspects of the treaty. Their marginalization can in part be explained by their weaker resources and bargaining power. However, if the majority of the non-aligned movement had perceived themselves as having actual security interests in the treaty outcome, it is likely that more would have found the resources to increase their bargaining effectiveness, as India, Pakistan and, indeed, Egypt, Iran and Mexico chose to do. Unlike landmines and cluster bombs, which are disproportionately used in developing countries (albeit largely manufactured and sold by the economically developed), nuclear disarmament and non-proliferation appear to be of marginal practical interest to the governments of the developing world. They do not have nuclear weapons, cannot use them, and do not believe they can have influence on the doctrines and policies of the dominant governments that do have them and must be prevented from using them. Though it is understandable that nuclear policies may seem remote from the day-to-day concerns of many governments, in fact the use of nuclear weapons on any scale would have global repercussions. That should be a good reason for non-nuclear-weapon governments to engage actively in nuclear disarmament, but the nuclear club has many ways to make other countries feel that their participation in nuclear-weapon-related matters is secondary. This is a factor that needs to be taken into account when considering which issues to address multilaterally, and under what rules and conditions.

Even among the middle-power regime-builders, many—particularly the Western allies of the United States, the United Kingdom and France—acted as though their interests in strengthening the regime carried less weight than the nuclear-weapon states' force-related interests. Although they clearly wanted a strong test ban, many middle powers appeared prepared to accept almost any version of a CTBT that the nuclear-weapon states were willing to sign and ratify. In contrast to the P-5 and D-3 pursuing their narrower interests, most of the Western middle powers were motivated by a desire to obtain a test-ban treaty that would prohibit the worst of nuclear testing, contribute to the NPT regime and deter nuclear aspirants. Even so, most non-nuclear delegations started the negotiations thinking that the zone of possible agreement was bounded by the demands and "needs" of the P-5. Tending to view the negotiations in zero-sum terms, they were therefore prepared to manage the process by facilitating confidence-building and concession trading, aiming to balance or split the differences between the dominant players for the sake of a workable treaty.

EXPANDING THE POSSIBILITIES FOR REACHING AGREEMENT

Negotiated outcomes are often—and traditionally—treated as zero sum, resulting in gains and losses being divided among the parties according to their relative economic or political power. Zero-sum approaches assume a rigid payoff structure that treats the zone within which agreements may be forged as bounded, with little flexibility to make solutions outside the fixed parameters. Agreements reached through zero-sum bargaining are known as distributive because they focus on apportioning benefits and constraints, usually through mechanisms of power or the trading of compromises and concessions. The training programmes that dominated international relations and diplomacy in the Cold War were underpinned by the expectations and limitations of distributive bargaining and, though this is beginning to change, there has been little exploration of the alternatives.[12]

Distributive convergence may be reached in various ways. At one extreme, a hegemon or other dominant actor might impose a settlement, which the rest are obliged to accept. For example, during the Cold War, arms control was developed as a mechanism to manage US–Soviet relations and mitigate insecurity. Other states were expected to fit in and accept the outcomes. This kind of unilateral or bilateral fiat does not really qualify as a process of negotiation, even if it involves a division of gains and losses.

A mechanism best described as "imposed convergence" is often seen in multilateral negotiations and institutions such as the UN Security Council. In imposed convergence a state or dominant group determines the parameters or specifics of an agreement or solution to a particular challenge, which could be negotiations on a resolution, treaty or some other cooperation or security challenge. In agreements reached through imposed convergence, a form of distributive negotiations may be conducted within a privileged group that reaches agreement on a particular outcome "on behalf" of a wider group. Although the others in the forum have little input, this does not necessarily mean that the outcome is to other states' detriment or that they must be coerced into accepting. The issue may come down to the perceived level of importance of the interests involved, for example, who possesses the weapons or capabilities concerned, and whether they are regarded as strategically crucial or of marginal utility. An imposed outcome will be accepted by other actors if the tangible or regime benefits are considered to be greater than the alternative of getting no agreement.[13]

The PTBT, for example, was negotiated between the Soviet Union, United Kingdom and United States, and then opened for other states to join. Most states had no nuclear weapon programmes at the time and saw the environmental benefits of a worldwide restriction on nuclear testing in the atmosphere, underwater and in outer space, even if the treaty did not prevent new weapons being designed using underground explosions. Even such a purportedly multilateral agreement as the NPT was negotiated in earnest only after the United States and Soviet Union submitted identical draft treaties to the Eighteen-Nation Disarmament Committee in August

1967.[14] Though the non-nuclear-weapon states played an important role in ensuring that the NPT would link disarmament with non-proliferation and not curtail access to nuclear energy and technology for non-military purposes, the superpowers maintained overall control in how they incorporated these provisions into their final joint draft treaty, which was adopted and opened for signature in 1968.

A number of the treaties negotiated during the Cold War lacked effective verification, in part because the two superpowers were relied on to use their national intelligence and technical means to verify compliance and their military and economic power to enforce and implement the agreements, at least within their spheres of influence (which during that time encompassed much of the world). Similar Cold War attitudes carried over to the start of the CTBT negotiations, where the P-5 conducted their own "minilateral" negotiations on issues relating most closely to their nuclear capabilities and facilities, such as scope and verification, especially on-site inspections. These P-5 negotiations epitomized the nuclear-weapon states' assumption that they could bargain privately with each other and then impose their preferred outcomes on all the other states. Contrary to their assumptions, they proved unable to impose agreement this way for most of the CTBT. The actual process of reaching convergence even on issues of primary importance to the P-5 generally involved other actors, strategies and tactics as well.

A further type of multilateral outcome may be brought about through "managed convergence". Common in negotiations where participants regard the possibilities for agreement as fixed or at least relatively inflexible, the process of bringing about convergence may be managed by dominant players or groups of states using a variety of negotiating techniques, such as concession trading and the control or manipulation of text, meaning and technical knowledge. Although capable of delivering mutual or regime benefits, such managed convergence has a tendency to result in lowest-common-denominator agreements where differences are split or the more powerful receive greater benefits.

Though many of the CD delegations negotiated as though they assumed the end results would be based on distributive convergence, there were other forces at work in the CTBT negotiations, leading to integrative outcomes for some of the important issues. Yet experience suggests that the approaches, techniques and benefits of integrative bargaining and convergence-building are generally overlooked by multilateral practitioners and training programmes in diplomacy. Drawing from the experiences of conflict resolution and with the aim of reducing the adversarial win–lose dynamic and consequences of traditional negotiations, integrative strategies place high priority on achieving mutually advantageous outcomes wherever possible. This does not mean that integrative solutions treat all states the same. While the objective is an outcome that benefits all or most of the participants or affected parties, some may be required to compromise or concede more than others, depending on the circumstances.

The integrative problem-solving approach does not accept the apparent limitations or boundaries assumed for a fixed or rigid payoff structure. Instead, integrative strategies are used to expand or change the framework or zone of possible agreement, for example, by constructing or presenting a different range of options than first appeared to be on the table.[15] In contrast to the zero-sum assumptions of distributive decision-making, integrative convergence does not regard expectations and interests as fixed, but as factors that can be manipulated or altered by teaching or recasting knowledge, values, norms and ideas. The cognitive and communications strategies of civil society frequently aim to foster integrative convergence by changing how negotiators view problems. Integrative approaches can help negotiators to gain more positive perceptions of the value and achievability of solutions that maximize common security and regime interests over the particular interests of individual governments.[16]

The CTBT negotiations illustrated examples of both distributive and integrative agreements. However, where integrative convergence occurred it was more likely the result of outside pressures, particularly from civil society. Reflecting Cold War power structures, the rules, assumptions and institutional practices of the CD negotiating forum and most if not all its member states have assumed and fostered zero-sum, distributive approaches to decision-making. In the CTBT the tendency was to privilege those states that asserted direct national security interests due to their possession or control of the weapons and military practices of concern. Those that had foregone or been denied access to nuclear weapons were perceived as having only secondary or indirect interests at stake. In effect, therefore, the CD marginalizes the lesser-armed states and those with fewer technical resources. Working within the terms of its establishment in 1978, this forum also appears unable to accommodate alternative approaches aimed at human security, more comprehensive disarmament and the transformation of power relations to reduce reliance on military capabilities and address global security threats. In its present form, the CD appears to foster adversarial interactions and suppress important factors such as perceptions, uncertainty, learning and change. Although some adaptation of multilateral institutions and rules has already occurred, largely driven by civil society campaigning, more needs to be done institutionally to maximize the opportunities for participatory regime-building.

The CTBT negotiations exposed the degree to which the system of regional groups within the CD has become dysfunctional, with group affiliation providing cover for some of the nuclear-weapon possessors (P-5 as well as D-3) while inhibiting the ability of regime-builders to organize effectively on a group basis. The Eastern European group's primary function was in nominating post holders. The Western group coordinated around NPT objectives, but though individual Western delegations played important roles during the test-ban negotiations, the group as a whole was constrained by the competing objectives of the three nuclear-weapon states in its midst. The G-21 caucused together frequently but, with India and Pakistan in dominant and adversarial roles, few statements rose above rhetoric and the reiteration of principles, often harking back to the First UN Special Session on Disarmament in 1978. If the group tried to address modern disarmament prospects and practicalities, they faced deep divisions. This was most clearly illustrated in the final year of negotiations, when some G-21 members tried to push for language in the preamble that would link the treaty's purpose and objectives more explicitly to disarmament and an end to the modernization and qualitative improvement of nuclear weapons. India declined to work with the rest of the G-21 on this, as it had its own strategy with the P-5 to pursue. Without India, the initiative had little chance of engaging the P-5 and thus failed.

With the exception of a few weeks in 1998, the CD has been unable to adopt a programme of work to carry out negotiations on any of its agenda items since the CTBT was concluded. The 12-year impasse has only confirmed that the CD is in dire need of reform. Ideas have been put forward for rethinking how consensus is applied and for alternative arrangements to manage decision-making and avoid paralysis, such as establishing similarly sized regional groups for allocating offices and posts and having sufficient flexibility to accommodate ad hoc issue-based groupings that could be developed to coordinate on substantive issues.[17] After looking at the political and institutional constraints, we turn now to an analysis of the prenegotiation phase and how the outcomes on scope, entry into force and verification were brought about.

Prenegotiations

Hopes and demands for a nuclear test ban were kept alive by the actions of tens of thousands, perhaps millions, of civil society actors throughout the Cold War. Although the long history leading up to the CTBT was undoubtedly important, for the purposes of this analysis it makes sense to limit this discussion of prenegotiations to the four-year period immediately preceding the January 1994 opening of negotiations.

Following the stand-off on the CTBT that prevented the adoption of a consensus final document at the 1990 NPT Review Conference, the major hold-outs against test-ban negotiations in the CD continued to be the United States and United Kingdom. France's accession to the NPT in 1992 affected the dynamic and generally reinforced the Western nuclear postures. China, which also joined the NPT in 1992, used rhetoric that echoed the Non-Aligned Movement on nuclear disarmament, while actually pursuing the modernization of its nuclear arsenal, which required it to keep on with its nuclear testing programme. Of the nuclear powers, Russia was the only real advocate of a CTBT.

Civil society played an important role in keeping nuclear testing in the public eye and raising the political stakes, leading to the moratoria. Their strategies narrowed the options for decision makers, deliberately tying support for the test ban (including the moratoria) with issues of direct personal, political or financial interest to the leaders in the target countries. During 1991–1992, each successive moratorium also helped to build momentum for the test ban and reel in further nuclear-weapon states. The French moratorium, for example, gave impetus to the campaign for a US moratorium driven by civil society and members of Congress. The US moratorium legislation explicitly called for CTBT negotiations, while at the same time imposing a moratorium on the United Kingdom, despite that country's political opposition to a test ban at the time. These moratoria thus became the tipping point that made CTBT negotiations possible.

Of course, civil society actions did not take place in a vacuum. It is true that there was no nuclear-related crisis or shock to bring conflicting parties to the table, as happened when the Cuban Missile Crisis focused US and

Soviet minds on the necessity for better cooperation and arms control, with the consequence that political leaders overcame domestic opposition and achieved the PTBT and NPT. In the case of CTBT prenegotiations in the 1990s, the end of the Cold War offered opportunities and the 1995 decision to extend the NPT imparted urgency. The factors that spurred both the French, Russian and US moratoria on testing and brought the major parties to the negotiating table were the geostrategic upheaval at the end of the Cold War, which opened up new challenges in security relations and nuclear policy, and the forthcoming NPT conference and extension decision in 1995. Where the moratoria were the result of the intentional actions of political players, both government and civil society, they used the opportunities provided by the exogenous developments. The reasons and dynamics were different for each case, but all three testing moratoria were the consequence of domestic decision-making in which civil society demands and strategies proved to be an important factor in shaping political leaders' preferences. Although it was the third state to announce a moratorium, the United States had the most impact on facilitating the start of negotiations. This was mainly a function of its pre-eminent political power and the lifting of US opposition to a CD negotiating mandate, which reversed a position that Washington had held since 1981.

As discussed in Chapter 3, the US moratorium was imposed on a president whose policy preference was to continue testing. The policy shift toward a CTBT was accomplished through a combination of public mobilization and legislative strategies. The US Senate legislation explicitly linked the moratorium to negotiations on a CTBT, providing a classic example of prenegotiations confidence-building. The initial duration of the moratorium was set at only nine months, which made it appear more feasible for senators to support than if it had been open-ended from the start. That they were only being asked to impose a relatively short, potentially temporary measure that included an option for up to 15 safety tests undoubtedly helped persuade those who might have balked at calling for a total, permanent cessation of nuclear testing at that time. As a modest confidence-building step that was reversible and not legally binding, a moratorium was an attractive option for those wanting to show support for the test ban and non-proliferation regime, without necessarily entailing commitment to all the steps to accomplish a treaty for the comprehensive prohibition and elimination of nuclear weapons. Once the United States halted testing and set a target date for conclusion of a CTBT, it became much harder for other reluctant states to avoid participating in the negotiations.

The US moratorium was sustained because of the election in November 1992 of a Democratic President. Had George H.W. Bush been re-elected, it is likely the moratorium legislation would have been reversed in 1993. Although we cannot assume that a second Bush administration would have continued to oppose test-ban negotiations in the CD, past experience suggests that it would have been harder to take the treaty negotiations forward if, in addition to China, the United States—and therefore also the United Kingdom—had continued to conduct periodic underground explosions. Even if the CD had managed to begin negotiations, it is possible that if three of the nuclear powers had continued to test, the other moratoria may not have held for long. Under such circumstances, it is reasonable to speculate that France might not have waited until 1995 to resume testing, and that it might not have made such efforts to limit the number and duration of those tests to avoid derailing the test ban negotiations. Because the moratoria of Russia and the United States remained in place, France's final series of nuclear tests did not derail the test-ban negotiations, and may even have precipitated the key decision on zero yield. If the context and timing of France's decision to resume testing had been different, the political impact may have been far worse.

Though not as decisive as the US moratorium in breaking the stand-off, the Soviet (then Russian) and especially the French moratoria were important in helping to create the conditions to push for the US moratorium in 1992, by fostering a sense that there was a "window of opportunity" that was worth the expenditure of political capital by the Democratic politicians who pushed through the moratorium legislation. As with the US Senate, the fact that a moratorium is by definition more temporary and revocable than a treaty may also have been a factor for Gorbachev and Mitterrand. As Chapters 2 and 3 explain, Gorbachev's moratorium was pragmatically determined, dictated by the nationalist–environmentalist popularity of an ad hoc civil society movement that blossomed briefly but effectively in reaction to contamination concerns from nuclear test venting in Kazakhstan. When the Nevada–Semipalatinsk Movement was formed in February 1989, the Cold War still dominated international relations. Within two years this Kazakh initiative, supported by physicians and scientists, had networked widely with the peace movements of the West, receiving resources and publicity in support of its demand for the closure of the principal Soviet test site. Amidst the political shifts and upheavals as the Soviet Union disintegrated, the nuclear testing programme in Kazakhstan was cancelled. It is interesting to note that though Gorbachev responded with a public commitment to close the Semipalatinsk test site, he did not immediately initiate a testing moratorium. The nuclear establishment intended to carry on testing at Novaya Zemlya. They were embarrassed, however, by Greenpeace's protests there and the environmental organization's revelations indicating a serious level of contamination at the Arctic test site. Moreover, Novaya Zemlya was increasingly expensive to use, a relevant factor at a time when the Soviet economy was being exposed as on the brink of collapse, in part due to the crippling costs of the nuclear arms race. With more than 30,000 nuclear weapons in the Soviet arsenal already, it is not surprising that Gorbachev concluded that a moratorium on further testing would be in Soviet interests, even though his 19-month moratorium in 1985–1986 had been ignored by the other nuclear powers. Though a mix of pressures influenced Gorbachev's decision to initiate another moratorium, the challenge posed by the Nevada–Semipalatinsk Movement undoubtedly played an important part in putting the Soviet establishment under pressure. Like France, there is little evidence that the Soviet moratorium was undertaken with a CTBT strategy in mind.

There are different views about why France suddenly declared a moratorium on nuclear testing in April 1992, but it served several purposes. It enabled Mitterrand to defuse a resurgent political challenge from Green Party environmentalists while allowing the French nuclear establishment to assess conditions and address problems at the Pacific test sites. As France's programme of tests (and justifications) in 1995 showed, it was unprepared for a total ban. This suggests that the moratorium had not been expected to provide more than a temporary halt in 1992. With Republicans in the White House and Conservatives in Downing Street, there was no reason why Mitterrand should have anticipated that the United States would follow suit, and it is probable that he expected to resume testing after a year or so.

Though each moratorium arose from the particular conditions in the respective nuclear-weapon states, taken together the three moratoria reflected and also promoted a confidence-building breathing space in nuclear testing, and so helped to pave the way for negotiations on the CTBT to begin in earnest. In this more positive atmosphere, the UN General Assembly was at last able to adopt consensus resolutions that fed into a growing perception that the CTBT's time had come. These resolutions promoted a positive atmosphere in the CD, which facilitated the achievement of consensus on a CTBT negotiating mandate.

In the 40 years leading up to the CTBT, civil society had played a variety of roles aimed at mobilizing public opinion and keeping a total test ban on the agenda as a necessary, viable and verifiable step towards nuclear disarmament. In the final phase characterized as prenegotiations, the mix of civil society strategies proved highly effective in raising the political stakes and narrowing the options for decision makers. It would be wrong to imply that these successes were the result of a unified transnational campaign or strategy, however. On the contrary, they were the product of an interplay of citizens from many countries working in different ways at different times, sometimes in coalition, sometimes adversarially, with a wide range of tools and tactics, not all of which were entirely compatible. Opening the CTBT for signature, UN Secretary-General Boutros Boutros-Ghali specifically acknowledged the contribution of civil society, paying tribute to its passion, pressure and support for the treaty.[18] As the action moved to the governments and diplomats in the CD, civil society also played an important role during the negotiations, particularly in determining the treaty's scope.

Scope

Regarding the scope and basic obligations of the treaty as the most fundamental determinant of its political role, a number of interest groups actively sought to influence national positions and achieve an outcome that would accord with their own objectives, which varied from narrow non-proliferation to disarmament. The P-5, among whom interests were both complementary and competitive, tried to keep scope negotiations within their own minilateral forum. As a concession to multilateral concerns and conscious of the approaching NPT Review and Extension Conference, they delivered occasional position statements in the CD and Nuclear Test Ban Committee, but beyond such token gestures there was little multilateral engagement on the issue of scope in the first year.

The core interest shared by all the nuclear powers was to preserve their nuclear weapon programmes while curbing the options of others. The non-nuclear negotiators were divided between what might be characterized as non-proliferation regime-builders, disarmament regime-builders and marginalized states. While none of these subscribed to the P-5's objective of maintaining nuclear infrastructures and options, their ability to mount a coherent opposition was diluted by the acceptance of nuclear deterrence by an influential group of nuclear allies. The approach of these non-proliferation regime-builders was pragmatic; they devoted themselves especially to getting the technical parts of the treaty worked out. At times they assisted the non-aligned states to promote disarmament objectives, but often they saw their role as keeping the nuclear-weapon states on track by reining in the more challenging disarmament-related proposals. Most G-21 members appeared to want a workable and disarmament-oriented treaty, preferably before the 1995 NPT Review Conference, but their effectiveness was diminished by inadequate resources and lack of unity on some of the major substantive issues. This was primarily due to the presence of India and Pakistan in the group, but there were others who also complicated G-21 attempts to advance substantive joint proposals because they put regional or national agendas above the disarmament goals.

Had the P-5 been able to cooperate more effectively during the first half of the negotiations, they might have been able to impose a scope outcome on the rest that would have represented their perceived interests better than the zero-yield scope that constituted the actual outcome. For more than half the negotiations they tried to forge agreement by means of concession trading over "activities not prohibited". They failed because their asymmetrical technological capabilities, political distrust and rivalries impeded their collective attempts to agree on even a threshold or maximum yield for hydronuclear experiments. Hence, having started off with ideas for a CTBT that would have been comprehensive in name but partial in application, the P-5 ended up with a zero-yield scope that reflected the hopes (if not expectations) of the structurally marginalized disarmament advocates more closely than their own perceived interests. To minimize the political and military impact of the scope decision, the nuclear powers sought to offset zero yield by declaring their intentions to ensure stockpile maintenance and enhancement without explosive testing (in many cases entailing an increase in resources to these areas of what the United States called stockpile stewardship). All but China also explicitly linked their supreme national interests with the condition of their nuclear arsenals, thereby preparing the ground for a future withdrawal if they chose to make the argument that the test ban had resulted in a degradation of nuclear forces.

The zero-yield outcome was not determined solely by those with the greatest political and military power. Perceptions of national self-interest and concerns about relative power need to be factored in to explain why the P-5 let their rivalry outweigh their mutual interests. This was a period of rapid geostrategic transformation and, despite the obvious military asymmetries, all of the P-5 wanted to retain their technological and military ground and, indeed, the political status and security they associated with nuclear weapons. Safety tests, for example, provided a context in which France and the United Kingdom could assert that they had responsibilities as nuclear-weapon states to maintain safe, reliable arsenals. Although the French delegation appeared to slipstream in their British counterpart's wake on safety tests, France's desire for such an option in the first 18 months of negotiations was actually greater than that of the United Kingdom. Since the late 1950s, the United Kingdom has benefited from nuclear cooperation with the United States,[19] but France has relied more on its own research and capabilities. American opposition to the Franco-British safety test provision posed a major problem for the credibility of the UK position "since Britain relies on the American test facility … it made no sense to insist on the right to carry out safety tests".[20]

France's position was more consistent with its nuclear doctrine and infrastructure, though that did not make it any more palatable to CTBT advocates.[21] Its perception was that nuclear weapons had secured for France a post-war international rank and strengthened its position within Europe, particularly vis-à-vis Germany and the United Kingdom. Nuclear weapons were considered necessary as an overt demonstration of France's status, national independence, technical prowess and willingness to defend itself.[22] Hence, France's support for a CTBT was made contingent on developing reliable simulation capabilities or retaining the option to conduct hydronuclear experiments up to a threshold of several hundred tonnes. The nuclear establishment was concerned that it would not be able to develop effective simulation capabilities without large hydronuclear experiments or a further programme of nuclear explosions. As Mitterrand had reportedly refused to be the first to break the moratorium, the nuclear establishment insisted that they needed to keep open the options of safety tests or a high threshold. Some officials also claimed that without further testing, three recently developed warheads would not be certified for deployment.[23] A provision for safety tests may therefore have been one approach to the problem that the French nuclear establishment later resolved when President Chirac agreed to break the moratorium and resume testing after June 1995.[24] In contrast to how the United Kingdom used its renunciation of the safety test proposal just before the NPT conference to demonstrate its credentials and claim to be a "good" nuclear-weapon state, France's Ambassador Errera characterized the move as "a very hard decision to come to".[25]

The United Kingdom appears to have been equivocal about the need for safety tests all along, as indicated by contradictory government statements at the time, discussed in Chapter 4. As a delaying mechanism the demand could only have played a small role, since discussion of safety tests took up relatively little time, but it can be understood as part of an overall strategy of delay, illustrated also in the tactics the British and French delegations employed to prevent Marín Bosch from issuing his Chair's text in July 1994, and the "reversed linkage" by which they countered any attempts to conclude the CTBT before the NPT Review and Extension Conference. The timing of the decision to drop the proposal was related to the desire to obtain the NPT's indefinite extension, suggesting that whatever the original intention, the proposal for safety tests had been kept in the rolling text so that it could be sacrificed with great fanfare in time for the NPT conference.[26] The dropping of this demand failed to impress as much as the British and French had hoped, however, since most of the other negotiators had already determined that a provision for safety tests, like Washington's proposal for a 10-year easy opt-out, would not be acceptable under any circumstance.

While the Franco-British demand for safety tests was held longer than expected, it was nothing compared to China's persistence on PNE. Rather than being a bargaining chip, as many CD diplomats had assumed, PNE came to occupy a central position in China's negotiating posture. But this may not have been the original intention.[27] Because China had no PNE programme and was well aware of the practical problems that had led the Russians and Americans to abandon their PNE programmes, it is unlikely that Beijing had suddenly developed an overriding interest in conducting such explosions. More plausibly, PNE were introduced into the negotiations to provide a peaceful-uses justification in case China decided to reject the treaty as it neared conclusion. As with China's argument for inclusion of its familiar demand for prohibiting the first use of nuclear weapons, the PNE proposal may have been intended initially to serve as a "best versus good" defection tactic.

If this analysis is correct, PNE started out being for China the equivalent of what linking entry into force with disarmament was for India—an ideologically defensible opt-out provision, if one were to be needed. The aim of the best-versus-good tactic is to provide a means of justifying defection from the treaty without losing credibility with important domestic constituents or international allies. Like India, China was equivocal about the CTBT when it entered the negotiations. Although initially the demand for PNE may have been intended as a tactic rather than a real objective, it appears that by the time Beijing had decided that it would be more in China's interests to join the rest of the P-5 in a CTBT than to remain outside, the negotiators' room to manoeuvre had become constricted. In other words, a feedback loop was created, in which the negotiators made such an appealing case for retaining the PNE option that they convinced domestic audiences, especially in the influential People's Liberation Army, that it was necessary. There is evidence for this conclusion in the fact that China's negotiators held out for a PNE mention in the final treaty that is purely symbolic, with no institutional weight and no chance of being successfully invoked.[28]

Apart from Russia's equivocation, the rest of the P-5 opposed PNE; yet when the zero-yield decision had swept away the various threshold options for conducting hydronuclear experiments, they were quite willing to do a trade-off with China to allow a more accessible provision for PNE in exchange for Chinese concessions on other issues, particularly relating to verification. It is clear from this that it was not in the minilateral P-5 bargaining that the demand for PNE was defeated, although it was undoubtedly helpful that China was quite isolated and the other nuclear powers had no significant interests at stake. As the history shows, when some form of PNE permission was on the verge of being accepted by the P-5, it was thwarted by the efforts of strategically placed civil society actors working in partnership with several key Western regime-builders, such as Australia, Canada, Germany and Japan. By recasting the proposed PNE permission as legitimizing continued research into nuclear explosions by the P-5 and D-3, this alliance of civil society and middle powers undermined the P-5 deal and the options for managed convergence put forward by Iran, Russia and others.

While it was important for the credibility of the CTBT to eliminate safety tests and PNE, the turning point in the negotiations was unquestionably the decision to go for zero yield, and this was almost entirely determined outside Geneva. According the resumption of French testing a decisive role in the zero-yield outcome, as some have claimed—not least the French themselves—would be consistent with theories about the role of crisis and exogenous shock in multilateral negotiations.[29] The evidence shows, however, that it was not the French decision to test as such, but international public reaction that provided the policy-shaping jolt that pushed Clinton to make the decision. The swiftness and intensity of public outrage, expressed through boycotts and demonstrations in many states, acres of newsprint, and thousands of letters to the White House, reminded the US President that a total test ban was an important and popular objective. The protests also conveyed the warning that if testing were not properly banned, there could be a revival of the kind of anti-nuclear protest movements witnessed in the 1980s. If perception of crisis was a factor in this case, it was not exogenous, but a politically generated crisis engineered mainly by transnational civil society.

A second important factor in shaping the zero-yield decision was the provision of technically relevant information by scientists and activists, especially in the United States. Several groups sought to influence the US nuclear-test-ban debate, but three played particularly significant roles. As in the past, some of the scientists and officials based in the US nuclear laboratories opposed the CTBT. Recognizing that this time a treaty was likely to be concluded, they fought for it to exempt certain types of nuclear testing, including hydronuclear experiments. Some went further, lobbying for the treaty to allow nuclear explosions below a certain threshold, such as 500t. They argued that the US stockpile would be at risk if it were not possible to conduct low yield nuclear tests. Instead of simply accepting such arguments, the US government commissioned the JASON Group, an independent group of scientists (including former nuclear weapon scientists) from both the governmental and non-governmental sectors. Both groups were ostensibly responsible to the Energy Secretary, Hazel O'Leary, but they offered different analyses and conclusions about the impact a zero-yield test ban would have on the US arsenal. Environmental and arms control organizations and individuals, including the Natural Resources Defense Council, Arms Control Association and Physicians for Social Responsibility also drew together technical information and arguments to show that a zero-yield treaty was feasible and would enhance US security.

Such groups resembled Peter Haas' "epistemic communities" in a number of ways,[30] with the caveat that in the CTBT case it would be inappropriate to regard the knowledge providers as a community. On the contrary, there appeared to be several knowledge-diffusing but politically fragmented groups of epistemic actors, offering competing information and advice. Significantly, advocates for and against zero yield were dispersed among US government laboratories and agencies and different kinds of non-governmental institutions. In consequence, because there were at least two sets of expert authorities pulling in different directions, O'Leary came to base her decisions largely on normative considerations, including the idea of putting in place a genuinely comprehensive test-ban regime. The expert arguments were used to defend and justify her choice but were not decisive in determining it. In the US interagency process, because O'Leary represented the Department of Energy, responsible for the nuclear laboratories, her decisions greatly reinforced the positions of regime-builders within the State Department, such as Tom Graham and John Holum, who were keen to see a CTBT that would be credible for the non-nuclear-weapon states and reinforce the nuclear non-proliferation regime.

The zero-yield decision became possible not only because the P-5 were deeply divided over threshold levels, with no managed convergence that would be acceptable to others in sight, but because there was also conflict within and between the various US agencies. Transgovernmental alliances between the nuclear scientists and military officials of more than one P-5 state further complicated things. In this situation, in which interests and power were fragmented and pressure was being exerted on all sides of the argument, President Clinton chose a scope more consistent with globalist views of a test ban that would contribute toward disarmament as well as non-proliferation and arms control.

This analysis of the shaping of the outcome on scope highlights two important aspects of multilateralism: the role of non-state actors and the importance of ideas. Though certain US government experts and officials were extremely influential, it was primarily civil society, using a range of cognitive and advocacy tactics, that succeeded in repositioning the issue of scope from a debate among the P-5 over activities not prohibited to one about the purpose of a test ban, thereby shifting the payoff matrix from thresholds and exempted activities to encompass the prohibition of all testing designed to produce a yield above zero.[31]

In doing so, they expanded the zone of possible agreements to include a ban on hydronuclear testing, which in 1994 had been thought impossible. This example of integrative convergence holds lessons for future multilateralism, particularly in relation to disarmament objectives. It was largely determined by normative considerations, but also reflected institutional objectives: it strengthened the chances of concluding a treaty that would be acceptable to the non-aligned states and so reinforced the non-proliferation regime. This was important, for although they had achieved the indefinite extension of the NPT in 1995 without actually delivering a finished CTBT, it was clear from the NPT agreements in 1995 that a CTBT continued to be a vital component of the non-proliferation regime. At the 2000 NPT Review Conference, the importance of the CTBT was emphasized again in the consensus final document, which also identified further measures that needed to be taken on disarmament and non-proliferation. At the same time, although institutional norms, ideas and epistemic strategies were more influential in determining the scope outcome than aggregate power and military interests, these considerations were not wholly swept aside. Both France's decision to obtain simulation capabilities through testing and the United States' six 'safeguards' and stockpile stewardship programme were conditioned on a perception of regime cooperation as mitigating the security dilemma by constraining others without significantly diminishing one's own relative power, capabilities and options. This belies claims by opponents of CTBT ratification that the treaty would weaken the US arsenal and capabilities.

Finally it must be noted that though the scope outcome provides a good example of integrative convergence in all its complexity, the United States then exerted its position of dominance to impose its decision on the rest of the P-5 and ensure that this became the authoritative interpretation of the majority-favoured Australian scope text from then on.

Entry into force

The high bar set for the CTBT's entry into force, combined with the negative attitude of the administration of George W. Bush, consigned the treaty to limbo for more than a decade. It is therefore interesting to reflect on how negotiations on this important requirement were neglected early on, with the assumption that (as happened with the Chemical Weapons Convention) the entry-into-force decisions would fall into place once other major contested issues had been resolved. With few actors engaged in finding ways to facilitate convergence, the zone of agreement was restricted by the competing expectations and interests among the P-5 and D-3, and positions became hardened in the endgame. Three of the nuclear-weapon states—China, Russia and the United Kingdom—succeeded in forcing through a stringent entry-into-force provision for narrow non-proliferation motivations, but a close look at the evidence suggests that none of these would have rejected the treaty if something a little less rigid on entry into force had been brokered. The most dogmatic positions were held by Pakistan, which wanted to ensure that India would have to accede, and several Middle

East states concerned about Israel. However, these countries lacked the political weight to force through their preferences and it is unlikely that any would have blocked conclusion if the treaty had contained a more flexible alternative.

Early in the negotiations, India had been hedging its bets over whether it would join a CTBT. The indefinite extension of the NPT in 1995 and election in May 1996 of a Bharatiya Janata Party-led government determined to show that India was a nuclear power, cemented India's opposition to the treaty. The justification for India's defection was couched in disarmament rhetoric, and the targeted entry-into-force requirement favoured by China, Russia, the United Kingdom and Pakistan provided a predictably contentious platform for a showdown and accusations of coercion. The consequence was that India not only walked away, but also derided the CTBT as a discriminatory instrument of the major powers. It was thus tarred with the same brush that India used to condemn the NPT, even though the CTBT was multilaterally negotiated in the CD, with shared responsibilities that included India and key non-aligned participants.

High-level political pressure from the United States might have made a difference, but Washington appeared disengaged on entry into force, its attention elsewhere until the very end. Although France became supportive of a more flexible entry-into-force approach in the final year, it had become less forceful in the P-5 minilateral dynamics after 1995. The rest of the CD was largely in favour of a provision that would enable early entry into force, but the regime-builders (like everyone else) did not realize the dangers until too late, and then they coordinated poorly and failed to unify around a credible alternative to the list proposals. Civil society likewise engaged very late and coordinated only weakly. The non-aligned were almost completely marginalized from the debate, in part because India and Pakistan were dominant—and rival—players in the G-21. Furthermore, because several Arab states wanted a stringent provision to bind Israel, the G-21 had little incentive to push for more flexible alternatives.

Politically viable options on entry into force were available to the CD negotiators, not least of which were the suggestions and proposals from the United States, Canada, the draft texts put forward by Iran and Australia, and the precedents set by the NPT and the Chemical Weapons Convention. However, there appeared to be little coherent pressure or strategy exerted in favour of a flexible option. No one took on the advocacy and expert roles that civil society used to change attitudes and shape the zones of agreement for scope and verification. Related to this absence of effective civil society engagement and ideas, there was insufficient high-level governmental and diplomatic attention until far too late. The Chair and his delegation were left to resolve the issue, but without adequate support or input from other regime-builders to offset the heavy pressure in favour of stringency. Of highest salience to the minority that sought rigidity, the determining factors were the specific regional and national interests of this small number of dominant states, who wanted to augment their positions by putting emphasis on a treaty binding the D-3. Hence, the outcome was the product of managed convergence: an unwieldy, unworkable provision, for which the chief justification was the hurry to meet the September 1996 deadline for conclusion of the treaty.

Verification

Early on, a number of states, notably Australia, Mexico and Russia, as well as NGOs, had argued that adequate verification could be provided by a combination of national technical means and existing open-sourced resources for seismic and radionuclide detection. Their position was that the verification regime was essentially for multilateral confidence-building, and need not be very expensive or elaborately defined. Arguments for a less-expansive verification system complemented the aspiration of the first year's Chair and some of the non-aligned states to conclude the CTBT before April 1995, but they dropped from view once the hope of an early treaty faded.

Apart from this divergence of perspective in the first year, there was little core conflict between the interests of the nuclear-weapon states and those of most non-nuclear-weapon states with regard to the international monitoring system, though there were of course disagreements over specifics. Unlike the negotiations on scope, entry into force or other aspects of verification, the process of reaching agreement on the IMS appeared genuinely multilateral and were generally conducted in a congenial atmosphere of shared responsibilities. In this, the IMS resembled the more standard treaty articles, such as redressing disputes, duration and withdrawal, signature, ratification and accession, rather than the more highly contested issues like scope or entry into force. Though there were differences in terms of technical expertise and opinion over capabilities and coverage, and some used the negotiations to pursue narrow national interests with regard to the location of specific stations and the supply of particular verification technologies, such conflicts as there were could be resolved through epistemic strategies and bridging tactics aimed at depoliticizing areas of contention. Disagreements were addressed with constructive, integrative approaches, and convergence largely achieved through multilateral cooperation, knowledge diffusion and the fostering of shared understandings about what would comprise a technically achievable, cost-effective system to provide verification confidence and collateral benefits. The principal actors were scientists attached to their government delegations; civil society was hardly involved.

By contrast, questions relating to on-site inspections and the use of NTM tapped into concerns about sovereignty and espionage, particularly among states with declared or de facto nuclear programmes. The ensuing arguments echoed the Cold War dichotomy of adequacy versus bearability, but pitted the United States more sharply against China than Russia, with the additional complication that other countries—most notably India, Israel and Pakistan—were seeking also to protect their national defence and nuclear assets from surveillance. The middle-power regime-builders tried to be brokers and assist in building knowledge and understanding of the implications of various options, but they were only weakly engaged on the issues of major political contention. The overall outcome was distributive, determined by the competing interests and requirements of the P-5 and D-3. Civil society was much less engaged on verification issues in the 1994–1996 CTBT negotiations than in the past, mainly because verification was far less politicized this time around.

By the end, the two dominant protagonists on OSI were China and the United States. US positions were strongly maintained because Ambassador Ledogar was open from the beginning about the need to have a sufficiently robust verification and inspection regime in order for the treaty to get through the process of ratification by the US Senate. The importance of this consideration was illustrated when the US delegation characterized less stringent proposals as "treaty-breakers", and dismissed ideas advocated by US allies on the grounds that they would not satisfy the Senate. Nevertheless, this was not a replay of the "impossibilist" verification arguments that some US administrations had resorted to in the Cold War. Although the United States negotiated hard on verification issues in the CTBT, its delegation was constructive and willing to find a solution that would be consistent with what it regarded as essential US requirements.

The power of verification arguments to derail agreements had weakened at the end of the Cold War. This was due not only to the changed political environment, but also to the technical advances and insights gained by verification exercises, including collaborative US–Soviet exchanges in the 1980s[32] and the bilateral inspections developed for the Intermediate-range Nuclear Forces Treaty in 1987. These developments and the precedent set by the Chemical Weapons Convention negotiations on inspections and NTM made it appear that "usage and custom" were moving in the direction of acceptance of verification norms in regime building.[33]

China also bargained effectively on these issues, in part through exerting "no agreement" leverage. By recognizing that it was important for the United States to have China join the CTBT from the very start, China was able to use this high-value card to augment its much weaker hand in terms of economic, military and diplomatic power, where it had fewer resources and clout than the United States. The final decision on OSI was a trade-off between China and the United States and imposed on the rest, who accepted.

Though less salient in the 1994–1996 negotiations, Cold War doubts about verification and verifiability were revived by test-ban opponents in the United States when they thwarted Senate ratification of the CTBT in 1999.[34] Their arguments, which also questioned the ability of the United States to maintain its nuclear arsenal under a test-ban treaty, took many by surprise. For the US delegation, criticisms of the verification outcome were particularly troubling because Ledogar and his team had been at pains to ensure that the verification regime would meet US intelligence requirements and provide confidence in treaty compliance.[35] The late 1990s were not, after all, the 1950s and 1960s, when highlighting verification problems had proven such a devastating weapon in the arms control opponents' armoury.[36]

LESSONS FOR FUTURE MULTILATERAL NEGOTIATIONS

Multilateralism does not require participation by all states, but it needs to be representative to be credible. Due to the differences among states, multilateralism must have structures and mechanisms for addressing asymmetries in a fair and cost-effective manner. It is not necessary that all state participants possess the weapons in question. In the case of landmines, possession was spread among a wide group of states from all regions and political groupings.[37] In other multilateral disarmament or arms control negotiations, such as those of the Biological and Toxin Weapons Convention and the Chemical Weapons Convention, the weapons in question were developed and possessed by a subset of states, generally with military or regional power or ambition. Nevertheless, the participants would all claim a security interest in the outcome of the negotiations. What distinguishes these examples of asymmetric possession from the case of nuclear weapons is that unlike the NPT-based nuclear regime, there existed no differential international legal barrier to possession or development of the weapons prior to the relevant treaty negotiations. National and economic resources, threat assessments, preferences of the public or policymakers, or some other set of conditions determined whether one state rather than another developed biological or chemical weapons; but given the appropriate conditions, any of them could have legally chosen to do so up to the point of concluding and signing the prohibition treaty.[38] The institutionalization of differential obligations in the nuclear non-proliferation regime makes gives rise to special challenges in negotiating nuclear weapons treaties.

In addition to the necessity to reform the CD and group system, various insights can be drawn out of the CTBT negotiations that have relevance for future multilateral disarmament and arms control negotiations. First, the power that matters in negotiations is issue-based rather than attributive, and reflects the ability to influence and control outcomes. This is a power *to do,* and should not be confused with traditional notions of power *over*. Power can be conceptualized in several ways, each of which has a role to play. Attributive or "absolute" power accords with the traditional view of power as derived from military and economic capabilities and exercised over adversaries or allies.[39] In some situations, it is the distributive pattern of military and economic power in the system that confers systemic or relational power, depending on the location of a particular state in relation to the others.[40] Charismatic power is associated with leadership and individual personality. Although this kind of power is less important in diplomacy than other kinds of politics, diplomats or officials with charisma can more effectively gather support or build alliances for particular initiatives, while an awkward or arrogant ambassador may provoke antagonism regardless of the merits of the case.

Many states enter negotiations assuming that those with the greatest levels of attributive power will dominate. The CTBT experience highlights the important role played by issue-based, bargaining power.[41] Attributive power that comes with dominant military, political or economic assets may be a significant component in the construction of issue-based power, but that does not mean that it is decisive in negotiations. In multilateralism, it appears that negotiators that can employ issue-based power and cognitive strategies are more likely to prevail, particularly if they structure their objectives around cooperative, integrative agreements rather than competitive, distributive outcomes. When negotiators are described as having "bargaining power" it means that they are successful in deploying their resources and capabilities either to change other actors' perceptions of what constitute acceptable gains or losses or to change the zone of possible agreements to integrate preferred options that had not previously been recognized as possibilities. Issue-based power is generally associated with controlling outcomes. Similarly, states with poor technological and diplomatic resources and capabilities (which is frequently but not always associated with having low attributive power) could be said to have low interactive capacity, contributing to low issue-based power and marginalization. To understand how actors with less attributive power, such as middle powers or civil society, are able to influence some agreements, it is necessary to focus on what they *do*, rather than on what they *are* or what they *have*.

Although absolute, attributive and relational power may be important components in the construction of issue-based power, other factors may be more relevant in determining a bargaining outcome. Such factors include a negotiator's ability to target information, recognize or develop effective strategies, and coordinate and utilize partnerships or alliances with other diplomats, governments or civil society; internal policy cohesion or division; the level of domestic political attention and support; geostrategic and political positioning; and communication and diplomatic capabilities, including the utilization of knowledge and expertise and the strategic importance of the weapon or practice under consideration. Individually and severally, these factors may augment or detract from the effective power that a party deploys in multilateral negotiations.

Second, multilateral diplomacy will deliver better outcomes in the context of human security and disarmament if negotiators pursue integrative negotiating strategies that shift the balance from zero-sum competition among the dominant states toward constructing shared, regime-enhancing outcomes that benefit a much broader spectrum of stakeholders. This point was amply illustrated in the processes that brought about the zero-yield scope and a strong, shared verification regime. Entry into force, by contrast, can be viewed as an exception that proves the rule. The "all or nothing" approaches taken by several of the key states created a rigid, zero-sum context that drastically narrowed the perceived zone of possible agreement during the endgame. The managed convergence that resulted has undermined the CTBT's objectives and put the treaty's viability in question for more than a decade.

Third, less-equipped states in military, economic, political or technological terms can counter their institutional marginalization and enhance their abilities to accomplish regime-building, human-security objectives through alliances with other states and with civil society actors. As this CTBT history demonstrates, though actors lacking absolute, attributive power may not control outcomes as directly as some of the P-5, they can have considerable effect in shaping outcomes if they make strategic use of knowledge and alliances. The parts played by non-nuclear-weapon middle powers such as Australia, Canada, Mexico, the Netherlands and Sweden, as well as South Africa's pivotal role during the 1995 NPT Conference, derived more from their issue-based alliances than from their attributive or issue-based power.

Fourth, following from the previous two observations and illustrated throughout this analysis of how the CTBT was brought to conclusion, it is clear that civil society, acting nationally and transnationally, can be of fundamental importance in fostering integrative convergence that reframes expectations and expands the zones of perceived and possible agreements. Such an understanding accords with post-Cold War analyses of the importance of transnational civil society in constructing political will and shaping interests through the strategic use of knowledge and public pressure to alter the zones of possible agreements and influence the selection of particular solutions.

In conclusion, taking all aspects of the CTBT negotiations into consideration, one can extrapolate from the lessons to suggest that for a given measure (treaty or agreement) of multilateral arms control to be successful, the effective, issue-based power of the regime-builder proponents, combined with the strategic engagement of civil society, must outweigh the issue-based power of dominant states that want to resist the constraints or retain the weapons or practices of concern. Those seeking to bring an issue to the negotiating table or carry multilateral arms control or disarmament negotiations forward successfully need to pay attention to all of these components.

CHAPTER 9

SECURING THE CTBT

Weapons of mass destruction cannot be uninvented. But they can be outlawed, as biological and chemical weapons already have been, and their use made unthinkable. Compliance, verification and enforcement rules can, with the requisite will, be effectively applied. And with that will, even the eventual elimination of nuclear weapons is not beyond the world's reach.

Weapons of Mass Destruction Commission, 2006[1]

On 9 October 2006, at 01h35 GMT, seismic stations across the world recorded tremors with the characteristics of a small underground nuclear explosion. Within two hours, states that had signed the CTBT were sent an automatic preliminary analysis, including information on time, location and magnitude. Sent out by the Provisional Technical Secretariat (PTS) of the Preparatory Commission for the CTBTO in Vienna, this information included data from more than 20 stations assigned to the IMS, placing the explosion within the Democratic People's Republic of Korea (North Korea) and indicating that it had a body wave magnitude between 3.58 and 4.2.

The way in which the PTS swung into action was an impressive example of what the negotiators working out the verification regime had intended the CTBTO to do if it detected a suspicious event that might be a nuclear explosion. Drawing on continuous monitoring by stations around the world, the International Data Centre's first tasks were to ascertain whether the seismic signature indicated a nuclear explosion or some other tremor-inducing activity (such as an earthquake, a chemical explosion or a mine collapse) and monitor for the release of radiation, either in the form of particulates or radioactive gases. After initial detection and analysis, the next stage is to sift information to identify the location and size of the suspected explosion as accurately as possible. If it is determined that a clandestine nuclear test has been carried out in violation of the treaty, an analysis of IMS data from all sources can provide valuable clues about the perpetrator and the type of device that was tested.

In the North Korean case, there had been a political indicator, as six days earlier a spokesperson had publicly announced that government's intention to conduct a nuclear test, though no date had been given. Later it was reported that China had been informed that North Korea planned an explosion with a yield of around 4kt.[2] After detecting the seismic signal early on 9 October, the PTS shared its data with states parties, organized a formal technical briefing and then issued a more detailed analysis on 11 October, confirming the preliminary information. The various monitoring technologies had enabled the location of the explosion to be narrowed down to an area of some 880km^2 in North Korea.[3] Two weeks after the event, the radionuclide monitoring station at Yellowknife in Canada recorded significant levels of xenon-133. As discussed in Chapter 7, xenon-133 is a radioactive gas that is a characteristic by-product of nuclear fission. The PTS used atmospheric transport models to confirm that the likely source of the xenon-133 was within the area of interest in North Korea. Detecting this radioactive gas also served to reinforce conclusions drawn from the seismic data that the explosion was conducted in hard rock and had a fission yield of less than 1kt.[4]

Of the many useful insights that resulted from the Secretariat's response to the North Korean test, three were particularly important:

- as the data indicates that the explosion was well below 1kt, this bears out the reassurances (and predictions) from many scientists during the CTBT negotiations that the different IMS technologies would work synergistically to provide detection and location of nuclear explosions significantly smaller than the verification system's baseline of 1kt;[5]
- the majority decision in the verification negotiations that resulted in the inclusion of noble gas sensors in some radionuclide monitoring stations was vindicated by the detection of elevated levels of xenon-133 in Canada, some 7,000km from the explosion;[6] and
- though remote sensing proved the effectiveness of the IMS, a prompt on-site inspection, as provided for once the treaty has entered into force, would likely have resolved most if not all remaining uncertainties and would have given more precise information about the explosion's exact location and yield.

In the absence of an on-site inspection and taking into account uncertainty regarding the geophysical characteristics of the test location (depth, hardness of rock and so forth), the magnitude range given by the IMS nevertheless indicated that the explosion was much smaller than the 4kt yield North Korea had apparently expected, if reports of the information provided to China are accurate.[7] While there has been some speculation that North Korea may have developed the technology and expertise to conduct a low-yield nuclear test on a device small enough to be delivered by its missiles, the most probable explanation is that the test was a "fizzle"—meaning that it failed to produce the expected yield. If the explosion "did not succeed as planned",[8] North Korea faced a difficult choice: to test again and risk even stronger international condemnation and sanctions; to abandon its attempts to develop a deliverable nuclear weapon; or to develop and deploy nuclear weapons without a reasonable degree of confidence about how they might work if used.

In view of the strong norm against testing that is being progressively embedded, even though the CTBT has not legally entered into force, the first option has been made more difficult. Considerable security and military problems are attached to the last option. That would leave the second option looking more attractive from the political, military, security and practical perspectives. Whether these suppositions are correct cannot yet be known, but within half a year North Korea had not only resumed negotiations under the auspices of the Six Party Talks, but had for the first time since 1994 agreed to a far-reaching "Denuclearization Action Plan", with first steps already taken toward dismantling its nuclear weapons programme and plutonium production facility and reinstating IAEA inspections.[9]

The noble gas monitoring station at Yellowknife played a decisive role in confirming that the seismic event in North Korea had been a nuclear explosion. This experience more than proved the case made during the CTBT negotiations for including noble gas sensors and a wide network of ground-based radionuclide stations. As will be recalled from Chapter 7, China questioned the need for noble gas monitoring, and Russia advocated having three specially equipped sampling planes to supplement a much less extensive network of ground-based monitors. As it turned out, the process of concession trading in the final stages of the negotiations resulted in both powers accepting the IMS architecture that was favoured by the majority. This established that sensors for detecting noble gases would be incorporated into 40 of the 80 designated radionuclide monitoring stations. At the time of the North Korean test, the Yellowknife radionuclide station was one of 10 where noble gas sensors had been installed and were being tested as part of an international experiment conducted under the auspices of the PTS.[10] The four closest stations to North Korea were in Canada, Mongolia, Norway and Sweden, but prevailing atmospheric currents carried the gases from west to east, so the other stations detected little or nothing above background levels.[11]

Despite the containment of the underground explosion, the distance travelled by the radioactive plume and the relatively short half life of xenon-133, the sensitivity of this equipment proved its worth even outside the 10-day window of opportunity that the IMS scientists had conservatively assumed. The small size and containment of the North Korean test may have prevented particulate matter from escaping, but they could not hide evidence from the seepage of radioactive gases. Not only did the detection of the released gases provide unmistakable evidence that a nuclear explosion had occurred, it also demonstrated to anyone considering a clandestine nuclear test in the future that the probability of detection is very high, even at great distance. As some of the delegations had argued during negotiations on the IMS, noble gas monitoring increases the costs and risks to a potential violator of the treaty and therefore greatly adds to the deterrent capacity of the verification regime.

North Korea's nuclear test, though highly undesirable from political and security standpoints, served as a proving ground for the effectiveness of the IMS, even when, according to the CTBTO, it was at the time only 60% established. In particular, the seismic and noble gas detection and identification of a nuclear explosion below 1kt yield demonstrated the effectiveness of the monitoring technologies. At the same time, the North Korean test has underscored the necessity of achieving the treaty's entry into force. If the CTBT had been in force in 2006 when the nuclear explosion had been detected, states parties would no doubt have decided to conduct an intrusive inspection in the area identified as the site of the suspected explosion, to provide more conclusive evidence.

FIELD EXERCISES IN ON-SITE INSPECTIONS

Unlike the IMS, which can be established and operated by the CTBTO on a provisional basis, on-site inspections cannot be carried out prior to the treaty's entry into force. Since 1997, however, the PTS has been working with signatories to the treaty to determine the technologies and procedures that could be required if an on-site inspection were to be requested under the treaty. Despite the difficulties caused by the Bush administration withholding for several years a portion of the US contribution to the CTBTO designated to fund work on OSI, representatives of states signatories continued to negotiate and draft a manual for inspections and to develop the techniques and equipment that would best fulfil the requirements contained in the verification article and protocol to the treaty. Where the finalized text of the treaty and its protocol are regarded as the legal basis for the inspections, the manual sets out the agreed procedures.

Several exercises have been held to train inspectors and test equipment and specific technologies: for example, radiological sampling was practised in areas near Chernobyl in June 2007, with careful attention paid to the health and safety of practitioners as well as the taking and testing of vegetation, soil and various different kinds of samples. In September 2008 the CTBTO for the first time held an integrated exercise utilizing all the basic technologies and techniques. To test out the adequacy of OSI operations and equipment as well as honing the skills of staff and inspectors, this integrated field exercise involved four weeks at the former Soviet test site of Semipalatinsk, Kazakhstan, in accordance with a realistically ambiguous fictional scenario involving rival governments and the real challenges of howling gales, driving rain and snow.[12]

The exercise scenario was launched when the IMS in Vienna registered a seismic event of magnitude 4 in the fictional state of "Arcania" in Central Asia, which was known to have conducted over 20 nuclear tests some decades earlier, but which had recently signed and ratified the CTBT. The fictional neighbouring state of "Fiducia" requested the CTBTO to carry out an on-site inspection and backed up this demand with additional evidence of radioactivity picked up by its national sensors. According to the scenario, a majority of at least 30 of the 51 "Executive Council" members agreed that an OSI would be necessary, and so 40 inspectors and some 50 tonnes of equipment were flown out to the Central Asian steppes. As far as possible, the Semipalatinsk field exercise had to be carried out in accordance with the treaty, its verification protocol and the draft on-site inspections manual.

In addition to testing and assessing all the technologies, techniques and procedures for CTBT on-site inspections, one purpose of the integrated field exercise was to test if the manual's provisions were appropriate for the field, including whether the negotiators had achieved a practical balance between the rights, responsibilities and needs of the inspection team and of the inspected state party. When the OSI provisions for the treaty were being negotiated in Geneva, it was thought that they were unlikely ever to be evoked. And yet it was still necessary to get them right: to achieve a balance between what was sufficient to ensure that non-compliance would be detected and what was politically bearable for the states parties who might one day find themselves the subject of an inspection request.

As demonstrated by its detection and identification of the North Korean nuclear test in October 2006, the IMS had proved itself to be sufficiently comprehensive and sensitive to act as a major deterrent to cheating since the likelihood of getting caught is very high. But deterrence does not always work. On-site inspections may be very rare, but they have to be robust and rigorous enough to provide confidence that treaty violations will be caught. Otherwise, it could be too tempting for someone to cheat and hope to brazen it out by claiming some other source for any seismic signals or radionuclides that were detected. In the exercise scenario, for example, Arcania maintained that the IMS had picked up a shallow earthquake and not a nuclear test. In submitting to the OSI, Arcania pointed out that the inspection area contained sites of current military sensitivity and boreholes from nuclear tests prior to 1989, and emphasized its intention to maintain its "right to protect confidential information".

Taking place at the interface between verification politics and technology, theory and practice, fact and fiction, the integrated field exercise was challenging for all sides. It was the first ever opportunity for the CTBTO to practise and integrate all the elements of an inspection in almost real time. Much was learned about the training and equipment needs and the feasibility of some approaches and timelines. As a consequence of a rigorous assessment of the challenges faced and the conduct of the exercise, the CTBTO is adapting its planning, procedures and manuals to be able to gather evidence and respond even more effectively should an OSI ever be required. As noted by Executive Secretary Tibor Tóth: "In a comparatively short period of time, a great wealth of knowledge has been created. ... Lessons have been learnt about equipment and scientific data, and about logistics and procedures." Characterizing on-site inspections as "an additional layer of the verification muscle of the CTBTO", he added, "It will bring the verification regime closer and closer to a state of readiness".[13]

CIVILIAN BENEFITS OF THE CTBT

The purpose of such verification readiness is not only to detect and provide evidence of clandestine nuclear explosions, but perhaps more importantly to deter any potential violator by increasing the costs and risks that they might face. Once the treaty enters into force, it is unlikely that any state will try to cheat. However, maintaining the verification regime will continue to be important. In addition to the security benefits of having an effectively verifiable CTBT, the complex architecture of sophisticated technologies is now being utilized to support civilian and scientific applications, such as dealing with disasters and climate change, and for uses of education, research and development. In November 2008, for example, despite the fact that Indonesia had not at that time ratified the CTBT it became the beneficiary of a vital Tsunami Warning Arrangement agreed with the CTBTO, in accordance with which the CTBTO would provide high-speed, relevant data transmissions from the IMS to Indonesia's Meteorological and Geophysical Agency to enhance its early warning capabilities.[14]

The civilian applications and benefits of the verification regime were barely discussed during the CTBT negotiations. Indeed, at the time, some delegations had insisted there should be stringent limits on what the CTBTO would be permitted to do with data received from the IMS. Their intention was to protect sensitive information, but the negative consequences of the restrictions became tragically apparent as a result of the tsunami that devastated coastal areas of several countries including Indonesia, Sri Lanka, Myanmar (Burma) and Thailand in December 2004. Following such loss of life, the states participating in the CTBTO's Preparatory Commission asked the PTS to investigate how data could be provided from the IMS for early warning of tsunami and other natural hazards. The agreement with Indonesia was the most recent, following on from arrangements initiated in November 2006 with Australia, Japan, Malaysia and the United States, and subsequently agreed also with the Philippines and Thailand.[15]

IMS radionuclide monitoring could also help in early warning and identification of nuclear accidents, thereby lessening the likelihood of the kinds of confusion and misinformation that delayed emergency responses in the aftermath of the Chernobyl accident in 1986. As the world becomes more aware of the impact and implications of climate change, IMS stations could also provide data for climate research and for understanding changes in weather patterns and the global atmospheric system. Although there are several thousand monitoring facilities operating as part of national meteorological networks, the value added by the IMS is that it has much wider coverage and can fill geographic gaps, since many IMS stations are in remote sites that have not been used for national monitoring because they are relatively inaccessible and underpopulated. The 60-station infrasound network would be particularly valuable in this regard, as it can detect and track severe storms, air and ocean waves, meteorites entering the earth's atmosphere, volcanic eruptions, as well as earthquakes and explosions.[16] Though the primary reason for the CTBT remains security and non-proliferation, it is now clear that the verification regime adds to international security in broader ways. The time may come when the international community decides that states that are impeding entry into force by delaying or refusing to sign or ratify the treaty will no longer be permitted to access or receive these civilian benefits associated with the CTBT.

UNFINISHED BUSINESS

The CTBT was a major objective of the Cold War, concluded in the first decade after its end. By any standard, this multilateral treaty is so widely supported that it should be judged a success. But it has not yet been able to enter into force, because only 35 of the 44 states listed in Annex II of the treaty have signed and ratified. Three of them—India, North Korea and Pakistan—have not yet even signed. As discussed in Chapter 6, the treaty's stringent entry-into-force provision requires all 44 states in Annex II to sign and ratify before the CTBT can enter into full legal force.

Because of this high barrier, the CTBT has suffered in legal limbo for more than a decade. The prolonged uncertainty over the treaty's future has already had a deleterious effect on the non-proliferation regime and on further efforts to pursue multilateral arms control and disarmament. Some regard the lack of a functional CTBT as indicative of bad faith on behalf of the nuclear powers. This was especially true of the United States during the Bush administration (2001–2009), which in its 2001 Nuclear Posture Review put capabilities rather than threat assessments at the heart of defence planning. In accordance with the neoconservative belief that US military options should be kept open, the Bush administration pursued policies that tended to undermine the international legal and non-proliferation regimes that provided some of the most effective tools for constraining adversaries and reducing threats to national and international security. Where the previous administration had made the CTBT an important plank of its arms control and non-proliferation efforts, the Bush administration voted against, criticized and withheld funding for the treaty. Though that is set to change with the Obama administration, the damage done to the credibility of the CTBT will need to be overcome.

Despite the CTBT having been a principal objective that India's former Prime Minister Jawaharlal Nehru had spearheaded on behalf of the non-aligned countries from the 1950s on, India has maintained its opposition to the treaty as negotiated in the CD and adopted by the General Assembly in 1996. Though Pakistan voted for the CTBT in 1996 and in the General Assembly in subsequent years, it too has made no effort to sign or ratify, instead maintaining its stance that Pakistan will join when India does. Pakistan's position may have disappointed those that hoped that the assurances embedded in Article XIV would enable that country to sign and ratify independently of its neighbour, but its failure to join has come as little surprise.

The world was shocked, however, in May 1998, when first India and then Pakistan conducted several underground tests and then proceeded to declare themselves to be "nuclear weapon states".[17] A further major setback occurred in October 1999, when the Clinton administration failed to muster the requisite two-thirds majority in the US Senate for ratification of the treaty.[18] Before the vote, test-ban opponents had questioned the treaty's verifiability and the constraints it set on the ability of the United States to maintain its arsenal. Though the failure to ratify was less related to the merits of the treaty than the unpropitious timing, in which the CTBT fell victim to a toxic political atmosphere that then characterized relations between the administration and the Republican Party, which held a narrow majority in the Senate, it must be acknowledged that the Clinton administration did not do enough at the time to promote information and debate about the importance, purpose and merits of the CTBT. After the ratification vote split along party lines, belated steps were taken by the administration to remedy those omissions.

Notwithstanding the fact that Russia, France and the United Kingdom had all ratified the treaty before the 2000 NPT Review Conference, however, there was not enough time or political will in the United States to rebuild the case for the CTBT and organize sufficient support to undertake a second attempt to ratify this treaty before the election of November 2000 resulted in George W. Bush being instated as the forty-third president. Publicly declaring opposition to this multilateral treaty, for eight years the Bush administration voted against any UN resolution that called on states to take the necessary steps to bring the CTBT into force and also boycotted political meetings of CTBT signatories such as the special conferences convened on entry into force in accordance with Article XIV of the treaty.

The first such conference was convened by state signatories in 1999, with the remit of considering how to facilitate entry into force. An Article XIV Conference was held every two years from then on, although the United States joined India and North Korea for some years in refusing to participate. The Preparatory Commission and Provisional Technical Secretariat, together with the first and second Executive Secretaries—Wolfgang Hoffmann from 1996 to 2005, succeeded by Tibor Tóth—set in place strategies and mechanisms to encourage governments to sign and ratify. In 2003, Jaap Ramaker, who had presided over the concluding year as Chair of the CTBT negotiations in 1996, was appointed Special Representative of the Ratifying States in 2003, with an EU-funded brief to explain the treaty's importance, encourage and facilitate ratification, and promote entry into force. It was an uphill struggle, however, as long as the US administration remained in active opposition to the treaty.

US hostility to the treaty made it very difficult for other countries to exert effective pressure on India and Pakistan to sign. It also let China, which had signed but not ratified, off the hook. For the past nine years, China has assured NPT and other meetings of its support for the CTBT but, though it participates fully in the PTS and votes in favour of the treaty in UN resolutions, China has still not ratified. The explanation given by diplomats is that the National People's Congress is still deliberating over the legislation required for ratification. At times, hints have been given that China may ratify soon, but this has so far not materialized. The impression given by this long hiatus is that China is waiting for the United States and perhaps even India to ratify.

Though nine national decisions must still be made, the political keys to entry into force lie in the hands of US and Indian leaders. With regard to the United States, the election of Obama and change of administration in 2009 offer new opportunities. President Obama and Secretary of State Hillary Clinton have both expressed support for the CTBT, but they will need to build bipartisan support to ensure that there is no chance of the treaty being defeated a second time by failing to reach the necessary two-thirds majority in the Senate. This would require support from all the Democrat Senators and votes in favour from some eight Republican Senators as well. While it would be desirable for the United States to have ratified the CTBT before the eighth Review Conference of the NPT in 2010, the domestic process needs to be carefully undertaken to ensure success next time the Senate votes on the treaty.

Obama does not need to reinvent the wheel to promote CTBT ratification. The politics surrounding nuclear issues have moved on since partisan rivalries defeated CTBT ratification in 1999. George Shultz, William Perry, Henry Kissinger, Sam Nunn and a group of about 20 other US statesmen and senior analysts from across the US political spectrum published an essay in the *Wall Street Journal* in January 2007 titled "A World Free of Nuclear Weapons",[19] which provoked considerable debate and was followed with a further essay in January 2008 that drew even more high-level support.[20] Making clear that their aim was to promote both international security and US national interests, these US foreign-policy leaders identified the core problems associated with nuclear weapons, deterrence and proliferation in the post-Cold War world and emphasized ratification of the CTBT as a high-priority step that the United States needed to take. To put the CTBT back on the US political agenda, they called for:

> a bipartisan review, first, to examine improvements over the past decade of the international monitoring system to identify and locate explosive underground nuclear tests in violation of the CTBT; and, second, to assess the technical progress made over the past decade in maintaining high confidence in the reliability, safety and effectiveness of the nation's nuclear arsenal under a test ban.[21]

As a first step, such a review could build on the work of General John Shalikashvili and the Commission President Clinton appointed him to lead in January 2000, after the ratification debacle. Mandated to consult with Senators and "lay the groundwork for future ratification of the treaty",[22] Shalikashvili devoted considerable energy to making the case for how and why the CTBT and its verification regime would enhance US security interests. Noting that "the value of a verification system extends well past the range where a monitor has high confidence of detecting, identifying, locating, and attributing a violation, and down into the gray area where a potential evader lacks certainty about the likelihood of discovery", the Shalikashvili Report concluded that the CTBT's verification regime would be able to detect explosions of 10 tons yield or lower at Russia's Novaya Zemlya test site; provide global coverage below 500 tons yield and much lower at all known test sites; and the right to use NTM to back up a request for an inspection.[23] In addition to Shalikashvili's report, independent studies were also undertaken by NGOs to assess the treaty's verifiability from a more technical and international standpoint, aiming not only to inform the US Congress, but officials and elected representatives in other countries whose ratification was essential for CTBT entry into force.[24]

As discussed above, the ability of the verification regime to detect, locate and identify even very-low-yield nuclear explosions was borne out in the case of the North Korean test. In developing a strategy to convince Senators that this treaty has widespread public support and would bring many benefits to the United States as well as the rest of the world, Obama may consider a new bipartisan review of the treaty and its verification regime or he may prefer to appoint an individual with knowledge of intelligence, verification, defence and security matters to lead the administration's efforts and line up the votes. Ideally, this needs to start early in 2009, and should address US security concerns while highlighting how these are best served by strengthening the multilateral regimes and tools for preventing nuclear proliferation and related dangers. Efforts will need to be made to counter the misconceptions about the treaty's purpose and verification regime that characterized the US debate on the CTBT in 1999.

In addition to updating the Shalikashvili Report, the administration should provide opportunities for Senators to meet the US officials responsible for protecting US interests in the negotiations, so that they can explain the provisions, limits and safeguards in the treaty. In October 1999, the head of the US delegation throughout the CTBT negotiations, Stephen Ledogar, gave compelling testimony to the US Senate Foreign Relations Committee. Pointing out that he had first been appointed as an ambassador by President Reagan, and had served under Presidents Bush and Clinton as chief negotiator for the Chemical Weapons Convention and CTBT respectively, Ledogar specifically addressed the criticisms from some Senators regarding the treaty's scope, verification and entry into force. He gave an overview of how these outcomes had been negotiated and what they meant, pointing out that the "zero means zero" yield decision was in US interests as it cut short the "squabbling" among the P-5 and ensured that there would be "no threshold for anybody. ... If what you did produced any nuclear yield whatsoever, it would not be allowed. If it didn't, it was allowed".[25] With regard to verification, Ledogar told the Committee:

> The point I would like to stress here is that the U.S. succeeded in the negotiations in getting virtually every thing the intelligence community and other parts of the government wanted from the treaty ... to strengthen our ability to detect and deter cheating and to seek appropriate redress if cheating did occur. At the same time, we succeeded in getting virtually everything the Defense Department and others wanted to insure the protection of sensitive national security information.[26]

With regard to the use of national technical means, for example, Ledogar acknowledged that there had been considerable opposition to the US position as providing "a clear advantage and a license to spy". The US delegation "crafted a complicated, highly detailed proposal that balanced our offensive and defensive needs". "[B]y the time we were through," Ledogar told the Committee, "the treaty read pretty much like the original U.S. position paper that had been put together jointly by the Departments of Defense, Energy and State, the intelligence community and the then existing Arms Control Agency".[27] Ledogar's testimony, substantiated by this book's analysis of the 1994–1996 negotiations in the CD, clearly shows that the US administration and delegation negotiated to get a CTBT that would be in US national security interests. The fact that the treaty is also in the wider non-proliferation and international security interests of the rest of the world does not detract from that fact.

As this history has shown, the CTBT negotiations were not a zero-sum game. The fact that so many other states have signed and ratified the CTBT indicates that it not only met US needs, but the security interests of other states as well. Most of civil society and the non-nuclear states have continued to support the CTBT, while recognizing that it is an interim step towards deeper disarmament. The CTBT is strong enough on its merits for the US Senate to ratify it on US security grounds. Despite speculation during late 2008 that Defense Secretary Robert Gates wanted CTBT ratification to be tied to commitments to develop a new "reliable replacement warhead" (RRW), such a trade-off would run counter to the administration's broader non-proliferation goals, and should not be pursued.

The nuclear and military establishments of the United States and some of the other nuclear powers were able to leverage their support for the CTBT in return for well-funded stockpile stewardship programmes, maintenance of some test sites and the expansion of technological capabilities to test and refine nuclear warheads using hydrodynamic and subcritical experiments, laser ignition and similar research and design techniques. The consequence of retaining such programmes is that the CTBT is not as far-reaching a disarmament instrument as it would have been twenty years earlier, but this does not mean that the CTBT is not an important and effective instrument to verifiably prohibit nuclear explosions, a necessary requisite for non-proliferation and disarmament. Such deals may at the time have been thought necessary to win over test-ban opponents in the respective countries. However, any further deal in the United States that included a trade-off involving new nuclear weapons in return for CTBT ratification could undermine both the CTBT and the NPT. It will be up to US civil society to take the lead in ensuring that such counter-productive trade-offs are not pursued, as they would undermine the NPT and be soundly condemned by other governments and international civil society.

The CTBT is a necessary—but not sufficient—component of non-proliferation and disarmament. It is a first step, not the last. To let the treaty fail now is not in the interests of anyone except a nuclear proliferator. These are the kinds of arguments that need to be made when the United States reconsiders ratification of the CTBT. While US ratification of the CTBT before the next Review Conference of the NPT in 2010 would be welcomed, it should not be rushed if the support has not been adequately marshalled. The worst outcome for the CTBT would be for another Senate vote to fail to reach the necessary majority for ratification. If, despite the administration's best efforts, it requires more time to marshal the numbers in the Senate for ratification to be achieved before the 2010 Review Conference, then the US administration would need to go to that conference with a strong message of support for the CTBT and demonstrate its political will and intention to achieve ratification in the near future. Together with initiatives on devaluing nuclear weapons and making further and deeper cuts in the arsenals, such an approach could still have a positive impact on the NPT.

If US support is restored, that would help bring about some of the remaining ratifications. If China, which has expressed support for the treaty since 1996, were willing to move ahead with its ratification and not wait for the United States, this would give positive momentum to efforts to persuade the US Senate to ratify the treaty. Chinese ratification in 2009 would demonstrate its international status as a leader, not a follower. It would set a positive example to North Korea and non-aligned countries such as Indonesia, Egypt and Iran, and help governments and civil society put greater political pressure on Washington and New Delhi—a win–win strategic move for Beijing.[28] The fact that the Obama administration appears eager to pursue deeper cuts in the US and Russian arsenals and displays noticeably less enthusiasm than George W. Bush about projects China considers threatening, such as ballistic missile defence, may go some way toward fostering a security context in which Chinese ratification can be finally achieved.

With a change of administration in the United States, India remains the hardest state to bring on board. Yet India's own security interests are such that it needs to move beyond its experience with the CTBT endgame and indefinite extension of the NPT and see the test-ban treaty for what it is now—a non-discriminatory treaty that provides global security benefits. Since declaring itself a nuclear-weapon state in May 1998, India has sought to be recognized as a responsible nuclear-weapon possessor. An obvious way to demonstrate its claim to exercise its weapon status responsibly would be to cement its current voluntary moratorium by signing and ratifying the CTBT. However, it was never challenged to reverse its opposition to the CTBT during the Bush administration. On the contrary, in 2007–2008, the United States promoted a far-reaching deal with India on civilian nuclear trade without any mention of the CTBT. The US–India nuclear cooperation deal divided members of the Nuclear Suppliers Group amidst fears that it would undermine the NPT. Though some would have liked to make India's signature and ratification of the CTBT a condition, this was not possible without US backing, so the agreement to facilitate nuclear trade with India went through without.

It may be too late to rewrite those agreements, but it is not too late late for individual states to offer inducements or exert pressure on India to sign and ratify the CTBT. It is likely that under the Nuclear Suppliers Group arrangements, India will be seeking nuclear-related supplies from countries such as Australia, Brazil, Canada, Japan, Russia, South Africa and members of the European Union such as France and the Netherlands. These are all strong supporters of the CTBT. If they decided to engage in nuclear trade, then at the very least they could make India's signature and ratification of the CTBT a minimum non-proliferation condition of any contracts that provided nuclear materials—or, for that matter, any form of defence-related technology or equipment. If these suppliers intend to trade, then they could make India's signature and ratification of the CTBT a minimum non-proliferation condition. There are precedents for this in long-standing European Union policies, in which adherence to EU rules on preventing weapons of mass destruction proliferation are inserted as conditions in certain trading contracts with parties outside the European Union. For the European Union to take the lead on this would be consistent with EU policy. In January 2007, the European Union's High Representative for the Common Foreign and Security Policy (CFSP), Javier Solana, emphasized the importance of entry into force and universality of the CTBT, which he described as "egalitarian". He noted: "All States have to comply with the same obligations and all have access, in the same way, to the most extensive global verification regime ever built".[29]

Civil society also has a role to play in persuading India to rethink the CTBT now and join. As a large and diverse democracy, India engaged in tumultuous debate about the CTBT during 1996. While majority opinion at that time seemed to favour rejection of the treaty and the subsequent testing of India's nuclear weapons in May 1998, the main arguments were based on national pride and opposition to what was portrayed as another discriminatory treaty that would compound India's exclusion from the nuclear club defined in the NPT regime. Now that the non-proliferation agenda is being transformed internationally into one that promotes the total abolition of nuclear weapons, Indian NGOs need to promote a new debate about nuclear policy in India, starting with the CTBT. For this, they need to re-engage India's diverse media and civil society leaders and link the CTBT to India's broader political and security goals, including its need for regional security and its national self-image as a progressive and ethical leader. Like the United States, India needs to undertake a non-partisan review of the CTBT's provisions, role, development and benefits as a first step toward rethinking its policy.

Among the remaining hold-outs there are geostrategic or client relationships that mean that ratification by one may make it more likely that others will follow. If India signs and ratifies, it is assumed from Pakistan's public statements that it will do so too. But that assumption may no longer hold. Pakistan's institutional and political interests are different from India's and Pakistan's governing elite is angry at being denied the nuclear trade benefits that it perceives India to be receiving through the nuclear deal spearheaded by the Bush administration. Pakistan may need to be dissuaded from seeking a high price or quid pro quo from the international community in return for signing and ratifying the CTBT. Though it is clear that accession to the CTBT is consistent with Pakistan's stated policies and security interests, in light of the destabilizing consequences of the US–India nuclear deal, it may be necessary for the international community to consider what kinds of inducements or incentives could be offered to Pakistan, in keeping with disarmament and non-proliferation objectives, that would facilitate that country's signature and ratification. It may also be necessary for India and Pakistan to harmonize their signatures and ratifications so that they join the treaty together, as France and the United Kingdom did in 1998.

Indonesia's inability to ratify the CTBT to date has been more difficult to understand, as it has long carried responsibility for coordinating the non-aligned states in disarmament and non-proliferation issues and was a significant player during the negotiations. Indonesia signed early, and now risks losing credibility if it continues without ratifying the treaty, particularly as it stands to benefit more than most from the civilian benefits of the IMS. Reassuringly, Indonesia signalled in 2008 that it planned to ratify soon, giving hope that this significant non-aligned country will not feel the need to wait for the United States or anyone else.

Signature and ratification of the CTBT would undoubtedly have been part of any Denuclearization Action Plan with North Korea had there not been declared opposition to the treaty from the Bush administration. There is now a chance to rectify that omission. Ideally, the Six Party Talks should include North Korea's accession to the CTBT as part of the Action Plan, but if this is not feasible then at the very least North Korea should be pressured into signing and ratifying the CTBT as a confidence-building measure to demonstrate its commitment to carrying through the irreversible dismantling of its nuclear weapon programme. Renewed leadership from China and the United States in this matter would be welcomed by Japan, Russia and South Korea, the other participants in the Six Party Talks, who have themselves ratified the CTBT.

That leaves the Middle East, where Egypt, Iran and Israel have all signed but not ratified the treaty. These three may be tough to bring on board. Though their reasons for not ratifying are linked, it is unlikely for political reasons that they would formally acknowledge this by trying to ratify together. Israel, like China, participates fully in the CTBTO and has a number of highly qualified personnel in staff or advisory positions. Like India and Pakistan, Israel has not joined the NPT. Unlike the South Asian states, however, Israel has never declared or admitted to having conducted a nuclear explosion and does not maintain a site on its territory where nuclear test explosions would be able to be carried out. There have been well-sourced suggestions that Israel would have ratified years ago if the Bush administration had not made use of its special relationship with the Israeli government to persuade it not to. If such speculation is true, then Israel might be more prepared to ratify now that the Obama administration has indicated its own intention to pursue CTBT ratification. Though Israel does not have a problem with the test ban as such, it has some remaining concerns about the prospect of intrusive inspections at sensitive sites such as Dimona. Its desire to participate fully in the CTBTO could be leveraged to persuade Israeli decision makers that they have more to gain by ratifying than by continuing to stall. While it might be unrealistic to assume that, when Israel ratifies, Iran and Egypt will quickly follow, it is even more unrealistic to think that either of these Middle East nations will undertake ratification of the CTBT unless they are sure that Israel is on board as well.

In view of concerns about Iran's nuclear programme, both Iran and its neighbours should have clear—if somewhat different—incentives to get the CTBT locked down. Ratifying the CTBT would be an important way to demonstrate that Iran is not—as many fear—planning to emulate North Korea in the future by withdrawing from the NPT and building and testing a nuclear weapon. As part of the ongoing negotiations over Iran's uranium enrichment programme, it would make sense at the very least for Iran to demonstrate its good faith as an NPT party by ratifying the CTBT. For years, the non-ratification of Israel and the United States (as well as Egypt) has provided Iran with a degree of cover. During the CTBT, Iran negotiated fully and constructively. Iranian diplomats were appointed to various responsibilities, including as Friend of the Chair on inspections. Though Iran's ratification of the CTBT would not alleviate all concerns, it is certain that if Tehran continues to hold out against joining the test ban this will compound suspicions that it harbours an ambition to pursue nuclear weapons under the guise of a nuclear energy programme.

Egypt has also delayed ratifying the CTBT, and is perceived to be waiting for Israel and perhaps also Iran. However understandable such linkage might be, the CTBT is far more in Egypt's interests than the political returns on a delay. To ratify early would put Egypt in a position to work with other major players to ensure that all relevant states in its region not only become bound by the test ban but also move toward its broader political goal of a nuclear-weapons-free zone in the Middle East.

Provisional application of the CTBT: only as a last resort

With a new president in the White House, the emphasis should now be on persuading the last nine hold-outs to join the treaty as it stands. Different strategies and tactics need to be tailored to the particular situation of each of these countries, to address their concerns and exert the right kind of pressure. However, even with concerted international and civil society action it is possible that the government of one or perhaps two of the 44 Annex II states may put narrow self-interest above collective security needs and refuse to sign and/or ratify. In accordance with how the treaty was written, just one of the 44 could indefinitely prevent the CTBT from entering into force, even if everyone else has ratified. This would be an intolerable state of affairs, in which a marginalized state was able to exercise a de facto veto to prevent the vast majority from fulfilling an agreed collective security objective. If, in a few years' time, most but not all of the nine have ratified and all reasonable efforts have been made to persuade the last one or two hold-outs to join the international community, it could be time for the states that have ratified to consider applying the treaty provisionally in all respects except Article XIV.[30]

Provisional application is a rarely employed but potentially useful mechanism to bypass extraordinary, temporary or unanticipated political obstacles impeding entry into force. It enables a treaty that is supported by a large and significant number of ratifiers to be implemented, at least for the consenting states. It is not a panacea or substitute for entry into force, but it can provide temporary reinforcement to bolster the legal authority of a treaty and prevent it from being undermined by circumstance. On the rare occasions that it has been invoked in relation to other treaties in the recent past, provisional application has contributed toward building confidence and helping to create more positive conditions and incentives to facilitate full entry into force.

According to Article 25 of the 1969 Vienna Convention on the Law of Treaties, "A treaty or part of a treaty is applied provisionally pending its entry into force if: (a) the treaty itself so provides"—which the CTBT does not—or if "the negotiating States have in some other manner so agreed".

Depending on how provisional application is entered into, this means that, pending entry into force, all or part of a treaty takes legal effect for those who wish to abide by the agreement. Though not binding on those who remain outside, a treaty that is provisionally applied by a large number of states has enhanced legal standing, increasing the political costs of violation.

The CTBT text does not specifically mention provisional application, but nor does it prohibit it. During the difficult negotiations over entry into force, provisional application was discussed as a way to prevent an individual state from exercising a de facto veto. Though it was not explicitly referred to publicly, an envisaged possible need to consider provisional application was subtext in the discussions among Canadian diplomats and others over proposals for special conferences in the event that the conditions specified in Article XIV were not met and the treaty was unable to enter into force in good time. Aware of the politics of the positions held by China, Russia, Pakistan and the United Kingdom on the one side and India on the other, the CD did not invest these Article XIV conferences with the power to waive the stringent entry-into-force requirements or the list of states in Annex II, but it did pave the way for participating states to agree on procedures for further measures. Potentially, such measures might include provisional application.

Provisional application would require the agreement of most but not all states that had ratified the treaty. There are several ways in which this could be taken forward. Most simply, a group of states could decide to convene a special conference and invite all states that had ratified (together with signatories, who would participate as non-voting observers) to negotiate and agree a protocol on provisional application. This could be done in conjunction with an Article XIV conference, or separately, in an extraordinary conference specially convened for the purpose.

Based on precedent and the particular needs of the CTBT, a provisional application agreement could be worded along the following lines and endorsed by a majority vote in the UN General Assembly:[31]

> 1. To promote the implementation of the Comprehensive Nuclear-Test-Ban Treaty, as opened for signature on September 24, 1996, hereinafter referred to as the Treaty, the States Parties hereby agree to the provisional application of certain provisions of the Treaty.

2. Without detriment to the provisions of Article XIV of the Treaty, the States Parties shall apply provisionally all other Articles, Protocols and Provisions of the Treaty.

3. The Treaty shall be applied provisionally by all States which have signed and ratified the Treaty, unless they notify the Depositary in writing that they do not consent to such provisional application.

4. The Treaty shall be applied provisionally by any State which has signed the Treaty, which consents to its provisional application by so notifying the Depositary in writing. Such provisional application shall become effective from the date of receipt of the notification by the Depositary.

5. Regardless of whether a signatory State has agreed to provisionally apply the Treaty, financial contributions for supporting Treaty implementation and verification shall be as agreed in the Schedule unless a State notifies the Depositary in writing of its intention to alter its financial contribution.

6. Provisional application shall terminate upon the entry into force of the Comprehensive Nuclear-Test-Ban Treaty. In conformity with Article IX of the Treaty, any State may also withdraw its consent from provisional application by notifying the Depositary in writing, and must include a statement of the extraordinary event or events related to the subject matter of this Treaty which the State regards as jeopardizing its supreme interests.

This approach has two advantages: an automatic co-option of all ratifiers (with a provision for opting out if a national decision is taken to that effect) plus a mechanism for signatories to opt in by executive decision. In the first case, states that have already ratified are not required to take additional national steps to be included in provisional application: it is simpler if the decision to provisionally apply the CTBT does not require additional legislative or judicial action (unless specific conditions have already been attached to a state's ratification). Whether additional legislation or agreement would be needed if a government wished to opt out would, of course, depend on national law or specific implementation procedures. The opt-in option for signatories could be used in cases where the executive branch of government wished to participate fully in the treaty's benefits but was impeded, as sometimes happens, if national ratification were to become bogged down in difficult legislative, judicial or bureaucratic processes.

Paragraph 2 is crucial—it means that the entire treaty, as concluded and signed, is applied, apart from the entry-into-force requirements. Since it is without detriment to Article XIV, every effort should continue to be made to fulfil the requirements and enable full entry into force. Although it would be hoped that none would seek to exercise the right of withdrawal, it is important to note that provisional application would not interfere with the withdrawal provisions in the treaty. According to Article IX of the CTBT, which would stand, withdrawal is possible after notice of six months if a state decides that extraordinary events related to the subject matter of the treaty have jeopardized its supreme interests.

Though the rules of procedure for Article XIV conferences currently require consensus among the ratifiers, decision-making in the case of provisional application would be according to rules determined by the participating states. With regard to amendments, for example, Article VII of the CTBT states that an amendment may be adopted by "a positive vote of a majority of states parties with no state party casting a negative vote". However, Article 9 of the Vienna Convention takes as general practice for treaty decision-making the less stringent requirement of a positive vote of two-thirds of the states participating and voting.

The next few years offer fresh opportunities to pursue full entry into force of the CTBT, in accordance with Article XIV, so it would be premature to consider provisional application until all efforts to persuade states to ratify have been exhausted. But if one or more of the Annex II states that have not yet ratified continue to hold the treaty hostage, the international community may need to act to secure the test ban and its verification system for the majority. This was recognized by the 2006 Weapons of Mass Destruction Commission, which acknowledged that the time might come for provisional entry into force or application to be seriously considered.[32]

If the CTBT is allowed to atrophy or die, either intentionally or as a side effect of some state's nuclear ambitions, it would be almost impossible to resurrect it. Losing the treaty would seriously damage international efforts toward nuclear disarmament and non-proliferation. Even if provisional application did not impose a sufficient deterrent to prevent all testing, a treaty in provisional force would have more chance of constituting a brake on testing by other states in response. Hence, there would be some hope of preventing a collapse of the test-ban norm, while at the same time the provisionally applied treaty would provide a stronger legal basis for collective UN action against the violator than is possible while the treaty remains not in force. Yet this should only be considered as a fallback position, a last resort if all efforts have failed to bear fruit by, say, the year 2012.

CONCLUSION

It is more than 50 years since the Japanese Parliament and India's Prime Minister backed growing public demands for a comprehensive nuclear-test-ban treaty, which became the centrepiece of disarmament advocacy for many decades. Just as today the idea of a nuclear weapons convention is dismissed by sceptics as a distant (if laudable) goal, the CTBT was delayed for years by arguments emanating from the nuclear-weapon states that it was impractical or unverifiable. By the time the CTBT was negotiated, however, it was perceived more as a non-proliferation measure than a disarmament step. Even if its significance for preventing the modernization of arsenals may have been diminished by technological advances in computer modelling and hydrodynamic experiments, the CTBT has a special role to fulfil in the promotion of disarmament and human security.

Thirteen years after the treaty was concluded it has been signed by more states than any other comparable agreement and yet has not been able to enter into force. At the same time a shift is underway in some of the nuclear-weapon states towards recognizing that reducing nuclear dangers will require the devaluing and progressive elimination of nuclear arsenals, not just reductions and counter-proliferation. As more leaders and opinion-formers line up behind the goal of a world free of nuclear weapons, the CTBT is not so much the next step as unfinished business. The continued failure to bring this important agreement into full legal effect leaves a dangerous door open and undermines collective efforts to prevent proliferation. Though the norm held sufficiently through the nuclear tests conducted by India and Pakistan in 1998 and by North Korea in 2006, any further nuclear explosions could derail disarmament efforts and destroy years of progress in non-proliferation.

With a change of heart in Washington real opportunities are opening up to bring the CTBT into force. Just as transnational civil society and some governments worked hard to bring the CTBT to the negotiating table in 1994 and secure a zero-yield scope, an intensification of effort will be needed to bring the treaty into force. As well as governments and civil society, parliamentarians may have a critical role to play, at least in facilitating debate in some of the hold-outs. In both India and the United States, for example, elected representatives will have a critical say in whether those countries ratify the treaty. In addition to paying close attention to the information they receive from the defence, nuclear and intelligence establishments, the respective parliamentarians and senators need to hear arguments in favour of the CTBT from their counterparts in other strategically relevant countries that have already voted themselves to ratify the treaty.

Though the next few years offer good opportunities for progress, that is not to say that it will be easy. There is, however, hope. In the past decade, civil society has worked in partnership with governments to achieve far-reaching bans on anti-personnel landmines and cluster munitions, despite opposition from some powerful states. In the case of the CTBT, an overwhelming majority of states have already signed and ratified the treaty. These governments need to exert leadership individually and in their roles as members of the Preparatory Commission for the CTBTO to develop and resource effective strategies to assist each of the nine key states to overcome their difficulties. For this to happen, transnational civil society may need to raise awareness for one final big push to bring the treaty into force. Achieving the CTBT after all these years will revive the credibility of multilateral arms control and pave the way for the next steps towards a world free of nuclear weapons to be undertaken.

ANNEX A

CTBT ANNEX II STATES

Article XIV, paragraph 1, of the CTBT states that "This Treaty shall enter into force 180 days after the date of deposit of the instruments of ratification by all States listed in Annex 2 to this Treaty, but in no case earlier than two years after its opening for signature". Annex II reads as follows:

LIST OF STATES PURSUANT TO ARTICLE XIV

> List of States members of the Conference on Disarmament as at 18 June 1996 which formally participated in the work of the 1996 session of the Conference and which appear in Table 1 of the International Atomic Energy Agency's April 1996 edition of "Nuclear Power Reactors in the World", and of States members of the Conference on Disarmament as at 18 June 1996 which formally participated in the work of the 1996 session of the Conference and which appear in Table 1 of the International Atomic Energy Agency's December 1995 edition of "Nuclear Research Reactors in the World":
>
> Algeria, Argentina, Australia, Austria, Bangladesh, Belgium, Brazil, Bulgaria, Canada, Chile, China, Colombia, Democratic People's Republic of Korea, Egypt, Finland, France, Germany, Hungary, India, Indonesia, Iran (Islamic Republic of), Israel, Italy, Japan, Mexico, Netherlands, Norway, Pakistan, Peru, Poland, Romania, Republic of Korea, Russian Federation, Slovakia, South Africa, Spain, Sweden, Switzerland, Turkey, Ukraine, United Kingdom of Great Britain and Northern Ireland, United States of America, Viet Nam, Zaire.

As of January 2009, nine of the states have yet to ratify the CTBT. These are:

China
The Democratic People's Republic of Korea
Egypt

India
Indonesia
The Islamic Republic of Iran
Israel
Pakistan
The United States of America

Of these, the Democratic People's Republic of Korea, India and Pakistan have also yet to sign the treaty.

ANNEX B

MEMBERSHIP OF THE WORKING GROUPS OF THE NUCLEAR TEST BAN COMMITTEE

January to September 1994
Chair: Miguel Marín Bosch (Mexico, G-21)

Working Group 1 on Verification

Chair: Wolfgang Hoffmann (Germany, Western Group)

Friend of the Chair on Seismic Verification: Ajit Kumar (India, G-21)

Friend of the Chair on Non-Seismic Verification: Peter Marshall (United Kingdom, Western Group)

Friend of the Chair on On-Site Inspections: Victor Slipchenko (Russia, Eastern European Group)

Friend of the Chair on Transparency: Bertil Roth (Sweden, in transition from G-21 to Western Group)

Working Group 2 on Legal and Institutional Issues

Chair: Ludwik Dembinski (Poland, Eastern European Group)

Friend of the Chair on Entry into Force: Alessandro Vattani (Italy, Western Group)

Friend of the Chair on Organization: Roberto Jaguaribe (Brazil, G-21)

January to September 1995
Chair: Ludwik Dembinski (Poland, Eastern European Group)

Working Group 1 on Verification

Chair: Lars Norberg (Sweden, ex-G-21, not yet accepted into Western Group)

Friend of the Chair on Technical Verification: Peter Marshall (United Kingdom, Western Group)

Friend of the Chair on International Monitoring System: Patrick Cole (Australia, Western Group)

Friend of the Chair on International Data Centre: Ralph Alewine (United States, Western Group)

Friend of the Chair on On-Site Inspections—consultation, clarification and trigger: Klaus Arnhold (Germany, Western Group)

Friend of the Chair on On-Site Inspections—access provisions, timelines: Victor Slipchenko (Russia, Eastern European Group)

Friend of the Chair on On-Site Inspections—reports, follow-up, sanctions: Hamid Baidi-Nejad (Iran, G-21)

Friend of the Chair on Transparency and Confidence-building: Richard Ekwall (Sweden, in transition from G-21 to Western Group)

<u>Working Group 2 on Legal and Institutional Issues</u>

Chair: Jaap Ramaker (Netherlands, Western Group)

Friend of the Chair on Entry into Force: Stephan Keller (Germany, Western Group)

Friend of the Chair on Implementing Organization: Ajit Kumar (India, G-21)

Organization team:[1] Magda Bauta Solés (Cuba, G-21), Donald Sinclair (Canada, Western Group) and Navtej Singh Sarna (India, G-21)

January to May 1996
Chair: Jaap Ramaker (Netherlands, Western Group)

<u>Working Group 1 on Verification</u>

Chair: Grigori Berdennikov (Russia, Eastern European Group)

Friend of the Chair on Technical Verification: Peter Marshall (United Kingdom, Western Group)

Friend of the Chair on On-Site Inspections: Mark Moher (Canada, Western Group)

Friend of the Chair on International Monitoring System: Patrick Cole (Australia, Western Group)

---

1 Because the issues relating to the implementing organization were considered rather broad and complex, Kumar coordinated an "organization team" of three other diplomats to assist in gathering and sifting information and practical requirements.

Friend of the Chair on International Data Centre: Ralph Alewine (United States, Western Group)

Friend of the Chair on Associated Measures, Transparency and Confidence-building: Richard Ekwall (Sweden—recently admitted to Western Group)

Working Group 2 on Legal and Institutional Issues

Chair: Mounir Zahran (Egypt, G-21)

Friend of the Chair on the Executive Council: Nacer Benjelloun-Touimi (Morocco, G-21)

Friend of the Chair on Entry into Force: Antonio de Icaza (Mexico, G-21)

Friend of the Chair on Funding: Yukiya Amano (Japan, Western Group)

Friend of the Chair on Preamble: Marshall Brown (United States, Western Group)

May–July 1996

After May 1996, the working groups were suspended, but the following people were retained to coordinate continuing negotiations on specific issues:

Preamble and Review: Mounir Zahran (Egypt, G-21)

Host Country Agreement: Stephen Ledogar (United States, Western Group)

Preparatory Commission: Wolfgang Hoffmann (Germany, Western Group), subsequently Don Sinclair (Canada, Western Group)[2]

Comprehensive Nuclear-Test-Ban Treaty Organization: Nacer Benjelloun-Touimi (Morocco, G-21)

International Monitoring System: Richard Starr (Australia, Western Group)

2 Near the end of the negotiations, Wolfgang Hoffmann was replaced by Don Sinclair of Canada because Ambassador Hoffmann was put forward as a candidate for the first Executive Secretary of the Preparatory Commission for the Comprehensive Nuclear-Test-Ban Treaty Organization. Hoffmann was subsequently confirmed as Executive Secretary when the Organization began to be established in Vienna.

ANNEX C

CORE TEXT OF THE COMPREHENSIVE NUCLEAR-TEST-BAN TREATY

The following is the core text of the CTBT, not including its Protocol.

PREAMBLE

The States Parties to this Treaty (hereinafter referred to as "the States Parties"),

Welcoming the international agreements and other positive measures of recent years in the field of nuclear disarmament, including reductions in arsenals of nuclear weapons, as well as in the field of the prevention of nuclear proliferation in all its aspects,

Underlining the importance of the full and prompt implementation of such agreements and measures,

Convinced that the present international situation provides an opportunity to take further effective measures towards nuclear disarmament and against the proliferation of nuclear weapons in all its aspects, and declaring their intention to take such measures,

Stressing therefore the need for continued systematic and progressive efforts to reduce nuclear weapons globally, with the ultimate goal of eliminating those weapons, and of general and complete disarmament under strict and effective international control,

Recognizing that the cessation of all nuclear weapon test explosions and all other nuclear explosions, by constraining the development and qualitative improvement of nuclear weapons and ending the development of advanced new types of nuclear weapons, constitutes an effective measure of nuclear disarmament and non-proliferation in all its aspects,

Further recognizing that an end to all such nuclear explosions will thus constitute a meaningful step in the realization of a systematic process to achieve nuclear disarmament,

Convinced that the most effective way to achieve an end to nuclear testing is through the conclusion of a universal and internationally and effectively verifiable comprehensive nuclear test-ban treaty, which has long been one of the highest priority objectives of the international community in the field of disarmament and non-proliferation,

Noting the aspirations expressed by the Parties to the 1963 Treaty Banning Nuclear Weapon Tests in the Atmosphere, in Outer Space and Under Water to seek to achieve the discontinuance of all test explosions of nuclear weapons for all time,

Noting also the views expressed that this Treaty could contribute to the protection of the environment,

Affirming the purpose of attracting the adherence of all States to this Treaty and its objective to contribute effectively to the prevention of the proliferation of nuclear weapons in all its aspects, to the process of nuclear disarmament and therefore to the enhancement of international peace and security,

Have agreed as follows:

ARTICLE I
BASIC OBLIGATIONS

1. Each State Party undertakes not to carry out any nuclear weapon test explosion or any other nuclear explosion, and to prohibit and prevent any such nuclear explosion at any place under its jurisdiction or control.

2. Each State Party undertakes, furthermore, to refrain from causing, encouraging, or in any way participating in the carrying out of any nuclear weapon test explosion or any other nuclear explosion.

ARTICLE II
THE ORGANIZATION

A. GENERAL PROVISIONS

1. The States Parties hereby establish the Comprehensive Nuclear-Test-Ban Treaty Organization (hereinafter referred to as "the Organization") to achieve the object and purpose of this Treaty, to ensure the implementation of its provisions, including those for international verification of compliance

with it, and to provide a forum for consultation and cooperation among States Parties.

2. All States Parties shall be members of the Organization. A State Party shall not be deprived of its membership in the Organization.

3. The seat of the Organization shall be Vienna, Republic of Austria.

4. There are hereby established as organs of the Organization: the Conference of the States Parties, the Executive Council and the Technical Secretariat, which shall include the International Data Centre.

5. Each State Party shall cooperate with the Organization in the exercise of its functions in accordance with this Treaty. States Parties shall consult, directly among themselves, or through the Organization or other appropriate international procedures, including procedures within the framework of the United Nations and in accordance with its Charter, on any matter which may be raised relating to the object and purpose, or the implementation of the provisions, of this Treaty.

6. The Organization shall conduct its verification activities provided for under this Treaty in the least intrusive manner possible consistent with the timely and efficient accomplishment of their objectives. It shall request only the information and data necessary to fulfil its responsibilities under this Treaty. It shall take every precaution to protect the confidentiality of information on civil and military activities and facilities coming to its knowledge in the implementation of this Treaty and, in particular, shall abide by the confidentiality provisions set forth in this Treaty.

7. Each State Party shall treat as confidential and afford special handling to information and data that it receives in confidence from the Organization in connection with the implementation of this Treaty. It shall treat such information and data exclusively in connection with its rights and obligations under this Treaty.

8. The Organization, as an independent body, shall seek to utilize existing expertise and facilities, as appropriate, and to maximize cost efficiencies, through cooperative arrangements with other international organizations such as the International Atomic Energy Agency. Such arrangements, excluding those of a minor and normal commercial and contractual nature, shall be set out in agreements to be submitted to the Conference of the States Parties for approval.

9. The costs of the activities of the Organization shall be met annually by the States Parties in accordance with the United Nations scale of assessments adjusted to take into account differences in membership between the United Nations and the Organization.

10. Financial contributions of States Parties to the Preparatory Commission shall be deducted in an appropriate way from their contributions to the regular budget.

11. A member of the Organization which is in arrears in the payment of its assessed contribution to the Organization shall have no vote in the Organization if the amount of its arrears equals or exceeds the amount of the contribution due from it for the preceding two full years. The Conference of the States Parties may, nevertheless, permit such a member to vote if it is satisfied that the failure to pay is due to conditions beyond the control of the member.

B. THE CONFERENCE OF THE STATES PARTIES

Composition, Procedures and Decision-making

12. The Conference of the States Parties (hereinafter referred to as "the Conference") shall be composed of all States Parties. Each State Party shall have one representative in the Conference, who may be accompanied by alternates and advisers.

13. The initial session of the Conference shall be convened by the Depositary no later than 30 days after the entry into force of this Treaty.

14. The Conference shall meet in regular sessions, which shall be held annually, unless it decides otherwise.

15. A special session of the Conference shall be convened:

(a) When decided by the Conference;

(b) When requested by the Executive Council; or

(c) When requested by any State Party and supported by a majority of the States Parties.

The special session shall be convened no later than 30 days after the decision of the Conference, the request of the Executive Council, or the attainment of the necessary support, unless specified otherwise in the decision or request.

16. The Conference may also be convened in the form of an Amendment Conference, in accordance with Article VII.

17. The Conference may also be convened in the form of a Review Conference in accordance with Article VIII.

18. Sessions shall take place at the seat of the Organization unless the Conference decides otherwise.

19. The Conference shall adopt its rules of procedure. At the beginning of each session, it shall elect its President and such other officers as may be required. They shall hold office until a new President and other officers are elected at the next session.

20. A majority of the States Parties shall constitute a quorum.

21. Each State Party shall have one vote.

22. The Conference shall take decisions on matters of procedure by a majority of members present and voting. Decisions on matters of substance shall be taken as far as possible by consensus. If consensus is not attainable when an issue comes up for decision, the President of the Conference shall defer any vote for 24 hours and during this period of deferment shall make every effort to facilitate achievement of consensus, and shall report to the Conference before the end of this period. If consensus is not possible at the end of 24 hours, the Conference shall take a decision by a two-thirds majority of members present and voting unless specified otherwise in this Treaty. When the issue arises as to whether the question is one of substance or not, that question shall be treated as a matter of substance unless otherwise decided by the majority required for decisions on matters of substance.

23. When exercising its function under paragraph 26 (k), the Conference shall take a decision to add any State to the list of States contained in Annex 1 to this Treaty in accordance with the procedure for decisions on matters of substance set out in paragraph 22. Notwithstanding paragraph 22, the Conference shall take decisions on any other change to Annex 1 to this Treaty by consensus.

Powers and Functions

24. The Conference shall be the principal organ of the Organization. It shall consider any questions, matters or issues within the scope of this Treaty, including those relating to the powers and functions of the Executive Council and the Technical Secretariat, in accordance with this Treaty. It may

make recommendations and take decisions on any questions, matters or issues within the scope of this Treaty raised by a State Party or brought to its attention by the Executive Council.

25. The Conference shall oversee the implementation of, and review compliance with, this Treaty and act in order to promote its object and purpose. It shall also oversee the activities of the Executive Council and the Technical Secretariat and may issue guidelines to either of them for the exercise of their functions.

26. The Conference shall:

(a) Consider and adopt the report of the Organization on the implementation of this Treaty and the annual programme and budget of the Organization, submitted by the Executive Council, as well as consider other reports;

(b) Decide on the scale of financial contributions to be paid by States Parties in accordance with paragraph 9;

(c) Elect the members of the Executive Council;

(d) Appoint the Director-General of the Technical Secretariat (hereinafter referred to as "the Director-General");

(e) Consider and approve the rules of procedure of the Executive Council submitted by the latter;

(f) Consider and review scientific and technological developments that could affect the operation of this Treaty. In this context, the Conference may direct the Director-General to establish a Scientific Advisory Board to enable him or her, in the performance of his or her functions, to render specialized advice in areas of science and technology relevant to this Treaty to the Conference, to the Executive Council or to States Parties. In that case, the Scientific Advisory Board shall be composed of independent experts serving in their individual capacity and appointed, in accordance with terms of reference adopted by the Conference, on the basis of their expertise and experience in the particular scientific fields relevant to the implementation of this Treaty;

(g) Take the necessary measures to ensure compliance with this Treaty and to redress and remedy any situation that contravenes the provisions of this Treaty, in accordance with Article V;

(h) Consider and approve at its initial session any draft agreements, arrangements, provisions, procedures, operational manuals, guidelines and any other documents developed and recommended by the Preparatory Commission;

(i) Consider and approve agreements or arrangements negotiated by the Technical Secretariat with States Parties, other States and international organizations to be concluded by the Executive Council on behalf of the Organization in accordance with paragraph 38 (h);

(j) Establish such subsidiary organs as it finds necessary for the exercise of its functions in accordance with this Treaty; and

(k) Update Annex 1 to this Treaty, as appropriate, in accordance with paragraph 23.

C. THE EXECUTIVE COUNCIL

Composition, Procedures and Decision-making

27. The Executive Council shall consist of 51 members. Each State Party shall have the right, in accordance with the provisions of this Article, to serve on the Executive Council.

28. Taking into account the need for equitable geographical distribution, the Executive Council shall comprise:

(a) Ten States Parties from Africa;

(b) Seven States Parties from Eastern Europe;

(c) Nine States Parties from Latin America and the Caribbean;

(d) Seven States Parties from the Middle East and South Asia;

(e) Ten States Parties from North America and Western Europe; and

(f) Eight States Parties from South-East Asia, the Pacific and the Far East.

All States in each of the above geographical regions are listed in Annex 1 to this Treaty. Annex 1 to this Treaty shall be updated, as appropriate, by the Conference in accordance with paragraphs 23 and 26 (k). It shall not be subject to amendments or changes under the procedures contained in Article VII.

29. The members of the Executive Council shall be elected by the Conference. In this connection, each geographical region shall designate States Parties from that region for election as members of the Executive Council as follows:

(a) At least one-third of the seats allocated to each geographical region shall be filled, taking into account political and security interests by States Parties in that region designated on the basis of the nuclear capabilities relevant to the Treaty as determined by international data as well as all or any of the following indicative criteria in the order of priority determined by each region:

(i) Number of monitoring facilities of the International Monitoring System;

(ii) Expertise and experience in monitoring technology; and

(iii) Contribution to the annual budget of the Organization;

(b) One of the seats allocated to each geographical region shall be filled on a rotational basis by the State Party that is first in the English alphabetical order among the States Parties in that region that have not served as members of the Executive Council for the longest period of time since becoming States Parties or since their last term, whichever is shorter. A State Party designated on this basis may decide to forgo its seat. In that case, such a State Party shall submit a letter of renunciation to the Director-General, and the seat shall be filled by the State Party following next-in-order according to this sub-paragraph; and

(c) The remaining seats allocated to each geographical region shall be filled by States Parties designated from among all the States Parties in that region by rotation or elections.

30. Each member of the Executive Council shall have one representative on the Executive Council, who may be accompanied by alternates and advisers.

31. Each member of the Executive Council shall hold office from the end of the session of the Conference at which that member is elected until the end of the second regular annual session of the Conference thereafter, except that for the first election of the Executive Council, 26 members shall be elected to hold office until the end of the third regular annual session of the Conference, due regard being paid to the established numerical proportions as described in paragraph 28.

32. The Executive Council shall elaborate its rules of procedure and submit them to the Conference for approval.

33. The Executive Council shall elect its Chairman from among its members.

34. The Executive Council shall meet for regular sessions. Between regular sessions it shall meet as may be required for the fulfilment of its powers and functions.

35. Each member of the Executive Council shall have one vote.

36. The Executive Council shall take decisions on matters of procedure by a majority of all its members. The Executive Council shall take decisions on matters of substance by a two-thirds majority of all its members unless specified otherwise in this Treaty. When the issue arises as to whether the question is one of substance or not, that question shall be treated as a matter of substance unless otherwise decided by the majority required for decisions on matters of substance.

Powers and Functions

37. The Executive Council shall be the executive organ of the Organization. It shall be responsible to the Conference. It shall carry out the powers and functions entrusted to it in accordance with this Treaty. In so doing, it shall act in conformity with the recommendations, decisions and guidelines of the Conference and ensure their continuous and proper implementation.

38. The Executive Council shall:

(a) Promote effective implementation of, and compliance with, this Treaty;

(b) Supervise the activities of the Technical Secretariat;

(c) Make recommendations as necessary to the Conference for consideration of further proposals for promoting the object and purpose of this Treaty ;

(d) Cooperate with the National Authority of each State Party;

(e) Consider and submit to the Conference the draft annual programme and budget of the Organization, the draft report of the Organization on the implementation of this Treaty, the report on the performance of its own activities and such other reports as it deems necessary or that the Conference may request;

(f) Make arrangements for the sessions of the Conference, including the preparation of the draft agenda;

(g) Examine proposals for changes, on matters of an administrative or technical nature, to the Protocol or the Annexes thereto, pursuant to

Article VII, and make recommendations to the States Parties regarding their adoption;

(h) Conclude, subject to prior approval of the Conference, agreements or arrangements with States Parties, other States and international organizations on behalf of the Organization and supervise their implementation, with the exception of agreements or arrangements referred to in sub-paragraph (i);

(i) Approve and supervise the operation of agreements or arrangements relating to the implementation of verification activities with States Parties and other States; and

(j) Approve any new operational manuals and any changes to the existing operational manuals that may be proposed by the Technical Secretariat.

39. The Executive Council may request a special session of the Conference.

40. The Executive Council shall:

(a) Facilitate cooperation among States Parties, and between States Parties and the Technical Secretariat, relating to the implementation of this Treaty through information exchanges;

(b) Facilitate consultation and clarification among States Parties in accordance with Article IV; and

(c) Receive, consider and take action on requests for, and reports on, on-site inspections in accordance with Article IV.

41. The Executive Council shall consider any concern raised by a State Party about possible non-compliance with this Treaty and abuse of the rights established by this Treaty. In doing so, the Executive Council shall consult with the States Parties involved and, as appropriate, request a State Party to take measures to redress the situation within a specified time. To the extent that the Executive Council considers further action to be necessary, it shall take, inter alia, one or more of the following measures:

(a) Notify all States Parties of the issue or matter;

(b) Bring the issue or matter to the attention of the Conference;

(c) Make recommendations to the Conference or take action, as appropriate, regarding measures to redress the situation and to ensure compliance in accordance with Article V.

D. THE TECHNICAL SECRETARIAT

42. The Technical Secretariat shall assist States Parties in the implementation of this Treaty. The Technical Secretariat shall assist the Conference and the Executive Council in the performance of their functions. The Technical Secretariat shall carry out the verification and other function entrusted to it by this Treaty, as well as those functions delegated to it by the Conference or the Executive Council in accordance with this Treaty. The Technical Secretariat shall include, as an integral part, the International Data Centre.

43. The functions of the Technical Secretariat with regard to verification of compliance with this Treaty shall, in accordance with Article IV and the Protocol, include inter alia:

(a) Being responsible for supervising and coordinating the operation of the International Monitoring System;

(b) Operating the International Data Centre;

(c) Routinely receiving, processing, analysing and reporting on International Monitoring System data;

(d) Providing technical assistance in, and support for, the installation and operation of monitoring stations;

(e) Assisting the Executive Council in facilitating consultation and clarification among States Parties;

(f) Receiving requests for on-site inspections and processing them, facilitating Executive Council consideration of such requests, carrying out the preparations for, and providing technical support during, the conduct of on-site inspections, and reporting to the Executive Council;

(g) Negotiating agreements or arrangements with States Parties, other States and international organizations and concluding, subject to prior approval by the Executive Council, any such agreements or arrangements relating to verification activities with States Parties or other States; and

(h) Assisting the States Parties through their National Authorities on other issues of verification under this Treaty.

44. The Technical Secretariat shall develop and maintain, subject to approval by the Executive Council, operational manuals to guide the operation of the various components of the verification regime, in accordance with Article IV and the Protocol. These manuals shall not constitute integral parts of this Treaty or the Protocol and may be changed by the Technical Secretariat

subject to approval by the Executive Council. The Technical Secretariat shall promptly inform the States Parties of any changes in the operational manuals.

45. The functions of the Technical Secretariat with respect to administrative matters shall include:

(a) Preparing and submitting to the Executive Council the draft programme and budget of the Organization;

(b) Preparing and submitting to the Executive Council the draft report of the Organization on the implementation of this Treaty and such other reports as the Conference or the Executive Council may request;

(c) Providing administrative and technical support to the Conference, the Executive Council and other subsidiary organs;

(d) Addressing and receiving communications on behalf of the Organization relating to the implementation of this Treaty; and

(e) Carrying out the administrative responsibilities related to any agreements between the Organization and other international organizations.

46. All requests and notifications by States Parties to the Organization shall be transmitted through their National Authorities to the Director-General. Requests and notifications shall be in one of the official languages of this Treaty. In response the Director-General shall use the language of the transmitted request or notification.

47. With respect to the responsibilities of the Technical Secretariat for preparing and submitting to the Executive Council the draft programme and budget of the Organization, the Technical Secretariat shall determine and maintain a clear accounting of all costs for each facility established as part of the International Monitoring System. Similar treatment in the draft programme and budget shall be accorded to all other activities of the Organization.

48. The Technical Secretariat shall promptly inform the Executive Council of any problems that have arisen with regard to the discharge of its functions that have come to its notice in the performance of its activities and that it has been unable to resolve through consultations with the State Party concerned.

49. The Technical Secretariat shall comprise a Director-General, who shall be its head and chief administrative officer, and such scientific, technical

and other personnel as may be required. The Director-General shall be appointed by the Conference upon the recommendation of the Executive Council for a term of four years, renewable for one further term, but not thereafter. The first Director-General shall be appointed by the Conference at its initial session upon the recommendation of the Preparatory Commission.

50. The Director-General shall be responsible to the Conference and the Executive Council for the appointment of the staff and for the organization and functioning of the Technical Secretariat. The paramount consideration in the employment of the staff and in the determination of the conditions of service shall be the necessity of securing the highest standards of professional expertise, experience, efficiency, competence and integrity. Only citizens of States Parties shall serve as the Director-General, as inspectors or as members of the professional and clerical staff. Due regard shall be paid to the importance of recruiting the staff on as wide a geographical basis as possible. Recruitment shall be guided by the principle that the staff shall be kept to the minimum necessary for the proper discharge of the responsibilities of the Technical Secretariat.

51. The Director-General may, as appropriate, after consultation with the Executive Council, establish temporary working groups of scientific experts to provide recommendations on specific issues.

52. In the performance of their duties, the Director-General, the inspectors, the inspection assistants and the members of the staff shall not seek or receive instructions from any Government or from any other source external to the Organization. They shall refrain from any action that might reflect adversely on their positions as international officers responsible only to the Organization. The Director-General shall assume responsibility for the activities of an inspection team.

53. Each State Party shall respect the exclusively international character of the responsibilities of the Director-General, the inspectors, the inspection assistants and the members of the staff and shall not seek to influence them in the discharge of their responsibilities.

E. PRIVILEGES AND IMMUNITIES

54. The Organization shall enjoy on the territory and in any other place under the jurisdiction or control of a State Party such legal capacity and such privileges and immunities as are necessary for the exercise of its functions.

55. Delegates of States Parties, together with their alternates and advisers, representatives of members elected to the Executive Council, together with their alternates and advisers, the Director-General, the inspectors, the inspection assistants and the members of the staff of the Organization shall enjoy such privileges and immunities as are necessary in the independent exercise of their functions in connection with the Organization.

56. The legal capacity, privileges and immunities referred to in this Article shall be defined in agreements between the Organization and the State Parties as well as in an agreement between the Organization and the State in which the Organization is seated. Such agreements shall be considered and approved in accordance with paragraph 26 (h) and (i).

57. Notwithstanding paragraphs 54 and 55, the privileges and immunities enjoyed by the Director-General, the inspectors, the inspection assistants and the members of the staff of the Technical Secretariat during the conduct of verification activities shall be those set forth in the Protocol.

ARTICLE III
NATIONAL IMPLEMENTATION MEASURES

1. Each State Party shall, in accordance with its constitutional processes, take any necessary measures to implement its obligations under this Treaty. In particular, it shall take any necessary measures:

(a) To prohibit natural and legal persons anywhere on its territory or in any other place under its jurisdiction as recognized by international law from undertaking any activity prohibited to a State Party under this Treaty;

(b) To prohibit natural and legal persons from undertaking any such activity anywhere under its control; and

(c) To prohibit, in conformity with international law, natural persons possessing its nationality from undertaking any such activity anywhere.

2. Each State Party shall cooperate with other States Parties and afford the appropriate form of legal assistance to facilitate the implementation of the obligations under paragraph 1.

3. Each State Party shall inform the Organization of the measures taken pursuant to this Article.

4. In order to fulfill its obligations under the Treaty, each State Party shall designate or set up a National Authority and shall so inform the Organization upon entry into force of the Treaty for it. The National Authority shall serve as the national focal point for liaison with the Organization and with other States Parties.

ARTICLE IV
VERIFICATION

A. GENERAL PROVISIONS

1. In order to verify compliance with this Treaty, a verification regime shall be established consisting of the following elements:

(a) An International Monitoring System;

(b) Consultation and clarification;

(c) On-site inspections; and

(d) Confidence-building measures.

At entry into force of this Treaty, the verification regime shall be capable of meeting the verification requirements of this Treaty.

2. Verification activities shall be based on objective information, shall be limited to the subject matter of this Treaty, and shall be carried out on the basis of full respect for the sovereignty of States Parties and in the least intrusive manner possible consistent with the effective and timely accomplishment of their objectives. Each State Party shall refrain from any abuse of the right of verification.

3. Each State Party undertakes in accordance with this Treaty to cooperate through its National Authority established pursuant to Article III, paragraph 4, with the Organization and with other States Parties to facilitate the verification of compliance with this Treaty by, inter alia:

(a) Establishing the necessary facilities to participate in these verification measures and establishing the necessary communication;

(b) Providing data obtained from national stations that are part of the International Monitoring System;

(c) Participating, as appropriate, in a consultation and clarification process;

(d) Permitting the conduct of on-site inspections; and

(e) Participating, as appropriate, in confidence-building measures.

4. All States Parties, irrespective of their technical and financial capabilities, shall enjoy the equal right of verification and assume the equal obligation to accept verification.

5. For the purposes of this Treaty, no State Party shall be precluded from using information obtained by national technical means of verification in a manner consistent with generally recognized principles of international law, including that of respect for the sovereignty of States.

6. Without prejudice to the right of States Parties to protect sensitive installations, activities or locations not related to this Treaty, States Parties shall not interfere with elements of the verification regime of this Treaty or with national technical means of verification operating in accordance with paragraph 5.

7. Each State Party shall have the right to take measures to protect sensitive installations and to prevent disclosure of confidential information and data not related to this Treaty.

8. Moreover, all necessary measures shall be taken to protect the confidentiality of any information related to civil and military activities and facilities obtained during verification activities.

9. Subject to paragraph 8, information obtained by the Organization through the verification regime established by this Treaty shall be made available to all States Parties in accordance with the relevant provisions of this Treaty and the Protocol.

10. The provisions of this Treaty shall not be interpreted as restricting the international exchange of data for scientific purposes.

11. Each State Party undertakes to cooperate with the Organization and with other States Parties in the improvement of the verification regime, and in the examination of the verification potential of additional monitoring technologies such as electromagnetic pulse monitoring or satellite monitoring, with a view to developing, when appropriate, specific measures to enhance the efficient and cost-effective verification of this Treaty. Such measures shall, when agreed, be incorporated in existing provisions in this Treaty, the Protocol or as additional sections of the Protocol, in accordance with Article VII, or, if appropriate, be reflected in the operational manuals in accordance with Article II, paragraph 44.

12. The States Parties undertake to promote cooperation among themselves to facilitate and participate in the fullest possible exchange relating to technologies used in the verification of this Treaty in order to enable all States Parties to strengthen their national implementation of verification measures and to benefit from the application of such technologies for peaceful purposes.

13. The provisions of this Treaty shall be implemented in a manner which avoids hampering the economic and technological development of the States Parties for further development of the application of atomic energy for peaceful purposes.

Verification Responsibilities of the Technical Secretariat

14. In discharging its responsibilities in the area of verification specified in this Treaty and the Protocol, in cooperation with the State Parties the Technical Secretariat shall, for the purpose of this Treaty:

(a) Make arrangements to receive and distribute data and reporting products relevant to the verification of this Treaty in accordance with its provisions, and to maintain a global communications infrastructure appropriate to this task;

(b) Routinely through its International Data Centre, which shall in principle be the focal point within the Technical Secretariat for data storage and data processing:

(i) Receive and initiate requests for data from the International Monitoring System;

(ii) Receive data, as appropriate, resulting from the process of consultation and clarification, from on-site inspections, and from confidence-building measures; and

(iii) Receive other relevant data from States Parties and international organizations in accordance with this Treaty and the Protocol;

(c) Supervise, coordinate and ensure the operation of the International Monitoring System and its component elements, and of the International Data Centre, in accordance with the relevant operational manuals;

(d) Routinely process, analyse and report on International Monitoring System data according to agreed procedures so as to permit the effective international verification of this Treaty and to contribute to the early resolution of compliance concerns;

(e) Make available all data, both raw and processed, and any reporting products, to all States Parties, each State Party taking responsibility for the use of International Monitoring System data in accordance with Article II, paragraph 7, and with paragraphs 8 and 13 of this Article;

(f) Provide to all States Parties equal, open, convenient and timely access to all stored data;

(g) Store all data, both raw and processed, and reporting products;

(h) Coordinate and facilitate requests for additional data from the International Monitoring system;

(i) Coordinate requests for additional data from one State Party to another State Party;

(j) Provide technical assistance in, and support for, the installation and operation of monitoring facilities and respective communication means, where such assistance and support are required by the State concerned;

(k) Make available to any State Party, upon its request, techniques utilized by the Technical Secretariat and its International Data Centre in compiling, storing, processing, analysing and reporting on data from the verification regime; and

(l) Monitor, assess and report on the overall performance of the International Monitoring System and of the International Data Centre.

15. The agreed procedures to be used by the Technical Secretariat in discharging the verification responsibilities referred to in paragraph 14 and detailed in the Protocol shall be elaborated in the relevant operational manuals.

B. THE INTERNATIONAL MONITORING SYSTEM

16. The International Monitoring System shall comprise facilities for seismological monitoring, radionuclide monitoring including certified laboratories, hydroacoustic monitoring, infrasound monitoring, and respective means of communication, and shall be supported by the International Data Centre of the Technical Secretariat.

17. The International Monitoring System shall be placed under the authority of the Technical Secretariat. All monitoring facilities of the International Monitoring System shall be owned and operated by the States hosting or otherwise taking responsibility for them in accordance with the Protocol.

18. Each State Party shall have the right to participate in the international exchange of data and to have access to all data made available to the International Data Centre. Each State Party shall cooperate with the International Data Centre through its National Authority.

Funding the International Monitoring System

19. For facilities incorporated into the International Monitoring System and specified in Tables 1-A, 2-A, 3 and 4 of Annex 1 to the Protocol, and for their functioning, to the extent that such facilities are agreed by the relevant State and the Organization to provide data to the International Data Centre in accordance with the technical requirements of the Protocol and relevant operational manuals, the Organization, as specified in agreements or arrangements pursuant to Part I, paragraph 4 of the Protocol, shall meet the costs of:

(a) Establishing any new facilities and upgrading existing facilities unless the State responsible for such facilities meets these costs itself;

(b) Operating and maintaining International Monitoring System facilities, including facility physical security if appropriate, and application of agreed data authentication procedures;

(c) Transmitting International Monitoring System data (raw or processed) to the International Data Centre by the most direct and cost effective means available, including, if necessary, via appropriate communications nodes, from monitoring stations, laboratories, analytical facilities or from national data centres; or such data (including samples where appropriate) to laboratory and analytical facilities from monitoring stations; and

(d) Analysing samples on behalf of the Organization.

20. For auxiliary network seismic stations specified in Table 1-B of Annex 1 to the Protocol the Organization, as specified in agreements or arrangements pursuant to Part I, paragraph 4 of the Protocol, shall meet the costs only of:

(a) Transmitting data to the International Data Centre;

(b) Authenticating data from such stations;

(c) Upgrading stations to the required technical standard, unless the State responsible for such facilities meets these costs itself;

(d) If necessary, establishing new stations for the purposes of this Treaty where no appropriate facilities currently exist, unless the State responsible for such facilities meets these costs itself; and

(e) Any other costs related to the provision of data required by the Organization as specified in the relevant operational manuals.

21. The Organization shall also meet the cost of provision to each State Party of its requested selection from the standard range of International Data Centre reporting products and services, as specified in Part I, Section F of the Protocol. The cost of preparation and transmission of any additional data or products shall be met by the requesting State Party.

22. The agreements or, if appropriate, arrangements concluded with States Parties or States hosting or otherwise taking responsibility for facilities of the International Monitoring System shall contain provisions for meeting these costs. Such provisions may include modalities whereby a State Party meets any of the costs referred to in paragraphs 19 (a) and 20 (c) and (d) for facilities which it hosts or for which it is responsible, and is compensated by an appropriate reduction in its assessed financial contribution to the Organization. Such a reduction shall not exceed 50 percent of the annual assessed financial contribution of a State Party, but may be spread over successive years. A State Party may share such a reduction with another State Party by agreement or arrangement between themselves and with the concurrence of the Executive Council. The agreements or arrangements referred to in this paragraph shall be approved in accordance with Article II, paragraphs 26 (h) and 38 (i).

Changes to the International Monitoring System

23. Any measures referred to in paragraph 11 affecting the International Monitoring System by means of addition or deletion of a monitoring technology shall, when agreed, be incorporated into this Treaty and the Protocol pursuant to Article VII, paragraphs 1 to 6.

24. The following changes to the International Monitoring System, subject to the agreement of those States directly affected, shall be regarded as matters of an administrative or technical nature pursuant to Article VII, paragraphs 7 and 8:

(a) Changes to the number of facilities specified in the Protocol for a given monitoring technology; and

(b) Changes to other details for particular facilities as reflected in the Tables of Annex 1 to the Protocol (including, inter alia, State responsible for the facility; location; name of facility; type of facility; and attribution of a facility between the primary and auxiliary seismic networks).

If the Executive Council recommends, pursuant to Article VII, paragraph 8 (d) that such changes be adopted, it shall as a rule also recommend pursuant to Article VII, paragraph 8 (g) that such changes enter into force upon notification by the Director-General of their approval.

25. The Director-General, in submitting to the Executive Council and States Parties information and evaluation in accordance with Article VII, paragraph 8 (b), shall include in the case of any proposal made pursuant to paragraph 24:

(a) A technical evaluation of the proposal;

(b) A statement on the administrative and financial impact of the proposal; and

(c) A report on consultations with States directly affected by the proposal, including indication of their agreement.

Temporary Arrangements

26. In cases of significant or irretrievable breakdown of a monitoring facility specified in the Tables of Annex 1 to the Protocol, or in order to cover other temporary reductions of monitoring coverage, the Director-General shall, in consultation and agreement with those States directly affected, and with the approval of the Executive Council, initiate temporary arrangements of no more than one year's duration, renewable if necessary by agreement of the Executive Council and of the States directly affected for another year. Such arrangements shall not cause the number of operational facilities of the International Monitoring System to exceed the number specified for the relevant network; shall meet as far as possible the technical and operational requirements specified in the operational manual for the relevant network; and shall be conducted within the budget of the Organization. The Director-General shall furthermore take steps to rectify the situation and make proposals for its permanent resolution. The Director-General shall notify all States Parties of any decision taken pursuant to this paragraph.

Cooperating National Facilities

27. States Parties may also separately establish cooperative arrangements with the Organization, in order to make available to the International Data

Centre supplementary data from national monitoring stations that are not formally part of the International Monitoring System.

28. Such cooperative arrangements may be established as follows:

(a) Upon request by a State Party, and at the expense of that State, the Technical Secretariat shall take the steps required to certify that a given monitoring facility meets the technical and operational requirements specified in the relevant operational manuals for an International Monitoring System facility, and make arrangements for the authentication of its data. Subject to the agreement of the Executive Council, the Technical Secretariat shall then formally designate such a facility as a cooperating national facility. The Technical Secretariat shall take the steps required to revalidate its certification as appropriate;

(b) The Technical Secretariat shall maintain a current list of cooperating national facilities and shall distribute it to all States Parties and;

(c) The International Data Centre shall call upon data from cooperating national facilities, if so requested by a State Party, for the purposes of facilitating consultation and clarification and the consideration of on-site inspection requests, data transmission costs being borne by that State Party.

The conditions under which supplementary data from such facilities are made available, and under which the International Data Centre may request further or expedited reporting, or clarifications, shall be elaborated in the operational manual for the respective monitoring network.

C. CONSULTATION AND CLARIFICATION

29. Without prejudice to the right of any State Party to request an on-site inspection, States Parties should, whenever possible, first make every effort to clarify and resolve, among themselves or with or through the Organization, any matter which may cause concern about possible non-compliance with the basic obligations of this Treaty.

30. A State Party that receives a request pursuant to paragraph 29 directly from another State Party shall provide the clarification to the requesting State Party as soon as possible, but in any case no later than 48 hours after the request. The requesting and requested States Parties may keep the Executive Council and the Director-General informed of the request and the response.

31. A State Party shall have the right to request the Director-General to assist in clarifying any matter which may cause concern about possible non-compliance with the basic obligations of this Treaty. The Director-General shall provide appropriate information in the possession of the Technical Secretariat relevant to such a concern. The Director-General shall inform the Executive Council of the request and of the information provided in response, if so requested by the requesting State Party.

32. A State Party shall have the right to request the Executive Council to obtain clarification from another State Party on any matter which may cause concern about possible non-compliance with the basic obligations of this Treaty. In such a case, the following shall apply:

(a) The Executive Council shall forward the request for clarification to the requested State Party through the Director-General no later than 24 hours after its receipt;

(b) The requested State Party shall provide the clarification to the Executive Council as soon as possible, but in any case no later than 48 hour after receipt of the request;

(c) The Executive Council shall take note of the clarification and forward it to the requesting State Party no later than 24 hours after its receipt;

(d) If the requesting State Party deems the clarification to be inadequate, it shall have the right to request the Executive Council to obtain further clarification from the requested State Party.

The Executive Council shall inform without delay all other States Parties about any request for clarification pursuant to this paragraph as well as any response provided by the requested State Party.

33. If the requesting State Party considers the clarification obtained under paragraph 32 (d) to be unsatisfactory, it shall have the right to request a meeting of the Executive Council in which States Parties involved that are not members of the Executive Council shall be entitled to take part. At such a meeting, the Executive Council shall consider the matter and may recommend any measure in accordance with Article V.

D. ON-SITE INSPECTIONS

<u>Request for an On-Site Inspection</u>

34. Each State Party has the right to request an on-site inspection in accordance with the provisions of this Article and Part II of the Protocol in

the territory or in any other place under the jurisdiction or control of any State Party, or in any area beyond the jurisdiction or control of any State.

35. The sole Purpose of an on-site inspection shall be to clarify whether a nuclear weapon test explosion or any other nuclear explosion has been carried out in violation of Article I and, to the extent possible, to gather any facts which might assist in identifying any possible violator.

36. The requesting State Party shall be under the obligation to keep the on-site inspection request within the scope of this Treaty and to provide in the request information in accordance with paragraph 37. The requesting State Party shall refrain from unfounded or abusive inspection requests.

37. The on-site inspection request shall be based on information collected by the International Monitoring System, on any relevant technical information obtained by national technical means of verification in a manner consistent with generally recognized principles of international law, or on a combination thereof. The request shall contain information pursuant to Part II, paragraph 41 of the Protocol.

38. The requesting State Party shall present the on-site inspection request to the Executive Council and at the same time to the Director-General for the latter to begin immediate processing.

Follow-up After Submission of an On-Site Inspection Request

39. The Executive Council shall begin its consideration immediately upon receipt of the on-site inspection request.

40. The Director-General, after receiving the on-site inspection request, shall acknowledge receipt of the request to the requesting State Party within two hours and communicate the request to the State Party sought to be inspected within six hours. The Director-General shall ascertain that the request meets the requirements specified in Part II, paragraph 41 of the Protocol, and, if necessary, shall assist the requesting State Party in filing the request accordingly, and shall communicate the request to the Executive Council and to all other states Parties within 24 hours.

41. When the on-site inspection request fulfils the requirements, the Technical Secretariat shall begin preparations for the on-site inspection without delay.

42. The Director-General, upon receipt of an on-site inspection request referring to an inspection area under the jurisdiction or control of a State

Party, shall immediately seek clarification from the State Party sought to be inspected in order to clarify and resolve the concern raised in the request.

43. A State Party that receives a request for clarification pursuant to paragraph 42 shall provide the Director-General with explanations and with other relevant information available as soon as possible, but no later than 72 hours after receipt of the request for clarification.

44. The Director-General, before the Executive Council takes a decision on the on-site inspection request, shall transmit immediately to the Executive Council any additional information available from the International Monitoring System or provided by any State Party on the event specified in the request, including any clarification provided pursuant to paragraphs 42 and 43, as well as any other information from within the Technical Secretariat that the Director-General deems relevant or that is requested by the Executive Council.

45. Unless the requesting State Party considers the concern raised in the on-site inspection request to be resolved and withdraws the request, the Executive Council shall take a decision on the request in accordance with paragraph 46.

Executive Council Decisions

46. The Executive Council shall take a decision on the on-site inspection request no later than 96 hours after receipt of the request from the requesting State Party. The decision to approve the on-site inspection shall be made by at least 30 affirmative votes of members of the Executive Council. If the Executive Council does not approve the inspection, preparations shall be stopped and no further action on the request shall be taken.

47. No later than 25 days after the approval of the on-site inspection in accordance with paragraph 46, the inspection team shall transmit to the Executive Council, through the Director-General, a progress inspection report. The continuation of the inspection shall be considered approved unless the Executive Council, no later than 72 hours after receipt of the progress inspection report, decides by a majority of all its members not to continue the inspection. If the Executive Council decides not to continue the inspection, the inspection shall be terminated, and the inspection team shall leave the inspection area and the territory of the inspected State Party as soon as possible in accordance with Part II, paragraphs 109 and 110 of the Protocol.

48. In the course of the on-site inspection, the inspection team may submit to the Executive Council, through the Director-General, a proposal to conduct drilling. The Executive Council shall take a decision on such a proposal no later than 72 hours after receipt of the proposal. The decision to approve drilling shall be made by a majority of all members of the Executive Council.

49. The inspection team may request the Executive Council, through the Director-General, to extend the inspection duration by a maximum of 70 days beyond the 60-day time-frame specified in Part II, paragraph 4 of the Protocol, if the inspection team considers such an extension essential to enable it to fulfil its mandate. The inspection team shall indicate in its request which of the activities and techniques listed in Part II, paragraph 6 of the Protocol it intends to carry out during the extension period. The Executive Council shall take a decision on the extension request no later than 72 hours after receipt of the request. The decision to approve an extension of the inspection duration shall be made by a majority of all members of the Executive Council.

50. Any time following the approval of the continuation of the on-site inspection in accordance with paragraph 47, the inspection team may submit to the Executive Council, through the Director-General, a recommendation to terminate the inspection. Such a recommendation shall be considered approved unless the Executive Council, no later than 72 hours after receipt of the recommendation, decides by a two-thirds majority of all its members not to approve the termination of the inspection. In case of termination of the inspection, the inspection team shall leave the inspection area and the territory of the inspected State Party as soon as possible in accordance with Part II, paragraphs 109 and 110 of the Protocol.

51. The requesting State Party and the State Party sought to be inspected may participate in the deliberations of the Executive Council on the on-site inspection request without voting. The requesting State Party and the inspected State Party may also participate without voting in any subsequent deliberations of the Executive Council related to the inspection.

52. The Director-General shall notify all States Parties within 24 hours about any decision by and reports, proposals, requests and recommendations to the Executive Council pursuant to paragraphs 46 to 50.

Follow-up after Executive Council Approval of an On-Site Inspection

53. An on-site inspection approved by the Executive Council shall be conducted without delay by an inspection team designated by the Director-General and in accordance with the provisions of this Treaty and the Protocol. The inspection team shall arrive at the point of entry no later than six days following the receipt by the Executive Council of the on-site inspection request from the requesting State Party.

54. The Director-General shall issue an inspection mandate for the conduct of the on-site inspection. The inspection mandate shall contain the information specified in Part II, paragraph 42 of the Protocol.

55. The Director-General shall notify the inspected State Party of the inspection no less than 24 hours before the planned arrival of the inspection team at the point of entry, in accordance with Part II, paragraph 43 of the Protocol.

The Conduct of an On-Site Inspection

56. Each State Party shall permit the Organization to conduct an on-site inspection on its territory or at places under its jurisdiction or control in accordance with the provisions of this Treaty and the Protocol. However, no State Party shall have to accept simultaneous on-site inspections on its territory or at places under its jurisdiction or control.

57. In accordance with the provisions of this Treaty and the Protocol, the inspected State Party shall have:

(a) The right and the obligation to make every reasonable effort to demonstrate its compliance with this Treaty and, to this end, to enable the inspection team to fulfil its mandate;

(b) The right to take measures it deems necessary to protect national security interests and to prevent disclosure of confidential information not related to the purpose of the inspection;

(c) The obligation to provide access within the inspection area for the sole purpose of determining facts relevant to the purpose of the inspection, taking into account sub-paragraph (b) and any constitutional obligations it may have with regard to proprietary rights or searches and seizures;

(d) The obligation not to invoke this paragraph or Part II, paragraph 88 of the Protocol to conceal any violation of its obligations under Article I; and

(e) The obligation not to impede the ability of the inspection team to move within the inspection area and to carry out inspection activities in accordance with this Treaty and the Protocol.

Access, in the context of an on-site inspection, means both the physical access of the inspection team and the inspection equipment to, and the conduct of inspection activities within, the inspection area.

58. The on-site inspection shall be conducted in the least intrusive manner possible, consistent with the efficient and timely accomplishment of the inspection mandate, and in accordance with the procedures set forth in the Protocol. Wherever possible, the inspection team shall begin with the least intrusive procedures and then proceed to more intrusive procedures only as it deems necessary to collect sufficient information to clarify the concern about possible non-compliance with this Treaty. The inspectors shall seek only the information and data necessary for the purpose of the inspection and shall seek to minimize interference with normal operations of the inspected State Party.

59. The inspected State Party shall assist the inspection team throughout the on-site inspection and facilitate its task.

60. If the inspected State Party, acting in accordance with Part II, paragraphs 86 to 96 of the Protocol, restricts access within the inspection area, it shall make every reasonable effort in consultations with the inspection team to demonstrate through alternative means its compliance with this Treaty.

Observer

61. With regard to an observer, the following shall apply:

(a) The requesting State Party, subject to the agreement of the inspected State Party, may send a representative, who shall be a national either of the requesting State Party or of a third State Party, to observe the conduct of the on-site inspection;

(b) The inspected State Party shall notify its acceptance or non-acceptance of the proposed observer to the Director-General within 12 hours after approval of the on-site inspection by the Executive Council;

(c) In case of acceptance, the inspected State Party shall grant access to the observer in accordance with the Protocol;

(d) The inspected State Party shall, as a rule, accept the proposed observer, but if the inspected State Party exercises a refusal, that fact shall be recorded in the inspection report.

There shall be no more than three observers from an aggregate of requesting States Parties.

Reports of an On-Site Inspection

62. Inspection reports shall contain:

(a) A description of the activities conducted by the inspection team;

(b) The factual findings of the inspection team relevant to the purpose of the inspection,

(c) An account of the cooperation granted during the on-site inspection;

(d) A factual description of the extent of the access granted, including the alternative means provided to the team, during the on-site inspection; and

(e) Any other details relevant to the purpose of the inspection.

Differing observations made by inspectors may be attached to the report.

63. The Director-General shall make draft inspection reports available to the inspected State Party. The inspected State Party shall have the right to provide the Director-General within 48 hours with its comments and explanations, and to identify any information and data which, in its view, are not related to the purpose of the inspection and should not be circulated outside the Technical Secretariat. The Director-General shall consider the proposals for changes to the draft inspection report made by the inspected State Party and shall wherever possible incorporate them. The Director-General shall also annex the comments and explanations provided by the inspected State Party to the inspection report.

64. The Director-General shall promptly transmit the inspection report to the requesting State Party, the inspected State Party, the Executive Council and to all other States Parties. The Director-General shall further transmit promptly to the Executive Council and to all other States Parties any results of sample analysis in designated laboratories in accordance with Part II, paragraph 104 of the Protocol, relevant data from the International Monitoring System, the assessments of the requesting and inspected States Parties, as well as any other information that the Director-General deems relevant. In the case of

the progress inspection report referred to in paragraph 47, the Director-General shall transmit the report to the Executive Council within the time-frame specified in that paragraph.

65. The Executive Council, in accordance with its powers and functions, shall review the inspection report and any material provided pursuant to paragraph 64, and shall address any concerns as to:

(a) Whether any non-compliance with this Treaty has occurred; and

(b) Whether the right to request an on-site inspection has been abused.

66. If the Executive Council reaches the conclusion, in keeping with its powers and functions, that further action may be necessary with regard to paragraph 65, it shall take the appropriate measures in accordance with Article V.

Frivolous or Abusive On-Site Inspection Requests

67. If the Executive Council does not approve the on-site inspection on the basis that the on-site inspection request is frivolous or abusive, or if the inspection is terminated for the same reasons, the Executive Council shall consider and decide on whether to implement appropriate measures to redress the situation, including the following:

(a) Requiring the requesting State Party to pay for the cost of any preparations made by the Technical Secretariat;

(b) Suspending the right of the requesting State Party to request an on-site inspection for a period of time, as determined by the Executive Council; and

(c) Suspending the right of the requesting State Party to serve on the Executive Council for a period of time.

E. CONFIDENCE-BUILDING MEASURES

68. In order to:

(a) Contribute to the timely resolution of any compliance concerns arising from possible misinterpretation of verification data relating to chemical explosions, and

(b) Assist in the calibration of the stations that are part of the component networks of the International Monitoring System, each State Party undertakes to cooperate with the Organization and with other States Parties in implementing relevant measures as set out in Part III of the Protocol.

ARTICLE V
MEASURES TO REDRESS A SITUATION AND TO ENSURE COMPLIANCE, INCLUDING SANCTIONS

1. The Conference, taking into account, inter alia, the recommendations of the Executive Council, shall take the necessary measures, as set forth in paragraphs 2 and 3, to ensure compliance with this Treaty and to redress and remedy any situation which contravenes the provisions of this Treaty.

2. In cases where a State Party has been requested by the Conference or the Executive Council to redress a situation raising problems with regard to its compliance and fails to fulfil the request within the specified time, the Conference may, inter alia, decide to restrict or suspend the State Party from the exercise of its rights and privileges under this Treaty until the Conference decides otherwise.

3. In cases where damage to the object and purpose of this Treaty may result from non-compliance with the basic obligations of this Treaty, the Conference may recommend to States Parties collective measures which are in conformity with international law.

4. The Conference, or alternatively, if the case is urgent, the Executive Council, may bring the issue, including relevant information and conclusions to the attention of the United Nations.

ARTICLE VI
SETTLEMENT OF DISPUTES

1. Disputes that may arise concerning the application or the interpretation of this Treaty shall be settled in accordance with the relevant provisions of this Treaty and in conformity with the provisions of the Charter of the United Nations.

2. When a dispute arises between two or more States Parties, or between one or more States Parties and the Organization, relating to the application or interpretation of this Treaty, the parties concerned shall consult together with a view to the expeditious settlement of the dispute by negotiation or by other peaceful means of the parties' choice, including recourse to

appropriate organs of this Treaty and, by mutual consent, referral to the International Court of Justice in conformity with the Statute of the Court. The parties involved shall keep the Executive Council informed of actions being taken.

3. The Executive Council may contribute to the settlement of a dispute that may arise concerning the application or interpretation of this Treaty by whatever means it deems appropriate, including offering its good offices, calling upon the States Parties to a dispute to seek a settlement through a process of their own choice, bringing the matter to the attention of the Conference and recommending a time-limit for any agreed procedure.

4. The Conference shall consider questions related to disputes raised by States Parties or brought to its attention by the Executive Council. The Conference shall, as it finds necessary, establish or entrust organs with tasks related to the settlement of these disputes in conformity with Article II, paragraph 26 (j).

5. The Conference and the Executive Council are separately empowered, subject to authorization from the General Assembly of the United Nations, to request the International Court of Justice to give an advisory opinion on any legal question arising within the scope of the activities of the Organization. An agreement between the Organization and the United Nations shall be concluded for this purpose in accordance with Article II, paragraph 38 (h).

6. This Article is without prejudice to Articles IV and V.

ARTICLE VII
AMENDMENTS

1. At any time after the entry into force of this Treaty, any State Party may propose amendments to this Treaty, the Protocol, or the Annexes to the Protocol. Any State Party may also propose changes, in accordance with paragraph 7, to the Protocol or the Annexes thereto. Proposals for amendments shall be subject to the procedures in paragraphs 2 to 6. Proposals for changes, in accordance with paragraph 7, shall be subject to the procedures in paragraph 8.

2. The proposed amendment shall be considered and adopted only by an Amendment Conference.

3. Any proposal for an amendment shall be communicated to the Director-General, who shall circulate it to all States Parties and the Depositary and

seek the views of the States Parties on whether an Amendment Conference should be convened to consider the proposal. If a majority of the States Parties notify the Director-General no later than 30 days after its circulation that they support further consideration of the proposal, the Director-General shall convene an Amendment Conference to which all States Parties shall be invited.

4. The Amendment Conference shall be held immediately following a regular session of the Conference unless all States Parties that support the convening of an Amendment Conference request that it be held earlier. In no case shall an Amendment Conference be held less than 60 days after the circulation of the proposed amendment.

5. Amendments shall be adopted by the Amendment Conference by a positive vote of a majority of the States Parties with no State Party casting a negative vote.

6. Amendments shall enter into force for all States Parties 30 days after deposit of the instruments of ratification or acceptance by all those States Parties casting a positive vote at the Amendment Conference.

7. In order to ensure the viability and effectiveness of this Treaty, Parts I and III of the Protocol and Annexes 1 and 2 to the Protocol shall be subject to changes in accordance with paragraph 8, if the proposed changes are related only to matters of an administrative or technical nature. All other provisions of the Protocol and the Annexes thereto shall not be subject to changes in accordance with paragraph 8.

8. Proposed changes referred to in paragraph 7 shall be made in accordance with the following procedures:

(a) The text of the proposed changes shall be transmitted together with the necessary information to the Director-General. Additional information for the evaluation of the proposal may be provided by any State Party and the Director-General. The Director-General shall promptly communicate any such proposals and information to all States Parties, the Executive Council and the Depositary;

(b) No later than 60 days after its receipt, the Director-General shall evaluate the proposal to determine all its possible consequences for the provisions of this Treaty and its implementation and shall communicate any such information to all States Parties and the Executive Council;

(c) The Executive Council shall examine the proposal in the light of all information available to it, including whether the proposal fulfils the requirements of paragraph 7. No later than 90 days after its receipt, the Executive Council shall notify its recommendation, with appropriate explanations, to all States Parties for consideration. States Parties shall acknowledge receipt within 10 days;

(d) If the Executive Council recommends to all States Parties that the proposal be adopted, it shall be considered approved if no State Party objects to it within 90 days after receipt of the recommendation. If the Executive Council recommends that the proposal be rejected, it shall be considered rejected if no State Party objects to the rejection within 90 days after receipt of the recommendation;

(e) If a recommendation of the Executive Council does not meet with the acceptance required under sub-paragraph (d), a decision on the proposal, including whether it fulfils the requirements of paragraph 7, shall be taken as a matter of substance by the Conference at its next session;

(f) The Director-General shall notify all States Parties and the Depositary of any decision under this paragraph;

(g) Changes approved under this procedure shall enter into force for all States Parties 180 days after the date of notification by the Director-General of their approval unless another time period is recommended by the Executive Council or decided by the Conference.

ARTICLE VIII
REVIEW OF THE TREATY

1. Unless otherwise decided by a majority of the States Parties, ten years after the entry into force of this Treaty a Conference of the States Parties shall be held to review the operation and effectiveness of this Treaty, with a view to assuring itself that the objectives and purposes in the Preamble and the provisions of the Treaty are being realized. Such review shall take into account any new scientific and technological developments relevant to this Treaty. On the basis of a request by any State Party, the Review Conference shall consider the possibility of permitting the conduct of underground nuclear explosions for peaceful purposes. If the Review Conference decides by consensus that such nuclear explosions may be permitted, it shall commence work without delay, with a view to recommending to States

Parties an appropriate amendment to this Treaty that shall preclude any military benefits of such nuclear explosions. Any such proposed amendment shall be communicated to the Director-General by any State Party and shall be dealt with in accordance with the provisions of Article VII.

2. At intervals of ten years thereafter, further Review Conferences may be convened with the same objective, if the Conference so decides as a matter of procedure in the preceding year. Such Conferences may be convened after an interval of less than ten years if so decided by the Conference as a matter of substance.

3. Normally, any Review Conference shall be held immediately following the regular annual session of the Conference provided for in Article II.

ARTICLE IX
DURATION AND WITHDRAWAL

1. This Treaty shall be of unlimited duration.

2. Each State Party shall, in exercising its national sovereignty, have the right to withdraw from this Treaty if it decides that extraordinary events related to the subject matter of this Treaty have jeopardized its supreme interests.

3. Withdrawal shall be effected by giving notice six months in advance to all other States Parties, the Executive Council, the Depositary and the United Nations Security Council. Notice of withdrawal shall include a statement of the extraordinary event or events which a State Party regards as jeopardizing its supreme interests.

ARTICLE X
STATUS OF THE PROTOCOL AND THE ANNEXES

The Annexes to this Treaty, the Protocol, and the Annexes to the Protocol form an integral part of the Treaty. Any reference to this Treaty includes the Annexes to this Treaty, the Protocol and the Annexes to the Protocol.

ARTICLE XI
SIGNATURE

This Treaty shall be open to all States for signature before its entry into force.

ARTICLE XII
RATIFICATION

This Treaty shall be subject to ratification by signatory States according to their respective constitutional processes.

ARTICLE XIII
ACCESSION

Any State which does not sign this Treaty before its entry into force may accede to it at any time thereafter.

ARTICLE XIV
ENTRY INTO FORCE

1. This Treaty shall enter into force 180 days after the date of deposit of the instruments of ratification by all States listed in Annex 2 to this Treaty, but in no case earlier than two years after its opening for signature.

2. If this Treaty has not entered into force three years after the date of the anniversary of its opening for signature, the Depositary shall convene a Conference of the States that have already deposited their instruments of ratification on the request of a majority of those States. That Conference shall examine the extent to which the requirement set out in paragraph 1 has been met and shall consider and decide by consensus what measures consistent with international law may be undertaken to accelerate the ratification process in order to facilitate the early entry into force of this Treaty.

3. Unless otherwise decided by the Conference referred to in paragraph 2 or other such conferences, this process shall be repeated at subsequent anniversaries of the opening for signature of this Treaty, until its entry into force.

4. All States Signatories shall be invited to attend the Conference referred to in paragraph 2 and any subsequent conferences as referred to in paragraph 3, as observers.

5. For States whose instruments of ratification or accession are deposited subsequent to the entry into force of this Treaty, it shall enter into force on the 30th day following the date of deposit of their instruments of ratification or accession.

ARTICLE XV
RESERVATIONS

The Articles of and the Annexes to this Treaty shall not be subject to reservations. The provisions of the Protocol to this Treaty and the Annexes to the Protocol shall not be subject to reservations incompatible with the object and purpose of this Treaty.

ARTICLE XVI
DEPOSITARY

1. The Secretary-General of the United Nations shall be the Depositary of this Treaty and shall receive signatures, instruments of ratification and instruments of accession.

2. The Depositary shall promptly inform all States Signatories and acceding States of the date of each signature, the date of deposit of each instrument of ratification or accession, the date of the entry into force of this Treaty and of any amendments and changes thereto, and the receipt of other notices.

3. The Depositary shall send duly certified copies of this Treaty to the Governments of the States Signatories and acceding States.

4. This Treaty shall be registered by the Depositary pursuant to Article 102 of the Charter of the United Nations.

ARTICLE XVII
AUTHENTIC TEXTS

This Treaty, of which the Arabic, Chinese, English, French, Russian and Spanish texts are equally authentic, shall be deposited with the Secretary-General of the United Nations.

ANNEX 1 TO THE TREATY

LIST OF STATES PURSUANT TO ARTICLE II, PARAGRAPH 28

Africa

Algeria, Angola, Benin, Botswana, Burkina Faso, Burundi, Cameroon, Cape Verde, Central African Republic, Chad, Comoros, Congo, Cote d'Ivoire,

Djibouti, Egypt, Equatorial Guinea, Eritrea, Ethiopia, Gabon, Gambia, Ghana, Guinea, Guinea-Bissau, Kenya, Lesotho, Liberia, Libyan Arab Jamahiriya, Madagascar, Malawi, Mali, Mauritania, Mauritius, Morocco, Mozambique, Namibia, Niger, Nigeria, Rwanda, Sao Tome & Principe, Senegal, Seychelles, Sierra Leone, Somalia, South Africa, Sudan, Swaziland, Togo, Tunisia, Uganda, United Republic of Tanzania, Zaire, Zambia, Zimbabwe.

Eastern Europe

Albania, Armenia, Azerbaijan, Belarus, Bosnia and Herzegovina, Bulgaria, Croatia, Czech Republic, Estonia, Georgia, Hungary, Latvia, Lithuania, Poland, Republic of Moldova, Romania, Russian Federation, Slovakia, Slovenia, The former Yugoslav Republic of Macedonia, Ukraine, Yugoslavia.

Latin America and the Caribbean

Antigua and Barbuda, Argentina, Bahamas, Barbados, Belize, Bolivia, Brazil, Chile, Colombia, Costa Rica, Cuba, Dominica, Dominican Republic, Ecuador, El Salvador, Grenada, Guatemala, Guyana, Haiti, Honduras, Jamaica, Mexico, Nicaragua, Panama, Paraguay, Peru, Saint Kitts and Nevis, Saint Lucia, Saint Vincent and the Grenadines, Suriname, Trinidad and Tobago, Uruguay, Venezuela.

Middle East and South Asia

Afghanistan, Bahrain, Bangladesh, Bhutan, India, Iran (Islamic Republic of), Iraq, Israel, Jordan, Kazakstan, Kuwait, Kyrgyzstan, Lebanon, Maldives, Oman, Nepal, Pakistan, Qatar, Saudi Arabia, Sri Lanka, Syrian Arab Republic, Tajikistan, Turkmenistan, United Arab Emirates, Uzbekistan, Yemen.

North America and Western Europe

Andorra, Austria, Belgium, Canada, Cyprus, Denmark, Finland, France, Germany, Greece, Holy See, Iceland, Ireland, Italy, Liechtenstein, Luxembourg, Malta, Monaco, Netherlands, Norway, Portugal, San Marino, Spain, Sweden, Switzerland, Turkey, United Kingdom of Great Britain and Northern Ireland, United States of America.

South East Asia, the Pacific and the Far East

Australia, Brunei Darussalam, Cambodia, China, Cook Islands, Democratic People's Republic of Korea, Fiji, Indonesia, Japan, Kiribati, Lao People's Democratic Republic, Malaysia, Marshall Islands, Micronesia (Federated States of), Mongolia, Myanmar, Nauru, New Zealand, Niue, Palau, Papua

New Guinea, Philippines, Republic of Korea, Samoa, Singapore, Solomon Islands, Thailand, Tonga, Tuvalu, Vanuatu, Viet Nam.

ANNEX 2 TO THE TREATY

LIST OF STATES PURSUANT TO ARTICLE XIV

List of States members of the Conference on Disarmament as at 18 June 1996 which formally participated in the work of the 1996 session of the Conference and which appear in Table 1 of the International Atomic Energy Agency's April 1996 edition of "Nuclear Power Reactors in the World", and of States members of the Conference on Disarmament as at 18 June 1996 which formally participated in the work of the 1996 session of the Conference and which appear in Table 1 of the International Atomic Energy Agency's December 1995 edition of "Nuclear Research Reactors in the World":

Algeria, Argentina, Australia, Austria, Bangladesh, Belgium, Brazil, Bulgaria, Canada, Chile, China, Colombia, Democratic People's Republic of Korea, Egypt, Finland, France, Germany, Hungary, India, Indonesia, Iran (Islamic Republic of), Israel, Italy, Japan, Mexico, Netherlands, Norway, Pakistan, Peru, Poland, Romania, Republic of Korea, Russian Federation, Slovakia, South Africa, Spain, Sweden, Switzerland, Turkey, Ukraine, United Kingdom of Great Britain and Northern Ireland, United States of America, Viet Nam, Zaire.

NOTES

Chapter 1
Introduction

1 Darlene Keju-Johnson, "For the Good of Mankind", in Zohl dé Ishtar (ed.), *Pacific Women Speak Out*, The Raven Press, 1998, p. 16.

2 1963 Treaty Banning Nuclear Weapon Tests in the Atmosphere, Outer Space and Under Water.

3 Though there may be some question of the number and type of nuclear tests conducted by India and Pakistan in May 1998, the prevailing view is that India detonated three nuclear devices on 11 May and a further two on 13 May, and that Pakistan conducted either five or six nuclear detonations on 28 May. See "India and Pakistan Nuclear Tests: Special Feature", *Disarmament Diplomacy*, no. 26, The Acronym Institute, 1998, pp. 2–21. For a comprehensive analysis, see George Perkovich, *India's Nuclear Bomb*, University of California Press, 1999.

4 Lee Chi-dong, "N. Korea claims success in nuclear test", *Yonhap News*, 9 October 2006, cited in Richard L. Garwin and Frank N. von Hippel, "A Technical Analysis: Deconstructing North Korea's October 9 Nuclear Test", *Arms Control Today*, vol. 36, no. 9, 2006.

5 George P. Shultz, William J. Perry, Henry A. Kissinger and Sam Nunn, "A World Free of Nuclear Weapons", *The Wall Street Journal*, 4 January 2007. George Shultz was President Reagan's Secretary of State in the 1980s, William Perry was President Clinton's Defense Secretary in the 1990s, Henry Kissinger was President Nixon's Secretary of State in the 1960s and 1970s, and Sam Nunn was a long-time Chair of the Senate Foreign Relations Committee and architect (with Richard Lugar) of legislative and political initiatives on cooperative threat reduction at the end of the Cold War.

6 George P. Shultz, William J. Perry, Henry A. Kissinger, Sam Nunn and others, "Toward a Nuclear-Free World", *The Wall Street Journal*, 15 January 2008.

7 Nuclear explosions are measured in terms of their TNT equivalent yield, given in kilogrammes (kg), tonnes or tons (t) and kilotonnes (kt). (US and European measurements and nomenclature differ, accounting for the occasional use of tons and kilotons in the text, as well as tonnes and kilotonnes.) A zero yield means that no nuclear test or explosion can

be carried out that would produce a fission or fusion yield of radiation energy or radioactive products. Though there is still some controversy over certain kinds of laboratory testing in which minute amounts of nuclear products may be released, the CTBT negotiators understood that the term "zero yield" ruled out the products of a nuclear chain reaction.

8 President George H.W. Bush, Speech to the Joint Session of Congress, 6 March 1991.

Chapter 2
Cold War attempts to ban nuclear explosions

1 President William J. Clinton, address to the United Nations General Assembly, 24 September 1996.

2 In 1996–1997, however, anti-personnel landmines attracted high public and political visibility, chiefly through an extremely effective awareness-raising campaign orchestrated by the International Campaign to Ban Landmines, and awareness-raising efforts by Diana, Princess of Wales, in the year before she died.

3 The Baruch Plan, presented to the United Nations Atomic Energy Commission, 14 June 1946.

4 A fourth phase, addressed in the next chapter, provided the "prenegotiations" conditions that enabled the CTBT negotiations finally to get underway in 1994.

5 The Bravo test was conducted on 1 March 1954. Glenn T. Seaborg, *Kennedy, Khrushchev and the Test Ban*, University of California Press, 1981, p. 4.

6 G. Allen Greb, "Survey on past nuclear test ban negotiations", in Jozef Goldblat and David Cox, *Nuclear Weapon Tests: Prohibition or Limitation?*, Oxford University Press, 1988, p. 96.

7 Glenn T. Seaborg, *Kennedy, Khrushchev and the Test Ban*, University of California Press, 1981, pp. 5–10. Following Stalin's death and a brief power struggle, Khrushchev consolidated his power by becoming General Secretary of the Soviet Communist Party in March 1958.

8 Valerian Zorin, the Soviet Ambassador to the United Nations at the time, noted that "parliaments, governments and a great many public organisations" regarded nuclear testing as "a burning political issue", quoted in G. Allen Greb, "Survey on past nuclear test ban negotiations", in Jozef Goldblat and David Cox, *Nuclear Weapon Tests: Prohibition or Limitation?*, Oxford University Press, 1988, p. 97.

[9] Two years later *The Bulletin of the Atomic Scientists* established the Doomsday Clock, which graphically depicts the risk of nuclear war in terms of minutes to midnight.

[10] In a period of post-world war uncertainty, the United States itself proposed non-proliferation measures in its 1946 Baruch Plan, including a halt to the production of plutonium and highly enriched uranium for weapons. See Lawrence Freedman, "The Post-War Assessments", in Philip Bobbitt, Lawrence Freedman and Gregory F. Treverton (eds), *US Nuclear Strategy*, New York University Press, 1989, pp. 46–53.

[11] The Pugwash scientists included many Nobel prize winners and some who had worked on the Manhattan Project. See Joseph Rotblat, *History of the Pugwash Conferences*, Taylor and Francis, 1962. Public concern turned nuclear testing into a dominant theme in the 1956 US elections. See Stanley A. Blumberg and Gwinn Owens, *Energy and Conflict: The Life and Times of Edward Teller*, G.P. Putnam's Sons, 1976, p. 396. The author is grateful to Daryl Kimball of the Arms Control Association, Washington DC, for sharing his unpublished research on the history of US NGOs and their work on the test ban.

[12] See *Radioactive Heaven and Earth*: *The Health and Environmental Effects of Nuclear Weapons Testing In, On, and Above the Earth, a Report of the IPPNW International Commission to Investigate the Heath and Environmental Effects of Nuclear Weapons Production and the Institute for Energy and Environmental Research*, Zed Books, 1991.

[13] The UK-based Direct Action Committee Against Nuclear War, for example, was active from 1957 to 1961, before being folded into the Committee of 100. During the late 1950s and early 1960s, these groups organized protests at the Ministry of Defence and nuclear bases in the United Kingdom, with the aim of developing a public campaign on civil disobedience against nuclear weapons.

[14] See Lawrence Freedman, *The Evolution of Nuclear Strategy*, 2nd ed., Macmillan Press, 1989, pp. 139–54.

[15] John Edmonds, "A Complete Nuclear Test Ban—Why Has it Taken so Long?", *Security Dialogue*, vol. 25, no. 4, 1994, pp. 375–88. As noted by Calvocoressi, the US and Soviet moratoria were possible in large part because both countries had just concluded their planned series of tests. Peter Calvocoressi, *World Politics since 1945*, 6th ed., Longman, 1991, p. 36. However, a US-wide Gallup poll in 1957 showed that 63% of Americans favoured a nuclear test ban, compared with only 20% in 1954. See Fen Osler Hampson with Michael Hart, *Multilateral*

Negotiations: Lessons from Arms Control, Trade and the Environment, The Johns Hopkins University Press, 1995, p. 57.

16 Glenn T. Seaborg, *Kennedy, Khrushchev and the Test Ban*, University of California Press, 1981, pp. 6–10.

17 The Geneva Experts Group outlined a network of about 170 control posts on land, each staffed by 30–40 technicians, and provisions for on-site inspections for events detected but not positively identified. It concluded "that it is technically feasible to establish with the capabilities and limitations indicated … a workable and effective control system to detect violations of an agreement on the worldwide suspension of nuclear weapon tests". Sir Michael Wright, *Disarm and Verify*, Chatto and Windus, 1964, appendix I: Report of the Conference of Experts to study the methods of detecting violations of a possible agreement on the suspension of nuclear tests, Geneva, 1st July to 21st August, 1958, p. 165. See also Glenn T. Seaborg, *Kennedy, Khrushchev and the Test Ban*, University of California Press, 1981, pp. 12–3.

18 Eisenhower's principal advisers from the nuclear laboratories were Edward Teller, Ernest Lawrence and Mark Mills, who argued forcefully against the idea of either a moratorium or a test ban, claiming that they could not be verified. As described in Stanley A. Blumberg and Gwinn Owens, *Energy and Conflict: The Life and Times of Edward Teller*, G.P. Putnam's Sons, 1976, pp. 395–400, in 1957, Teller and Lawrence turned an appearance before the Senate Subcommittee on Military Applications of the Joint Committee on Atomic Energy, intended to address nuclear reactor products, into an impassioned plea about "the great damage which would occur if all testing were stopped". Invited to meet with Eisenhower, Teller made a strong pitch for underground nuclear testing and development of a "clean bomb" which would "destroy an intended target without releasing radioactivity to be carried by the winds to do damage indiscriminately where no damage was intended". On the basis of such arguments, in July 1957 Teller initiated Project Plowshare to show that "these 'clean' explosives can also be used in peace as powerful workhorses in mammoth construction jobs".

19 Killian, who was President of the Massachusetts Institute of Technology (MIT), was additionally given the newly created position of Special Assistant to the President for Science and Technology. Fen Osler Hampson with Michael Hart, *Multilateral Negotiations: Lessons from Arms Control, Trade and the Environment*, The Johns Hopkins University Press, 1995, p. 58. For a number of these scientists, trained mainly in physics and weapons engineering and centred around Harvard University and MIT,

involvement with PSAC gave them first-hand experience in arms control through their participation in the test-ban talks. They included Herbert York, Jerome Wiesner, Paul Doty, Hans Bethe, Eugene Rabinowitch, George Rathgens, Spurgeon Keeny and Wolfgang Panovsky, many of whom continued to be active on arms control issues well past their age of professional retirement. Emanuel Adler, "The emergence of cooperation: national epistemic communities and the international evolution of the idea of nuclear arms control", in Peter M. Haas (ed.), *Knowledge, Power and International Policy Coordination*, University of South Carolina Press, 1992, pp. 111–24.

20 John Edmonds, "A Complete Nuclear Test Ban—Why Has it Taken so Long?", *Security Dialogue*, vol. 25, no. 4, 1994, p. 376.

21 It is relevant to note here that on 3 July 1958, the United States and the United Kingdom signed an Agreement of Cooperation on nuclear research and information. Macmillan needed the United States to understand that British public opinion strongly favoured a nuclear test ban. One reason for the United Kingdom's strong advocacy of a test-ban treaty at the time may have been to divert public attention away from the wider calls for nuclear disarmament. G. Allen Greb, "Survey on past nuclear test ban negotiations", in Jozef Goldblat and David Cox, *Nuclear Weapon Tests: Prohibition or Limitation?*, Oxford University Press, 1988, pp. 96–7.

22 Ibid., p. 99; and Stanley A. Blumberg and Gwinn Owens, *Energy and Conflict: The Life and Times of Edward Teller*, G.P. Putnam's Sons, 1976, pp. 406–10. Stanley Kubrik's Dr Strangelove is widely believed to have been based on Edward Teller.

23 The 1960 Eisenhower proposal covered atmospheric, underwater and outer space tests, as well as underground tests greater than a magnitude of some 10–30kt, depending on the geological conditions. See G. Allen Greb, "Survey on past nuclear test ban negotiations", in Jozef Goldblat and David Cox, *Nuclear Weapon Tests: Prohibition or Limitation?*, Oxford University Press, 1988, pp. 98–101.

24 This so-called "U-2 incident" strengthened hawks and test-ban opponents in the Soviet Union's powerful military, reducing what little room to manoeuvre Khrushchev might have had. G. Allen Greb, "Survey on past nuclear test ban negotiations", in ibid., p. 101. In an alternative view, Calvocoressi acknowledges that the U-2 incident contributed to the failure of Khrushchev's policy of rapprochement, but suggests that Khrushchev might have "deliberately engineered this stop on his own policies, possibly in response to pressures from military and pro-

Chinese lobbies". Peter Calvocoressi, *World Politics since 1945*, 6th ed., Longman, 1991, pp. 28–9.

25 The Ten-Nation Disarmament Committee functioned only briefly, 1959–1960, and comprised five states from each side of the Iron Curtain. Founded by the Foreign Ministers of France, the Soviet Union, United Kingdom and United States, it also included Bulgaria, Canada, Czechoslovakia, Italy, Poland and Romania.

26 Drawn up by senior diplomats John McCloy and Valerian Zorin, the "McCloy–Zorin recommendations" were summarily dismissed as "unreal plans". Peter Calvocoressi, *World Politics since 1945*, 6th ed., Longman, 1991, p. 36.

27 In 1962, the United Kingdom began using the Nevada Test Site under US auspices to conduct underground nuclear tests.

28 Mandated to report to the UN General Assembly, the ENDC (1962–1969) added eight non-aligned, neutral states to the five NATO and five Warsaw Pact states in the short-lived Ten-Nation Disarmament Committee. The members of the ENDC were Brazil, Bulgaria, Burma, Canada, Czechoslovakia, Ethiopia, India, Italy, Mexico, Nigeria, Poland, Romania, the Soviet Union, Sweden, the United Arab Republic, the United Kingdom and the United States. France was an invited member but declined to attend. The People's Republic of China was only admitted into the United Nations in 1971, at which time it also joined the Committee on Disarmament (successor to the ENDC and precursor to the CD) and took up a permanent seat on the Security Council.

29 The US–UK draft accepted several Soviet demands, including a total ban on tests in space, despite the verification limitations; parity of on-site inspections for the Soviet Union, the United Kingdom and the United States; and examination of devices intended for "peaceful nuclear explosions". On four crucial areas of verification, however, the Anglo-American position and the Soviets were still far apart: the West wanted an annual quota of 20 on-site inspections but the USSR would accept only 3; the Soviets would accept 15 seismic stations on their territory, staffed by the host country, but the US–UK side wanted 19, staffed internationally. While they eventually agreed on an 11-member Control Commission, (four each for the Soviet Union and the United States; three for the United Kingdom), the US–UK negotiators wanted a single "neutral" administrator. Khrushchev argued that there was no such thing, and called for a "troika" of administrators from the three original parties, each of which would have the ability to exercise a veto. This mirrored Soviet demands for troika leadership of the United

Nations, which it eventually abandoned. The United States and United Kingdom argued against a troika for the Control Commission on grounds that a right to veto would be used to avoid any inspections of suspect events. See Glenn T. Seaborg, *Kennedy, Khrushchev and the Test Ban*, University of California Press, 1981.

30 The US–UK draft partial-test-ban treaties were tabled in August 1962. Fen Osler Hampson with Michael Hart, *Multilateral Negotiations: Lessons from Arms Control, Trade and the Environment*, The Johns Hopkins University Press, 1995, p. 67.

31 McGeorge Bundy, national security adviser to President Kennedy, as quoted in G. Allen Greb, "Survey on past nuclear test ban negotiations", in Jozef Goldblat and David Cox, *Nuclear Weapon Tests: Prohibition or Limitation?*, Oxford University Press, 1988, p. 102.

32 Fen Osler Hampson with Michael Hart, *Multilateral Negotiations: Lessons from Arms Control, Trade and the Environment*, The Johns Hopkins University Press, 1995, p. 68.

33 Ibid., pp. 69–72.

34 Arthur M. Schlesinger Jr., *A Thousand Days: John F. Kennedy in the White House*, Andre Deutsch, 1965, pp. 754–70. The conciliatory effect of these overtures was somewhat dented by his "Ich bin ein Berliner" speech later that month, however.

35 In the United States the PTBT is more commonly known as the Limited Test Ban Treaty (LTBT).

36 The Irish resolution, A/RES/1665, was adopted unanimously and the Swedish resolution, A/RES/1664, by 58 votes to 10, with 23 abstentions, on 4 December 1961. For background, see Alva Myrdal, *The Game of Disarmament: How the United States and Russia Run the Arms Race*, Manchester University Press, 1977, pp. 166–77. See also Jan Prawitz, *From Nuclear Option to Non-nuclear Promotion: The Sweden Case*, The Swedish Institute of International Affairs, Research Report no. 20, 1995, pp. 12–8; and Bo K. A. Huldt, "Swedish Disarmament and Security Policy from the 1920s to the 1980s", in *Neutrality and Defence: the Swedish Experience*, Revue internationale d'histoire militaire no. 57, Edition de la Commission Suedoise d'Histoire Militaire, 1984, pp. 47–53.

37 For a detailed history on the NPT negotiations, see Mohammed Shaker, *The Nuclear Non-Proliferation Treaty: Origin and Implementation, 1959–1979*, Oceana, 1980.

38 Alva Myrdal, *The Game of Disarmament: How the United States and Russia Run the Arms Race*, Manchester University Press, 1977, p. 167.

39 Ibid.

40 Ibid.

41 ENDC/152 and ENDC/152.Add.1 (US draft), and ENDC/164 and ENDC/175 (Soviet draft). See Savita Pande, *The Future of NPT*, Institute for Defence Studies and Analyses, 1995, p. 7 and p. 23, note 15.

42 ENDC/192 (US Draft) and ENDC/193 (Soviet draft). See Savita Pande, *The Future of NPT*, Institute for Defence Studies and Analyses, 1995, pp. 3–22, and p. 23, note 28 .

43 Alva Myrdal, *The Game of Disarmament: How the United States and Russia Run the Arms Race*, Manchester University Press, 1977, p. 168. This had previously been tabled at the ENDC on 11 March 1968; see Savita Pande, *The Future of NPT*, Institute for Defence Studies and Analyses, 1995, p. 15.

44 Ibid., p. 17. Myrdal herself derided the NPT as a "grossly discriminatory treaty", citing a lack of balance between obligations and benefits for the non-nuclear-weapon states. See Alva Myrdal, *The Game of Disarmament: How the United States and Russia Run the Arms Race*, Manchester University Press, 1977, pp. 168–71. Four also voted against: Albania, Cuba, Tanzania and Zambia. Of those who abstained or spoke against the NPT in 1968, all but India have now acceded. Israel, Pakistan and South Africa voted in favour of the resolution but did not sign at the time. South Africa eventually joined the NPT in 1992 after a fundamental political shift away from apartheid led to the dismantlement of its nuclear weapon facilities and small number of nuclear weapons.

45 The idea that nuclear explosions could ever be peaceful has been challenged by many. Defined in Article V of the NPT, the concept of peaceful nuclear explosions caused problems for the CTBT negotiations until the final few months.

46 John Edmonds, "A Complete Nuclear Test Ban—Why Has it Taken so Long?", *Security Dialogue*, vol. 25, no. 4, 1994, pp. 377–8.

47 In support of her view, Myrdal quotes the American Academy of Arts and Sciences Bulletin, vol. 28, no. 1, 1974, reporting on the 1974 US–Soviet summit: "The ultimate mockery at the summit was the 'threshold test ban' … that, in the guise of restraint, permits underground explosives equivalent to 150,000 tons of TNT. That is ten times larger than the bomb that obliterated Hiroshima, and larger than almost all the tests conducted by the United States and the Soviet Union in recent years". Alva Myrdal, *The Game of Disarmament: How the United States and Russia Run the Arms Race*, Manchester University Press, 1977, p. 210.

[48] G. Allen Greb, "Survey on past nuclear test ban negotiations", in Jozef Goldblat and David Cox, *Nuclear Weapon Tests: Prohibition or Limitation?*, Oxford University Press, 1988, p. 108. Jozef Goldblat, one of the most knowledgeable observers of Cold War arms control and multilateral negotiations, offers a plausible analysis that the TTBT was hastily conceived to give the appearance of arms control for public consumption after the United States and Soviet Union had failed to reach a more important agreement on strategic offensive arms limitations. Jozef Goldblat, *Arms Control: A Guide to Negotiations and Agreements*, Sage Publications, 1994, p. 46.

[49] Alva Myrdal, *The Game of Disarmament: How the United States and Russia Run the Arms Race*, Manchester University Press, 1977, p. 210.

[50] Roland Timerbaev, "A Hostage to Political Realities: a Russian Commentary", *Security Dialogue*, vol. 25, no. 4, 1994, pp. 389–92, quoted in Nancy W. Gallagher, *The Politics of Verification*, The Johns Hopkins University Press, 1999, p. 165.

[51] Ibid., p. 164.

[52] John Edmonds, "A Complete Nuclear Test Ban—Why Has it Taken so Long?", *Security Dialogue*, vol. 25, no. 4, 1994, p. 378.

[53] Callaghan requested UK participation in the test-ban talks, speaking directly to Carter and using the Downing Street hotline to the Kremlin for the first time in five years. Author's private communication with John Edmonds, 24 April 2002.

[54] Though they agreed that would be desirable, the United Kingdom and the United States considered the prospect of accession by France and China rather remote, since neither had yet joined either the PTBT or the NPT. John Edmonds, "A Complete Nuclear Test Ban—Why Has it Taken so Long?", *Security Dialogue*, vol. 25, no. 4, 1994, p. 378.

[55] Ibid., p. 379.

[56] April Carter, *Success and Failure in Arms Control Negotiations*, Oxford University Press/SIPRI, 1989, pp. 86–91.

[57] Quoted in John Edmonds, "A Complete Nuclear Test Ban—Why Has it Taken so Long?", *Security Dialogue*, vol. 25, no. 4, 1994, p. 379. As a consequence, the US chief negotiator, Paul Warnke, resigned and was replaced by Herbert York, one of Eisenhower's original President's Science Advisory Committee scientists and a former director of the Livermore nuclear weapons laboratory.

[58] Calvocoressi notes that "The election of Ronald Reagan to the presidency of the United States in 1980 owed a great deal to the feeling that the United States ought to be making better use of its power instead of

striking deals with an adversary who was getting stronger and was not to be trusted". Peter Calvocoressi, *World Politics since 1945*, 6th ed., Longman, 1991, p. 49.

59 Ibid., pp. 49–52.

60 It was, for example, considered possible to limit nuclear use to the territory of allies, exempting the "homeland" territories of the superpowers. Lawrence Freedman, *The Evolution of Nuclear Strategy*, 2nd ed., Macmillan Press, 1989, pp. 406–24.

61 According to the zero option, NATO would forgo the planned deployment of cruise and Pershing missiles in Europe if the Soviet Union removed all its intermediate range missiles (the older SS-4s and SS-5s as well as the modern SS-20s) not only from the areas adjacent to Europe, but from the rest of the Soviet bloc. Rejecting the zero option as such, General Secretary Brezhnev proposed a bilateral freeze on intermediate range missiles in Europe, but that was rejected by Washington. Calvocoressi argues that the zero option was constructed to be impossible for the Soviets to accept. Peter Calvocoressi, *World Politics since 1945*, 6th ed., Longman, 1991, p. 52. Freedman argues that the zero option was not just "a cynical political move designed to wrong-foot both the Soviet Union and the disarmament movement", but reflected a European view that the cruise and Pershing II missiles were actually unnecessary. Lawrence Freedman, *The Evolution of Nuclear Strategy*, 2nd ed., Macmillan Press, 1989, p. 418.

62 McGeorge Bundy, George F. Kennan, Robert S. McNamara and Gerard Smith, "The President's Choice: Star Wars or Arms Control", in William G. Hyland (ed.), *The Reagan Foreign Policy*, Meridian Books and the Council on Foreign Relations, 1987, pp. 165–79.

63 See, for example, Diana Johnstone, *The Politics of Euromissiles*, Verso, 1984, pp. 33–78; and Mary Kaldor and Dan Smith (eds), *Disarming Europe*, The Merlin Press, 1982.

64 Lawrence Freedman, *The Evolution of Nuclear Strategy*, 2nd ed., Macmillan Press, 1989, p. 419.

65 Ibid.

66 When Reagan formally abandoned the tripartite talks, he had taken up the TTBT and PNET, expressing a desire to renegotiate the verification terms of these two bilateral treaties. John Edmonds noted that Moscow condemned this as "no more than a pretext for sabotaging the CTB negotiations", while *Time* magazine reasoned that "the Administration wants to keep on testing America's nuclear warheads". The United States, supported by the United Kingdom, blocked all attempts to work

on a test ban at the Conference on Disarmament, which since 1978 had put the CTBT at the top of its agenda. See John Edmonds, "A Complete Nuclear Test Ban—Why Has it Taken so Long?", *Security Dialogue*, vol. 25, no. 4, 1994, p. 380.

67 Prior to the sinking of the Rainbow Warrior, Greenpeace had directed attention at the human cost of nuclear testing by evacuating Rongelap islanders (at their request), victims of 1950s atmospheric testing in the Marshall Islands, to a safer, less contaminated site. Afterwards, to raise attention in Europe, Greenpeace flew a hot air balloon over East and West Berlin, demanding a halt to nuclear testing. Greenpeace, which had started in Canada in 1971 as (according to some of its employees) a "boys' sailing club with a conscience", was one of the few organizations to maintain a focus against nuclear testing during the 1970s and 1980s. See Michael Szabo, *Making Waves: The Greenpeace New Zealand Story*, Reed Books, 1992, pp. 28–35 and 109–43.

68 The President of the Conference, Ambassador Mohammed Shaker of Egypt, managed to bypass Greenpeace's strategy with the unusual but effective tactic of obtaining consensus for a compromise document that reflected views rather than enshrining actual agreements.

69 The scientists and advocates involved in the joint verification project had a range of motives, from confidence-building to testing new seismological equipment, data interpretation and measuring assumptions. On the US side, Thomas Cochran, a prime mover from NRDC, together with Frank von Hippel of the Federation of American Scientists, wanted to confront the inconsistencies in US and Soviet approaches to verification and show the effectiveness of verification capabilities. The driving force from the Soviet side, Evgeny Velikhov, vice president of the Soviet Academy of Sciences, believed the joint verification project could demonstrate the sincerity of Soviet disarmament proposals and have impact on the domestic American debate by showing Soviet openness and cooperation. This summary of the joint verification experiments derives primarily from Nancy W. Gallagher, *The Politics of Verification*, The Johns Hopkins University Press, 1999, pp 196–205.

70 Ibid., pp. 200–4. Though noting that "the NRDC-SAS joint monitoring project was the most innovative move in the politics of test ban verification [but] it failed to have an immediate impact on US policy …", Gallagher quotes one of Richard Perle's assistants as admitting that NRDC "wanted to prove that a CTB is verifiable, while we'd made verification into the main public objection to a CTB".

71 The *Washington Post*, for example, carried this assessment: "No more could governments pretend that a [CTBT] would be unverifiable ... . The NRDC has given hope ... by showing that determined private citizens can lead even superpower governments out of the deadly traps they fashion for themselves". Robert Park, "A Bold Plan for Testing the Test Ban", *Washington Post*, 22 January 1989, quoted in Nancy W. Gallagher, *The Politics of Verification*, The Johns Hopkins University Press, 1999, p. 203. It is interesting to note that after the INF Treaty was signed, the United States and Soviet Union agreed to conduct official Joint Verification Experiments (JVE), using hydrodynamic methods and seismology.

Chapter 3
Putting the test ban back on the table

1 UN press release, "Secretary-General Declares Comprehensive Nuclear-Test-Ban Treaty Open for Signature", UN document SG/SM/6062, 24 September 1996. Wherever possible, the quotations in the text are referenced to official UN documentary sources. Some, however, are from working papers of the CD or NTB Committee or informal papers or "non-papers" that were circulated by delegations but not formally issued with a CD document number. In that case, references identify the source (whether a delegation or a Friend of the Chair, for example) and the title of the paper as written, with the date if identified on the paper or known by other means. Occasionally quotations taken from a contemporaneously issued statement or notes of a speech do not correspond exactly with the official verbatim record from the CD or UN, which may be due to differences between oral interpreters and text translators or revisions inserted by delegations prior to the verbatim records being formally issued. Dates given in the references for documents or UN resolutions the date of official issuance and do not necessarily indicate the date of adoption by the CD or UN General Assembly or Security Council.

2 This observation was by Andy Johnson, legislative aide to Senator Exon, in an interview with Hugh Gusterson on 4 December 1997. Quoted with permission from Gusterson, the interview was part of his research for a book that has not yet been published. See also Dunbar Lockwood, "Nuclear Arms Control", in Stockholm International Peace Research Institute, *SIPRI Yearbook 1993: World Armaments and Disarmament*, Oxford University Press, 1993, p. 562.

[3] George Bush, "Statement on Signing the Energy and Water Development Appropriations Act, 1993", P.L. 102-377, 2 October 1992. See Dunbar Lockwood, "Nuclear Arms Control", in Stockholm International Peace Research Institute, *SIPRI Yearbook 1993: World Armaments and Disarmament*, Oxford University Press, 1993, p. 562.

[4] See above and Dunbar Lockwood, "Nuclear Arms Control", in Stockholm International Peace Research Institute, *SIPRI Yearbook 1993: World Armaments and Disarmament*, Oxford University Press, 1993, p. 561.

[5] Ragnhild Ferm, "Nuclear Explosions 1945–92", in *SIPRI Yearbook 1993: World Armaments and Disarmament*, Oxford University Press, 1993, p. 254. See excerpts from the August 1992 letter from Sir Robin Renwick (UK Ambassador to Washington) to Senate sponsors of test-ban legislation, President Bush's 19 January 1993 letter to Les Aspin, Chair of the House Armed Services Committee, and President Clinton's 12 February 1993 letter to Senate Majority Leader George Mitchell, in "Nuclear Testing Issue: Three Letters", *Arms Control Today*, vol. 23, no. 2, 1993, p. 29.

[6] United States, *Congressional Record*, 24 September 1992, p. H9424.

[7] This is the indigenous Maohi (Tahitian) spelling of Moruroa (which means "place of a great secret"), which is used in preference to the French phonetic approximation "Mururoa".

[8] Bruno Barrillot, "French finesse nuclear future", *The Bulletin of the Atomic Scientists*, vol. 48, no. 7, 1992, pp. 22–6. This point was also made by then Deputy Head of the US Arms Control and Disarmament Agency Thomas Graham. See Thomas Graham Jr., *Disarmament Sketches*, University of Washington Press, 2002, p. 238.

[9] China and France did not accede to the NPT until after the 1990 Review Conference.

[10] The special consultations were undertaken among the most active participants on the issue: the United States, the United Kingdom and the Soviet Union, and Australia, Canada, New Zealand, Poland, Sweden, Indonesia, Iran, Mexico, Nigeria, Peru, Sri Lanka, Venezuela and Yugoslavia. See William Epstein, "Conference a qualified success", *The Bulletin of the Atomic Scientists*, vol. 46, no. 10, 1990, pp. 45–7.

[11] Ibid.

[12] According to a senior Iranian diplomat who was present during the intensive private negotiations in the final hours before the Fourth NPT Review Conference collapsed, the British delegation indicated at around 4h00 that it would accept the President's compromise language

on the CTBT as accepted by the non-aligned states. The United States remained adamant on its additional paragraph, and so the Review Conference was allowed to fail. Author's conversation with Ali Asghar Soltanieh, Annecy, 14 July 2002. See also William Epstein, "Conference a qualified success", *The Bulletin of the Atomic Scientists*, vol. 46, no. 10, 1990, pp. 45–7.

13 See, for example, John Simpson, "The 1990 Review Conference of the Nuclear Non-Proliferation Treaty", *The Round Table*, vol. 80, no. 318, 1991; Leonard S. Spector and Jacqueline R. Smith, "Treaty review: Deadlock damages nonproliferation", *The Bulletin of the Atomic Scientists*, vol. 46, no. 10, 1990, pp. 39–44; and, for an alternative view, William Epstein, "Conference a qualified success", *The Bulletin of the Atomic Scientists*, vol. 46, no. 10, 1990, pp. 45–7.

14 As subsequent events have shown, he also had political ambitions and saw the testing issue as a way to mobilize Kazakh nationalism, using raised awareness of the health and environmental damage from nuclear testing to foster outrage and fuel opposition to the Soviet military presence and political system. Author's conversation with Suleimenov's aide, St. Petersburg, 24 June 1999.

15 Author's conversation with Olzhas Suleimenov, January 1991.

16 Much of this section is derived from contemporaneous notes of meetings between the author and members of the Nevada–Semipalatinsk Movement. The author participated in the 1990 Citizens Congress. See also Peter Zheutlin, "Nuclear victims of the world unite", *The Bulletin of the Atomic Scientists*, vol. 46, no. 7, 1990, p. 3; "Testing decision on Semipalatinsk by Kazakhstan", *Soviet Weekly*, 10 January 1991; and Vladimir Iakimets and Olzhas Suleimenov, "New tests mean new nukes", *The Bulletin of the Atomic Scientists*, vol. 48, no. 8, 1992, pp. 12–3, 45.

17 Much less was known about China's test site at Lop Nor in Xinjiang Province.

18 Importantly, in terms of reaching wider public opinion, both actions were covered extensively (and positively) in the British popular press, as well as the political dailies. One of the women, Lorna Richardson, was the niece of a prominent Labour Member of Parliament, Jo Richardson, who recruited her fellow Shadow Cabinet members to put pressure on the UK Foreign and Commonwealth Office and US Department of Energy to have the test cancelled on safety grounds after US surveillance failed for two days to locate the hikers. Examples of the press coverage included: "Protest Dive off Tower Bridge", *The Daily*

Express, 13 November 1990; "Nuke Ban Daredevils Jump off Deep End", *The Daily Star*, 13 November 1990; Margaret Hall, "Greenham girl halts nuclear blast 7 minutes from death", *Today*, 15 November 1990; "N-bomb halted by women", *The Daily Mirror*, 15 November 1990; John Hiscock, "Nuclear test delayed after three women infiltrate site", *The Daily Telegraph*, 15 November 1990; "Nevada Blast is Delayed", *The Times*, 15 November 1990; Robert Lowes, "British Women Conquer NTS", *The Death Valley Gateway Gazette*, 16–22 November 1990. The Greenpeace/Greenham women's action also resulted in a pair of editorials for and against a nuclear test ban, published in a widely read US newspaper as "Face-Off: Testing and Protesting", *USA Today*, 16–18 November 1990.

19 *Testimonies: Witnesses of French nuclear testing in the South Pacific*, Greenpeace International, August 1990.

20 *Memorandum: Preliminary proposals for research on nuclear test sites in French Polynesia (Moruroa and Fangataufa)*, Greenpeace International, October 1990.

21 See Michael Szabo, *Making Waves: The Greenpeace New Zealand Story*, Reed Books, 1992, pp. 201–13.

22 Sampling provided a motivation for entering the test-site zone other than the publicity-seeking desire to have a confrontation with the French military. In this regard, Greenpeace campaigners set themselves up for a win–win strategy: if they got in and took samples they calculated that they would find enough radioactivity to justify their demand for an independent study; if they were arrested, the media would give coverage to the "return" of the *Rainbow Warrior*. As it turned out, they were successful in doing both.

23 The PTBT amendment conference was the brainchild of Aaron Tovish, who drove it forward under the leadership of the President of the Parliamentarians for Global Action, Ólafur Grimsson, and two successive PGA Secretary-Generals, Nick Dunlop and Kennedy Graham.

24 Yugoslavia was among the six to take up the initiative in 1988 but, as the Federation disintegrated into nationalism and war, was unable to play a role in the 1990s.

25 "Britons held", *The Times*, 7 January 1991; "250 Nevada Test Site arrests", *The Morning Star*, 7 January 1991. The Nevada conference and actions, organized by Greenpeace and the American Peace Test network, brought together many of the international activists and anti-testing NGOs, including Kazakhs from the Nevada–Semipalatinsk Movement and indigenous Maohi activists from Tahiti-Polynesia. The Conference

was a means both of information exchange and networking, and also served as a way of funding international activists' travel to New York to attend the PTBT Amendment Conference at the United Nations. See also "Nuclear conference to debate total test ban", *The Independent*, 8 January 1991; "UN Conferees Press for Test Ban", *International Herald Tribune*, 8 January 1991; and "Testing time for treaty", *The Independent*, 14 January 1991.

26 See William Epstein, "CTB: Two paths, one goal", *The Bulletin of the Atomic Scientists*, vol. 49, no. 8, 1993, pp. 3–5.

27 *Scientific and Technical Aspects of the Verification of a Comprehensive Test Ban Treaty*, VERTIC, April 1990. At that time, VERTIC, stood for Verification Technology Information Centre. The name of the London-based NGO was changed in 1998 to the Verification Research, Training and Information Centre.

28 Acting as a "temporary mechanism that provides for the change itself on a transitional and provisional basis", the moratoria fit Zartman's characterization of a "downpayment on confidence". I. William Zartman, "Prenegotiation: Phases and Functions", in Janice Gross Stein (ed.), *Getting to the Table: The Processes of International Prenegotiation*, The Johns Hopkins University Press, 1989, p. 13. On prenegotiations theory, see also Harold Saunders, "The pre-negotiation phase", in D.B. Bendahmane and J.W. McDonald (eds), *International Negotiation: Art and Science*, Foreign Service Institute, Department of State, 1984; and I. William Zartman and Maureen R. Berman, *The Practical Negotiator*, Yale University Press, 1982.

29 Though not directly involved by the time this initiative bore fruit, Greenpeace had been working with Solange Fernex and other Members of the European Parliament, churches and other NGOs on resolutions and reports on nuclear testing in the European Parliament for the several years just prior to the formation of the launch of the European Campaign for a Moratorium on French Nuclear Tests in the Pacific.

30 Barrillot notes that a poll in June 1992 indicated that nearly 60% of the French public opposed nuclear testing. Bruno Barrillot, "French finesse nuclear future", *The Bulletin of the Atomic Scientists*, vol. 48, no. 7, 1992, pp. 24–5.

31 Tom A. Zamora, "Moruroa-torium", *The Bulletin of the Atomic Scientists*, vol. 48, no. 5, 1992, pp. 11–3.

32 François Mitterrand, from a press conference on 12 April, reported in *Le Monde*, 14 April 1992, as quoted in Bruno Barrillot, "French finesse

nuclear future", *The Bulletin of the Atomic Scientists*, vol. 48, no. 7, 1992, pp. 24–5.

33 "Decree of the Russian Federation President on the Novaya Zemlya test site", The Kremlin, Moscow, 27 February 1992, unofficial translation. See also "Russia urged by US to resume nuclear tests", *North American News Report*, 23 April 1992. Also putting pressure on Yeltsin, Nobel Prize winners from IPPNW received international publicity for its 44-page report about nuclear-related problems, based on a two-week mission to four former Soviet republics in late spring.

34 General Assembly, *Comprehensive nuclear-test-ban treaty*, UN document A/RES/47/47, 9 December 1992.

35 Tom A. Zamora, "Moruroa-torium", *The Bulletin of the Atomic Scientists*, vol. 48, no. 5, 1992, pp. 11–3. See also George Perkovich, "Weapons complexes v. democracy", *The Bulletin of the Atomic Scientists*, vol. 48, no. 5, 1992, pp. 16–7. Additional information was provided by unpublished research from Hugh Gusterson and Daryl Kimball.

36 John Isaacs, "The Senate that can say no", *The Bulletin of the Atomic Scientists*, vol. 48, no. 8, 1992, pp. 6–8.

37 Tom A. Zamora, "Moruroa-torium", *The Bulletin of the Atomic Scientists*, vol. 48, no. 5, 1992, pp. 11–3. These included $4.5 billion for a supercollider in Bush's home state of Texas. Hugh Gusterson also reports speculation that President Bush signed after being assured by his aides that China would test, thereby allowing the United States to resume. China did not do so, however, until October 1993, by which time the Clinton administration decided not to react in kind. From correspondence with Hugh Gusterson.

38 The Hatfield-Exon-Mitchell Amendment, section 507 of the Energy and Water Appropriations Act for Fiscal Year 1993. See also the *UK Defence Committee Report, 1992–3*, House of Commons; "Congress seeks nuclear test ban", *The Times*, 26 September 1992; "Bush signs nuclear test moratorium", *The Independent*, 3 October 1992; "No more nuclear tests", *The Washington Post*, 28 September 1992.

39 Referring to the Russian and French moratoria, Clinton said "I think … we ought to get out there and join the parade on working toward a comprehensive test ban". Speech by President Clinton, Sandia National Laboratories, 18 September 1992, quoted by Frank von Hippel and Tom Zamora-Collina, "Nuclear Junkies: Testing, Testing, 1-2-3—Forever", *The Bulletin of the Atomic Scientists*, vol. 49, no. 6, 1993, pp. 28–32.

40 Thomas Graham Jr., *Disarmament Sketches*, University of Washington Press, 2002, pp. 239–40.

41 HR 1146, bill to provide that any foreign nation that conducts a test of a nuclear weapon in the United States shall pay the costs resulting from the test, introduced by Michael J Kopetski, Representative of Oregon, in the House of Representatives, 25 February 1993. It was not voted on. NGOs also circulated the text of correspondence with Kopetski including a letter to UK Prime Minister John Major from Michael Kopetski, 22 February 1993, and a letter to Congressman Kopetski from CJR Meyer, Chargé d'affaires, British Embassy, Washington, 17 March 1993.

42 Thomas Graham Jr., *Disarmament Sketches*, University of Washington Press, 2002, p. 242. Ambassador Graham was appointed by Clinton to lead US efforts to obtain the indefinite extension of the NPT in 1995.

43 According to Hugh Gusterson's unpublished research, former Defense Secretary James Schlesinger argued the Anglo-American relations case, and Sidney Drell raised the argument about Senate ratification.

44 Von Hippel's position was based on the physics. In hydronuclear experiments most of the fissile material in the device (highly enriched uranium or plutonium) is replaced by non-fissile isotopes with similar material properties. When this is compressed with high explosives, the device barely reaches criticality and so nuclear yields are kept very low. As discussed further in Chapter 4, the US threshold of 1.8kg for hydronuclear experiments was presented as a margin for potential error rather than a limit for permitted tests.

45 This point was made by Daryl Kimball, in private communication with the author, 20 June 2008.

46 This account derives mainly from Thomas Graham Jr., *Disarmament Sketches*, University of Washington Press, 2002, pp. 237–56.

47 Daryl Kimball cites these poll figures in his unpublished research which he shared with the author. how can the text say that the poll data was published, but the reference refers to unpublished research?

48 See, for example, "US to scrap test ban", *The Guardian*, 18 May 1993. This followed earlier reports in the *Washington Post* on April 30 and in other US newspapers.

49 Most of the Ministry of Defence's efforts to overturn the US moratorium had been kept out of the US and UK media, but this changed in early July, when 13 women associated with the Aldermaston Women's Peace Camp(aign) climbed over the Buckingham Palace walls and gate-crashed a royal Garden Party with placards and banners protesting against British nuclear testing in what they claimed was violation of Western Shoshone land in Nevada. After logistical problems forced the original plans to

be delayed, the Buckingham Palace protest was out of time for the US debate, but it was instrumental in focusing British attention on the issue of nuclear testing. Since the Queen and most of the Royal Family were in Buckingham Palace on the chosen date, there was a large number of guests and attendant journalists on the premises. The women's action gained unusually prominent front page coverage in the United Kingdom and publicity around the world. Media discussions and evidence given at the trial of the women at Bow Street Magistrates Court, as well as polls taken by CND following this action, suggested that most British people had no idea that their government or anyone else still conducted nuclear tests, but if so, then they thought that nuclear testing should be banned. See, for example, "Mass Break-in at the Palace—The Queen in Residence as Protest Women Scale the Walls", *Evening Standard*, 6 July 1993. See also Alexander MacLeod, "Clinton's Stay of Nuclear Tests Irks the United Kingdom", *Christian Science Monitor*, 7 July 1993.

50 VERTIC's project was initiated by its director, Dr Patricia Lewis, with funding from Carnegie Corporation of New York and the Ploughshares Fund. The author, who had for the previous four years directed Greenpeace International's nuclear testing campaign, was project coordinator, responsible for political and media strategy and outreach. The imaging and technical coordination was carried out by Vipin Gupta (Imperial College), with support from Professor Michael Barnett (his thesis supervisor at Imperial College) and Dr Roger Clarke (University of Leeds), as well as Philip McNab (VERTIC). See Vipin Gupta and Philip McNab, "Tracking Down a Chinese Nuclear Test", in J.B. Poole and R. Guthrie (eds), *Verification 1994: Arms Control, Peacekeeping and the Environment*, Brasseys, 1994; and Vipin Gupta and Philip McNab, "Sleuthing from home", *The Bulletin of the Atomic Scientists*, vol. 49, no. 10, 1993, pp. 44–7.

51 The First Committee comprises all members of the United Nations General Assembly and deals with issues relating to disarmament and international security.

52 "The United Kingdom Scores First on Rumbling Tests", *The Guardian*, 6 October 1993; "China Explodes Nuclear Device Despite US Plea", *The Financial Times*, 6 October 1993; and "Waiting for the Earth to Move", *The Independent*, 11 October 1993. See also Dingli Shen, "China", in Eric Arnett (ed.), *Nuclear Weapons After the Comprehensive Test Ban*, Oxford University Press/SIPRI, 1996, pp. 24–30. See also Vipin Gupta and Philip McNab, "Sleuthing from Home", *Bulletin of the Atomic Scientists*, vol. 49, no. 10, 1993, pp. 44–7.

53 Known as the Conference of the Committee on Disarmament (CCD) for six years from 1978, it was formally constituted as the Conference on Disarmament in 1984.

54 *Final Document, Special Session of the General Assembly on Disarmament 1978*, United Nations, 1988, paragraph 120, pp. 41–3. The first Special Session on Disarmament was held from 23 May to 1 July 1978, and though the session ran over by a day, it adopted its Final Document by consensus, unlike the two subsequent Special Sessions on Disarmament, in 1982 and 1988, which were unable to reach agreement.

55 Excerpt from the mandate, as contained in Conference on Disarmament, *Decision on agenda item 1 "Nuclear test ban" adopted by the CD at its 659th plenary meeting on 10 August 1993*, CD document CD/1212, 10 August 1993. Cold War habits died hard, so this mandate was based on a bilateral draft circulated by Russia and the United States and agreed among the P-5 before it was multilaterally negotiated among the wider CD. See the full Mandate for an Ad Hoc Committee under Agenda Item 1 "Nuclear Test Ban", adopted in Conference on Disarmament, *Report of the Ad Hoc Committee on a Nuclear Test Ban*, CD document CD/1220, 24 August 1993.

56 As a result of the disintegration of the Soviet Union and political changes in a number of Eastern European countries, by the time the CD opened negotiations in 1994, its membership stood at 38, with Yugoslavia forbidden to occupy its seat. France, which had boycotted the ENDC, began participating in 1979, followed, a year later, by China. From January 1994 to June 1996, therefore, CD membership included: the United Kingdom, China, France, Russia, the United States, India, Pakistan, Argentina, Australia, Belgium, Canada, Germany, Italy, Japan, the Netherlands, Sweden, Bulgaria, Hungary, Poland, Romania, Algeria, Brazil, Cuba, Egypt, Ethiopia, Indonesia, Iran, Kenya, Mexico, Mongolia, Myanmar, Nigeria, Peru, Sri Lanka, Venezuela, Yugoslavia (denied its seat) and Zaire (now the Democratic Republic of the Congo). During the negotiations, some 30–40 further states participated as observers, of whom fewer than 10 engaged actively in the test-ban negotiations.

57 Proposed by Argentina and adopted at the 739th plenary, the CD decided in June 1996 "to admit Austria, Bangladesh, Belarus, Cameroon, Chile, Colombia, the Democratic People's Republic of Korea, Finland, Iraq, Israel, New Zealand, Norway, the Republic of Korea, Senegal, Slovakia, South Africa, Spain, Switzerland, Syria, Turkey, Ukraine, Viet Nam and Zimbabwe as members of the Conference on Disarmament on 17 June 1996"; Conference on Disarmament, *Decision on Expansion*

of *Membership of the Conference*, CD document CD/1406, 17 June 1996. Following a further decision on CD enlargement in August 1999 to admit five new members—Ecuador, Ireland, Kazakhstan, Malaysia and Tunisia—the membership (as of 1 September 1 2008) stands at 66.

58 Inga Thorsson, "Multilateral Forums", in Arthur S. Lall, *Multilateral Negotiation and Mediation: Instruments and Methods*, Pergamon Press/International Peace Academy, 1985, pp. 93–114; and Jozef Goldblat, *Arms Control: A Guide to Negotiations and Agreements*, Sage Publications, 1994, pp. 8–11 and 189–90.

59 As of August 1996, when the CTBT was finalized, the division of CD members among the groups was as follows—Group of Western States and Others: Argentina, Australia, Austria, Belgium, Canada, Germany, Finland, France, Israel, Italy, Japan, the Netherlands, New Zealand, Norway, the Republic of Korea, Spain, Sweden, Switzerland, Turkey, the United Kingdom and the United States (21); Group of Eastern European States and Others: Belarus, Bulgaria, Hungary, Poland, Romania, Russia, Slovakia, Ukraine (eight—not counting Yugoslavia); The Group of Non-Aligned States and Others was called the G-21 when it had 21 members, and the name has remained, although the numbers have fluctuated. In August 1996, the G-21 comprised: Algeria, Bangladesh, Brazil, Cameroon, Chile, Colombia, Cuba, the Democratic People's Republic of Korea, Egypt, Ethiopia, India, Indonesia, Iraq, Iran, Kenya, Mexico, Mongolia, Morocco, Myanmar, Nigeria, Pakistan, Peru, Senegal, South Africa, Sri Lanka, Syria, Venezuela, Viet Nam, Zaire, Zimbabwe (30). The five states added in 1999 were: Ireland (Western Group); Kazakhstan (Eastern European Group); and Ecuador, Malaysia and Tunisia (G-21). China, as noted, often refers to itself as the "group of one".

60 The G-21, for example, used to be called the Group of Non-Aligned and Neutral States, as it was a CD subset of the Movement of Non-Aligned States. The common factor among states in the Non-Aligned Movement, formalized in 1961 in Belgrade, was supposed to be a foreign policy that was independent of the superpowers or their associated blocs. Though some political coordination was envisaged, it was not intended to form a third bloc. See Richard L. Jackson, *The Non-Aligned, the UN and the Superpowers*, Praeger, 1983; and Leo Mates, *Nonalignment*, Oceana Publications, 1972.

61 Argentina and Sweden left the G-21 and joined the Western group midway in the CTBT negotiations, and Mongolia left the Eastern

European group for the G-21. As more and more erstwhile members of the Eastern European Group have joined or applied to join the European Union or NATO, that group has practically ceased to have separate political relevance, but is loath to disband itself entirely, as it retains the right to nominate candidates for chairs and other positions. With posts still allocated equally among the Western, Eastern European and G-21 groups, the anomalous position of the Eastern European group is increasingly causing resentment among non-aligned states, particularly after Eastern European membership slipped to fewer than one third that of the G-21.

62 The United States withheld consensus from the decision to enlarge the CD in September 1993 because it was concerned that Iraq, which was on the O'Sullivan List, would exercise a de facto veto to sabotage agreements and block the work of the CD as a means of exerting leverage on the United States and others to lift UN Security Council sanctions. To bypass the US objections while maintaining the integrity of the O'Sullivan List, South Africa crafted a device whereby all the new members signed an undertaking that for the first two years they would not individually obstruct any action of the CD: in so doing they suspended their individual right to prevent consensus, although more than one of the new members could withhold consensus if they acted in concert. Together with Chile (leader of the 23 countries on O'Sullivan's list), New Zealand, and CD member Argentina, South Africa managed to persuade the United States to accept this compromise. See Rebecca Johnson, "Geneva Update No. 29", *Disarmament Diplomacy*, no. 6, The Acronym Institute, 1996, pp. 24–7 for a fuller account of the expansion decision.

63 Clocks can be stopped by the chair before midnight on the final day if there is sufficient hope that an agreement can be reached, as was done at the NPT Review Conference in May 2000 (although new UN rules now aim to prevent this technique). Delegations caught in difficult decision-making dilemmas can delay discussions by insisting that they need to consult with their capitals or that they need new instructions. With different time zones to navigate, this can be effective during the late stages of negotiations. Stopping the clock is a way of undercutting such tactics.

64 R.P. Barston, *Modern Diplomacy*, 2nd ed., Addison Wesley Longman, 1997, pp. 6 and 87–98.

65 This is similar to a point made by Kahler with regard to consensus, in Miles Kahler, "Multilateralism with Small and Large Numbers", in John

Gerard Ruggie (ed.), *Multilateralism Matters*, Columbia University Press, 1993, pp. 318–9.

66 The tactics identified here draw in the first instance on Johan Kaufmann's analysis of multilateralism in the North–South context, in which he focused mainly on obstructive tactics. See Johan Kaufmann, *The Diplomacy of International Relations: Selected Writings*, Kluwer Law International, 1998, especially pp. 11–30. While retaining some of Kaufmann's typology of tactics, including the names he gave them, the list has been considerably expanded as a result of the author's observations of multilateral arms control negotiations during the past 20 years.

67 Dean Pruitt calls this concession-trading tactic "logrolling", a term adopted by Hampson. However, shifting a logjam can sometimes be accomplished by the removal of just one strategically placed log, which is a rather different matter than trading the removal of obstructive logs in more than one place, though either method may eventually get the logs rolling. On logrolling and bridging tactics, see Dean G. Pruitt, *Negotiation Behaviour*, Academic Press, 1981, especially pp. 153–5; and Fen Osler Hampson with Michael Hart, *Multilateral Negotiations: Lessons from Arms Control, Trade and the Environment*, The Johns Hopkins University Press, 1995, especially pp. 40–3.

68 This is similar to what Hampson called "issue decomposition and sequencing". See ibid., especially the introduction and conclusion.

69 The 1997 Mine Ban Treaty enshrined a multilateral but not universal ban on anti-personnel landmines. Taking place in parallel with the CTBT, the "Ottawa Process" that led to the treaty was noted for having created a negotiating forum outside both the CD and the CCW. See Maxwell A. Cameron, Robert J. Lawson and Brian W. Tomlin (eds), *To Walk Without Fear: The Global Movement to Ban Landmines*, Oxford University Press, 1998; Kenneth Anderson, "The Ottawa Convention Banning Landmines, the Role of International Non-Governmental Organizations and the Idea of International Civil Society", *European Journal of International Affairs*, vol. 2, no. 1, 2000; and Richard Price, "Reversing the Gun Sights: Transnational Civil Society Targets Landmines", *International Organization*, vol. 53, no. 3, 1998, pp. 613–44.

Chapter 4
The struggle for a zero-yield test ban

1 Conference on Disarmament, *Final Record of the Six Hundred and Sixty-sixth Plenary Meeting*, CD document CD/PV.666, 25 January 1994, statement by John D. Holum, Director of the US Arms Control and Disarmament Agency, p. 14.

2 General Assembly, *Comprehensive test-ban treaty*, UN document A/RES/48/70, 16 December 1993.

3 Conference on Disarmament, *Mandate for an Ad Hoc Committee under Agenda Item 1, "Nuclear Test Ban"*, CD document CD/1238, 25 January 1994. See Appendix B for the list of diplomats appointed as Chairs and Friends of the Chair on specific aspects.

4 Conference on Disarmament, *Final Record of the Six Hundred and Sixty-ninth Plenary Meeting*, CD document CD/PV.669, 3 February 1994, statement by Stephen Ledogar (USA), p. 13.

5 See Tom Zamora Collina and Ray E. Kidder, "Shopping spree softens test-ban sorrows", *The Bulletin of the Atomic Scientists*, vol. 49, no. 6, 1993, pp. 23–9; and Katherine Magraw, "The United States", in Eric Arnett (ed.), *Nuclear Weapons After the Comprehensive Test Ban*, Oxford University Press/Stockholm International Peace Research Institute, 1996.

6 For a while there were concerns that Russia wanted the PTBT language because it could allow a loophole for above-ground, contained or laboratory testing. Vladimir Iakimets, a Russian adviser to the Nevada–Semipalatinsk Movement, alerted NGOs that testing in an above-ground, contained environment such as a laboratory might be legalistically construed as neither underground nor in the atmosphere, underwater or outer space.

7 Conference on Disarmament, *Final Record of the Six Hundred and Sixty-eighth Plenary Meeting*, CD document CD/PV.668, 1 February 1994, statement by Grigori Berdennikov (Russia), p. 9.

8 Interview with Sir Michael Weston, Matfield, 11 June 2002. See also Zou Yunhua, *China and the CTBT Negotiations*, Stanford University Center for International Security and Cooperation, 1998.

9 Conference on Disarmament, *Final Record of the Six Hundred and Seventy-sixth Plenary Meeting*, CD document CD/PV.676, 24 March 1994, statement by Hou Zhitong (China), p. 20.

10 Zou Yunhua, *China and the CTBT Negotiations*, Stanford University Center for International Security and Cooperation, 1998, p. 12.

11 Conference on Disarmament, *Final Record of the Six Hundred and Seventy-sixth Plenary Meeting*, CD document CD/PV.676, 24 March 1994, statement by Hou Zhitong (China), p. 20.

12 Conference on Disarmament, *Final Record of the Six Hundred and Sixty-sixth Plenary Meeting*, CD document CD/PV.666, 25 January 1994, statement by Sir Michael Weston (UK), pp. 22–3.

13 Though the United Kingdom envisaged this provision as applying to the P-5 and not the D-3, the proposal was not explicit and, if accepted, could have led to a CTBT being used by non-NPT parties like India to claim parallel rights. Interview with Sir Michael Weston, Matfield, 11 June 2002.

14 Gérard Érrera, "Approche Générale de la Négociation d'un Traité d'Interdiction Complète des Essais Nucléaires", 7 February 1994 (informal paper to the NTB Committee).

15 The Franco-British harmonization of positions may have been cemented through their Joint Commission on nuclear policy and doctrine, established in 1992. See Camille Grand, *A French Nuclear Exception?*, The Henry L. Stimson Center, Occasional Paper no. 38, 1998.

16 *Some key elements of a Comprehensive Nuclear Test Ban Treaty: working paper*, CD document CD/1252, 22 March 1994.

17 Sweden and Australia were particularly active in this regard. Sweden updated the draft CTBT it had first proposed in 1984, and tabled again in 1991 and in 1993. Australia first issued a "draft structural outline" for a CTBT and then circulated a "non-paper", which was published as a "Resource Paper on draft treaty elements" on 30 March 1994, with accompanying notes. The Australian non-paper built on the Swedish drafts of 1991 and 1993 and incorporated ideas from the recent experience of the 1993 Chemical Weapons Convention, especially with regard to verification provisions. Canada took its familiar role of promoting wider understanding of the technical and political aspects of verification by drawing attention to the papers it had circulated the previous year on "verification synergies". See Sweden, *Letter dated 93/12/06 from the Head of delegation of Sweden addressed to the Secretary-General of the Conference on Disarmament transmitting the text of a draft comprehensive nuclear test ban treaty and its annexed draft Protocol*, CD document CD/1232–CD/NTB/WP.33, 6 December 1993. See also Sweden, *Letter dated 91/07/09 from the head of the Swedish Delegation addressed to the Secretary-General of the Conference on Disarmament transmitting the text of a draft Comprehensive Test-ban Treaty and its annexed protocols*, CD document CD/1089–CD/NTB/

WP.14, 31 July 1991; and Sweden, *Letter dated 93/06/03 from the Head of the Swedish Delegation addressed to the Secretary-General of the Conference on Disarmament transmitting the text of a draft Comprehensive Test-ban Treaty*, CD document CD/1202–CD/NTB/WP.19, 3 June 1993; Australia, *Letter dated 94/01/04 from the Permanent Representative of Australia to the United Nations for disarmament matters addressed to the President of the Conference on Disarmament transmitting the text of a working paper entitled "Comprehensive nuclear test ban treaty: a draft structural outline"*, CD document CD/1235, 5 January 1994; Australia, *Comprehensive test ban treaty: Australian resource paper on draft treaty elements: working paper*, CD document CD/NTB/WP.49, 30 March 1994; and Australia, *Comprehensive test ban treaty: Australian resource paper on draft treaty elements: explanatory notes: working paper*, CD document CD/NTB/WP.50, 30 March 1994; and Canada, *Letter dated 93/06/03 from the Permanent Representative of Canada addressed to the Secretary-General of the Conference on Disarmament transmitting a booklet entitled "Constraining proliferation: the contribution of verification synergies"*, CD document CD/1201–CD/NTB/WP.18, 3 June 1993.

18 Conference on Disarmament, *Final Record of the Six Hundred and Sixty-sixth Plenary Meeting*, CD document CD/PV.666, 25 January 1994, statement by Lars Norberg (Sweden), p. 11.

19 Though initiated by Sweden, it was Germany that made most of the running on behalf of preparations, trying as late as February 1996 to include the investigation of "concerns regarding apparently imminent non-compliance" into the treaty sections on consultation and clarification and on the powers and functions of the Executive Council. Germany issued a draft Working Paper, *Germany's proposed new Treaty language regarding the imminent preparation of a nuclear test explosion in the context of a CTBT*, 9 February 1996, which was not formally tabled with a CD number.

20 Conference on Disarmament, *Final Record of the Six Hundred and Eighty-third Plenary Meeting*, CD document CD/PV.683, 23 June 1994, statement by Sirous Nasseri (Iran), pp. 17–22.

21 Conference on Disarmament, *Final Record of the Six Hundred and Seventieth Plenary Meeting*, CD document CD/PV.670, 10 February 1994, statement by Soemadi D.M. Brotodiningrat (Indonesia), p. 12.

22 Ibid.

23 "1. Each State Party undertakes not to carry out any nuclear weapon test or any nuclear explosion and to prohibit and prevent any such nuclear

test or nuclear explosion at any place under its jurisdiction or control. 2. Each State Party undertakes, furthermore, to refrain from causing, encouraging, or in any way participating in the carrying out of such nuclear weapon test or nuclear explosion, as specified in paragraph 1 above"; see Indonesia, *Draft article on scope: working paper*, CD document CD/NTB/WP.243, 29 June 1995.

24 The reasons for the September 1996 target date included the US fiscal year and election timetables: four years would give time for negotiations and ensure that the treaty could be concluded during one US presidential term.

25 Author's discussions with French diplomats, 1994–1995. See also Camille Grand, *A French Nuclear Exception?*, The Henry L. Stimson Center, Occasional Paper no. 38, 1998.

26 As discussed in Chapter 3, China's statement supporting this target date came after its public relations debacle over the nuclear test exposed by VERTIC. See "Britain scores first on rumbling tests", *The Guardian*, 6 October 1993; and "China explodes nuclear device despite US plea", *The Financial Times*, 6 October 1993.

27 According to a senior Chinese official, there was a continuing debate between the military and political establishments and no definite decision had yet been taken on whether to join the CTBT or not. Interview by the author, Beijing, 13 October 2000.

28 Taken from Gérard Érrera, "Approche Générale de la Negociation d'un Traité d'Interdiction Complète des Essais Nucléaires", 7 February 1994, (informal paper to the NTB Committee); the English quote given here is from Rebecca Johnson and Sean Howard, *A Comprehensive Test Ban: Disappointing Progress*, ACRONYM Report, no. 3, The Acronym Consortium, 1994, p. 10.

29 China said little but the delegation suddenly tabled seven working papers with draft treaty language that it insisted must be included in the rolling text. If anything, this confirmed the Chair's instinct that it was necessary to concentrate the negotiators' minds on an actual text and force the critical issues out from the camouflage of endless discussions.

30 The opinions of Ambassador Érrera and Sir Michael Weston were given in an informal meeting, reported to the author by diplomats from several delegations and recorded contemporaneously in the author's weekly e-mailed reports to international NGOs, known as *Acronym Emails*. According to these sources, Weston's remarks offended not only Marín Bosch, but also the Swedish and Australian delegations, who cherished

the view that their drafts had helped to lay a useful groundwork for the early negotiations.

31 Interview with Stephen Ledogar, New York, 5 November 2000. Despite the Franco-British alliance on issues like safety tests and timing, with which many EU countries disagreed, German diplomats privately confirmed to the author that they had instructions to reassure France and ensure its continued participation in the negotiations. This was understood to be in the context of Bonn's foreign policy priorities in relation to the Franco-German relationship in the European Union.

32 See Chapter 7 for explanations of the relevance of and debates on these various verification technologies.

33 As with previous test-ban negotiations, time was spent on considering improbable evasion scenarios in remote locations around the world, dreamed up by nuclear weapon technicians and presented as if, being theoretically possible, they were technically feasible or militarily significant.

34 Conference on Disarmament, *Final Record of the Six Hundred and Eighty-fourth Plenary Meeting*, CD document CD/PV.684, 30 June 1994, statement by Hendrik Wagenmakers (Netherlands), p. 8.

35 See *Report of the Ad Hoc Committee on a Nuclear Test Ban to the Conference on Disarmament*, CD document CD/1273/Rev.1, 5 September 1994.

36 See Appendix B for the full list of Chairs and Friends of the Chair.

37 Australia, *Draft article on scope: working paper*, CD document CD/NTB/WP.222, 9 March 1995.

38 France, *Proposal to Working Group 2 on Legal and Institutional Issues on Withdrawal*, 17 August 1994.

39 The G-21 issued a statement opposing the easy opt-out provision, 16 December 1994. A number of US allies made representations to the US government behind the scenes. Though these were off the record and not made public, diplomats from several European and Asia–Pacific countries told the author about their initiatives on this.

40 The Campaign comprised 18 of the most influential Washington-based NGOs at the time: the Arms Control Association, British-American Security Information Council, Center for Defense Information, Committee for National Security, Council for a Livable World, Institute for Science and International Security, Lawyers Alliance for World Security, Manhattan Project II, Natural Resources Defense Council, Nuclear Control Institute, Peace Action, Physicians for Social Responsibility, Plutonium Challenge, Public Education Center, Henry L. Stimson Center, Union of Concerned

Scientists, Washington Council on Non-Proliferation, and Women's Action for New Directions.

41 The Campaign for the NPT had been initiated by Michael Krepon of the Henry L. Stimson Center, together with the W. Alton Jones Foundation, a major US funder of arms control projects with the twofold purpose of facilitating international support for indefinite extension of the NPT and getting an effective CTBT by September 1996. By 1994, Joseph Cirincione, a former Senate aide to the Committee on Foreign Relations had been hired to lead the Campaign and coordinate political and media strategies.

42 See Conference on Disarmament, *Final Record of the Six Hundred and Ninety-third Plenary Meeting*, CD document CD/PV.693, 31 January 1995, statement by Ralph Earle (USA).

43 Author's conversation with Miguel Marín Bosch in Geneva, January 1995. Contrary to this perception, the proposal was taken more seriously in Washington than many CTBT negotiators and watchers thought at the time. Author's conversations with Stephen Ledogar, New York, 5 November 2000, and with Edward Ifft, Washington DC, June 2007.

44 This is how the UK–French proposal for safety tests appeared in the rolling text. See *Report of the Ad Hoc Committee on a Nuclear Test Ban to the Conference on Disarmament*, CD document CD/1273/Rev.1, 5 September 1994, p. 32.

45 According to senior British officials at the time, requests should be carefully defined and have to meet rigorous criteria; they would have to be considered on a special-case basis, granted by the implementing authority and duly verified to ensure that testing was solely for the purposes stated and not new development.

46 Group of 21, *Some key elements of a Comprehensive Nuclear Test Ban Treaty: working paper*, CD document CD/1252, 22 March 1994. Following this statement, India and Pakistan underlined their opposition to safety tests in individual statements to the CD. India specified that "no test should be carried out under the pretext of safety purposes" and that the CTBT "should be comprehensive and not establish thresholds". Conference on Disarmament, *Final Record of the Six Hundred and Eightieth Plenary Meeting*, CD document CD/PV.680, 2 June 1994, statement by Satish Chandra (India), p. 3. Pakistan, for its part, argued that permitting exceptions for continued nuclear tests for safety or other purposes "would be unacceptable, as they would be against the very spirit of the treaty [and] leave the treaty open to exploitation and abuse".

In Pakistan's view, weapons whose safety had become doubtful should be dismantled, which would "be a positive contribution to the goal of nuclear disarmament". Conference on Disarmament, *Final Record of the Six Hundred and Eighty-first Plenary Meeting*, CD document CD/PV.680, 9 June 1994, statement by Ahmad Kamal (Pakistan), p. 5.

47 UK House of Commons, *Hansard*, vol. 244, 14 June 1994, column 536W.

48 Interview with Sir Michael Weston, reported in Rebecca Johnson, *Acronym Email 13*, 17 June 1994 (contemporaneous report, distributed electronically).

49 UK House of Lords, *Hansard*, vol. 556, 21 June 1994, column 169. Perhaps the words were chosen deliberately, since it could be argued that the UK's position was to *include* a provision for safety tests in the treaty.

50 President François Mitterrand was committed to maintaining the French moratorium and had publicly stated on French television that despite China's continuing nuclear tests, France would conduct no further tests while he was in power. In contrast, Jacques Chirac, the Gaullist front-runner for the presidency, had condemned his own party for submitting to Mitterrand's moratorium and had called for 20 more tests before France would accept a CTBT. Rebecca Johnson and Sean Howard, *A Comprehensive Test Ban Within Reach*, ACRONYM Report, no. 1, The Acronym Consortium, 1994, p. 18.

51 Conference on Disarmament, *Final Record of the Seven Hundred and Fifth Plenary Meeting*, CD document CD/PV.705, 6 April 1995, statement by Sir Michael Weston (UK), p. 20. The Australian scope formulation was contained in Australia, *Draft article on scope: working paper*, CD document CD/NTB/WP.222, 9 March 1995.

52 Conference on Disarmament, *Final Record of the Seven Hundred and Fifth Plenary Meeting*, CD document CD/PV.705, 6 April 1995, statement by Sir Michael Weston (UK), p. 21.

53 Although France had endorsed the proposal for safety tests from very early on, and negotiations on it had been coordinated between the two European powers, the United Kingdom was officially the owner of the text and so was able to withdraw it without formal corroboration from France. The decision was jointly coordinated however, as confirmed by both Érrera and Weston. See also Rebecca Johnson, *Strengthening the Non-Proliferation Regime: Ends and Beginnings*, ACRONYM Report, no. 6, The Acronym Consortium, 1995, p. 10.

54 Rebecca Johnson, *Indefinite Extension of the Non-Proliferation Treaty: Risks and Reckonings*, ACRONYM Report, no. 7, The Acronym Consortium, 1995, pp. 16 and 38–40.

55 See Rebecca Johnson, "Advocates and Activists: Conflicting Approaches on Non-proliferation and the Test Ban Treaty", in Ann M. Florini (ed.), *The Third Force: The Rise of Transnational Civil Society*, Japan Center for International Exchange and Carnegie Endowment for International Peace, 2000.

56 Ibid. The quotations are taken from General Debate and Main Committee statements given at the 1995 NPT Review and Extension Conference, as summarized in Rebecca Johnson, *Indefinite Extension of the Non-Proliferation Treaty: Risks and Reckonings*, ACRONYM Report, no. 7, The Acronym Consortium, 1995 and a series of 21 daily reports published by the author during the 1995 NPT Review and Extension Conference.

57 The Chair of Main Committee III at the NPT Review and Extension Conference was Jaap Ramaker, then Chair of the Nuclear Test Ban Committee's Working Group 2, and later chosen to chair the final year of the CTBT negotiations in 1996.

58 In full, Article V of the NPT states; "Each Party to the Treaty undertakes to take appropriate measures to ensure that, in accordance with this Treaty, under appropriate international observation and through appropriate international procedures, potential benefits from any peaceful applications of nuclear explosions will be made available to non-nuclear-weapon States Party to the Treaty on a non-discriminatory basis and that the charge to such Parties for the explosive devices used will be as low as possible and exclude any charge for research and development. Non-nuclear-weapon States Party to the Treaty shall be able to obtain such benefits, pursuant to a special international agreement or agreements, through an appropriate international body with adequate representation of non-nuclear-weapon states. Negotiations on this subject shall commence as soon as possible after the Treaty enters into force. Non-nuclear-weapon States Party to the Treaty so desiring may also obtain such benefits pursuant to bilateral agreements".

59 *Article V: Working paper submitted by Algeria, Australia, Austria, Belarus, Cambodia, Canada, Croatia, the Czech Republic, Denmark, Finland, Hungary, Indonesia, Ireland, Kazakhstan, Kenya, Kyrgyzstan, Latvia, Lebanon, Malaysia, the Netherlands, New Zealand, Norway, Papua New Guinea, the Philippines, the Republic of Korea, Romania, Slovakia, South*

Africa, Sri Lanka, Sweden and Ukraine, UN document NPT/CONF.1995/MC.III/WP.6, 3 May 1995.

60 Ibid. See also NPT/CONF.1995/MC.III/WP.6/Add.1, 9 May 1995, adding the following to the list of countries that submitted the working paper: Bulgaria, Colombia, Japan, the Marshall Islands, Palau, Poland, Switzerland, Tonga, Tuvalu and Uruguay. Both working papers are reproduced in *1995 Review and Extension Conference of the Parties to the Treaty on the Non-Proliferation of Nuclear Weapons, Final Document*, UN document NPT/CONF.1995/32 (Part II), 1995, pp. 401–3.

61 See ibid., p. 386.

62 For the paragraphs as agreed by Main Committee III and the Drafting Committee, see ibid., pp. 385–6.

63 For more information, see Jayantha Dhanapala with Randy Rydell, *Multilateral Diplomacy and the NPT: An Insider's Account*, UN Institute for Disarmament Research and SIPRI, Geneva, 2005.

64 Paragraph 4 reads: "The achievement of the following measures is important in the full realization and effective implementation of article VI, including the programme of action as reflected below: (a) The completion by the Conference on Disarmament of the negotiations on a universal and internationally and effectively verifiable Comprehensive Nuclear-Test-Ban Treaty no later than 1996. Pending the entry into force of a Comprehensive Test-Ban Treaty, the nuclear-weapon States should exercise utmost restraint"; *1995 Review and Extension Conference of the Parties to the Treaty on the Non-Proliferation of Nuclear Weapons, Final Document*, UN document NPT/CONF.1995/32 (Part II), 1995, p. 10.

65 Interview with Jayantha Dhanapala, President of the 1995 NPT Review and Extension Conference, conducted by the author and Jim Wurst of *Disarmament Times*, New York, 13 May 1995. These views are also discussed in Jayantha Dhanapala with Randy Rydell, *Multilateral Diplomacy and the NPT: An Insider's Account*, UN Institute for Disarmament Research and SIPRI, Geneva, 2005.

66 Jonathan Mirsky, "Neighbours condemn Chinese nuclear test", *The Times*, 16 May 1995; and Ian Black, "China snubs world with nuclear test", *The Guardian*, 16 May 1995 Black quotes an unnamed UK official acknowledging that China's test, so soon after the NPT Conference had closed, was "certainly indelicate, because it looks as if the nuclear powers have got what they wanted and are back to business as usual".

67 From author's off-the-record conversations with diplomats from all the P-5 states, New York, 17 May 1995. See Rebecca Johnson, *Indefinite*

Extension of the Non-Proliferation Treaty: Risks and Reckonings, ACRONYM Booklet, no. 7, The Acronym Consortium, September 1995, p. 62. Although the author could not get formal confirmation of the internal discussions (or lack thereof) on the timing of nuclear tests from the Chinese delegation, it was elicited that the Chinese military determines its testing schedule according to need and conditions, which suggested that diplomatic sensitivities would not normally be considered (and, indeed, that diplomats were unlikely to be told in advance, which suggests that knowledge of the preparations to test in early May derived from US intelligence reports, as the above-mentioned off-the-record conversations had intimated). China conducted a further, 60–80kt explosion (its forty-third) on 17 August 1995, the date of the CD plenary at which the US ambassador formally presented President Clinton's zero yield scope decision to the test-ban negotiators. This was almost certainly a coincidence, providing more evidence of a lack of communication between the nuclear test decision makers and China's Geneva negotiators.

68 Statements by the representatives of various delegations, Conference on Disarmament, *Final Record of the Seven Hundred and Eighth Plenary Meeting*, CD document CD/PV.708, 15 June 1995 and Conference on Disarmament, *Final Record of the Seven Hundred and Ninth Plenary Meeting*, CD document CD/PV.709, 22 June 1994. See also Roger Highfield, "How France could limit the fall-out", *The Daily Telegraph*, 12 July 1995; Philippe Séguin, "A rebuttal: why France's nuclear plan is serious", *International Herald Tribune*, 6 September 1995; and Alan Riding, "Despite Wave of Protest, France Defends Pacific Nuclear Test", *New York Times*, 7 September 1995.

69 Conference on Disarmament, *Final Record of the Seven Hundred and Eighth Plenary Meeting*, CD document CD/PV.708, 15 June 1995, statement by Yukiya Amano (Japan), quoting a statement made in Tokyo by Japan's Deputy Prime Minister Yohei Kono, p. 10. See also Ian Black, "France rejects Japan's test plea", *The Guardian*, 20 June 1995.

70 Conference on Disarmament, *Final Record of the Seven Hundred and Eighth Plenary Meeting*, CD document CD/PV.708, 15 June 1995, statement by Wade Armstrong (New Zealand), p. 11. The use of a strong word like "outrage" is rare in the CD, where whole days can be spent on deciding whether to "note" a particular action or event, express "regret" or go so far as to "deplore" or "condemn".

[71] Conference on Disarmament, *Final Record of the Seven Hundred and Eighth Plenary Meeting*, CD document CD/PV.708, 15 June 1995, statement by Richard Starr (Australia), pp. 11–4.

[72] Conference on Disarmament, *Final Record of the Seven Hundred and Ninth Plenary Meeting*, CD document CD/PV.709, 22 June 1994, statement by Friedrich Moser (Switzerland), pp. 12–3.

[73] Ibid., statement by Antonio de Icaza (Mexico), p. 14. His reference to a "senior United States representative" was understood to mean William J. Perry, US Secretary of Defense, who made reference to the reopening of US interagency debates over higher thresholds at a press conference on 18 June. See, for example, R. Jeffrey Smith, "Administration debates Pentagon proposal to resume nuclear tests", *Washington Post*, 18 June 1995. It was widely believed that the United States had used Mexico's vulnerability during a serious financial crisis to insist that the Mexican government replace Marín Bosch as Ambassador to the CD, in large part due to his opposition to indefinite extension of the NPT.

[74] The gist of the long statement from Ambassador Nasseri is illustrated by these short extracts: "attempts at nuclear testing run contrary to the basic objective of the indefinite extension" of the NPT, and that "it was not only the moratorium that kept nuclear tests at bay but that the concerns about the outcome of the NPT Conference also served as a very essential deterrence to nuclear testing". Conference on Disarmament, *Final Record of the Seven Hundred and Eighth Plenary Meeting*, CD document CD/PV.708, 15 June 1995, statement by Sirous Nasseri (Iran), p. 24.

[75] See Rebecca Johnson, *Strengthening the Non-Proliferation Treaty: Decisions Made, Decisions Deferred*, ACRONYM Booklet, no. 4, The Acronym Consortium, September 1994, pp. 12–4.

[76] William J. Perry, US Secretary of Defense, press conference, Washington DC, 18 June 1995. Text supplied by *United States Information Service Facsimile Transmission*.

[77] While most of the United Kingdom's efforts were carried out behind the scenes, some reached the media. See, for example, James Adams, "Britain presses US to resume nuclear tests", *The Times*, 25 June 1995.

[78] Newspaper articles illustrate the development of this US debate during June 1995. Representative articles include Martin Walker and Ian Black, "Pentagon steps up fight to resume nuclear tests", *The Guardian*, 7 June 1995; "Pentagon seeks resumption of nuclear tests", *Armed Forces Newswire Service*, 8 June 1995; "Nuclear commitments", *New York Times*, 12 June 1995; Jessica Mathews, "Waffling on the test ban",

Washington Post, 12 June 1995; "Pentagon officials want underground nuclear tests", *AP Datastream*, 17 June 1995; "Administration debating whether small blasts should be conducted", *AP Datastream*, 17 June 1995; R. Jeffrey Smith, "Administration debates Pentagon proposal to resume nuclear tests", *Washington Post*, 18 June 1995; "Japan asks US not to resume nuclear tests", *Agence France-Presse International News*, 19 June 1995; Tom Rhodes, "Pentagon's nuclear tests plan raises concern for treaty", *The Times*, 20 June 1995; John Carlin, "Clinton drops nuclear bombshell", *The Independent*, 20 June 1995; Stephen Robinson, "US military urges Clinton to resume nuclear testing", *The Daily Telegraph*, 20 June 1995; and Martin Walker, "Clinton sacrifices principle in drive for second term", *The Guardian*, 20 June 1995.

79 Thomas Graham Jr., *Disarmament Sketches*, University of Washington Press, 2002, p. 247.

80 See Chapter 3.

81 Unpublished notes of an NGO meeting with Bob Bell, involving members of the Campaign for the NPT (reconstituted as the Working Group on the CTBT) and Greenpeace, Washington DC, 21 July 1995, made available to the author by Daryl Kimball.

82 In addition to ruling out hydronuclear experiments, Indonesia's text encompassed hydrodynamic experiments and, potentially, computer simulations and other forms of non-destructive assays, as well as PNE. Indonesia, *Draft article on scope: working paper*, CD document CD/NTB/WP.243, 29 June 1995.

83 India, *Draft article on scope: working paper*, CD/NTB/WP.244, 29 June 1995.

84 India had modified some essential elements of the original NRDC scope formulation, which read as follows: "Each State Party undertakes not to carry out any nuclear weapon test explosion, any other nuclear explosion, or any release of nuclear energy caused by the assembly or compression of fissile or fusion material by chemical high explosive means, and to prohibit and prevent such explosions or releases at any place under its jurisdiction or control". Thomas B. Cochran and Christopher Paine, *The Role of Hydronuclear Tests and Other Low-Yield Nuclear Explosions and Their Status Under a Comprehensive Test Ban*, Natural Resources Defense Council, 1995, p. vi. NRDC's objectives had also moved forward, as by June 1995 the battle in Washington was between zero yield and 500t. Author's conversations with NRDC scientists and lobbyists, Washington DC, July 1995.

[85] Contemporaneous report, distributed electronically, Rebecca Johnson, *Acronym Email*, 3 July 1995. In that email, written from notes summarizing extensive off-the-record discussions that week with diplomats from all the key CD members, the following reasons for the change in the non-nuclear-weapon states attitudes were identified: i) a threshold of tens or hundreds of tonnes, as reportedly discussed among the P-5 and in renewed inter-agency debates in the United States, would not be tolerated by the non-nuclear-weapon states; ii) information provided by NGOs identifying the role hydronuclear experiments and other experiments could play in nuclear weapon research and development had caused a rethink among some non-nuclear countries about the value and meaning of a CTBT that permitted hydronuclear experiments; iii) there was a sense of betrayal over the indecent haste with which the NPT extension decision had been followed by P-5 activities—notably, the Chinese nuclear test of 15 May and the 13 June announcement of the French resumption of testing—and discussions that were viewed as incompatible with the commitments made at the NPT conference; iv) the non-nuclear states were no longer willing to trust the "grey areas" in their dealings with the nuclear states, and wanted everything explicitly agreed; and v) ascribing the date 1996 had caused governments on all sides to feel that they had room to manoeuvre before finalizing the CTBT, giving space in which the nuclear states were testing out high threshold numbers and the non-nuclear delegations were trying out definitions.

[86] Conference on Disarmament, *Final Record of the Seven Hundred and Tenth Plenary Meeting*, CD document CD/PV.710, 29 June 1995, statement by Satish Chandra (India), speaking on behalf of the G-21, p. 14. Since India was not a member of the NPT, it appeared strange to have a statement that focused so particularly on the NPT being delivered by an Indian ambassador, but Chandra was at that time coordinator of the G-21 group in the CD.

[87] Ibid.

[88] The Acronym Consortium played a significant role in providing CD delegations and their governments (usually the foreign or defence ministries in capitals) with detailed, fortnightly summaries of the CTBT negotiations through *Nuclear Proliferation News*, which also highlighted relevant analysis from other NGOs regarding debates or developments relating to nuclear weapons or testing.

[89] Conference on Disarmament, *Final Record of the Seven Hundred and Tenth Plenary Meeting*, CD document CD/PV.710, 29 June 1995,

statement by Satish Chandra (India), speaking on behalf of the G-21, p. 14.

90 Widespread anger and civil society reaction to the French and Chinese testing decisions, especially in Japan and Australia, put pressure on both these governments to make stronger public statements of condemnation than the normally polite diplomatic expressions of regret. In the CD, this caused (or was used to justify) a public deterioration of relations, on the one hand, between the French and Australian delegations, and, on the other, between the Chinese and Japanese. Seeking to deflect criticism and embarrass Japan for taking a "moralistic" stance, the Chinese ambassador resorted to reminding the Japanese ambassador of war crimes committed by Japan against China during the 1930s and 1940s. For various national expressions condemning the French and Chinese tests, see the verbatim records of the CD for the periods 1 June to 6 July 1995 (CD documents CD/PV.706 to CD/PV.711) and 3 August to 21 September 1995 (CD documents CD/PV.712 to CD/PV.719). See especially Conference on Disarmament, *Final Record of the Seven Hundred and Seventeenth Plenary Meeting*, CD document CD/PV.717, 5 September 1995, statement by Sha Zukang (China).

91 Conversation with the author, Geneva, June 1995. The diplomat gave permission to be quoted but not named in Rebecca Johnson, *Indefinite Extension of the Non-Proliferation Treaty: Risks and Reckonings*, ACRONYM Report, no. 7, The Acronym Consortium, 1995, p. 65.

92 Author's conversation with Gérard Érrera, Geneva, August 1995.

93 Civil Society contributions in this regard included input from the author (Acronym) in Geneva, scientists such as Annette Schaper at the Peace Research Institute, Frankfurt (PRIF), Eric Arnett at the Stockholm International Peace Research Institute (SIPRI), Patricia Lewis at VERTIC, and US non-governmental scientists and lobbyists, including Frank von Hippel, Hal Feiveson, Steve Fetter, Richard Garwin, Stan Norris, Tom Cochran, Michael Krepon, Joe Cirincione and Daryl Kimball, associated variously with Princeton University, NRDC and the Campaign for the NPT.

94 See Eric Arnett, "The Comprehensive Nuclear Test Ban", in *SIPRI Yearbook 1995: Armaments, Disarmament and International Security*, Oxford University Press/Stockholm International Peace Research Institute, 1995, pp. 699–702.

95 Conference on Disarmament, *Final Record of the Six Hundred and Ninety-third Plenary Meeting*, CD document CD/PV.693, 31 January 1995, Statement of Miguel Marín Bosch (Mexico).

96 Eric Arnett and Annette Schaper, "No hydronuclear ban", *The Bulletin of the Atomic Scientists*, vol. 50, no. 6, 1994, pp. 22–3.

97 Thomas B. Cochran and Christopher Paine, *The Role of Hydronuclear Tests and Other Low-Yield Nuclear Explosions and Their Status Under a Comprehensive Test Ban*, Natural Resources Defense Council, 1995, p. i.

98 Ibid.

99 Ibid., p. vi.

100 Ibid., pp. vi–vii. NRDC was at pains to distance itself from the Indian proposal, and in conversations with the author and others, Cochran and Paine let it be known that India's text had garbled key elements and was potentially counterproductive to their intentions.

101 UK House of Lords, *Hansard*, vol. 565, 20 June 1995, columns 147–9.

102 Interviews with Sha Zukang, Beijing, 13 October 2000; Stephen Ledogar, New York, 5 November 2000; Grigori Berdennikov, Vienna, 17 July 2001; and Sir Michael Weston, Matfield, 11 June 2002; and conversations with a senior French official, Washington DC, November 2000.

103 See Ann Devroy and R. Jeffrey Smith, "White House defuses nuclear test proposal", *Washington Post*, 23 June 1995; Declan Butler, "Dispute over 'threshold' explosions could disrupt test ban negotiations", *Nature*, vol. 376, no. 6538, 1995; and Rebecca Johnson, "CTB Negotiations—Geneva Update 20", *Nuclear Proliferation News 28*, 30 June 1995.

104 Fact sheets were brought out by VERTIC, Scientists for Global Responsibility, the CTB Clearinghouse and the Working Group on the CTB (formerly the Campaign for the NPT) and possibly others of which the author is not aware.

105 This strategy echoed the pressure exerted by Linus Pauling and Pugwash for a CTBT 35 years earlier.

106 See, for example, Peter Gray, "O'Leary v. Deutsch", *The Bulletin of the Atomic Scientists*, vol. 50, no. 6, 1994, pp. 10–2; and Nancy W. Gallagher, *The Politics of Verification*, The Johns Hopkins University Press, 1999, p. 227.

107 The NRDC report of March 1995 built on the 1994 report from the JASON group on stockpile stewardship. The JASON Group, as it was called, comprised eminent scientists, including nuclear weapon scientists, and spanned a spectrum of political and technical perspectives. It was headed by Sidney Drell and coordinated through the JASON division of the MITRE Corporation, and was generally viewed as authoritative and more independent than the nuclear laboratories. See Sidney Drell et al,

Science Based Stockpile Stewardship, JASON/The MITRE Corporation, November 1994, especially p. 22.

108 Ibid. The JASON Group was chaired by Sidney Drell and at this time comprised John Cornwall, Freeman Dyson, Douglas Eardley, Richard Garwin, David Hammer, John Kammerdiener, Robert LeLevier, Robert Peurifoy, John Richter, Marshall Rosenbluth, Seymour Sack, Jeremiah Sullivan and Fredrik Zachariasen.

109 In downplaying the benefits from low yield nuclear tests, the JASON report proposed additional funding for the laboratories to develop other kinds of nuclear weapon-related research. For a critique of these compromises and programmes, which caused grave concern to some disarmament NGOs, see Andrew Lichterman and Jacqueline Cabasso, *Faustian Bargain 2000: Why 'Stockpile Stewardship' Is Fundamentally Incompatible with the Process of Nuclear Disarmament*, Western States Legal Foundation, May 2000.

110 Daryl Kimball, unpublished research.

111 Reporting on the boycott of French products in Japan, Hong Kong and other Asian and Pacific countries, including cancellation of hotel reservations in France by some Asian tourists, the *Washington Post* quoted a senior French official as saying "We expected a few angry outbursts, but we never thought it would get this bad"; William Drozdiak, "France's nuclear storm: plan to resume testing in Pacific unleashes typhoon of anger", *Washington Post*, 8 July 1995.

112 The International Peace Bureau and IPPNW, for example, produced stickers in various European languages, to identify French goods on the shelves with a message against nuclear testing. In the United States, Peace Action, the Women's Action for New Directions (WAND), the Fellowship of Reconciliation and others formed a boycott coalition, which asked French-owned companies to make public statements denouncing the tests or risk being included on lists encouraging the public to boycott their goods as a protest. The lists were disseminated through the internet, but there has been no systematic assessment of their impact.

113 Craig R. Whitney, "Paris defends seizing ship in atom test zone", *New York Times*, 11 July 1995. The sounds of the forcible boarding and arrests, which included chilling screams from campaigners being manhandled by French commandos, were broadcast by the BBC. They occurred on the tenth anniversary of the French secret service bombing of the first *Rainbow Warrior* in Auckland Harbour on 10 July 1985, which increased the embarrassment factor for France. Graham, who was then

in the United States, particularly recalls hearing the "young woman staffer broadcast to the world over the radio the sounds of the French military crudely storming the ship". Thomas Graham Jr., *Disarmament Sketches*, University of Washington Press, 2002, p. 248.

114 Camille Grand, *A French Nuclear Exception?*, The Henry L. Stimson Center, Occasional Paper no. 38, 1998.

115 Thomas Graham Jr., *Disarmament Sketches*, University of Washington Press, 2002, pp. 246–7.

116 "Worldview", WBEZ, Chicago, 9 August 1995.

117 See Conference on Disarmament, *Final Record of the Seven Hundred and Thirteenth Plenary Meeting*, CD document CD/PV.713, 10 August 1995. France's acceptance of the Australian scope formulation was not immediately associated with zero yield. Instead, the announcement was assumed to mean that France was dropping its demand for a threshold of up to 300t and would abide by whatever decision the P-5 could agree on "activities not prohibited". According to the recollections of a senior French official (in conversations with the author in November 2000), since the United Kingdom and the United States had already endorsed the Australian text, while continuing to wrangle within the P-5 sidebar negotiations about threshold levels, France's statement was not intended to mean that it was abandoning the option of conducting very low yield hydronuclear tests. See also Hervé de Charette, "For both non-proliferation and a credible French deterrent", *International Herald Tribune*, 22 August 1995.

118 Statement by President William J. Clinton and fact sheet from the Office of the Press Secretary, 11 August 1995, reproduced in *Letter dated 17 August 1995 from the Permanent Representative of the United States Of America to the Conference addressed to the Deputy Secretary-General of the Conference On Disarmament transmitting the text of a statement by the President of the United States made on 11 August 1995 concerning United States nuclear testing policy and a White House fact sheet issued also on 11 August 1995 concerning United States CTBT safeguards*, CD document CD/1340, 17 August 1995.

119 Ibid. Article IX in the finalized CTBT states that the treaty is of unlimited duration, but "Each State Party shall, in exercising its national sovereignty, have the right to withdraw from this Treaty if it decides that extraordinary events related to the subject matter of this Treaty have jeopardized its supreme interests". See also R. Jeffrey Smith, "US to back total nuclear test ban", *Washington Post*, 11 August 1995.

[120] It is not clear to what extent the United States and France harmonized their announcements, but there had been a high-level delegation of US officials to France in the period immediately before 10–11 August 1995, and the author was told that President Clinton discussed the policy shift in a phone call with President Chirac just before the announcements were made public.

[121] Conference on Disarmament, *Final Record of the Seven Hundred and Eighteenth Plenary Meeting*, CD document CD/PV.718, 14 September 1995, statement by Sir Michael Weston (UK), p. 15.

[122] Russian diplomats expressed anger at the way in which the United States had abruptly and—as they saw it—unilaterally or in collaboration with France gone outside the P-5 negotiations and pushed the scope to zero. They complained that Russia was not consulted before Clinton made his decision, and that the US delegation gave less than a day's notice of Clinton's announcement. As a consequence, Russia not only delayed giving its agreement to the Australian text and zero yield understanding, but also put forward additional proposals relating to the international monitoring system, and took a harder line than expected over on-site inspections and entry into force (discussed in later chapters). These insights come from the author's discussions with diplomats during late 1995 and early 1996, confirmed in interviews with Victor Slipchenko, formerly the Deputy Ambassador for the Russian Federation in the CTBT negotiations, Vienna, 8 October 1999, and Ambassador Grigori Berdennikov, Vienna, 17 July 2001.

[123] President William J. Clinton, Press Conference, Moscow Nuclear Safety and Security Summit, Moscow, 21 April 1996.

[124] President Boris Yeltsin, Press Conference, Moscow Nuclear Safety and Security Summit, Moscow, 21 April 1996.

[125] Conference on Disarmament, *Final Record of the Seven Hundred and Thirty-fourth Plenary Meeting*, CD document CD/PV.734, 14 May 1996, statement by Grigori Berdennikov (Russia), pp. 17–8.

[126] Ibid., pp. 17–9.

[127] Conference on Disarmament, *Final Record of the Seven Hundred and Thirty-third Plenary Meeting*, CD document CD/PV.733, 28 March 1996, statement by Sha Zukang (China).

[128] Ibid.

[129] See *Report of the Ad Hoc Committee on a Nuclear Test Ban to the Conference on Disarmament*, CD document CD/1346/Rev.1, 6 September 1995.

130 "New contractor announced for Nevada Test Site: Secretary outlines plans for site", US Department of Energy, press release, 27 October 1995.

Chapter 5
Making the treaty ban civilian as well as military nuclear explosions

1 Conference on Disarmament, *Final Record of the Seven Hundred and Thirty-third Plenary Meeting*, CD document CD/PV.733, 28 March 1996, statement by Sha Zukang (China), p. 20.

2 General Assembly, *Comprehensive nuclear-test-ban-treaty*, UN document A/RES/50/65, 9 January 1996. The first draft of the resolution had identified "not later than 30 June" as the target date for completing the treaty, and though this was left out of the final version, as adopted, the end of June was treated by most delegations as a de facto target date for a finalized text in order to meet the 30 September 1996 deadline identified in the 1992 US moratorium legislation.

3 Conference on Disarmament, *Final Record of the Six Hundred and Sixty-sixth Plenary Meeting*, CD document CD/PV.666, 25 January 1994, statement by John Holum (USA), p. 16.

4 France's rejection of Starr in late 1994 because he was too "active" on behalf of a test ban (at a time when France's strategy was for delay), was exacerbated during 1995 by Australia's strongly expressed opposition to the resumption of French testing in the Pacific. According to the author's interviews with US and UK diplomats, many delegations, including the United States and the United Kingdom, would have been happy to see Australia chair the NTB Committee in 1996, but they considered it counterproductive to try to override the French hostility, and were, in fact, quite comfortable with the choice of Ramaker, who was well respected and regarded as a "safe pair of hands".

5 See Appendix B or a list of key appointments.

6 President Jacques Chirac, address on French television, 29 January 1996. The final test, on 27 January 1996, was also the largest, at 120kt, and was detonated beneath the Fangataufa atoll, adjacent to Moruroa.

7 Conference on Disarmament, *Final Record of the Seven Hundred and Twenty-first Plenary Meeting*, CD document CD/PV.721, 23 January 1996, contained in the statement by John Holum (USA), p. 12.

8 "New contractor announced for Nevada Test Site: Secretary outlines plans for site", US Department of Energy, press release, 27 October 1995. Confirmed also in author's interviews with US diplomats.

9 Conference on Disarmament, *Final Record of the Seven Hundred and Twenty-first Plenary Meeting*, CD document CD/PV.721, 23 January 1996, statement by John Holum (USA), p. 14.

10 See ibid., statement by Munir Akram (Pakistan), pp. 9–11; Conference on Disarmament, *Final Record of the Seven Hundred and Twenty-third Plenary Meeting*, CD document CD/PV.723, 1 February 1996, statement by Bernard Goonetilleke (Sri Lanka), pp. 18–22; and Conference on Disarmament, *Final Record of the Seven Hundred and Twenty-third Plenary Meeting*, CD document CD/PV.723, 1 February 1996, statement by Mounir Zahran (Egypt), pp. 6–10. The first of the subcritical tests had been scheduled for June 1996, which would have placed it in the middle of the critical final phase of negotiations. In addition to representations from a number of US and international NGOs to have the tests called off, Jaap Ramaker made a personal appeal to the Clinton administration not to conduct any such tests during the negotiations. The June subcritical test, codenamed "Rebound", was subsequently postponed. Though the Department of Energy press statement linked the postponement with the CTBT negotiations, it also underlined that the tests were "an essential ingredient" of the stockpile stewardship programme and did not "technically violate a zero yield ban". See "DOE opts to postpone NTS weapon test", *Inside Energy*, 10 June 1996.

11 Tim Weiner, "US suspects India prepares to conduct nuclear test", *New York Times*, 15 December 1995; and "India may be preparing for nuclear test", *Armed Forces Newswire*, 18 December 1995. See also Rebecca Johnson, "CTB negotiations—Geneva Update No. 25", p. 6, and "Concerns rise over India nuclear stance", pp. 37–8, in *Disarmament Diplomacy*, no. 1, The Acronym Institute, 1996.

12 For a comprehensive discussion, see George Perkovich, *India's Nuclear Bomb*, University of California Press, 1999, especially chp. 13.

13 Conference on Disarmament, *Final Record of the Seven Hundred and Twenty-second Plenary Meeting*, CD document CD/PV.722, 25 January 1996, statement by Arundhati Ghose (India), p. 2.

14 India, *Indian draft language on preamble: working paper*, CD document CD/NTB/WP.295, 29 January 1996; India, *Indian draft language on review: working paper*, CD document CD/NTB/WP.296, 29 January 1996; and India, *Indian draft language on entry into force: working paper*, CD document CD/NTB/WP.297, 29 January 1996.

15 Atal Behari Vajpayee, Member of Parliament and Member of the Indian Delegation, Statement to the Fiftieth United Nations General Assembly, at the First Committee, New York, 26 October 1995.

16 India had proposed that "… this Treaty shall enter into force only after all states parties have committed themselves to the attainment of the goal of total elimination of all nuclear weapons within a well defined time framework (of ten years)"; India, *Indian draft language on entry into force: working paper*, CD document CD/NTB/WP.297, 29 January 1996.

17 Ghose made an oblique reference to these corridor discussions, calling the CD a "hall with trick mirrors in which nothing is what it seems to be". Following a strategy that relied on combining best-versus-good and hide-and-seek tactics, she complained that "Those who want a truly comprehensive treaty are labelled spoilers. Those who want to eliminate nuclear weapons are being seen as a threat to disarmament. A time-bound framework to eliminate nuclear weapons is seen as a diabolical plot to stall negotiations on the CTBT". Conference on Disarmament, *Final Record of the Seven Hundred and Twenty-fifth Plenary Meeting*, CD document CD/PV.725, 15 January 1996, statement by Arundhati Ghose (India), p. 4.

18 During the 1950s and 1960s, the United States carried out its "Plowshares" programme of nuclear explosions for civilian purposes, but abandoned it in 1977, deeming that the costs and problems outweighed any benefits. Before giving up its programme in the 1980s, amid growing economic and environmental concerns, the Soviet Union conducted more than a hundred explosions, mostly for large scale excavation and construction work. Iris Y. P. Borg, "Nuclear explosions for peaceful purposes", in Jozef Goldblat and David Cox, *Nuclear Weapon Tests: Prohibition or Limitation?*, Oxford University Press, 1988, pp. 59–74. For an early defence of PNE, see Edward Teller, *The Legacy of Hiroshima*, Doubleday, 1962, pp. 81–92.

19 General Qian Shaojun, statement to the NTB Committee, 26 January 1996, quoted in Zou Yunhua, *China and the CTBT Negotiations*, Stanford University Center for International Security and Cooperation, 1998, p. 63.

20 Statement by Ambassador Sha Zukang, at the Olof Palme International Centre, Stockholm, 5 February 1996.

21 India maintained that the 1974 explosion was for peaceful purposes until it conducted an explicit series of nuclear weapons test explosions in May 1998, after which it admitted that the 1974 explosion had also been a nuclear weapon test.

22 China's proposal from March 1995 and India's additional language were included in the rolling text issued by the NTB Committee in its 1995

Report to the Conference on Disarmament. Appendix 1, Volume 3, texts of documents issued by the Conference on Disarmament, CD document CD/1364/AppendixI/VolumeIII, 26 September 1995, p. 31. A footnote recorded that a number of delegations opposed any inclusion in a CTBT of a section on "so-called 'peaceful nuclear explosions'".

23 Conference on Disarmament, *Final Record of the Six Hundred and Eighty-first Plenary Meeting,* CD document CD/PV.681, 9 June 1994, statement by Ahmad Kamal (Pakistan), p. 4. Pakistan's position on this indicated that denying India a loophole was more important than supporting China's preference.

24 *Draft comprehensive nuclear test ban treaty: Islamic Republic of Iran*, CD document CD/1384, 21 February 1996.

25 Author's conversations with a senior German diplomat regarding the views of different delegations, Geneva, February 1996.

26 Author's conversations with two Iranian diplomats, Geneva, February 1996.

27 Rebecca Johnson, "CTB negotiations—Geneva Update No. 26", *Disarmament Diplomacy*, no. 2, The Acronym Institute, 1996, pp. 7–18.

28 Conference on Disarmament, *Final Record of the Seven Hundred and Thirty-first Plenary Meeting,* CD document CD/PV.731, 21 March 1996, statement by Sergio González Gálvez (Mexico), p. 7.

29 Conference on Disarmament, *Final Record of the Seven Hundred and Thirty-third Plenary Meeting,* CD document CD/PV.733, 28 March 1996, statement by Sha Zukang (China), p. 22.

30 Ibid.

31 At the same time, China was seeking leverage with the United States over on-site inspections, which the US delegation had declared its priority in the endgame.

32 Conference on Disarmament, *Final Record of the Seven Hundred and Thirty-seventh Plenary Meeting,* CD document CD/PV.737, 6 June 1996, statement by Sha Zukang (China), p. 8. Emphasis in delivery.

33 China, *Article 2, Peaceful Nuclear Explosions*, 18 June 1996. Informal proposals like this, the Canadian counter-proposal and the compromise text, as noted below, were not introduced as official documents and, though distributed at the time, they were not assigned an official CD number.

34 Two years later, a senior Chinese negotiator confirmed to the author that it was important for China that the phrase "nuclear explosions for

peaceful purposes" was mentioned as an issue which could be raised in the future. Private conversation, New York, October 1998.

35 Mark Moher, Canada's ambassador to the CD at the time, used this term in interventions in the CD as well as in informal conversation to describe Canada's position on PNE.

36 Canada, *Suggested Changes to Article VIII*, 25 June 1996.

37 *Compromise text*, 26 June 1996. This informal paper did not identify Canada and China as authors, but they put the text forward to the NTB Committee together. Incorporated into the June 28 draft text, it survived unamended to become part of Article VIII of the final treaty. See Appendix C.

38 See Trevor Findlay, *Peace through Chemistry*, Australian National University, 1993.

39 Conference on Disarmament, *Final Record of the Seven Hundred and Twenty-sixth Plenary Meeting*, CD document CD/PV.726, 22 February 1996, statement by Ali Akbar Velayati (Iran), p. 5.

40 Conference on Disarmament, *Final Record of the Seven Hundred and Twenty-seventh Plenary Meeting*, CD document CD/PV.727, 29 February 1996, statement by Michael Costello (Australia), p. 9.

41 Ibid., statement by Sirous Nasseri (Iran), p. 21.

42 Australia, *Comprehensive nuclear test ban treaty: model treaty text*, CD document CD/1386, 29 February 1996; and Australia, *Comprehensive nuclear test ban treaty: explanatory notes accompanying model treaty text (as contained in CD/1386)*, CD document CD/1387, 29 February 1996.

43 Iran, *Draft comprehensive nuclear test ban treaty*, CD document CD/1384, 21 February 1996.

44 Ghose stressed that while every delegation has the right to present their national positions of what would constitute a balanced text, "there is only one text on the basis of which we can hope to get consensus and that is the current rolling text. Any change of this basis could temporarily exclude my delegation from the negotiations, a development which we would view with dismay and disappointment". She concluded that "In our efforts to speed up negotiations, we may very well end up by delaying them". Conference on Disarmament, *Final Record of the Seven Hundred and Twenty-seventh Plenary Meeting*, CD document CD/PV.727, 29 February 1996, p. 30. China's views were expressed informally until its first major policy statement of 1996, in late March. Warning against an artificial climate of urgency, Sha Zukang implied that the Iranian and Australian texts—and indeed, the Chair's working

paper—were just reference materials, though he characterized them as valuable. Sha argued that "As the CTBT will have a long-term bearing on international peace and security, we are against wrapping up these issues in a simplistic, hasty manner for the sake of mere political expediency". Conference on Disarmament, *Final Record of the Seven Hundred and Thirty-third Plenary Meeting*, CD document CD/PV.733, 28 March 1996, p. 21.

45 As reflected in the author's contemporaneous reports on the negotiations, senior diplomats from several Western delegations privately commented that on a number of issues they liked Iran's proposed solutions better than Australia's. See, for example, Rebecca Johnson, "CTB negotiations—Geneva Update No. 26", *Disarmament Diplomacy*, no. 2, The Acronym Institute, 1996, p. 8. This observation was subsequently confirmed in interviews with Stephen Ledogar, New York, 5 November 2000, and Sir Michael Weston, Matfield, 11 June 2002.

46 Chairman of the Ad Hoc Committee on a Nuclear Test Ban, *Outline of a draft Comprehensive Nuclear Test-Ban Treaty: working paper*, CD document CD/NTB/WP.321, 21 March 1996.

47 Author's contemporaneous notes of conversation with a senior member of the Dutch delegation, reporting on Ramaker's statement to the NTB Committee, 28 March 1996.

48 Chairman of the Ad Hoc Committee on a Nuclear Test Ban, *Draft comprehensive nuclear test-ban treaty: working paper*, CD document CD/NTB/WP.330, 28 March 1996.

49 Conference on Disarmament, *Final Record of the Seven Hundred and Thirty-fifth Plenary Meeting*, CD document CD/PV.735, 23 May 1996, statement by Munir Akram (Pakistan), p. 2.

50 Author's contemporaneous notes of conversation with a senior member of the Dutch delegation, 28 May 1996.

51 Unofficial working paper from the delegations of Brazil, Cuba, Indonesia, Iran, Kenya, Mexico, Mongolia, Myanmar, Nigeria, Pakistan, Peru, Sri Lanka and Venezuela, entitled *Amendment proposals to Chairman's WP.330 and 335 on Preamble*, 25 June 1996. To the embarrassment of the United States, an article in the *Washington Post* on 17 June had leaked news of a "secret" agreement signed by the United States and France on the exchange of nuclear-related data, especially ensuring access to data related to computer-simulated nuclear tests. R. Jeffrey Smith, "France, U.S. Secretly Enter Pact to Share Nuclear Weapons Data", *Washington Post*, 17 June 1996, See also, "France, US sign

secret deal to exchange nuclear information", *Agence France-Presse International News*, 17 June 1996; "Franco-US deal covers technical cooperation—Ministry", *Agence France-Presse International News*, 17 June 1996; and "US and France said to deepen nuclear-weapons cooperation", *Disarmament Diplomacy*, no. 7, The Acronym Institute, 1996, p. 51.

52 Jaap Ramaker, Informal statement to the NTB Committee, 28 May 1996.

Chapter 6
Entry into force and the endgame

1 Conference on Disarmament, *Final Record of the Seven Hundred and Fortieth Plenary Meeting*, CD document CD/PV.740, 20 June 1996, p. 16.

2 Arundhati Ghose, verbal statement to the Nuclear Test Ban Committee, 28 June 1996, cited in Jaap Ramaker, Jenifer Mackby, Peter D. Marshall and Robert Geil, *The Final Test*, Preparatory Commission for the Comprehensive Nuclear-Test-Ban Treaty Organization, 2003. This detailed account of the CTBT negotiations has not yet been made available for public distribution.

3 For a thought-provoking analysis of India's nuclear-related dilemmas at the time of CTBT finalization, see William Walker, "Viewpoint: India's Nuclear Labyrinth", *The Nonproliferation Review*, Fall 1996, pp. 61–77. See also George Perkovich, *India's Nuclear Bomb*, University of California Press, 1999.

4 This characterization came from a German diplomat in conversation with the author, Geneva, August 1996. The revenge was supposedly against the United States for the moratorium that prevented further testing at the Nevada Test Site after 1992. The British nuclear weapon and defence establishment had planned at least three further warhead tests for Trident, and were unhappy to find they had insufficient influence in Washington to prevent their plans being ignominiously derailed.

5 Trevor Findlay, *Peace through Chemistry*, Australian National University, 1993, pp. 15–9.

6 Treaty Banning Nuclear Weapon Tests in the Atmosphere, in Outer Space and Under Water, article III. See also the discussion in Kim Tay, "Entry into Force", *Verification Matters*, no. 6, VERTIC, 1994.

7 Treaty on the Non-Proliferation of Nuclear Weapons, article IX.

8 The CWC eschewed the specification of certain states and provided for entry into force 180 days after the sixty-fifth state deposited its instruments of ratification, but not earlier than two years after being opened for signature. Convention on the Prohibition of the Development, Production, Stockpiling and Use of Chemical Weapons and on Their Destruction, article XXI.

9 Post-1990 accessions to the NPT include a number of countries that for different reasons gave up substantial capabilities or nuclear weapon options, including Argentina, Algeria, Brazil, South Africa, as well as Belarus, Ukraine, and Kazakhstan after the Soviet Union's disintegration. China and France also chose to join in 1992, although their case was somewhat different, as they were recognized under the NPT as nuclear-weapon states.

10 Sweden, *Letter dated 6 December 1993 from the Head of delegation of Sweden addressed to the Secretary-General of the Conference on Disarmament transmitting the text of a draft comprehensive nuclear test ban treaty and its annexed draft Protocol*, CD document CD/1232–CD/NTB/WP.33, 6 December 1993. This draft was based on earlier drafts dating back to 1983. See especially Sweden, *Letter dated 9 July 1991 from the head of the Swedish Delegation addressed to the Secretary-General of the Conference on Disarmament transmitting the text of a draft Comprehensive Test-ban Treaty and its annexed protocols*, CD document CD/1089–CD/NTB/WP.14, 31 July 1991; and Sweden, *Letter dated 3 June 1993 from the Head of the Swedish Delegation addressed to the Secretary-General of the Conference on Disarmament transmitting the text of a draft comprehensive test-ban treaty*, CD document CD/1202–CD/NTB/WP.19, 3 June 1993. See also Maurice A. Mallin, *The June 1993 Swedish Draft Comprehensive Nuclear Test-Ban Treaty: Implications and Issues for Negotiations*, The Center for National Security Negotiations, 1994.

11 Conference on Disarmament, *Final Record of the Six Hundred and Sixty-sixth Plenary Meeting*, CD document CD/PV.666, 25 January 1994, statement by Sir Michael Weston (UK), p. 23.

12 Conference on Disarmament, *Final Record of the Six Hundred and Sixty-eighth Plenary Meeting*, CD document CD/PV.668, 1 February 1994, statement by Grigori Berdennikov (Russia), p. 10.

13 Conference on Disarmament, *Final Record of the Six Hundred and Sixty-sixth Plenary Meeting*, CD document CD/PV.666, 25 January 1994, statement by Sir Michael Weston (UK), p. 23.

14 See the Vienna Convention on the Law of Treaties, §3, article 24.

15 As noted in Chapter 3, expansion of the CD had been expected in 1993, but failed to go through as a result of a last minute decision by the United States to prevent consensus because of its concerns about admitting Iraq. The United Kingdom and France preferred the expanded CD option over the IAEA list, which also covered the P-5, D-3 and a number of other states with potential nuclear ambitions or capabilities, on the normative grounds that participation in the negotiations should confer an added incentive and interest in acceding to the treaty. The stand-off with the United States over Iraq took so long to resolve that France and the United Kingdom had abandoned their proposal by the end of 1994. The enlargement decision was not adopted by the CD until June 1996, just in time for the CTBT negotiations' difficult endgame. To address the United States' concerns about Iraq and ensure that none of the incoming states would be able to disrupt the CTBT negotiations, all the new members had to sign an undertaking that for the first two years they would not individually obstruct any action of the CD—in other words, that since the CD makes decisions by consensus, they would not exercise their individual power to prevent consensus. See Rebecca Johnson, "CTB Negotiations—Geneva Update No. 29", *Disarmament Diplomacy*, no. 6, The Acronym Institute, 1996, pp. 24–7.

16 Friend of the Chair, *Working paper on signature, ratification, accession, entry into force*, CD document CD/NTB/WG.2/9, 10 March 1994.

17 This discussion of the various suggestions derives from the author's conversations at the time with American and other diplomats in Geneva. The author has not been able to obtain papers detailing the suggestions, and it is possible that they were not circulated in writing.

18 China, *Entry into force of the CTBT: working paper*, CD document CD/NTB/WP.123, 20 June 1994.

19 Mexico's comment is referred to in Jaap Ramaker, Jenifer Mackby, Peter D. Marshall and Robert Geil, *The Final Test*, Preparatory Commission for the Comprehensive Nuclear-Test-Ban Treaty Organization, 2003, p. 243. This detailed account of the CTBT negotiations has not yet been made available for public distribution.

20 Zou Yunhua, *China and the CTBT Negotiations*, Stanford University Center for International Security and Cooperation, 1998, p. 21.

21 Conference on Disarmament, *Final Record of the Seven Hundred and Seventeeth Plenary Meeting*, CD document CD/PV.717, 5 September 1995, statement by Sha Zukang (China), p. 5. In the end, China stopped testing after signing the CTBT in September 1996. That does not, however, mean that the concerns about the possibility of China

continuing to test until entry into force were unfounded. Colonel Zou Yunhua acknowledged that China wanted "at least a few more tests", and until late in the negotiations China's diplomats were careful to leave open the possibility of testing after conclusion of the treaty, either through delaying signature (while declaring willingness not to impede entry into force) or through defying the norm established by the Vienna Convention on Treaties and Conventions, which China has not signed. See Zou Yunhua, *China and the CTBT Negotiations*, Stanford University Center for International Security and Cooperation, 1998, p. 26.

22 The quotes, which confirmed Jaap Ramakers recollections when interviewed by the author in Vienna, 16 July 2001, are taken from Jaap Ramaker, Jenifer Mackby, Peter D. Marshall and Robert Geil, *The Final Test*, Preparatory Commission for the Comprehensive Nuclear-Test-Ban Treaty Organization, 2003, pp. 242–3. This detailed account of the CTBT negotiations has not yet been made available for public distribution.

23 The Tlatelolco Treaty negotiators were conscious that two important target states—Brazil and Argentina—were at that time engaged in a race to acquire the technology for a nuclear weapon option (a potentially deadly rivalry that the treaty was intended to assist in defusing), and that this could affect the decisions taken by some of their neighbours. Moreover, Cuba's relative isolation and military relationship with the Soviet Union made its accession difficult to influence and impossible to predict. To address this potentially destabilizing dilemma, Mexico, with help from UN-based lawyers, notably William Epstein, developed the unusual waiver formula to facilitate early establishment of the nuclear-weapon-free zone. The formal EIF conditions required ratification by all the states in the zone of application, plus ratification of Additional Protocols I and II. However the treaty contained a provision whereby states that had ratified could choose to waive the specified EIF conditions, thereby enabling the treaty to enter into force for those that chose to abide by it. The treaty therefore became "operative" in April 1968. This formula was able to act as a confidence-building measure, allowing a credible treaty regime and implementing authority (*Organismo para la Proscripcion de las Armas Nucleares en la America Latina*—OPANAL) to be developed as the adherents grew in number. Jozef Goldblat, *Arms Control: A Guide to Negotiations and Agreements*, Sage Publications, 1994, pp. 149–53.

24 This summary was based on conversations with the Australian delegation during 1995, during which the author was given sight of a

draft document which she was not permitted to retain and which, to her knowledge, was never introduced as an official CD document.

25 Australia's national preference was still for a simple number, but the delegation acknowledged that the opposition to this appeared entrenched. The Australian model text therefore proposed that the basic condition should specify ratification by all CD members plus observers (which would have been some 75 states, including the P-5 and D-3), but that the EIF article should explicitly provide for a conference to consider whether to waive this stringent condition, even if a few states on the list had not yet joined, and inaugurate the verification system. The conference could be initiated any time after two years from the treaty being opened for signature, and would be called by decision of those who had ratified. This was a modified version of the US waiver conference proposal, but without the US condition requiring all P-5 on board. Australia, *Comprehensive nuclear test ban treaty: model treaty text,* CD document CD/1386, 29 February 1996; and Australia, *Comprehensive nuclear test ban treaty: explanatory notes accompanying model treaty text (as contained in CD/1386)*, CD document CD/1387, 29 February 1996.

26 Iran based entry into force on the full IAEA list of all 68 states that have or have had any level of nuclear technology or capability, and specified that the treaty should enter into force if 65 out of these 68 states ratified (a modified version of the percentage option). Iran, *Draft comprehensive nuclear test ban treaty*, CD document CD/1384, 21 February 1996.

27 India, *Indian draft language on entry into force: working paper*, CD document CD/NTB/WP.297, 29 January 1996.

28 The quote was taken from an informal non-paper provided to the author by the British delegation.

29 Author's conversation with Israeli diplomat, Geneva, June 1996.

30 Conference on Disarmament, *Final Record of the Seven Hundred and Thirty-third Plenary Meeting*, CD document CD/PV.733, 28 March 1996, statement by Harald Kreid (Austria), pp. 2–6; and Austria, *Draft Treaty Language on Provisional Application: working paper*, CD document CD/NTB/WP.242, 16 June 1995.

31 This question, discussed in the CD corridors, had the situation of Pakistan or some of the Middle East countries in mind, though they did not openly raise it themselves.

32 Author's interview with Jaap Ramaker, Vienna, 16 July 2001.

33 The IMS stations, listed in an annex to the verification protocol, were intended to be part of an easily amended, flexible protocol to the

treaty that could evolve as required. Although the EIF provision in the Chair's 28 May draft had referred only to primary seismic stations and radionuclide laboratories, India actually withdrew all its IMS-designated facilities, consisting of one primary seismic station, one auxiliary station, a radionuclide station and an infrasound station. See Annex 1 to the Protocol, tables 1-A, 1-B, 2-A and 4, in Conference on Disarmament, *Draft Comprehensive Nuclear Test-ban Treaty*, CD document CD/NTB/WP.330/Rev.2, 14 August 1996. The gaps left by India's withdrawal are marked "to be determined".

34 Author's conversations with senior Dutch officials in Geneva, 28–30 May 1996; and confirmed by author's interview with Jaap Ramaker, Vienna, 16 July 2001.

35 Conference on Disarmament, *Final Record of the Seven Hundred and Thirty-sixth Plenary Meeting*, CD document CD/PV.736, 30 May 1996, statement by Jaap Ramaker (Netherlands), p. 6.

36 Ibid.

37 Perkovich quotes sources that say that at least one nuclear device had already been put into a test shaft during the previous test preparations at Pokharan in December 1995, and so scientists believed they could conduct the explosion quite quickly. George Perkovich, *India's Nuclear Bomb*, University of California Press, 1999, pp. 374–5.

38 Ibid., pp. 353–4.

39 Robert Bell, from a transcript of a Coalition to Reduce Nuclear Dangers press conference coinciding with the start of US Senate Hearings on the CTBT. See "The Issues Behind the CTB Ratification Debate", *Arms Control Today*, vol. 27, no. 7, Arms Control Association, 1997.

40 Author's interview with Sha Zukang, Beijing, 15 October 2000.

41 Author's interview with Grigori Berdennikov, Vienna, 17 July 2001.

42 The memo is reportedly classified, and the author relies on information from a former US official close to the negotiations, provided during a conversation in Washington DC, April 2002. When questioned about this in Stockholm, September 2002, Berdennikov recalled hearing "something" of a memo along these lines, but said he had not seen it and appeared to doubt its authenticity. In a follow-up discussion with Jaap Ramaker in Washington DC, November 2002, it is clear that he knew nothing of such a Russian memo. The full truth of this matter has not yet been ascertained, but is included here, with these caveats, because of the credibility of the original informant and potential significance of such a communication between Moscow and Washington in assessing Russia's true bottom line on EIF. If Moscow sent this memo to Washington

it implies that Russia would not have actually rejected the Chair's draft text or wrecked the negotiations as long as the EIF provision ensured accession by all the P-5.

43 Author's interview with Sir Michael Weston, Matfield, 11 June 2002.

44 The speculation, rife among UK NGOs at the time, that the Ministry of Defence rather than the Foreign and Commonwealth Office was the driving force behind the United Kingdom's refusal to compromise over EIF was confirmed by Sir Michael Weston. Author's interview, Matfield, 11 June 2002.

45 Author's discussions with Sir Michael Weston and others, Geneva, June 1996.

46 Explanation of vote by H.E. Mr Munir Akram, Ambassador and Permanent Representative of Pakistan to the European Office of the United Nations in Geneva, New York, 10 September 1996. After this statement, the author spoke to Weston outside the General Assembly, and he told her that he was very disappointed in Pakistan's decision not to sign the treaty. When questioned about this years later, Weston referred to a specific undertaking given to the British government by Pakistan, the gist of which was that it would join the treaty if India's accession were made a condition. It was apparently on the basis of this undertaking that the United Kingdom believed that the "eight condition", as some delegations called accession by the P-5 plus D-3, would work because India would be left isolated, which the United Kingdom thought New Delhi would find untenable over time. Author's interview with Sir Michael Weston, Matfield, 11 June 2002.

47 With the Tlatelolco Treaty and the experience of Brazil and Argentina in mind, some thought this could work for the P-5 with respect to each other, Pakistan with respect to India, Egypt with respect to Israel, and so on.

48 The Russian Duma, for example, insisted that US ratification of START II and the Memorandum of Understanding were necessary for the treaty to take effect.

49 Memo from George Perkovich on "EIF and India", 2 June 1996. Perkovich was at the time a senior staff member of the W. Alton Jones Foundation, which funded many of the NGOs working on the CTBT and NPT, including partners of the Acronym Consortium.

50 Ibid.

51 See Chapter 3. For a full account of the final negotiations on CD enlargement in 1996, see Rebecca Johnson, "CTB Negotiations—

Geneva Update No. 29", *Disarmament Diplomacy*, no. 6, The Acronym Institute, 1996, pp. 24–7.

52 Israel and several other CD candidate states participated in all major sessions of the NTB Committee, and were able to have their working papers and proposals considered on an equal basis. The non-members were less well represented in group meetings and the more formal management structures for decision-making in the CD, although the United States made sure that Israel's interests were represented where necessary.

53 The quotations in this and the following paragraphs are all from Conference on Disarmament, *Final Record of the Seven Hundred and Fortieth Plenary Meeting*, CD document CD/PV.740, 20 June 1996, pp. 14–6.

54 Ibid., p. 16. The relevant part of Ghose's statement continued: "Under such circumstances, it is natural that our national security considerations become a key factor in our decision-making. Our capability is demonstrated but, as a matter of policy, we exercise restraint. Countries around us continue in their weapon programmes, either openly or in a clandestine manner. In such an environment, India cannot accept any restraints on its capability if other countries remain unwilling to accept the obligation to eliminate their nuclear weapons". She reminded CD members that India had refused to accede to the NPT, despite various kinds of pressure. "The same conviction is reflected in our stand on the CTBT. Last year we expressed our dismay at the indefinite extension of the NPT because, in our view, it sought to legitimize the indefinite possession of nuclear weapons by five countries. Today, the right to continue development and refinement of their arsenals is being sought to be legitimized through another flawed and eternal treaty. Such a treaty is not conceived as a measure toward universal nuclear disarmament and is not in India's national security interest". Ibid., p. 15–6.

55 Ibid., p. 16.

56 Chairman of the Ad Hoc Committee on a Nuclear Test Ban, *Chairman's working paper: Ad Hoc Committee on a Nuclear Test Ban*, CD document CD/NTB/WP.334, 20 June 1996.

57 UK House of Commons, *Hansard*, vol. 131, 27 June 1996, columns 197.

58 Ibid.

59 Ibid., column 198.

60 Antonio de Icaza, statement to the NTB Committee, 20 June 1996.

[61] In one of the strange, almost comedic vignettes of the CTBT negotiations, as the author and three observers from the Women's International League for Peace and Freedom, American Peace Test and Greenpeace, waited for news outside the doors of the Council Chamber, the blow-by-blow account of the EIF meeting was relayed by diplomats escaping the room, not only for the usual reasons of a cigarette or the toilet, but to check up on the score of an England versus Germany football match (the semi-final of the European Championship), relayed over the Greenpeace representative's small radio. The final score, after extra time, was England 1: Germany 1.

[62] Author's conversations with officials from several delegations that were present at the meeting, 26 June 1996; confirmed in conversations with senior Dutch officials, The Hague, 29 March 2002.

[63] Idem.

[64] Author's interview with Sir Michael Weston, Matfield, 11 June 2002. While the written statement was said to contain the "wriggling on a hook" reference, Weston's comment about Japan and Germany and others being in the negotiations mainly to pay for the treaty was recalled as an extemporaneous remark, which he later regretted.

[65] Author's conversations with senior Dutch officials, The Hague, 29 March 2002.

[66] Michael Krepon, communication to the author, 1 April 2002. Krepon, who had been trying to bring the high-level group together for several weeks, also commented on how difficult it was to get anyone interested in taking up what they viewed as a procedural issue, as compared with the clearly political, substantive issue of scope.

[67] Author's conversations with senior Dutch diplomats, 29 March 2002.

[68] Author's conversations with UK and French delegation members, 28 June 1996.

[69] Author's interview with Sir Michael Weston, Matfield, 11 June 2002.

[70] The Chair's clarifications and assurances regarding the entry-into-force provisions and several other elements in the draft treaty were put on record in the *Report of the Ad Hoc Committee on a Nuclear Test Ban to the Conference on Disarmament*, CD document CD/1425, 16 August 1996. These quotes are taken from that report.

[71] Australia, Austria, Belgium, Bulgaria, Canada, Chile, Denmark, Finland, Germany, Hungary, Ireland, Italy, Japan, New Zealand, Norway, Poland, Slovakia, Spain, Sweden and Switzerland.

[72] Chairman of the Ad Hoc Committee on a Nuclear Test Ban, *Draft Comprehensive Nuclear Test Ban Treaty*, CD document CD/NTB/WP.330/Rev.1, 28 June 1996.

[73] The relevant part of this Chinese government statement read: "China successfully conducted a nuclear test today. The Chinese government hereby solemnly declares that it will start a moratorium from July 30, 1996. Such an important decision by China is not only a response to the appeal of the vast number of non nuclear weapon states, but also a concrete action to promote nuclear disarmament." *Statement of the Government of the People's Republic of China*, 29 July 1996. Originally issued through the *Xinhua News Agency*, this statement is now archived on the website of the Nuclear Threat Initiative.

[74] For international reactions to the test, see "China tests, declares moratorium", *Disarmament Diplomacy*, no. 7, The Acronym Institute, 1996, p. 46.

[75] Author's conversation with Grigori Berdennikov, 1 August 1996, and confirmed in Jaap Ramaker, Jenifer Mackby, Peter D. Marshall and Robert Geil, *The Final Test*, Preparatory Commission for the Comprehensive Nuclear-Test-Ban Treaty Organization, 2003, p. 34. This detailed insiders' account of the CTBT negotiations has not yet been made available for public distribution.

[76] Sha Zukang announced on 6 June that China would be willing to accept "a temporary ban on PNEs" and endorse the Australian scope text, wanting only a reference to a future possibility of reconsideration at a review conference. Conference on Disarmament, *Final Record of the Seven Hundred and Thirty-seventh Plenary Meeting*, CD document CD/PV.737, 6 June 1996, pp. 8–9. See Chapter 5.

[77] Author's interview with Arundhati Ghose, New Delhi, 20 February 2000.

[78] The working paper was delayed by attempts to persuade India to support a joint G-21 proposal. The 13 delegations that co-sponsored the proposal in the end were Brazil, Cuba, Indonesia, Iran, Kenya, Mexico, Mongolia, Pakistan, Peru, Sri Lanka, Nigeria, Myanmar and Venezuela; *Proposed amendments to the Preamble in the Chairman's Working Papers (CD/NTB/WP.330 and CD/NTB/WP.335)*, CD document CD/NTB/WP.336, 27 June 1996. See also CD/NTB/WP.336/Rev.1, dated 18 July 1996.

[79] The quotes in this paragraph are from the Conference on Disarmament, *Draft Comprehensive Nuclear Test Ban Treaty*, CD document CD/NTB/

WP.330/Rev.2, 14 August 1996, preamble, and were finalized as part of the CTBT text.

80 This quote, as with those above, is from the final text of the CTBT.

81 Author's contemporaneous notes from off the record conversations and interviews, June 1996.

82 Sometimes called the G-28 proposal, this programme of action was supported by Algeria, Bangladesh, Brazil, Cameroon, Colombia, Cuba, Democratic People's Republic of Korea, Egypt, Ethiopia, India, Indonesia, Iraq, Islamic Republic of Iran, Kenya, Mexico, Mongolia, Morocco, Myanmar, Myanmar, Nigeria, Pakistan, Peru, Senegal, Sri Lanka, Syrian Arab Republic, Venezuela, Viet Nam, Zaire and Zimbabwe. *Proposal for a programme of action for the elimination of nuclear weapons*, CD document CD/1419, 7 August 1996. See also, Conference on Disarmament, *Final Record of the Seven Hundred and Forty-fourth Plenary Meeting*, CD document CD/PV.744, 8 August 1996, statement by Mounir Zahran (Egypt) on behalf of 28 delegations, pp. 5-6. The two G-21 delegations that did not support this proposal were Chile and South Africa, who said they strongly supported nuclear disarmament but were sceptical of the proposed time frame.

83 Ibid., statement by Arundhati Ghose (India), pp. 10–1.

84 For example, Bangladesh, an NPT party whose "renunciation of the option for acquiring nuclear weapons is unequivocal", complained about being included as one of the 44 listed states and argued that "as a least developed country", its decision on ratification would have to be based on "budgetary arithmetic". Conference on Disarmament, *Final Record of the Seven Hundred and Forty-fifth Plenary Meeting*, CD document CD/PV.745, 15 August 1996, statement by Anwar Hashim (Bangladesh), pp. 6–9.

85 *Report of the Ad Hoc Committee on a Nuclear Test Ban to the Conference on Disarmament*, August 16, 1996, CD/1425, Section V Conclusions of the Chairman on his Consultations, pp 13-16.

86 Ibid., section VI, national statements of position, pp. 16–37.

87 Ibid., statement by the Islamic Republic of Iran, section VI, paragraph 28, pp. 27–30.

88 Ibid., statement by India, section VI, paragraph 20, pp. 19–20.

89 Conference on Disarmament, *Final Record of the Seven Hundred and Forty-sixth Plenary Meeting*, CD document CD/PV.746, 20 August 1996, statement by Jaap Ramaker (Netherlands), pp. 3–4.

90 Ibid., statement by Arundhati Ghose (India), pp. 4–7.

91 Ibid., statement by Munir Akram (Pakistan), pp. 8–9.

92 Conference on Disarmament, *Final Record of the Seven Hundred and Forty-seventh Plenary Meeting*, CD document CD/PV.747, 22 August 1996, statement by Sirous Nasseri (Iran), pp. 7–9.

93 Though the report was technical in essence, describing the course of negotiations factually, as India had demanded, it referred to the draft treaty and included mention of "a new negotiating framework" following presentation of the Chair's first draft text (CD/NTB/WP.330) on 28 May, thereby signifying that this draft text did in fact replace the rolling text as the basis of negotiations, even if no formal decision to do this was taken. For these reasons, India decided that, even shorn of the draft treaty itself, the NTB Committee Report could provide a basis for the UN General Assembly to approve the treaty and would therefore have to be blocked as well.

94 Conference on Disarmament, *Final Record of the Seven Hundred and Forty-sixth Plenary Meeting*, CD document CD/PV.746, 20 August 1996, statement by Munir Akram (Pakistan), pp. 8–9.

95 Conference on Disarmament, *Final Record of the Seven Hundred and Forty-seventh Plenary Meeting*, CD document CD/PV.747, 22 August 1996, pp. 2–5

96 Ibid., statement by Richard Starr (Australia), p. 26.

97 Ibid., pp. 26–8.

98 Ibid., statement by Mounir Zahran (Egypt), p. 36.

99 Ibid., statement by Baron Alain Guillaume (Belgium), pp. 38–9. The author was informed that this tactic had been agreed in a private meeting of Western delegations, and spearheaded by Belgium in part because their ambassador, Baron Guillaume, was due to retire and would not therefore suffer if there was any backlash against the manoeuvre.

100 Conference on Disarmament, *Letter dated 22 August 1996 from the Permanent Representative of Belgium addressed to the President of the Conference transmitting the text of a Draft Comprehensive Nuclear Test-Ban Treaty*, CD document CD/1427, 22 August 1996.

101 General Assembly, *Letter dated 22 August 1996 from the Permanent Representative of Australia to the United Nations addressed to the President of the General Assembly*, UN document A/50/1024, 22 August 1996.

102 General Assembly, *Letter dated 22 August 1996 from the Permanent Representative of Australia to the United Nations addressed to the Secretary-General*, UN document A/50/1027, 26 August 1996.

103 General Assembly, *Comprehensive Test-Ban Treaty*, UN document A/50/L.78, 6 September 1996.

[104] The quotation, from my contemporaneous notes of the General Assembly meeting, was attributed to the representative of Ghana, but no independent documentary confirmation has been obtainable.

[105] See General Assembly, *Advisory opinion of the International Court of Justice on the legality of the threat or use of nuclear weapons, Note by the Secretary-General*, UN document A/51/218, 15 October 1996.

[106] General Assembly, *Letter dated 9 September 1996 from the Permanent Representative of India to the United Nations addressed to the President of the General Assembly*, UN document A/50/1036, 9 September 1996.

[107] Diplomatic absence can be for reasons other than non-attendance. In view of the Democratic People's Republic of Korea's subsequent failure to sign the CTBT, it should be noted that it was also counted as absent from the vote. For others the reasons may have been procedural: on this occasion a number of the resolution's co-sponsors and Iraq were not permitted to vote because their payments to the United Nations were in serious arrears.

[108] Explanation of vote by H.E. Mr Munir Akram, Ambassador and Permanent Representative of Pakistan to the European Office of the United Nations in Geneva, New York, 10 September 1996.

[109] Prakash Shah, Ambassador of India to the United Nations General Assembly, 9 September 1996.

[110] Arundhati Ghose, Ambassador of India to the UN in Geneva, to the United Nations General Assembly, New York, 10 September 1996.

[111] Boutros Boutros-Ghali, Secretary-General of the United Nations, to the United Nations General Assembly, New York, 24 September 1996.

[112] Bill Clinton, US President, to the United Nations General Assembly, 24 September 1996.

[113] Yevgeni Primakov, Minister of Foreign Affairs of the Russian Federation, to the United Nations General Assembly, 24 September 1996.

[114] Qian Qichen, Minister of Foreign Affairs of the People's Republic of China, to the United Nations General Assembly, 24 September 1996.

[115] Hervé de Charette, Minister of Foreign Affairs of France, to the United Nations General Assembly, 24 September 1996.

[116] Malcolm Rifkind, UK Secretary of State for Foreign and Commonwealth Affairs, to the United Nations General Assembly, 24 September 1996.

Chapter 7
Designing a robust verification regime

1 Jacques Chirac, Tony Blair and Gerhard Schröder, "A Treaty We All Need", *New York Times*, 8 October 1999.

2 It was later decided that treaty parties should themselves make the determination of what was a false alarm, but the ability to distinguish was one of the criteria for the verification system.

3 For fuller detail, see Rebecca Johnson, "Verifying a Comprehensive Test Ban Treaty: Key Issues in the 1994 Negotiations", in J.B. Poole and R. Guthrie (eds), *Verification 1995: Arms Control, Peacekeeping and the Environment*, Westview Press/VERTIC, 1995, pp. 37–54.

4 The Verification Technology Information Centre, *Scientific and Technical Aspects of the Verification of a Comprehensive Test Ban Treaty*, VERTIC, 1990. VERTIC's detailed study on verifying a CTBT had been commissioned by Parliamentarians for Global Action for dissemination to governments and diplomats prior to the PTBT Amendment Conference.

5 Sir Michael Wright, *Disarm and Verify*, Chatto and Windus, 1964, p. 76.

6 See Nancy W. Gallagher, *The Politics of Verification*, The Johns Hopkins University Press, 1999.

7 Informal paper, dated February 1994, distributed to delegations (and received by the author), attached to the Chairman's Paper, Working Group on Verification, Ad Hoc Committee on a Nuclear Test Ban, CD document CD/NTB/WG.1/1, 18 February 1994.

8 Grigori Berdennikov, Statement to the Ad Hoc Committee on a Nuclear Test Ban, 6 June 1994 (unofficial translation).

9 Established by the UN Conference of the Committee on Disarmament (the CD's predecessor), with a mandate to conceptualize and test an international seismic data-exchange system, the Group of Scientific Experts, chaired by Swedish scientist Ola Dahlman, had toiled since 1976 at seismic verification, hampered by a mandate that severely restricted its work to a narrowly conceived technical realm of seismic measuring. By early 1994 the GSE was ready to conduct its third technical test (known as GSETT-3), incorporating a three tier network of seismic stations, relying on "alpha stations" transmitting data continuously to an international data centre, "beta stations" to be connected into national data centres and accessed as required by the international system, and "gamma stations" which would only supply supplementary data from

national and regional networks. Although there was some truth to the criticism that the GSE mandate left the scientists in a political vacuum which diminished the usefulness of their work, the GSE's technical tests were able to provide a basis for the seismic network of primary and auxiliary stations which were eventually incorporated into the treaty. During the CTBT negotiations, the GSE continued in parallel with the work of the NTB Committee, reporting periodically to the CD plenaries.

10 This chapter deals with the principal political disputes and outcomes. A more detailed account of the development of the negotiations on verification and organization issues, including key states' positions and working papers, is contained in Jaap Ramaker, Jenifer Mackby, Peter D. Marshall and Robert Geil, *The Final Test*, Preparatory Commission for the Comprehensive Nuclear-Test-Ban Treaty Organization, 2003. This detailed account of the CTBT negotiations has not yet been made available for public distribution.

11 Joachim Schulze, "Verification for CTBT Compliance: Developments during the 1995 Negotiations", in J.B. Poole and R. Guthrie (eds), *Verification 1996: Arms Control, Peacekeeping and the Environment*, Westview Press/VERTIC, 1996, pp. 105–24. Dr Schulze served on the German delegation to the CD as a scientific adviser and participated in that capacity in the CTBT negotiations.

12 It was judged that a 5kt baseline would require around 25 primary seismic stations with three other technologies, whereas the lower baseline of 100t would need at least 150 primary seismic stations and increased coverage from a range of other technologies.

13 Friend of the Chair (Non-Seismic Verification), *Illustration of possible networks of sensors to detect, locate, and identify explosions underground, underwater and in the atmosphere based on the reports of experts: working paper*, CD document CD/NTB/WP.181, 6 September 1994.

14 Joachim Schulze, "Verification for CTBT Compliance: Developments during the 1995 Negotiations", in J.B. Poole and R. Guthrie (eds), *Verification 1996: Arms Control, Peacekeeping and the Environment*, Westview Press/VERTIC, 1996, p. 106.

15 Conference on Disarmament, *Final Record of the Seven Hundred and Twenty-eighth Plenary Meeting*, CD document CD/PV.728, 7 March 1996, statement by Grigori Berdennikov (Russia), p. 14. Since France had announced closure of the Pacific test site after it completed its final test series, Russia subsequently agreed to drop the requirement for additional monitors at Moruroa.

16 Author's conversations with Russian officials, January 1996, confirmed by interviews with Victor Slipchenko (Vienna, 8 October 1999) and Grigori Berdennikov (Vienna, 17 July 2001). See also Rebecca Johnson, "CTB Negotiations—Geneva Update No. 25", *Disarmament Diplomacy*, no. 1, The Acronym Institute, 1996, p. 10, and Rebecca Johnson, *Comprehensive Test Ban Treaty: The Endgame*, ACRONYM Report no. 9, The Acronym Institute, 1996, p. 18.

17 Zou Yunhua, *China and the CTBT Negotiations*, Stanford University Center for International Security and Cooperation, 1998, p. 16.

18 According to a senior British official, Sha Zukang was adamant that no stations in China would be relocated to accommodate the Russian complaint, and then "opted out" of discussions concerning other changes, thereby passively accepting the repositioning of the Kazakhstan station. Conversation with the author, May 2002.

19 Joachim Schulze, "Verification for CTBT Compliance: Developments during the 1995 Negotiations", in J.B. Poole and R. Guthrie (eds), *Verification 1996: Arms Control, Peacekeeping and the Environment*, Westview Press/VERTIC, 1996, p. 115.

20 During the Cold War, the frequent venting from underground tests was routinely denied by the nuclear-weapon states but, in 1975, when Edward Kennedy introduced a resolution into the US Senate on a CTBT, he reiterated the claims of civil society scientists in the United States in a press release that asserted that "about one-fifth of our tests have vented, sending radioactive particles into the air". *Statement by Senator Edward M. Kennedy on Introducing a Resolution Urging the Negotiation of a Comprehensive Test Ban Treaty*, 20 May 1975.

21 With regard to atmospheric tests, China argued that noble gas sensors would be superfluous because tests in the atmosphere could be detected, located and identified through other means, including monitoring for more long-lived radioactive particulates or aerosols. Zou Yunhua, *China and the CTBT Negotiations*, Stanford University Center for International Security and Cooperation, 1998, p. 15.

22 China, *The question of including noble gas monitoring capacity in the atmospheric radionuclide monitoring network: working paper*, CD document CD/NTB/WP.268, 5 September 1995; and Working Group on Verification, *Report based on technical discussions held from 22 to 25 August 1995*, CD document CD/NTB/WP.269, 15 September 1995. See also Zou Yunhua, *China and the CTBT Negotiations*, Stanford University Center for International Security and Cooperation, 1998, p. 16.

[23] Russian Federation, *The use of aircraft for detecting radioactive products in radioactivity monitoring: working paper*, CD document CD/NTB/WP.199, 14 December 1994.

[24] The explosions generate sound waves that propagate through water and can be detected at great distances. Hydroacoustic monitoring makes particular use of a layer in the oceans where sound travel is especially efficient. Known as the Sound Fixing and Ranging Channel (SOFAR), this low sound velocity layer is at approximately 1km depth.

[25] Joachim Schulze, "Verification for CTBT Compliance: Developments during the 1995 Negotiations", in J.B. Poole and R. Guthrie (eds), *Verification 1996: Arms Control, Peacekeeping and the Environment*, Westview Press/VERTIC, 1996, p. 111.

[26] China, *Establishment of a global electromagnetic pulse monitoring system: working paper*, CD document CD/NTB/WP.217, 20 February 1995; and China, *Further views on a global EMP monitoring system: working paper*, CD document CD/NTB/WP.267, 5 September 1995.

[27] China challenged Marshall's calculation that an option comprising 18 satellites would add $2,700 million to the cost of the IMS. Arguing for sensors to be combined with commercial satellites, China put forward its own assessment that nuclear-explosion sensors placed on 45 of the 66 satellites planned by Motorola Cellular Telecommunications for 1996–1998 would provide full CTBT coverage for around $50 million. See China, *Establishment of a global satellite monitoring system: working paper*, CD document CD/NTB/WP.188, 13 November 1994.

[28] China, *Establishment of a global electromagnetic pulse monitoring system: working paper*, CD document CD/NTB/WP.217, 20 February 1995; and Joachim Schulze, "Verification for CTBT Compliance: Developments during the 1995 Negotiations", in J.B. Poole and R. Guthrie (eds), *Verification 1996: Arms Control, Peacekeeping and the Environment*, Westview Press/VERTIC, 1996.

[29] See, for example, Australia, *Making CTBT verification information accessible: incorporation of automated preliminary event identification into international data centre bulletins: working paper*, CD document CD/NTB/WP.223, 13 March 1995. In June 1995, the G-21 issued a statement calling for the IDC to be empowered to analyse the data. From their point of view, it was not merely legitimate but desirable for the IDC to analyse the data into comprehensible bulletins, even highlighting anomalous events and providing preliminary identification with probability values, and that far from usurping, this would assist states in fulfilling their assessment responsibilities. The statement was

intended to flag the non-aligned states' concerns and did not propose an alternative approach. *Statement of the Group of 21 on a Nuclear Test Ban*, CD document CD/1329–CD/NTB/WP.248, 30 June 1995.

30 In option 1, close to the US position during 1995, the IDC would send out just the raw data, with no standardized event screening. Individual states parties would be responsible for filtering and analysing the data. Option 2 would provide for internationally standardized event screening according to criteria established by the CTBTO. For states parties requiring additional filtering, some technical assistance could be provided. Option 3 would provide the highest level of IDC support to states parties, with internationally standardized event analysis, screening according to nationally requested criteria, technical expert evaluation to assist in identifying events in the IDC screened event bulletin, and further technical assistance to set up data analysis at national data centres. Friend of the Chair, *International Data Center Progress Report 3: function and products of the International Data Center: working paper*, CD document CD/NTB/WP.312, 27 February 1996.

31 Germany, *IDC–Products*, CD document CD/NTB/WP.320, 12 March 1996. For a fuller account of this debate, see Rebecca Johnson, *Comprehensive Test Ban Treaty: The Endgame*, ACRONYM Report, no. 9, The Acronym Institute, 1996, pp. 19–21.

32 Tables 1-A, 2-A, 3 and 4 of Annex 1 to the Protocol to the Comprehensive Nuclear Test Ban Treaty, Part I, The International Monitoring System and International Data Centre Functions.

33 Sidney N. Graybeal and Michael Krepon, "On-Site Inspections", in Michael Krepon and Mary Umberger (eds), *Verification and Compliance*, Macmillan Press, 1988, p. 94.

34 Timothy Pounds, "Proposals for On-Site Inspection over the Years: From the Baruch Plan to the Reagan Initiatives", in Lewis A. Dunn and Amy E. Gordon (eds), *Arms Control Verification and the New Role of On-Site Inspection*, Lexington Books/Science Applications International Corporation, 1990, pp. 69–91.

35 Prior to this, the NPT had incorporated safeguards agreements with the IAEA, entailing inspections at declared nuclear facilities, but these were obligatory only for the non-nuclear-weapon states and did not cover weapons-related sites at all. The 1976 Peaceful Nuclear Explosions Treaty included a protocol providing for "routine" and "discretionary" rights of observation, according to which both sides would have a so-called routine right to have observers present if the planned aggregate yield of a notified PNE exceeded 150kt and discretionary rights of observation

and limited inspection in the event of PNE of 100–150kt. As it turned out, these OSI provisions were never evoked or implemented.

36 Jessica Eve Stern, "All's Well that Ends Well? Verification and the CWC", in J.B. Poole and R. Guthrie (eds), *Verification 1993: Peacekeeping, Arms Control and the Environment*, Brassey's/VERTIC, 1993, p. 33. As noted above, Sir Michael Wright first characterized the verification dilemma as adequate versus bearable in negotiations on the PTBT. See Sir Michael Wright, *Disarm and Verify*, Chatto and Windus, 1964.

37 Most of this account was drawn from Gordon M. Burck, "The Chemical Weapons Convention Negotiations", in J.B. Poole and R. Guthrie (eds), *Verification Report 1992: Yearbook on Arms Control and Environmental Agreements*, VERTIC, 1992, especially pp. 122–30; and Trevor Findlay, *Peace through Chemistry*, Australian National University, 1993, particularly pp. 8–9 and 31–6.

38 Trevor Findlay, *Peace through Chemistry*, Australian National University, 1993, pp. 31–6.

39 Ibid., pp. 8–9 and 31–6; Gordon M. Burck, "The Chemical Weapons Convention Negotiations", in J.B. Poole and R. Guthrie (eds), *Verification Report 1992: Yearbook on Arms Control and Environmental Agreements*, VERTIC, 1992, pp. 122–30.

40 Trevor Findlay, *Peace through Chemistry*, Australian National University, 1993, p. 31.

41 Russian Federation, *On-Site Inspections under a CTBT: the Russian Federation's approach: working paper*, CD document CD/NTB/WP.249, 30 June 1995. The similarity between US and Russian positions on technical issues was due not only to Russia's political shift but also because the nuclear superpowers had greater experience than most other participants of inspection technologies and evasion scenarios.

42 Where the United States and Soviet Union had disagreed in the Cold War over cooperative *proverka* and intelligence-collecting *kontrol*, the CTBT witnessed China and the non-NPT weapon states juxtaposing principles like sovereignty and non-discrimination against the United States' desire to watch, know and have the option to control other states that might impinge on its national security. In essence, this had become the modern equivalent of what Sir Michael Wright had called the "adequate versus bearable" disputes of the Cold War. See Nancy W. Gallagher, *The Politics of Verification*, The Johns Hopkins University Press, 1999, pp. 29–30.

43 See, for example, Israel, *On-site inspection: draft text covering some procedural elements of OSI: working paper*, CD document CD/NTB/

WP.132, 29 June 1994; and Israel, *Access regime: proposed treaty language for the Protocol: working paper*, CD document CD/NTB/WP.204, 16 December 1994.

44 *Report of the Working Group of Experts on On-Site Inspection to Working Group 1 on Verification, On-site inspection for the Comprehensive Test Ban Treaty: phenomena, technology, OSI examples, costs*, CD document CD/NTB/WP.198, 15 December 1994.

45 As previously noted, two isotopes of xenon were of particular importance for early detection of a clandestine nuclear explosion: xenon-133 (half-life 5 days) and xenon-135 (half-life 9 hours).

46 Argon-37, another nuclear explosion indicator, has a half-life of 35 days.

47 *Report of the Working Group of Experts on On-Site Inspection to Working Group 1 on Verification, On-site inspection for the Comprehensive Test Ban Treaty: phenomena, technology, OSI examples, costs*, CD document CD/NTB/WP.198, 15 December 1994.

48 Gordon M. Burck, "The Chemical Weapons Convention Negotiations", in J.B. Poole and R. Guthrie, (eds), *Verification Report 1992: Yearbook on Arms Control and Environmental Agreements*, VERTIC, 1992, p. 124.

49 Canada also suggested that "black boxes" (automated detectors) could be installed at certain mining sites. See Canada, *The Comprehensive Test Ban Treaty and large chemical explosions: working paper*, CD document CD/NTB/WP.233, 31 March 1995. See also Australia, *The identification of Australian mining explosions: a study of spectral characteristics: working paper*, CD document CD/NTB/WP.232, 31 March 1995; Australia, *Chemical explosions: Some implications for CTBT verification drawing on Australian experiences*, CD document CD/NTB/WP.231, 31 March 1995; and Australia, *Mining explosions in Australia and CTBT verification: working paper*, CD document CD/NTB/WP.230, 31 March 1995.

50 The United States proposed mandatory provision of information on sites where large chemical explosions were planned, but avoided mention of transparency and confidence-building measures at previously used nuclear test sites. This test-site-based confidence-building measure, proposed by Canada and Australia, received widespread support from the non-aligned countries, many of whom would have preferred the test sites to be closed down altogether, if that had been a viable option to push for in this treaty. Instead, the United States suggested that further voluntary information should be encouraged in the event of large explosions, after unforeseen seismic events such as earthquakes or mine

collapses, and if there has been any accidental release of radioactivity which could raise alarms. See Rebecca Johnson, "The CTBT Endgame: the Major Obstacles", in J.B. Poole and R. Guthrie (eds), *Verification 1996: Arms Control, Peacekeeping and the Environment*, Westview Press/VERTIC, 1996, pp. 87–104.

51 The early US proposal for phased on-site inspections comprised: an initial phase within seven days to catch the short-lived phenomena; an optional extended phase, using sensors and collecting samples; and an optional drilling phase, on grounds that the "only conclusive evidence of a nuclear explosion is the retrieval of a radioactive sample containing certain characteristic isotopes". United States of America, *"Challenge" on-site inspection concept: working paper*, CD document CD/NTB/WP.90, 8 June 1994.

52 The US two-phase OSI proposal encompassed an initial phase, of "relatively short duration and low intrusiveness" and a second, more intrusive phase, of longer duration. Arguing the importance of speed to obtain time-critical evidence, the Americans proposed that the first phase should go ahead on a "red light" basis, meaning that it would proceed automatically unless stopped by a two-thirds majority of the Executive Council. This initial phase would involve aerial overflight, visual inspection and seismological and radioactivity measurements; it should be undertaken if possible within seven days of detecting an ambiguous event, and be conducted within two weeks. If more evidence were required, the second phase would be requested but could only go ahead if given a positive "green light" by a simple majority of the Executive Council voting in favour. The second phase, less time sensitive but more intrusive, would employ a greater range of measuring equipment, including the placement of unattended sensors for considerable periods of time, and drilling if deemed necessary. See United States of America, *U.S. approach to on-site inspections: working paper*, CD document CD/NTB/WP.238, 9 June 1995; United States of America, *U.S. draft language on on-site inspection provisions for the rolling test of the treaty: working paper*, CD document CD/NTB/WP.239, 9 June 1995; and United States of America, *Basic U.S. principles for an effective OSI regime: working paper*, CD document CD/NTB/WP.253, 10 July 1995.

53 Trying to persuade sceptics, the US argued that initial inspection could well provide enough evidence to dispel or confirm the suspicions which had triggered the OSI request, thereby obviating the need for further

inspections. Only if the first phase failed to resolve the ambiguity would the longer, more intrusive and expensive inspection go ahead. Ibid.

54 Ibid.

55 United States of America, *U.S. approach to on-site inspections: working paper*, CD document CD/NTB/WP.238, 9 June 1995; United States of America, *U.S. draft language on on-site inspection provisions for the rolling test of the treaty: working paper*, CD document CD/NTB/WP.239, 9 June 1995; and United States of America, *Basic U.S. principles for an effective OSI regime: working paper*, CD document CD/NTB/WP.253, 10 July 1995.

56 *Statement of the Group of 21 on a Nuclear Test Ban*, CD document CD/1329–CD/NTB/WP.248, 30 June 1995, p. 2.

57 Author's conversations with delegation members from the P-5, June–September 1995. See also China, *China's position on CTBT on-site inspections: working paper*, CD document CD/NTB/WP.266, 5 September 1995.

58 See Russian Federation, *On-site inspections under a CTBT: the Russian Federation's approach: working paper*, CD document CD/NTB/WP.249, 30 June 1995. Though the United Kingdom shared some aspects of Russia's approach, it did not put in a working paper at this stage.

59 See ibid.

60 Conference on Disarmament, *Final Record of the Seven Hundred and Eighteenth Plenary Meeting*, CD document CD/PV.718, 14 September 1995, statement by Munir Akram (Pakistan), p. 31.

61 According to one senior British official, interviewed off the record in May 2002, Israel—designated to host IMS stations—chose to feed its ideas or concerns about the IMS direct through the Friend of the Chair, Peter Marshall.

62 Israel, *On-site inspection: draft text covering some procedural elements of OSI: working paper*, CD document CD/NTB/WP.132, 29 June 1994; and Israel, *Health and safety during on-site inspection: proposed treaty language for the Protocol: working paper*, CD document CD/NTB/WP.190, 1 December 1994.

63 Israel, *Access regime: proposed treaty language for the Protocol: working paper*, CD document CD/NTB/WP.204, 16 December 1994.

64 United States of America, *"Challenge" on-site inspection concept: working paper*, CD document CD/NTB/WP.90, 8 June 1994.

65 Russia suggested excluding certain areas from aerial reconnaissance, or shrouding or removing from the inspected area sensitive installations unconnected with the ambiguous event, as well as closing off particular

buildings, structures or premises. Russian Federation, *On-Site Inspections under a CTBT: the Russian Federation's approach: working paper*, CD document CD/NTB/WP.249, 30 June 1995.

66 United States response to questionnaire, informal paper dated 16 March 1994.

67 Despite being a party to the NPT and appearing to comply with IAEA safeguards, including inspections, after the 1990–1991 Gulf War, Iraq was found to have developed a significant nuclear weapons programme. This discovery prompted a rethink on the IAEA's inspection powers, leading to negotiations on an Additional Protocol to strengthen the previous safeguards regime. The United States' belief in its NTM capabilities derives from the Pentagon's confidence in having the most advanced intelligence technology and resources, and goes back as far as nuclear arms control. One reason for concluding the PTBT in 1963, rather than achieving a comprehensive test ban, was the US view that tests in the atmosphere, outer space and underwater would be easier to detect without any institutionalized or cooperative verification provisions. Such was his confidence in US national intelligence means that when President John F. Kennedy recommended the PTBT to Congress for ratification, he promised: "The risks in clandestine violations under this treaty are far smaller than the risks in unlimited testing … No nation tempted to violate the treaty can be certain that an attempted violation will go undetected, given the many means of detecting nuclear explosions. The risks of detection outweigh the potential gains from violation, and the risk to the United States from such violation is outweighed by the risk of a continued unlimited nuclear arms race". John F. Kennedy, Statement to US Senate when transmitting the 1963 Partial Test Ban Treaty for their advice and consent, quoted in Michael Krepon, *Arms Control, Verification and Compliance*, Foreign Policy Association, 1984, p. 16.

68 Conference on Disarmament, *Final Record of the Seven Hundred and Seventeenth Plenary Meeting*, CD document CD/PV.717, 5 September 1995, statement by Sha Zukang (China), p. 6. China, Pakistan and India, in particular, rooted their opposition to NTM in incidents of alleged harassment and accusations based on what they regarded as unconfirmed, unverifiable (or unfalsifiable) intelligence, invariably from the United States. On several occasions, Chinese officials obliquely cited the *Yin He* incident of 1993, when US military personnel, with the assistance of Saudi Arabia, forcibly boarded and detained a Chinese vessel en route to Iran, to search for precursor chemicals for chemical

weapon production—which they did not find. The *Yin He* was detained in the Saudi port of Dammam from 26 August to 4 September. See *Statement by the Ministry of Foreign Affairs of the People's Republic of China on the "Yin He" Incident, Dated 4 September 1993*, (circulated to the Preparatory Commission for the OPCW, 25 September 1993, available at <www.nti.org/db/china/engdocs/ynhe0993.htm>. See also Celes Eckerman, "Inspection of Chinese Cargo Ship Yields No Evidence of Chemicals", *Arms Control Today*, vol. 23, no. 9, 1993, p. 19. Pakistan's Foreign Minister, Sardar Aseff Ahmad Ali, referred to Pakistan's "historical experience of undue harassment" when he told the CD that information from NTM should not be allowed a role in triggering an OSI, as it could be "subjective, selective and unreliable"; See Conference on Disarmament, *Final Record of the Seven Hundred and Thirty-third Plenary Meeting*, CD document CD/PV.733, 28 March 1996, statement by Sardar Aseff Ahmad Ali (Pakistan), p. 12. India also alluded to incidents in which it was accused by media innuendo on the grounds of "leaked" US intelligence sources, without being provided with evidence that could be directly contested. India's complaint was a two-edged sword, as the *New York Times* reports of its test preparations at Rajasthan in late 1995, widely understood to have been deliberately leaked by US intelligence, turned out to have been accurate. For contemporaneous reports of the test preparations and reactions in India, see Tim Weiner, "U.S. Suspects India Prepares to Conduct Nuclear Test", *New York Times*, 15 December 1995; C. Raja Mohan, "Ploy to pressure India on CTBT", *The Hindu*, 17 December 1995; Aziz Hanliffa, "N-leak was to trap India into CTBT", *The Hindu*, 30 December 1995. See also News Review compiled by Sean Howard in *Disarmament Diplomacy*, no. 1, The Acronym Insitute, 1996, pp. 37–8. For the full story, see George Perkovich, *India's Nuclear Bomb*, University of California Press, 1999, pp. 353–77. Iranian delegates reiterated their objections to US intelligence being evoked to deprive Iran of nuclear technology or assistance under Article IV of the NPT, despite its compliance with the basic (INFCIRC 153) IAEA safeguards under the NPT's Article III.

69 Conference on Disarmament, *Final Record of the Seven Hundred and Seventeenth Plenary Meeting*, CD document CD/PV.717, 5 September 1995, statement by Sha Zukang (China), p. 7.

70 The G-21 argued that "CTBT judgement should be based on data received from the IMS" and that NTM should "not be used on a case-by-case and selective basis". *Statement of the Group of 21 on a Nuclear Test Ban*, CD document CD/1329–CD/NTB/WP.248, 30 June 1995. See

also Conference on Disarmament, *Final Record of the Seven Hundred and Tenth Plenary Meeting*, CD document CD/PV.710, 29 June 1995, statement on behalf of the G-21 by Satish Chandra.

71 The Nuclear Test Ban Committee's mandate's exact wording—"a universal and multilaterally and effectively verifiable comprehensive nuclear test ban treaty"—appears consistent with both these interpretations.

72 Ledogar used the term "treaty-breaker" frequently during the final stage of the OSI negotiations, and later confirmed that this was not just diplomatic hyperbole, but that his instructions were to ensure the widest possible permissibility for NTM, encompassing all nationally sourced information, including COMINT and HUMINT. Interview with Stephen Ledogar, New York, 5 November 2000.

73 In effect, France argued that a requested OSI could go ahead on a "red light" procedure if backed up with IMS data, but that any request based on NTM would have to undergo the more stringent "green light" process, requiring the positive decision of the Executive Council before it could proceed. French Statement to Working Group 1, 18 August 1995.

74 Although kept from CD membership until June 1996 by US opposition to Iraq's inclusion on the "O'Sullivan list", as discussed in Chapter 3, South Africa's participation in the CTBT negotiations had begun to establish its reputation for constructive, disarmament-oriented, regime-strengthening positions among the non-aligned states. South Africa, *Comprehensive Test Ban Treaty (CTBT): The International Monitoring System (IMS) and On-Site Inspections (OSI): working paper*, CD document CD/NTB/WP.300, 8 February 1996.

75 Israel, *Supplementary monitoring data from co-operating national facilities: working paper*, CD document CD/NTB/WP.251, 6 July 1995.

76 Conference on Disarmament, *Final Record of the Seven Hundred and Seventeenth Plenary Meeting*, CD document CD/PV.717, 5 September 1995, statement by Sha Zukang (China), p. 7.

77 Islamic Republic of Iran, *Draft comprehensive test ban treaty*, CD document CD/1384, 21 February 1996. In similar ways, Australia's model treaty proposed that an on-site inspection could be based on data from the IMS or "other elements of the treaty verification regime … [including] any relevant supplementary data or information". Australia also proposed associated measures promoting access by all states parties to "other technical information and data relevant to the verification of the basic obligations of the treaty". Australia, *Comprehensive nuclear*

test ban treaty: model treaty text, CD document CD/1386, 29 February 1996; and Australia, *Comprehensive nuclear test ban treaty, explanatory notes accompanying model treaty text (as contained in CD/1386)*, CD document CD/1387, 29 February 1996.

78 Jaap Ramaker, statement to the Ad Hoc Committee on a Nuclear Test Ban, 9 August 1996. These assurances were placed on the record in *Report of the Ad Hoc Committee on a Nuclear Test Ban to the Conference on Disarmament*, CD document CD/1425, 16 August 1996, pp. 13–6.

79 This early, time-critical phase would consist of visual inspection, overflights and more targeted monitoring. If this inspection failed to clarify the ambiguities, a further, more intrusive inspection would be considered. See Islamic Republic of Iran, *Draft comprehensive test ban treaty*, CD document CD/1384, 21 February 1996; Australia, *Comprehensive nuclear test ban treaty: model treaty text*, CD document CD/1386, 29 February 1996; and Australia, *Comprehensive nuclear test ban treaty, explanatory notes accompanying model treaty text (as contained in CD/1386)*, CD document CD/1387, 29 February 1996.

80 Jaap Ramaker, interview with the author, Vienna, 16 July 2001.

81 Conference on Disarmament, *Final Record of the Seven Hundred and Thirty-seventh Plenary Meeting*, CD document CD/PV.737, 6 June 1996, statement by Sha Zukang (China), p. 10–1.

82 Ibid., statement by Sha Zukang (China), p. 9. The author's contemporaneous notes of this plenary session indicate that "make or break" was the idiomatic expression provided in English by the interpreters on the day, but this phrase does not appear in the corrected version of the verbatim records. However, Sha used the phrase "make or break" in conversations with the author and also in interventions on OSI in the NTB Committee during June–July 1996, according to diplomats that were present at the time.

83 Jaap Ramaker, interview with the author, Vienna, 16 July 2001.

84 Beijing had calculated the balance on the Executive Council and considered that 30 out of the 51 members was the minimum assurance it needed that the United States and its allies did not have the automatic weight to vote for an OSI request unless they had sufficient supporting evidence to persuade others.

85 Chairman of the Ad Hoc Committee on a Nuclear Test Ban, *Draft Comprehensive Nuclear Test-ban Treaty*, CD document CD/NTB/WP.330/Rev.2, 14 August 1996.

86 See the Protocol to the Comprehensive Nuclear Test Ban Treaty, Part II, On-Site Inspections.

87 Jaap Ramaker, statement to the Ad Hoc Committee on a Nuclear Test Ban, 9 August 1996. These assurances were placed on the record in *Report of the Ad Hoc Committee on a Nuclear Test Ban to the Conference on Disarmament*, CD document CD/1425, 16 August 1996, pp. 13–6.

88 Jaap Ramaker, interview with the author, Vienna, 16 July 2001.

89 There had been considerable debate about whether the word "nuclear" needed to be in the formal title of the treaty and organization. In the end it was included, so the organization is formally the Comprehensive Nuclear-Test-Ban Treaty Organization but the common abbreviation CTBT was retained in CTBTO.

90 The Comprehensive Nuclear-Test-Ban Treaty, Article II, The Organization.

91 The negotiations on these aspects of the institutional arrangements and establishment of the CTBTO are explained in greater detail in Jaap Ramaker, Jenifer Mackby, Peter D. Marshall and Robert Geil, *The Final Test*, Preparatory Commission for the Comprehensive Nuclear-Test-Ban Treaty Organization, 2003. This detailed account of the CTBT negotiations has not yet been made available for public distribution, but is available through the governments that participate in the CTBTO.

Chapter 8
Lessons for future multilateral security negotiations

1 George P. Shultz, William J. Perry, Henry A. Kissinger and Sam Nunn, "A World Free of Nuclear Weapons", *The Wall Street Journal*, 4 January 2007.

2 See the essays in John Borrie and Vanessa Martin Randin (eds), *Thinking Outside the Box in Multilateral Disarmament and Arms Control Negotiations*, UNIDIR, 2006, including Rebecca Johnson, "Changing perceptions and practice in multilateral arms control negotiations".

3 Paul Taylor, "The United Nations and international order", in John Baylis and Steve Smith (eds), *The Globalization of World Politics*, 2nd ed., Oxford University Press, 2001, p. 338; Charles Beitz, *Political Theory and International Relations*, Princeton University Press, 1979; Terry Nardin, *Law, Morality and the Relations of States*, Princeton University Press, 1983; and Michael Walzer, *Just and Unjust Wars: A Moral Argument with Historical Illustration*, Basic Books, 1977.

4 Andrew Moravcsik, "Taking Preferences Seriously: A Liberal Theory of International Politics", in Paul R. Viotti and Mark V. Kauppi, *International Relations Theory*, 3rd ed., Allyn and Bacon, 1987, p. 250.

5 Updating Allison's 1971 analysis that influentially challenged notions of rationality in foreign policy decision-making, see Graham T. Allison with Philip Zelikow, *Essence of Decision: Explaining the Cuban Missile Crisis*, 2nd ed., Longman, 1999. Also Morton H. Halperin, *Bureaucratic Politics and Foreign Policy*, Brookings Institution, 1974; John Steinbruner, *The Cybernetic Theory of Decision*, Princeton University Press, 1974; Amy Sands, "The Impact of Governmental Context on Negotiation and Implementation: Constraints and Opportunities for Change", in Nancy W. Gallagher (ed.), *Arms Control: New Approaches to Theory and Policy*, Frank Cass, 1998; and the articles in James N. Rosenau (ed.), *Domestic Sources of Foreign Policy*, The Free Press, 1967.

6 See Jeffrey W. Knopf, "Beyond two-level games: domestic-international interaction in the intermediate-range nuclear forces negotiation", *International Organization*, vol. 47, no. 4, 1993, pp. 599–628; and Robert D. Putnam "Diplomacy and Domestic Politics: The Logic of Two-Level Games", in Peter B. Evans, Harold K. Jacobson and Robert D Putnam (eds), *Doubled Edged Diplomacy: International Bargaining and Domestic Politics*, University of California Press, 1993. Also Barry Buzan, Charles Jones and Richard Little, *The Logic of Anarchy: Neorealism to Structural Realism*, Columbia University Press, 1993.

7 Accepting NPT language that characterized disarmament as an "ultimate goal" of the non-proliferation regime only slightly masked that the nuclear-weapon states at the time actually considered disarmament to be remote, unachievable and, in real terms, undesirable.

8 This phrase was attributed to a senior P-5 diplomat, who reportedly used it in an informal NTB Committee meeting, and it was then taken up by others to characterize the CTBT's limits, as "to ban the bangs not to ban the bomb".

9 See William Walker, "India's Nuclear Labyrinth", *The Nonproliferation Review*, vol. 4, no. 1, 1996, pp. 61–77; and George Perkovich, *India's Nuclear Bomb*, University of California Press, 1999.

10 In the stag-hunt analogy, the group has agreed in advance (coordinated) to a cooperation scenario that requires each to participate. The mutual benefit is food for all, but there is no certainty of collective success. Collective failure means hunger for all. Defection by one assures collective failure but provides at least a one-meal benefit for the defector. From Jean-Jacques Rousseau, *Discourse On the Origin and Foundations of Inequality Among Men*.

11 For more on the value of non-discrimination and diffuse reciprocity in multilateralism, see John Gerard Ruggie, "Multilateralism: the Anatomy

of an Institution", in John Gerard Ruggie (ed.), *Multilateralism Matters*, Columbia University Press, 1993.

12 Analysed by Robert Jervis in *Perception and Misperception in International Politics*, Princeton University Press, 1976; the authors' interviews with diplomats and officials demonstrated that training programmes for foreign policy practitioners continue to be dominated by the worldviews associated with the theories of realism, neorealism and neoliberalism.

13 On no-agreement dilemmas and alternatives to accepting agreement, see James K. Sebenius, "Challenging conventional explanations of international cooperation: negotiation analysis and the case of epistemic communities", in Peter M. Haas, *Knowledge, Power, and International Policy Coordination*, University of South Carolina Press, 1992, pp. 334–5.

14 This was despite the fact that the idea originated in an Irish–Swedish resolution to the UN General Assembly in 1961. See especially ENDC/192 (US Draft) and ENDC/193 (Soviet draft), which superseded US–Soviet drafts from 1965.

15 Richard Walton and Robert McKersie are credited with coining the term and defining the term "integrative bargaining", in Richard Walton and Robert McKersie, *A Behavioral Theory of Labour Negotiations*, McGraw-Hill, 1965. See also James K. Sebenius, "Challenging conventional explanations of international cooperation: negotiation analysis and the case of epistemic communities", in Peter M. Haas, *Knowledge, Power, and International Policy Coordination*, University of South Carolina Press, 1992, p. 329. On integrative bargaining and mixed-motive games, see Thomas C. Schelling, *The Strategy of Conflict*, Harvard University Press, 1980 (first published 1960).

16 James K. Sebenius, "Challenging conventional explanations of international cooperation: negotiation analysis and the case of epistemic communities", in Peter M. Haas, *Knowledge, Power, and International Policy Coordination*, University of South Carolina Press, 1992, pp. 346–65.

17 See Tariq Rauf, "PrepCom Opinion: Farewell to the NPT's Strengthened Review Process?", *Disarmament Diplomacy*, no. 26, The Acronym Institute, 1998, p. 26. See also "Breaking the CD Impasse: Statements by Vladimir Petrovsky And Rebecca Johnson", *Disarmament Diplomacy*, no. 53, The Acronym Institute, 2001, pp. 16–23.

18 "Secretary-General Declares Comprehensive Test Ban Treaty Open for Signature", *United Nations Press Release*, September 24, 1996, SG/SM/6062.

19 The 1958 Agreement between Government of the United States of America and the Government of the United Kingdom of Great Britain and Northern Ireland and the for Cooperation on the Uses of Atomic Energy for Mutual Defence Purposes, often called the Mutual Defence Agreement, provides for the exchange of classified information concerning nuclear weapons to improve "design, development and fabrication capability". First signed in Washington, 3 July 1958, the Mutual Defence Agreement has been updated and renewed frequently, most recently in 1994 and 2004.

20 Michael Evans, "Britain ends 40 years of nuclear test explosions", *The Times*, 7 April 1995.

21 On the argument that, because of technical problems, France has learned less from its nuclear tests than the United States, see "France keeps the experts guessing", *Nature*, vol. 376, no. 6538, 1995. For an alternative view on the relative independence of French nuclear development, see William Drozdiak and R. Jeffrey Smith, "French Nuclear Program Closely Tied to U.S.", *Washington Post*, 19 September 1995.

22 Marie-Hélène Labbé, "France", in Eric Arnett (ed.), *Nuclear Weapons After the Comprehensive Test Ban*, Oxford University Press/SIPRI, 1996, p. 33.

23 Marie-Hélène Labbé, "France", in Eric Arnett (ed.), *Nuclear Weapons After the Comprehensive Test Ban*, Oxford University Press/SIPRI, 1996, p. 35. The new warheads were the M-5, the M-45 and the TN-75.

24 In particular, the interests of the *Direction des applications militaires* (DAM, the Office of Military Applications) must be taken into consideration. Apparently caught off guard by Mitterrand's decision to declare a nuclear test moratorium in April 1992, DAM feared losing resources, staffing and expertise. The French nuclear establishment became concerned for its future, fearing that it would come under domestic political and economic pressure to close down the test facilities at Moruroa and Fangataufa if a CTBT did not contain some provisions justifying the retention of the test site, either through periodic safety tests or by permitting hydronuclear testing at yields high enough to require specially constructed and reinforced facilities. Their fear was well founded, for after acceding to the CTBT, France closed the Pacific Test Site and undertook clean-up programmes with IAEA assistance and oversight. France's options were further constrained because

the Clinton administration had already rejected a 1kt threshold and appeared adamantly opposed to the high level of threshold that France's nuclear weapon scientists wanted. See Marie-Hélène Labbé, "France", in Eric Arnett (ed.), *Nuclear Weapons After the Comprehensive Test Ban*, Oxford University Press/SIPRI, 1996, pp. 37–8.

25 Gérard Érrera, conversation with the author, quoted in Rebecca Johnson, *Strengthening the Non-Proliferation Regime: Ends and Beginnings*, ACRONYM Report, no. 6, The Acronym Consortium, 1995, p. 10.

26 Unlike the CD, which works according to the rule of consensus, the NPT specified that the decision on the extension of the NPT could be taken by a simple majority of states parties, with each state having a vote of equal value. The nuclear-weapon states knew that they would need something to show, as from past NPT Review Conferences it was clear that progress on nuclear disarmament would be an important factor for many of the non-nuclear-weapon states whose votes they needed to win. In addition to abandoning the unpopular Franco-British proposal for safety tests, the nuclear-weapon states undertook several other initiatives to win favour among the marginalized non-nuclear-weapon states. See Rebecca Johnson, *Indefinite Extension of the Non-Proliferation Treaty: Risks and Reckonings*, ACRONYM Report, no. 7, The Acronym Consortium, 1995, pp. 40–2. Michael Evans, "Britain ends 40 years of nuclear test explosions", *The Times*, 7 April 1995.

27 Writing several years after conclusion of the CTBT negotiations, Jing-Dong Yuan backs up this observation with his analysis of China's negotiating posture on PNE and verification. Jing-Dong Yuan, "Culture Matters: Chinese Approaches to Arms Control and Disarmament", in Keith R. Krause, *Culture and Security: Multilateralism, Arms Control and Security Building*, Frank Cass, 1999, p. 110.

28 Jing-Dong Yuan, "Culture Matters: Chinese Approaches to Arms Control and Disarmament", in Keith R. Krause, *Culture and Security: Multilateralism, Arms Control and Security Building*, Frank Cass, 1999.

29 See, for example, See Fen Osler Hampson, with Michael Hart, *Multilateral Negotiations: Lessons from Arms Control, Trade and the Environment*, The Johns Hopkins University Press, 1995, especially pp. 34–6 and 350–1.

30 Peter M. Haas (ed.), *Knowledge, Power and International Policy Coordination*, University of South Carolina Press, 1992. In the case of the CTBT, most specialists viewed as having authoritative knowledge about nuclear science or verification were either government employees or had served for part of their career in their countries' nuclear laboratories

or establishments. Although some became formidable advocates and some formed networks; they did not necessarily have a commonality of purpose as implied in the concept of a community. Governments or pressure groups called on the scientists' knowledge and expertise to give authority to arguments for or against a proposed approach or provision for the treaty. Epistemic actors operated not only in a domestic policy environment, but transnationally. See Emanuel Adler, "The emergence of cooperation: national epistemic communities and the international evolution of the idea of nuclear arms control", in Peter M. Haas (ed.), *Knowledge, Power and International Policy Coordination*, University of South Carolina Press, 1992.

31 Analysing the mechanisms of decision-making, Goldstein and Keohane concluded that "ideas influence policy when the principles or causal beliefs they embody provide road maps that increase actors' clarity about goals or ends–means relationships, when they affect outcomes of strategic situations in which there is no unique equilibrium, and when they become embedded in political institutions". Judith Goldstein and Robert O. Keohane, "Ideas and Foreign Policy", in Paul R. Viotti and Mark V. Kauppi, *International Relations Theory*, 3rd ed., Allyn and Bacon, 1987, p. 297.

32 As discussed in Chapter 2, the joint verification experiments started as non-governmental exchanges initiated by the Soviet Academy of Sciences and US Natural Resources Defense Council and were then taken over by the two governments, helping to build confidence.

33 For a discussion of how "usage and custom" contribute to regime building, see Stephen D. Krasner (ed.), *International Regimes*, Cornell University Press, 1983.

34 See Daryl Kimball, "How the US Senate Rejected CTBT Ratification", *Disarmament Diplomacy*, no. 40, The Acronym Institute, 1999, pp. 8–15.

35 Interview with Stephen Ledogar, New York, 5 November 2000. See also Prepared Testimony of Ambassador Stephen J. Ledogar (Ret.), Chief US Negotiator of the CTBT, Before the Senate Foreign Relations Committee, Washington DC, 7 October 1999. available at <www.fas.org/nuke/control/ctbt/text/ctbtsenate.htm>.

36 See Nancy W. Gallagher (ed.), *Arms Control: New Approaches to Theory and Policy*, Frank Cass, 1998.

37 This presented a range of targets that could more easily be persuaded to take action, which then helped to give momentum to efforts at controlling or banning the weapons. For some states, and often as

a result of pressure from transnational civil society, the unilateral, voluntary renunciation of the export or production of landmines signalled their commitment to negotiate the ban. For accounts of the role of civil society and states in achieving the 1997 Mine Ban Treaty, see Maxwell A. Cameron, Robert J. Lawson and Brian W. Tomlin (eds), *To Walk Without Fear: The Global Movement to Ban Landmines*, Oxford University Press, 1998; Kenneth Anderson, "The Ottawa Convention Banning Landmines, the Role of International Non-Governmental Organizations and the Idea of International Civil Society", *European Journal of International Affairs*, vol. 2, no. 1, 2000; and Motoko Mekata, "Building Partnerships toward a Common Goal: Experiences of the International Campaign to Ban Landmines", in Ann M. Florini (ed.), *The Third Force: The Rise of Transnational Civil Society*, Japan Center for International Exchange and Washington D.C. Carnegie Endowment for International Peace, 2000, pp. 143–76.

38 Earlier laws, such as the Geneva Protocol, prohibited use but not possession.

39 Hans J. Morgenthau, *Politics Among Nations: The Struggle for Power and Peace*, revised by Kenneth W. Thompson, brief ed., McGraw-Hill Inc., 1993 (first published 1948).

40 Kenneth N. Waltz, *Theory of International Politics*, McGraw-Hill, 1979.

41 See also Barry Buzan, "Beyond Neorealism: Interaction Capacity", in Barry Buzan, Charles Jones, and Richard Little, *The Logic of Anarchy: Neorealism to Structural Realism*, Columbia University Press, 1993, pp. 66–80.

Chapter 9
Securing the CTBT

1 *Weapons of Terror: Freeing the World of Nuclear, Biological and Chemical Arms*, Weapons of Mass Destruction Commission, 2006, p. 17. The Commission was chaired by Dr Hans Blix, former Director-General of the IAEA (1981–1997) and head of the United Nations Monitoring, Verification and Inspection Commission in Iraq (UNMOVIC, 2000–2003).

2 Mark Mazzetti, "Preliminary Samples Hint at North Korean Nuclear Test", *New York Times*, 14 October 2006.

3 A paper from the Preparatory Commission for the CTBTO put the location at 41.43º N, 129.02º E. See Andreas Becker, G. Wotawa and P.R.J. Saey, "On the meteorological situation governing the emission and

atmospheric transport conditions during the announced October 2006 event in North Korea", *Geophysical Research Abstracts*, vol. 9, 2007. See also Robert G. Pearce, "North Korea: a real test for the CTBT Verification System?", *CTBTO Spectrum*, no. 9, 2007, pp. 24–5; and Paul R.J. Saey, Andreas Becker and Gerhard Wotawa, "North Korea: a real test for the CTBT Verification System? Part II: noble gas observations", *CTBTO Spectrum*, no. 10, 2007, pp. 20–1. It should also be noted that seismic facilities attached to universities and other civilian establishments also detected and identified the test, which—like VERTIC's project with regard to the Chinese test in 1993—provides additional confidence in test-ban verification and increases the uncertainty and deterrence for a would-be violator.

4 P.R.J. Saey, M. Bean, A. Becker, J. Coyne, R. d'Amours, L.-E. De Geer, R. Hogue, T.J. Stocki, R.K. Ungar and G. Wotawa, "A long distance measurement of radioxenon in Yellowkife, Canada, in late October 2006", *Geophysical Research Letters*, vol. 34, 2007. The authors provide a detailed analysis, including methodology and reasons for dismissing nuclear activities other than the North Korean test as plausible sources for the levels of xenon-133 detected by the Yellowknife station.

5 See Chapter 7.

6 See Chapter 7.

7 North Korean sources appear to have given alternative, potentially contradictory assessments. For example, one North Korean diplomat told the South Korean newspaper *Hankyorch* that the test was "smaller than expected"; Dafna Linzer and Walter Pincus, "U.S. Detects Signs of Radiation Consistent With Test", *Washington Post*, 14 October 2006. Another source said nothing about yield but claimed that they "successfully conducted an underground nuclear test under secure conditions". See Lee Chi-dong, "N. Korea claims success in nuclear test", *Yonhap News*, 9 October 2006, cited in Richard L. Garwin and Frank N. von Hippel, "A Technical Analysis: Deconstructing North Korea's October 9 Nuclear Test", *Arms Control Today*, vol. 36, no. 9, 2006.

8 Richard L. Garwin and Frank N. von Hippel, "A Technical Analysis: Deconstructing North Korea's October 9 Nuclear Test", *Arms Control Today*, vol. 36, no. 9, 2006. See also, "CIA says North Korea nuclear test a failure: report", *Reuters*, 28 March 2007.

9 Anna Fifield, "N Korea agrees to shut nuclear plant", *Financial Times*, 13 February 2007. It should be noted that many analysts and media sources also credited increased US flexibility in the Six Party Talks with

the agreement in February 2007 on the Denuclearization Action Plan. See, for example, David E. Sanger and Thom Shanker, "Rice Is Said to Have Speeded North Korea Deal", *New York Times*, 16 February 2007; and Nicola Butler, "North Korea Nuclear Agreement: Can it Work?", *Disarmament Diplomacy*, no. 84, The Acronym Institute, 2007, pp. 70–6.

10 The noble gas stations that were working at that time were one in Australia, three in Canada (Ottawa, Yellowknife and St. John's), and one each in Germany, Tahiti, Mongolia, Norway, Russia (Dubna) and Sweden. An eleventh station at Tarasaki in Japan was not yet up and running, although it began functioning less than a month after the North Korean nuclear test.

11 P.R.J. Saey, M. Bean, A. Becker, J. Coyne, R. d'Amours, L.-E. De Geer, R. Hogue, T.J. Stocki, R.K. Ungar and G. Wotawa, "A long distance measurement of radioxenon in Yellowkife, Canada, in late October 2006", *Geophysical Research Letters*, vol. 34, 2007.

12 The author participated in this exercise, known as the Integrated Field Exercise 2008 (IFE08), as an observer and designated "science writer"; see the dispatches from the field on the websites of the *Bulletin of the Atomic Scientists* and *Disarmament Diplomacy*, September 2008.

13 Tibor Tóth, Executive Secretary of the CTBTO, quoted in "Integrated on-site inspection exercise in Kazakhstan reaches a successful conclusion", CTBTO Press release, 9 October 2008.

14 "Signing of tsunami warning arrangement with Indonesia", CTBTO press release, 11 November 2008.

15 *Annual Report 2007*, CTBTO, 2008, p. 20.

16 See Helga Kromp-Kolb, "The importance of IMS data for global climate change research", *CTBTO Spectrum*, no. 10, 2007, pp. 22–3. The IMS technologies continue to be developed and augmented. See the CTBTO website at <www.ctbto.org> for the most up to date information on developments in the IMS coverage, technologies and in programmes to enhance the civilian and scientific benefits.

17 See George Perkovich, *India's Nuclear Bomb*, University of California Press, 1999; and Rebecca Johnson, "International Implications of the India-Pakistan Tests", *Disarmament Diplomacy*, no. 28, The Acronym Institute, 1998, pp. 26–35.

18 See Daryl Kimball, "How the US Senate Rejected CTBT Ratification", *Disarmament Diplomacy*, no. 40, The Acronym Institute, 1999, pp. 8–15.

[19] George P. Shultz, William J. Perry, Henry A. Kissinger and Sam Nunn, "A World Free of Nuclear Weapons", *Wall Street Journal*, 4 January 2007. George Shultz was President Reagan's Secretary of State in the 1980s, William Perry was President Clinton's Defense Secretary in the 1990s, Henry Kissinger was President Nixon's Secretary of State in the 1960s and 1970s, and Sam Nunn was a long-time Chair of the Senate Foreign Relations Committee and architect (with Richard Lugar) of legislative and political initiatives on cooperative threat reduction at the end of the Cold War.

[20] George P. Shultz, William J. Perry, Henry A. Kissinger, Sam Nunn and others, "Toward a Nuclear-Free World", *The Wall Street Journal*, 15 January 2008.

[21] Ibid.

[22] John M. Shalikashvili, "Findings and Recommendations Concerning the Comprehensive Nuclear Test Ban Treaty", *Arms Control Today*, vol. 31, no. 1, 2001, pp. 18–28, especially p. 21.

[23] Ibid., p. 21.

[24] The most comprehensive of the non-governmental studies was the Independent Commission on the Verifiability of the CTBT, carried out under the auspices of VERTIC. See *Final Report, Independent Commission on the Verifiability of the CTBT*, VERTIC, 2000.

[25] US Senate Committee on Foreign Relations, *Final Review of the Comprehensive Nuclear Test Ban Treaty (Treaty Doc. 105-28)*, US Government Printing Office document S. Hrg. 106-262, 7 October 1999, pp. 17–8.

[26] Ibid., p. 18.

[27] Ibid.

[28] See Rebecca Johnson, "Renewed opportunities to bring the CTBT into force", *CTBTO Spectrum*, no. 10, 2007, pp. 10–1.

[29] Javier Solana, "The importance of CTBT universalization", *CTBTO Spectrum*, no. 9, 2007, p. 5.

[30] The following section is largely drawn from Rebecca Johnson, "Beyond Article XIV: Strategies to Save the CTBT", *Disarmament Diplomacy*, no. 73, The Acronym Institute, 2003; and Rebecca Johnson, "Is it time to consider provisional application of the CTBT?", *Disarmament Forum*, no. 2, UNIDIR, 2006.

[31] The following section is taken from Rebecca Johnson, "Beyond Article XIV: Strategies to Save the CTBT", *Disarmament Diplomacy*, no. 73, The Acronym Institute, 2003.

[32] *Weapons of Terror: Freeing the World of Nuclear, Biological and Chemical Arms*, Weapons of Mass Destruction Commission, 2006, p. 108. William Perry, one of the four principal authors of the *Wall Street Journal* essays, was the US member on the Commission, and endorsed the conclusion regarding provisional entry into force in the knowledge that it might be invoked if another US president hostile to the CTBT were elected in 2008. In view of President Obama's support for the CTBT, it is now more likely that if provisional entry into force were needed it would be to bypass the opposition of a non-P-5 state.

ACRONYMS

CD	Conference on Disarmament
CND	Campaign for Nuclear Disarmament
CTBT	Comprehensive Nuclear-Test-Ban Treaty
CTBTO	Comprehensive Nuclear-Test-Ban Treaty Organization
CWC	Chemical Weapons Convention
D-3	India, Israel and Pakistan—the de facto nuclear-weapon states
EIF	entry into force
END	European Nuclear Disarmament
ENDC	Eighteen-Nation Disarmament Committee
G-21	Group of Non-Aligned States and Others
IAEA	International Atomic Energy Agency
IMS	International Monitoring System
INF	Intermediate-Range Nuclear Forces Treaty
IPPNW	International Physicians for the Prevention of Nuclear War
NATO	North Atlantic Treaty Organization
NGO	non-governmental organization
NPT	Treaty on the Non-Proliferation of Nuclear Weapons
NRDC	Natural Resources Defense Council
NTB	Nuclear Test Ban Committee
NTM	national technical means
P-5	China, France, Russia, the United Kingdom and the United States—the nuclear-weapon states, and also the permanent members of the UN Security Council
PNE	peaceful nuclear explosion
PNET	Peaceful Nuclear Explosions Treaty
PSAC	President's Science Advisory Committee
PTBT	Partial Test Ban Treaty
PTS	Provisional Technical Secretariat
SANE	National Committee for a Sane Nuclear Policy
T-BAG	Test Ban Action Group
TTBT	Threshold Test Ban Treaty
VERTIC	Verification Research, Training and Information Centre